# DEMOCRATIC REPRESENTATION IN INTERNATIONAL ORGANIZATIONS

International organizations (IOs) play a central role in contemporary international law making: they institutionalize most of the processes through which international law is adopted today. From the perspective of the democratic legitimacy of international law, this raises the question of the conditions under which those IOs may be regarded as democratic representatives of their Member States' peoples. Curiously, given its important international and domestic stakes, however, the democratic representativeness of IOs, but also of States and other public and private institutions within those IOs does not seem to be much of a concern in practice. Even more curiously, and by contrast to other issues of democratic legitimacy it is necessarily related to, such as participation or deliberation inside IOs, representation has only rarely been addressed as such in scholarly debates. It is this gap in theory and practice that this volume purports to fill. It is the first one bringing global democracy theorists and international lawyers into dialogue on the topic and in English language. This title is also available as open access on Cambridge Core.

Samantha Besson holds the Chair Droit international des Institutions at the College of France, Paris and is Professor of Public International Law and European Law at the University of Fribourg (Switzerland). She is a member of the Institute of International Law and was co-Chair of the ILA Study Group on the International Law of Regional Organizations (2021–24).

## ASIL Studies in International Legal Theory



The purpose of the ASIL Studies in International Legal Theory series is to clarify and improve the theoretical foundations of international law. Too often the progressive development and implementation of international law has foundered on confusion about first principles. This series raises the level of public and scholarly discussion about the structure and purposes of the world legal order and how best to achieve global justice through law.

This series grows out of the International Legal Theory project of the American Society of International Law. The ASIL Studies in International Legal Theory series deepens this conversation by publishing scholarly monographs and edited volumes of essays considering subjects in international legal theory.

**Books in the series**

*Democratic Representation in International Organizations* Edited by Samantha Besson

*States, Firms, and Their Legal Fictions: Attributing Identity and Responsibility to Artificial Entities* Edited by Melissa J. Durkee

*Rethinking the Relationship between International, EU and National Law* Lando Kirchmair

*Consenting to International Law* Edited by Samantha Besson

*The Death Penalty's Denial of Fundamental Human Rights* John Bessler

*Theories of International Responsibility Law* Edited by Samantha Besson

*Human Dignity in International Law* Ginevra Le Moli

*Tipping Points in International Law: Commitment and Critique* Edited by Jean d'Aspremont and John D. Haskell

*Ethical Leadership in International Organizations: Concepts, Narratives, Judgment, and Assessment* Edited by Maria Varaki and Guilherme Vasconcelos Vilaca

*Whither the West?: Concepts on International Law in Europe and the United States* Edited by Chiara Giorgetti and Guglielmo Verdirame

*International Law as Behavior* Edited by Harlan Grant Cohen and Timothy Meyer

*Space and Fates of International Law: Between Leibniz and Hobbes* Ekaterina Yahyaoui Krivenko

*Why Punish Perpetrators of Mass Atrocities?: Purposes of Punishment in International Criminal Law* Edited by Florian Jeßberger and Julia Geneuss

*The Challenge of Inter-Legality* Edited by Jan Klabbers and Gianluigi Palombella

*The Nature of International Law* Miodrag A. Jovanović

*Reexamining Customary International Law* Edited by Brian D. Lepard

*Theoretical Boundaries of Armed Conflict and Human Rights* Edited by Jens David Ohlin

*Human Rights in Emergencies* Edited by Evan J. Criddle

*The Theory of Self-Determination* Edited by Fernando R. Tesón

*Negotiating State and Non-State Law: Global and Local Legal Pluralism* Edited by Michael A. Helfand

*Jus Post Bellum and Transitional Justice* Edited by Larry May and Elizabeth Edenberg

*Normative Pluralism and International Law: Exploring Global Governance* Edited by Jan Klabbers and Touko Piipaerinen

*The Future of International Law: Global Government* Joel P. Trachtman

*Morality, Jus Post Bellum, and International Law* Edited by Larry May and Andrew T. Forcehimes

*Global Justice and International Economic Law: Opportunities and Prospects* Edited by Chios Carmody, Frank J. Garcia, and John Linarelli

*Parochialism, Cosmopolitanism, and the Foundations of International Law* Edited by M. N. S. Sellers

*The Role of Ethics in International Law* Edited by Donald Earl Childress III

*The New Global Law* Rafael Domingo

*Customary International Law: A New Theory with Practical Applications* Brian D. Lepard

*International Criminal Law and Philosophy* Edited by Larry May and Zachary Hoskins

# Democratic Representation in International Organizations

*Edited by*

SAMANTHA BESSON

*Collège de France, Paris*

*With the assistance of*

MATHILDE VIGNÉ

CAMBRIDGE
UNIVERSITY PRESS

CAMBRIDGE
UNIVERSITY PRESS

Shaftesbury Road, Cambridge CB2 8EA, United Kingdom

One Liberty Plaza, 20th Floor, New York, NY 10006, USA

477 Williamstown Road, Port Melbourne, VIC 3207, Australia

314–321, 3rd Floor, Plot 3, Splendor Forum, Jasola District Centre, New Delhi – 110025, India

Cambridge University Press is part of Cambridge University Press & Assessment, a department of the University of Cambridge.

We share the University's mission to contribute to society through the pursuit of education, learning and research at the highest international levels of excellence.

www.cambridge.org
Information on this title: www.cambridge.org/9781009710541

DOI: 10.1017/9781009710558



When citing this work, please include a reference to the DOI 10.1017/9781009710558

First published 2026

Cover image: Three keys to the International Labour Organization's gate in Geneva, symbol of tripartism, 1929. ILO Historical Archives.

*A catalogue record for this publication is available from the British Library*

*Library of Congress Cataloging-in-Publication Data*
NAMES: Besson, Samantha, 1973– editor
TITLE: Democratic representation in international organizations / Samantha Besson, College of France, Paris.
DESCRIPTION: Cambridge, United Kingdom ; New York, NY : Cambridge University Press, 2026. | Includes bibliographical references and index.
IDENTIFIERS: LCCN 2025051234 | ISBN 9781009710541 hardback | ISBN 9781009710527 paperback | ISBN 9781009710558 ebook
SUBJECTS: LCSH: International agencies – Law and legislation | International agencies – Membership | International law | Representative government and representation – Law and legislation
CLASSIFICATION: LCC KZ4852.D46 2026
LC record available at https://lccn.loc.gov/2025051234

ISBN 978-1-009-71054-1 Hardback

# Contents

# Contributors

JOCHEN VON BERNSTORFF is Professor of Public International Law at the University of Tübingen.

SAMANTHA BESSON is Professor at College of France where she holds the Chair International Law of Institutions, and Professor of Public International Law and European Law at the University of Fribourg.

FRANCIS CHENEVAL is Professor of Philosophy at the University of Zurich.

JACOB KATZ COGAN is Professor of Law at the University of Cincinnati.

ÉDOUARD DUBOUT is Professor of European Law at the Paris-Panthéon-Assas University.

MELISSA J. DURKEE is Professor of Law at Washington University in St. Louis.

OLIVIER DE FROUVILLE is Professor of Public Law and Director of the Paris Human Rights Center (CRDH) at Paris-Panthéon-Assas University.

ÉVELYNE LAGRANGE is Professor of Public Law, member of the Sorbonne Research Institute for International and European Law (IREDIES) at Paris I-Panthéon-Sorbonne University.

MARIEKE LOUIS is Associate Professor in Political Science and International Relations at Sciences Po Lille (CERAPS), and an associate researcher at the Center Marc Bloch in Berlin.

TERRY MACDONALD is Associate Professor of International Relations at the University of Melbourne.

JOSÉ LUIS MARTÍ is Associate Professor of Philosophy of Law at the University of Pompeu Fabra.

ANNE PETERS is Director at the Max Planck Institute for Comparative Public Law and International Law and Professor at the University of Heidelberg.

PHILIP PETTIT is L. S. Rockefeller Professor of Politics and Human Values at Princeton University and Distinguished Professor of Philosophy at the Australian National University.

DOMINIQUE RITLENG is Professor of Public Law at the University of Strasbourg.

PIERRE ROSANVALLON is Honorary Professor at College of France, where he held the Chair Modern and Contemporary History of the Political.

MARIE-CLOTILDE RUNAVOT is Professor of Public Law at the University of Toulouse Capitole.

MATHILDE VIGNÉ is a former Research Assistant at the Chair International Law of Institutions, College of France.

# Preface

Many contemporary international organizations (IOs) are empowered to adopt international law that claims to bind their Member States and, as a result, those States' peoples. Certain IOs have also become members of other IOs or, at least, active participants in international lawmaking processes that claim to bind those IOs and their Member States (and, by extension, the latter's peoples). Generally speaking, IOs play a central role in contemporary international lawmaking: they institutionalize most of the processes through which international law is adopted today, be it through international lawmaking conferences, international courts, or as IO secondary law. From the perspective of the democratic legitimacy of international law, this raises the question of the conditions under which those IOs may be regarded as democratic representatives of their Member States' peoples and, accordingly, under which the international law they have the right or, at least, the discretion to adopt inside and outside of IO organs and processes may claim to bind those peoples legitimately.

When one knows how powerful and even dominating certain IOs and certain States and their governments (usually not the most democratic ones) within those IOs have become politically, the stakes of those IOs' democratic representativeness are extremely high. As a matter of fact, those stakes are not only international. As we know by now, the deficit in democratic representation in and/or by IOs has also fuelled the so-called crisis of democratic representation domestically, including its populist critique and the new alternative claims of constructivist, statistic, altruistic, or epistemic representation that critique has given rise to.

Curiously, given those important international and domestic stakes, however, the democratic representativeness of IOs does not seem to be much of a concern of IOs and their Member States, at least if one refers to the international law of IOs. The question of democratic representation (by [the representatives of] Member States and/or [the representatives of] other public or private institutions involved in their lawmaking and decision-making processes, such as cities, regions, indigenous peoples, non-governmental organizations [NGOs], multinational corporations, employer's associations, trade unions, or patients' associations) in IOs, but also by IOs in and of themselves remains moot, to say the least. Even more curiously, while the question of democratic representation in and by IOs is straightforward enough from a democratic legitimacy perspective, it has only rarely been addressed as such in scholarly debates pertaining to the democratic legitimacy of international law. This is true in global or international democratic theory as much as in international democracy law.

It is this gap not only in the practice of democratic representation in IOs, but also in the literature, that the proposed volume purports to fill. Specialists of representation in both international democratic theory and IO law were invited to explore those issues and many others in a conference that took place at College of France in Paris on 22–23 June 2023. This volume gathers the thirteen chapters presented at the conference, together with an introduction and conclusions, as the first edited volume on the topic in English language and as the first one bringing global democracy theorists and IO law specialists into a dialogue on the issue.

The volume could not have come into existence without the support of a great number of people and institutions. First, and foremost, I would like to express my gratitude to Dr Mathilde Vigné, former research assistant at College of France, for her tremendous and unfailing assistance throughout the editorial process during the academic year 2023–24. Many thanks also to Mr Louis Hill, former research assistant at College of France, for his help in finalizing the volume's first building blocks in the summer of 2023; to Ms Shpresa Salihu, research assistant at the University of Fribourg, for her assistance in proofreading the edited manuscript in 2024; and to Ms Camille Michel, research assistant at College of France, for her assistance in putting the final editorial touches on the reviewed manuscript, indexing and proofreading in 2025–26. Special thanks are also due to my administrative assistant at College of France, Ms Sylvie Sportouch, who helped organize the June 2023 conference. I am also extremely grateful to Dr Sévrine Knuchel for translating four of the volume's contributions.

I would like to thank Ms Natasha Burton and Mr Edgar Mendez from Cambridge University Press for their support and kind forbearance during the process of putting this book together, as well as Professor Mortimer Sellers for his willingness to include this volume in the ASIL Studies in International

Legal Theory series. I am particularly grateful to three anonymous reviewers for their feedback on the book proposal and for making me reflect further upon the project. I hope they will be able to find traces of some of their constructive suggestions in the volume. Finally, I would like to express my gratitude to the College of France's Foundation for providing vital financial support for the June 2023 conference and for the English translation of four of the contributions, as well as to the Swiss National Science Foundation for its financial support to the Open Access publication of the volume.

Last but not least, special thanks are owed to all contributors and to the commentators, Professors Franck Petiteville, Charles Girard, and Yves Sintomer who decided not to publish with us, for making this ambitious project such a stimulating, formative, and worthwhile experience, and for their lively and engaging discussions at a memorable conference in Paris.

# 1

# Democratic Representation in, through, and by International Organizations: An Introduction

Samantha Besson

## 1.1 INTRODUCTION

Many contemporary international organizations (IOs) are empowered to adopt international law that claims to bind their Member States and, as a result, those States' peoples. Certain IOs have also become members of other IOs or, at least, active participants in international lawmaking processes that claim to bind those IOs and their Member States (and, by extension, the latter's peoples). Generally speaking, IOs play a central role in contemporary international lawmaking: they institutionalize most of the processes through which international law is adopted today, be it through international lawmaking conferences, international courts, or as IO secondary law.

From the perspective of the democratic legitimacy of international law, this raises the question of the conditions under which those IOs may be regarded as democratic representatives of their Member States' peoples and, accordingly, under which the international law they have the right or discretion to adopt inside and outside of IO organs and processes may claim to bind those peoples legitimately.

When one knows how powerful and even dominating certain IOs and certain States and their governments (usually not the most democratic ones) within those IOs have become politically,[1] the stakes of those IOs' democratic

Many thanks to Louis Hill and Mathilde Vigné for their editorial assistance.

[1] See Athena D. Efraim, *Sovereign (In)equality in International Organizations* (Leiden: Martinus Nijhoff, 2000); Andrew Hurrell, 'Power, Institutions, and the Production of Inequality', in Michael Barnett and Raymond Duvall (eds.), *Power in Global Governance* (Cambridge: Cambridge University Press, 2004), pp. 33–58; Andrew Hurrell and Nicholas Lees, 'International Organizations and the Idea of Equality', in Bob Reinalda (ed.), *Routledge Handbook of International Organization* (London: Routledge, 2013), pp. 106–118; Lora A. Viola, Duncan Snidal and Michael Zürn, 'Sovereign (In)equality in the Evolution of the International System', in Stefan Leibfried, Evelyne Huber, Matthew Lange, Jonah D. Levy and

representativeness are extremely high. One should also mention, of course, and it is related to the concentration of oligarchic power by and in IOs, the increasing 'capture' of IOs' organs, funding, and lawmaking processes by private organizations, be it multinational corporations, philanthropists, or non-governmental organizations (NGOs).[2] Ironically, the private capture of IOs sometimes even proceeds in the name of the greater 'inclusion' or 'participation' of 'stakeholders' in those IOs,[3] stakeholders who are deemed as self-representing or, at least, self-authorized.

As a matter of fact, the stakes of the democratic representativeness of IOs are not only international. As we know by now, the deficit in democratic representation in and/or by IOs has also fuelled the so-called 'crisis' of democratic representation domestically. This is the case of the populist critique of both governments and parliaments[4] and of the new alternative claims of constructivist, statistic, altruistic, or epistemic[5] representation that critique has given

John D. Stephens (eds.), *The Oxford Handbook of Transformations of the State* (Oxford: Oxford University Press, 2015), pp. 221–236; Lora A. Viola, *The Closure of the International System: How Institutions Create Political Equalities and Hierarchies* (Cambridge: Cambridge University Press, 2020); Samantha Besson, 'L'égalité des États membres de l'Union européenne: un nouveau départ en droit international de l'organisation des États?', in Édouard Dubout (ed.), *L'égalité des États membres de l'Union européenne* (Brussels: Bruylant, 2022), pp. 261–298.

2 See Samantha Besson, 'What makes International Organizations "Public"? A Plea for a Public International Law of Organisation' (2026) *Leiden Journal of International Law* in press; Samantha Besson, 'What can Public international Law do against Privatization?' (2024) 15(3) *Transnational Legal Theory* 341–369; Samantha Besson, 'The International Public: A Farewell to Functions in International Law' (2021) 115 *American Journal of International Law Unbound* 307–311; Samantha Besson, 'COVID-19 and the WHO's Political Moment' (2020) *EJIL:Talk!* www.ejiltalk.org/covid-19-and-the-whos-political-moment/, last accessed 2 August 2023. On private capture of IOs, see Melissa J. Durkee, 'Industry Lobbying and "Interest Blind" Access Norms at International Organizations' (2017) 111 *American Journal of International Law Unbound* 119–124; Ayelet Berman, 'Between Participation and Capture in International Rule-Making: The WHO Framework of Engagement with Non-State Actors' (2021) 32(1) *European Journal of International Law* 227–254; Olga Kovarzina and Martino Maggetti, 'Stakeholder Participation Reforms in Global Finance Governance', in Joost Pauwelyn, Martino Maggetti, Tim Büthe and Ayelet Berman (eds.), *Rethinking Participation in Global Governance: Voice and Influence after Stakeholder Reforms in Global Finance and Health* (Oxford: Oxford University Press, 2022), pp. 91–110.

3 See e.g. Pauwelyn *et al.*, fn. 2.

4 See Nadia Urbinati, *Me the People: How Populism Transforms Democracy* (Cambridge, MA: Harvard University Press, 2019); Joachim Blatter and Johannes Schulz, 'Intergovernmentalism and the Crisis of Representative Democracy: The Case for Creating a System of Horizontally Expanded and Overlapping National Democracies' (2022) 28(3) *European Journal of International Relations* 722–747; Kilian Spandler and Fredrik Söderbaum, 'Populist (De) Legitimation of International Organizations' (2023) 99(3) *International Affairs* 1023–1041.

5 On those different categories of alternative political representation, see Besson and Martí, Chapter 12 in this volume.

rise to domestically.[6] The future of domestic representation is therefore bound to that of international representation, and vice versa.[7]

Curiously given those important international and domestic stakes, however, the democratic representativeness of IOs does not seem to be much of a concern of IOs and their Member States, at least if one refers to the international law of IOs. Even more curiously, while the question of democratic representation in and by IOs is straightforward enough from a democratic legitimacy perspective, it has only rarely been addressed as such in scholarly debates pertaining to the democratic legitimacy of international law. It is this gap not only in the practice of democratic representation by IOs, but also in the literature, that the present volume purports to fill.

This introduction sets the stage for the book's argument: first, it unpacks the reasons that led to putting this collection together and introduces the main issues it addresses (Section 1.2); second, it identifies the specificities of the volume and explains what it hopes to achieve (Section 1.3); third, it provides some information about how the book is structured and its different parts articulated (Section 1.4); and, finally, it sketches out the contents of its successive chapters (Section 1.5).

## 1.2 THE BACKGROUND TO THE VOLUME

The question of democratic representation (by [the representatives of] Member States and/or [the representatives of] other public or private institutions involved in their lawmaking and decision-making processes, such as

6 See e.g. Lisa Disch, 'Introduction: The End of Representative Politics', in Lisa Disch, Mathijs van de Sande and Nadia Urbinati (eds.), *The Constructivist Turn in Political Representation* (Edinburgh: Edinburgh University Press, 2019), pp. 1–18; Jonathan W. Kuyper, 'Systemic Representation: Democracy, Deliberation, and Nonelectoral Representatives' (2016) 110(2) *American Political Science Review* 308–324; Michael Saward, *The Representative Claim* (Oxford: Oxford University Press, 2010). For a critique, see Sofia Näsström, 'Where is the Representative Turn Going?' (2011) 10(4) *European Journal of Political Theory* 501–510; Nadia Urbinati, 'Representative Democracy and its Critics', in Sonia Alonso, John Keane and Wolfgang Merkel (eds.), *The Future of Representative Democracy* (Cambridge: Cambridge University Press, 2011), pp. 23–49; Nadia Urbinati and Mark Warren, 'The Concept of Representation in Contemporary Democratic Theory' (2008) 11 *Annual Review of Political Science* 387–412; Nadia Urbinati, 'Representative Constructivism's Conundrum', in Disch *et al.*, fn. 6., pp. 182–202.

7 On the continuity between domestic and international democracy, see Samantha Besson, 'The Authority of International Law: Lifting the State Veil' (2009) 31(3) *Sydney Law Review* 343–380; Samantha Besson, 'Theorizing the Sources of International Law', in Samantha Besson and John Tasioulas (eds.), *The Philosophy of International Law* (Oxford: Oxford University Press, 2010), pp. 163–185; Samantha Besson, 'Investment Citizenship and Democracy in a Global Age: Towards a Democratic Interpretation of International Nationality Law' (2019) 29(4) *Swiss Review of International and European Law* 525–547; Samantha Besson, *Reconstructing the International Institutional Order* (Paris: OpenEdition Books/College of France, 2021).

cities, regions, indigenous peoples, NGOs, multinational corporations, employer's associations, trade unions, or patients' associations) in IOs, but also by IOs in and of themselves has not always been that moot. After all, the issue of equal representation and its modalities were hotly debated at the United Nations (UN) from the 1940s to the 1960s.[8] Even today, the neglect of the issue does not affect all IOs equally. Thus, the discussion is much more advanced in and regarding the International Labour Organization (ILO)[9] or the European Union (EU)[10] where (democratic) representation in and/or by the IO is a requirement of the respective IOs' constitutive treaty, than it is in and with respect to the World Health Organization (WHO)[11] or the International Organization for Migration (IOM).[12]

There are many reasons one may venture for the contemporary sidelining of the question of democratic representation *by* and *in* IOs in the law of international organizations and its practice.

[8] On those debates, see e.g. Boutros Boutros-Ghali, 'Le principe d'égalité des États et les organisations internationales' (Volume 100) *Collected Courses of the Hague Academy of International Law*, 1960, pp. 3–73; Ulrich K. Preuss, 'Equality of States: Its Meaning in a Constitutionalized Global Order' (2008) 9(1) *Chicago Journal of International Law* 17–49.

[9] See e.g. Francis Maupain, *The Future of the International Labour Organization in the Global Economy* (Oxford: Hart, 2013); Marieke Louis, *Qu'est-ce qu'une bonne représentation? L'Organisation internationale du travail de 1919 à nos jours* (Paris: Dalloz, 2016); Marieke Louis, 'Who Decides? Representation and Decision-Making at the International Labour Organization' (2019) 11 *International Development Policy* 40–58.

[10] See e.g. Christopher Lord, 'Externalities and Representation beyond the State: Lessons from the European Union', in Dario Castiglione and Johannes Pollak (eds.), *Creating Political Presence: The New Politics of Democratic Representation* (Chicago: Chicago University Press, 2018), pp. 254–275; Richard Bellamy, 'Representing the Peoples of Europe: Addressing the *Demoi*cratic Disconnect', in Richard Bellamy, *A Republican Europe of States: Cosmopolitanism, Intergovernmentalism and Democracy in the EU* (Cambridge: Cambridge University Press, 2019), pp. 97–130.

[11] See e.g. Lukasz Gruszczynski and Margherita Melillo, 'The Uneasy Coexistence of Expertise and Politics in the World Health Organization: Learning from the Experience of the Early Response to the covid-19 Pandemic' (2022) 19(2) *International Organizations Law Review* 301–331. For an exception, see Besson, 'COVID-19 and the WHO's Political Moment', fn. 2; Samantha Besson, 'Pour une représentation démocratique multiple au sein de l'Organisation mondiale de la Santé', in Olivier de Frouville and Dominique Rousseau (eds.), *Démocratiser l'Espace-Monde* (Le Kremlin Bicêtre: Mare & Martin, 2024), pp. 199–218; Samantha Besson and José Luis Martí, 'From Equal State Consent to Equal Public Participation in International Organizations: Institutionalizing Multiple International Representation', in Samantha Besson (ed.), *Consenting to International Law* (Cambridge: Cambridge University Press, 2023), pp. 314–346; Samantha Besson, 'We the Peoples of the United Nations: From Single Separate Instituent Powers to Multiple Nested Instituted Publics', in Peter Niesen, Marcus Patberg and Lucia Robinelli (eds.), *The Oxford Handbook of Constituent Power* (Oxford: Oxford University Press, 2026), pp. 531–544.

[12] See e.g. Jan Klabbers, 'Notes on the Ideology of International Organizations Law: The International Organization for Migration, State-Making, and the Market for Migration' (2019) 32(3) *Leiden Journal of International Law* 383–400.

One of the main reasons for the neglect of democratic representation *by* IOs is that their capacity to represent has mostly been approached as 'non-political' in international law.[13] Representation by IOs is indeed often organized so as to follow a 'functional' approach to legitimacy, that is, an approach to legitimacy by output only: representation by IOs should ensure the implementation of delegated States' functions and hence the protection of their Member States' interests. When it is exceptionally framed by reference to input legitimacy, representation by IOs remains functional, however. It relies on IOs' integrated or independent organs' expertise, for instance, in implementing States' functions and protecting their interests.

Moreover, to the extent that IO Member States, but also other public and private institutions participate in IO procedures and hence are to be represented *in* IO organs according to IO law, it is usually as such, and not necessarily as representatives of their respective constituencies.[14] In the increasing number of cases where their representativeness in IOs is required, it is mostly functional and measured by reference to certain characteristics of States or civil society organizations (CSOs) that may be of instrumental relevance for the IO. One may think here of the economic, financial, military, or technoscientific power of some of its Member States (usually a few of them) in the IO's interstate organs, on the one hand, and of the expertise and financial resources of some CSOs (usually just a few as well), on the other.[15] For the rest, the emphasis has been on 'participation' and 'inclusion' in IOs,[16] for instance of the so-called 'affected persons' and other 'stakeholders'.[17] This is

13 See also Marieke Louis and Lucile Maertens, *Why International Organizations Hate Politics: Depoliticizing the World* (London: Routledge, 2021).

14 There are exceptions, of course, such as the ILO's representative tripartism (see Louis, *Qu'est-ce qu'une bonne représentation?*, fn. 9 and Louis, 'Who Decides?', fn. 9) but they are rare.

15 This is the case, for instance, in the WHO, 'Framework of Engagement with Non-State Actors' (FENSA) (28 May 2016), WHA69.10 (see Besson, 'Pour une représentation démocratique multiple au sein de l'Organisation mondiale de la Santé', fn. 11).

16 See Angelo Golia and Anne Peters, 'The Concept of International Organization', in Jan Klabbers (ed.), *The Cambridge Companion to International Organizations Law* (Cambridge: Cambridge University Press, 2022), pp. 25–49; Klaus Dingwerth and Patrizia Nanz, 'Participation', in Jacob Katz Cogan, Ian Hurd and Ian Johnstone (eds.), *The Oxford Handbook of International Organizations* (Oxford: Oxford University Press, 2016), pp. 1126–1145.

17 See Terry Macdonald, 'Citizens or Stakeholders? Exclusion, Equality and Legitimacy in Global Stakeholder Democracy', in Daniele Archibugi, Mathias Koenig-Archibugi and Raffaele Marchetti (eds.), *Global Democracy: Normative and Empirical Perspectives* (Cambridge: Cambridge University Press, 2011), pp. 47–68; Coline Ruwet, 'Que représentent les *stakeholders*?: Le cas de l'élaboration d'ISO 26000' (2010) 60(6) *Revue Française de Science Politique* 1115–1135; Jochen von Bernstorff, 'New Responses to the Legitimacy Crisis of International Institutions: The Role of "Civil Society" and the Rise of the Principle of

usually done without reference to the representative credentials of those participants in IO processes except as self-representing or as self-appointed representatives, however, and without any concern about their impact on the concurrent representation of the very same people(s) by States within those IOs.

Even more curiously, while the question of democratic representation in and by IOs is straightforward enough from a democratic legitimacy perspective, it has only rarely been addressed as such in debates pertaining to the democratic legitimacy of international law. This is true in global or international (both terms being used interchangeably in this introduction) democratic theory as much as in international democracy law.

Starting with democratic theory, first, the so-called representative 'turn' or 'renaissance' of the last fifteen years or so[18] has not included international representation so far. This is most probably because there has rarely been an overlap of expertise in the same persons between international democracy theorists and democratic representation theorists.[19] When there has been such

Participation of the "Most Affected" in International Institutional Law' (2021) 32(1) *European Journal of International Law* 125–157, at 141ff.

18 See e.g. Hanna F. Pitkin, *The Concept of Representation* (Berkeley: University of California Press, 1972); Bernard Manin, *The Principles of Representative Government* (Cambridge: Cambridge University Press, 1997); Anne Phillips, *The Politics of Presence* (Oxford: Oxford University Press, 1998); Pierre Rosanvallon, *Le peuple introuvable: Histoire de la représentation démocratique en France* (Paris: Gallimard, 1998); Jane Mansbridge, 'Rethinking Representation' (2003) 97(4) *American Political Review* 515–528; Nadia Urbinati, *Representative Democracy: Principles and Genealogy* (Chicago: University of Chicago Press, 2006); Urbinati and Warren, fn. 6; Saward, fn. 6; Jane Mansbridge, 'Clarifying the Concept of Representation' (2011) 105(3) *American Political Science Review* 621–630; Näsström, fn. 6; Alonso *et al.*, fn. 6; Yves Sintomer, 'Le sens de la représentation politique: Usages et mésusages du débat contemporain' (2013) 50 *Raisons politiques* 13–34; Samuel Hayat and Yves Sintomer, 'Repenser la représentation politique' (2013) 50 *Raisons politiques* 5–11; Dario Castiglione and Mark E. Warren, 'Rethinking Democratic Representation: Eight Theoretical Issues', in Disch *et al.*, fn. 6, pp. 21–47; Castiglione and Pollak, fn. 10; Disch *et al.*, fn. 6; Samuel Hayat, Corinne Péneau and Yves Sintomer, *La représentation avant le gouvernement représentatif* (Rennes: Presses Universitaires de Rennes, 2020); Felipe Rey, 'The Representative System' (2023) 26(6) *Critical Review of International Social and Political Philosophy* 831–854; Manuela Albertone and Michel Troper, 'Penser la représentation', in Manuela Albertone and Michel Troper (eds.), *La représentation politique. Anthologie* (Paris: Classiques Garnier, 2021), pp. 7–32; Lisa Disch, *Making Constituencies: Representation as Mobilization in Mass Democracy* (Chicago: University of Chicago Press, 2021); Felipe Rey, *El sistema representativo: Las representaciones políticas y la transformación de la democracia parlamentaria* (Barcelona: Gedisa, 2023).

19 There have been exceptions, of course, see e.g. Andrew Kuper, *Democracy Beyond Border: Justice and Representation in Global Institutions* (Oxford: Oxford University Press, 2004); Terry Macdonald, *Global Stakeholder Democracy: Power and Representation Beyond Liberal*

an overlap, moreover, the democratic representation by IOs has not been the centre of attention, except in discussions of the EU[20] or the ILO.[21]

In a nutshell, international democracy theorists have divided into two groups over the years. The first and original group of so-called ideal international democracy theorists whose writings date back to the 1990s was actually concerned with international democratic representation. However, its focus was mostly cosmopolitan, for example on a world parliamentary assembly, and monistic, for example on a world State-like public institution, at the expense of the plurality of States and of other representative institutions active in international lawmaking.[22] At the turn of the millennium, and in reaction, a second group of theorists turned to non-ideal international democratic theory, defending both non-cosmopolitan and pluralist accounts of international democracy. However,

*States* (Oxford: Oxford University Press, 2008); Philip Pettit, 'Legitimate International Institutions: A Neorepublican Perspective', in Besson and Tasioulas, fn. 7, pp. 139–161; Philip Pettit, 'A Republican Law of Peoples' (2010) 9(1) *European Journal of Political Theory* 70–94; Richard Bellamy, '"An Ever Closer Union Among the Peoples of Europe": Republican Intergovernmentalism and *Demoi*cratic Representation within the EU' (2013) 35(5) *Journal of European Integration* 499–516; Bellamy, 'Representing the Peoples of Europe', fn. 10; Bellamy, *A Republican Europe of States*, fn. 10; Kuyper, fn. 6; Samantha Besson and José Luis Martí, 'Legitimate Actors of International Law-Making: Towards a Theory of International Democratic Representation' (2018) 9(3) *Jurisprudence* 504–540; Eva Erman, 'Political Legitimacy of Global Governance and the Proper Role of Society Actors' (2018) 24 *Res Publica* 133–155; Eva Erman and Jonathan W. Kuyper, 'Open Access: Global Democracy and Feasibility' (2020) 23(3) *Critical Review of International Social and Political Philosophy* 311–331; Samantha Besson and José Luis Martí, 'Cities as Democratic Representatives in International Law-Making', in Helmut P. Aust and Janne E. Nijman (eds.), *Research Handbook on International Law and Cities* (London: Edward Elgar, 2021), pp. 341–353; Besson, 'L'égalité des États membres de l'Union européenne', fn. 1; Samantha Besson, 'Democratic Representation within International Organizations: From International Good Governance to International Good Government' (2022) 19(3) *International Organizations Law Review* 489–527; Besson and Martí, 'From Equal State Consent to Equal Public Participation in International Organizations', fn. 11; Besson, 'Pour une représentation démocratique multiple au sein de l'Organisation mondiale de la Santé', fn. 11; Samantha Besson, 'The Politics of Regional International Organizations: A New Dawn for the Political Legitimacy of International Law' (2024) 21(1) *International Organizations Law Review* 87–114; Besson, 'We the Peoples of the United Nations', fn. 11.

20 See Lord, fn. 10; Bellamy, '"An Ever Closer Union Among the Peoples of Europe"', fn. 19; Bellamy, 'Representing the Peoples of Europe', fn. 10.

21 See Louis, *Qu'est-ce qu'une bonne représentation?*, fn. 9; Louis, 'Who Decides?', fn. 9.

22 See Robert A. Dahl, 'Can International Organizations Be Democratic? A Skeptic's View', in Ian Shapiro and Casiano Hacker-Cordón (eds.), *Democracy's Edges* (Cambridge: Cambridge University Press, 1999), pp. 19–36; Richard Falk and Andrew Strauss, 'Toward Global Parliament' (2001) 80(1) *Foreign Affairs* 212–220; David Held, 'Restructuring Global Governance: Cosmopolitanism, Democracy and the Global Order' (2009) 37(3) *Millennium Journal of International Studies* 535–547; Daniele Archibugi, 'Cosmopolitan Democracy: A Restatement' (2012) 42(1) *Cambridge Journal of Education* 9–20; Luis Cabrera (ed.), *Institutional Cosmopolitanism* (Oxford: Oxford University Press, 2018).

falling prey to the (common but mistaken) reduction of democratic representation to electoral representation[23] and hence to the latter's perceived lack of feasibility on an international scale, most authors in that vein have focused instead on issues of democratic deliberation, participation, accountability, and/or stakeholderism in international relations.[24] And this has been at the expense of a discussion of international democratic representation itself, of its inherent, complementary, and mutual relations with international democratic participation and deliberation and, more generally, of its conceptual relationship to international democratic legitimacy itself.

Turning to international democracy law and its literature, second, the issue of international democratic representation has generally been obliterated[25] by a similar and almost exclusive focus on democratic inclusion, participation and/or deliberation,[26] except for discussions of international parliamentary assemblies (wrongly) regarded again as the sole form of international democratic representation.[27] To that extent, the literature has fallen prey to the same

23 For this critique, see Nadia Urbinati, 'Representative Democracy and Its Critics', in Alonso *et al.*, fn. 18, pp. 23–49. See also Besson and Martí, Chapter 12 in this volume.

24 See Jens Steffek, 'The Legitimation of International Governance: A Discourse Approach' (2003) 9(2) *European Journal of International Relations* 249–275; James Bohman, *Democracy Across Borders: From Dêmos to Dêmoi* (Cambridge, MA: MIT Press, 2007); John S. Dryzek, 'Transnational Democracy in an Insecure World' (2006) 27(2) *International Political Science Review* 101–119; Macdonald, *Global Stakeholder Democracy*, fn. 19; Eva Erman, 'In Search of Democratic Agency in Deliberative Governance' (2013) 19(4) *European Journal of International Relations* 847–868; Erman and Kuyper, fn. 19; Thomas Hale and Mathias Koenig-Archibugi, 'Are Europeans Ready for a More Democratic European Union? New Evidence on Preference Heterogeneity, Polarisation, and Crosscuttingness' (2016) 55(2) *European Journal of Political Research* 225–245; Dominik Zaum, 'Legitimacy', in Cogan *et al.*, fn. 16, pp. 1107–1125; John S. Dryzek and Ana Tanasoca, *Democratizing Global Justice: Deliberating Global Goals* (Cambridge: Cambridge University Press, 2021).

25 There has been more literature on (non-democratic) representation in international law in general, albeit not much by comparison to domestic law. See e.g. Angelo Piero Sereni, 'La représentation en droit international' (Volume 73) *Collected Courses of The Hague Academy of International Law*, 1948, pp. 69–166; Riad Daoudi, *La représentation en droit international public* (Paris: LGDJ, 1980); Jean Salmon, 'Representatives of States in International Relations', in Rüdiger Wolfrum (ed.), *Max Planck Encyclopedia of Public International Law* (Oxford: Oxford University Press, 2007).

26 See Anne Peters, 'Dual Democracy', in Jan Klabbers, Anne Peters and Geir Ulfstein (eds.), *The Constitutionalization of International Law* (Oxford: Oxford University Press, 2009), pp. 263–341; Steven Wheatley, *The Democratic Legitimacy of International Law* (Oxford: Hart, 2010); Olivier de Frouville, *From Cosmopolitanism to Human Rights* (Oxford: Hart, 2022); Pauwelyn *et al.*, fn. 2; Ian Johnstone, 'Deliberation', in Klabbers, fn. 16, pp. 173–198; Bhupinder S. Chimni, 'Inclusion and Exclusion in International Organizations', in Klabbers, fn. 16, pp. 76–97. For a critique, see Besson and Martí, Chapter 12 in this volume.

27 See Laurence Dubin and Marie-Clotilde Runavot, 'Représentativité, efficacité, légitimité: Des organisations internationales en crise?', in Évelyne Lagrange and Jean-Marc Sorel (eds.), *Droit des organisations internationales* (Paris: LGDJ, 2013), pp. 77–103; Bjørn Høyland,

conflation between democratic representation and electoral representation, on the one hand, and hence to the related separation and sterile alternative opposition between (electoral) representation and (non-electoral) participation and deliberation, on the other.

Moreover, IOs have not been central to those discussions[28] and when they have, it has mostly been as institutional fora of democratic participation by CSOs, and not as representatives in and of themselves.[29] This focus may be explained by the compensatory approach that has long dominated international democracy law and the relevant literature: its aim has been to compensate for the insufficient democratic legitimacy of States in international lawmaking by the inclusion and participation of CSOs. And this, without any attempt at articulating those CSOs' 'participation' with the State-based representation of the same peoples and, hence, without addressing the risks of over-representation or under-representation of those peoples by those CSOs, and actually assuming their democratic representativeness.

It is this gap not only in the practice of representation by and in IOs, but also in the literature in international democratic theory and international democracy law, that the present volume purports to fill. More specifically, the volume is organized around three sets of issues: representation *in*, *through*, and *by* IOs.[30]

'Parliaments', in Cogan *et al.*, fn. 16, pp. 782–801; Marie-Clotilde Runavot (ed.), *La démocratie appliquée au droit international: de quoi parle-t-on?* (Paris: Pedone, 2018). See also Runavot, Chapter 6 in this volume; Lagrange, Chapter 14 in this volume. For a critique, see Besson and Martí, Chapter 12 in this volume.

28 On (mostly non-democratic) representation in and by IOs, see e.g. Évelyne Lagrange, *La représentation institutionnelle dans l'ordre international: Une contribution à la théorie de la personnalité morale des organisations internationales* (The Hague: Kluwer Law International, 2002); Jacob Katz Cogan, 'Representation and Power in International Organization: The Operational Constitution and its Critics' (2009) 103(2) *American Journal of International Law* 209–263; Dubin and Runavot, fn. 27; Louis, *Qu'est-ce qu'une bonne représentation?*, fn. 9; David P. Rapkin, Jonathan R. Strand and Michael W. Trevathan, 'Representation and Governance in International Organizations' (2016) 4(3) *Politics and Governance* 77–89; Louis, 'Who Decides?', fn. 9; Damien Bouvier, *La représentation internationale de l'Union européenne* (Brussels: Bruylant, 2020); Stephen Mathias and Stadler Trengove, 'Membership and Representation', in Cogan *et al.*, fn. 16, pp. 962–984. See also Cogan, Chapter 4 in this volume.

29 See Anne Peters, 'International Organizations and International Law', in Cogan *et al.*, fn. 16, pp. 33–59; Martin Krajewski, 'International Organizations or Institutions, Democratic Legitimacy', in Rüdiger Wolfrum (ed.), *Max Planck Encyclopedia of Public International Law* (Oxford: Oxford University Press, 2019); Anne Peters, 'Constitutional Theories of International Organisations: Beyond the West' (2021) 20(4) *Chinese Journal of International Law* 649–698; Chimni, fn. 26. For a recent exception, see von Bernstorff, fn. 17.

30 On this distinction and those three issues, see my previous work, as a single author or with José Luis Martí: Besson and Martí, 'Legitimate Actors of International Law-Making', fn. 19; Besson, 'COVID-19 and the WHO's Political Moment', fn. 2; Besson and Martí, 'Cities as Democratic

First of all, democratic representation *in* IOs. To the extent that IOs include Member States in their interstate organs and also increasingly allow for the participation of other public and private institutions in their deliberation and/or decision-making processes, the issue of the democratic representation by those institutions inside IOs arises.

Their democratic representativeness is already required by certain IOs' constitutive treaties,[31] but also, arguably, by international democracy law or, at least, by international human rights law.[32] One may think here of the democratic credentials required of State representatives in a given IO, for example at the time of accreditation of those representatives in the UN General Assembly[33] or

Representatives in International Law-Making', fn. 19; Besson, 'L'égalité des États membres de l'Union européenne', fn. 1; Besson, 'Democratic Representation within International Organizations', fn. 19; Besson and Martí, 'From Equal State Consent to Equal Public Participation in International Organizations', fn. 11; Besson, 'Pour une représentation démocratique multiple au sein de l'Organisation mondiale de la Santé', fn. 11; Samantha Besson and José Luis Martí, 'Republican Sovereignty', in Mortimer Sellers and Frank Lovett (eds.), *The Oxford Handbook of Republicanism* (Oxford: Oxford University Press, in press, 2027) (online edn, Oxford Academic, 23 January 2024, https://doi.org/10.1093/oxfordhb/9780197754115.013.35, last accessed 16 January 2026); Besson, 'We the Peoples of the United Nations', fn. 11. See also Besson and Martí, Chapter 12 in this volume.

31 See e.g. Articles 3(1) and 5 of the ILO Constitution on the representativeness of the Members' 'delegates', be they representative of 'governments', 'employers', or 'workpeople', in the General Conference of representatives, see International Labour Organization Constitution. www.ilo.org/dyn/normlex/en/f?p=1000:62:0::NO:62:P62_LIST_ENTRIE_ID:2453907:NO, last accessed 8 November 2023; Art. 10 of the Treaty on the European Union (hereafter TEU) on the representation of 'citizens' and 'States' by their 'representatives', 'governments', or 'heads of government', in the EU Parliament, Council, or European Council, see Consolidated Version of the Treaty on the European Union, OJ 2012 No. C326, 26 October 2012, p. 13. See also Louis, *Qu'est-ce qu'une bonne représentation?*, fn. 9.

32 See e.g. UN Human Rights Committee (UNHRC), 'CCPR General Comment No. 25: Article 25 (Participation in Public Affairs and the Right to Vote), The Right to Participate in Public Affairs and the Right of Equal Access to Public Service' (12 July 1996), CCPR/C/21/Rev.1/Add.7, para. 5; UNGA Res. 75/178 (16 December 2020), paras. 6(g), 6(h), 6(i). See also Nahuel Maisely, 'The International Right of Rights? Article 25(a) of the ICCPR as a Human Right to Take Part in International Law-Making' (2017) 28(1) *European Journal of International Law* 89–113; Hilary Charlesworth, 'International Legal Encounters with Democracy' (2017) 8(S6) *Global Policy* 34–43.

33 See Jean d'Aspremont, 'Legitimacy of Governments in the Age of Democracy' (2006) 38(4) *New York University Journal of International Law and Politics* 877–917; Jean d'Aspremont, 'The Rise and Fall of Democratic Governance in International Law: A Reply to Susan Marks' (2011) 22(2) *European Journal of International Law* 549–570; Hilary Charlesworth, 'Democracy and International Law' (Volume 371) *Collected Courses of the Hague Academy of International Law*, 2015, pp. 43–152; Charlesworth, fn. 32. For a recent discussion, see Catherine Armirfar, Romain Zamour and Duncan Pickard, 'Representation of Member States at the United Nations: Recent Challenges' (2022) 26(6) *ASIL Insights*. www.asil.org/insights/volume/26/issue/6, last accessed 3 August 2023. See also Runavot, Chapter 6 in this volume; Cogan, Chapter 4 in this volume.

of the democratic regime conditions for State membership in a given IO, for instance at the time of accession to or suspension from the UN.[34] Those democratic credentials are also sometimes required of representatives of CSOs such as, for example, trade unions and organizations of employers in the interstate organs of the ILO[35] and, arguably, of accredited NGOs in most UN organs and agencies.[36]

Second, democratic representation *through* IOs. The next issue the volume addresses pertains to the additional legal and institutional requirements IOs could and, one may argue, should pose to the democratic representativeness of States and of other public and private institutions, and of their respective representatives, inside IOs' lawmaking organs and processes. Indeed, it is precisely because IOs organize competing forms of public and private representation separately *in* the IOs' organs, as I have just explained, that they could also be deemed to be in a position to correct those other representatives' respective democratic deficits when they arise.[37] Furthermore, IOs could and, one may argue, should also contribute to articulate those multiple forms of public and private representation in such a way as to ensure their complementarity. This could circumvent the risks of under- and over-representation of the same peoples, and thereby contribute to turn IOs themselves into genuine 'systems of multiple international representation'[38] in the future.

After all, many IOs are general organizations (at least insofar as they guarantee the equality of their Member States) and are public ones (at least insofar as they have public institutions, the States, as members) or, at any rate, have the capacity to be. As such, IOs are ideally placed to organize or orchestrate international democratic representation in their midst from a general and public point of view. They already have to some extent, but, as explained before, this is not a general feature yet and it is arguably one that should be developed. Worse, certain IOs have even contributed to undermine the democratic representation of or by some of their Member States, for instance through privatization requirements or through orchestrating inegalitarian representation in

34 See Alison Duxbury, *The Participation of States in International Organisations: The Role of Human Rights and Democracy* (Cambridge: Cambridge University Press, 2011); Mathias and Trengove, fn. 28.

35 See Louis, *Qu'est-ce qu'une bonne représentation?*, fn. 9; Louis, 'Who Decides?', fn. 9.

36 See von Bernstorff, fn. 17.

37 See Besson and Martí, 'Legitimate Actors of International Law-Making', fn. 19; Besson, 'Democratic Representation within International Organizations', fn. 19. See also Besson and Martí, Chapter 12 in this volume.

38 On that system, see Besson and Martí, 'Legitimate Actors of International Law-Making', fn. 19; Besson, 'Democratic Representation within International Organizations', fn. 19. See also Besson and Martí, Chapter 12 in this volume.

integrated IO organs or secretariats.[39] And the same may be said of the often selected number of NGOs that are given functional precedence in their involvement in certain IOs.[40]

As examples of the enhancement of democratic representation through IOs, one may think of the legal constitution of transnational CSOs by IOs in order to enhance the international representation of national ones in their midst. This may be illustrated by the constitution of the International Organization of Employers (IOE) in the framework of the ILO.[41] Another example of the contribution of IOs to the enhancement of the democratic representativeness of other private or public institutions they include as representatives in their lawmaking processes may be the consolidation of an international private or public law status of those institutions and their international institution or re-institution as a result,[42] as it has been the case for small organizations of farmers by the Food and Agriculture Organization[43] (FAO) or for refugee organizations by the UN High Commissioner for Refugees[44] (UNHCR).

Third, democratic representation *by* IOs. Besides organizing the democratic representation by Member States and other public and private institutions they include in or associate to their respective decision-making procedures and besides articulating those multiples forms of democratic representation in their midst, and actually in order to do so democratically, IOs themselves could and should be regarded as democratic representatives.[45] This is the case both internally inside IO lawmaking procedures and externally when IOs engage in international lawmaking with third States and others IOs. This is the most difficult of all three questions and the one where most work is still needed, both on a theoretical and on a practical plane. In turn, this raises the further issue of the democratic representation *of* IOs, that is, the democratic representativeness of the 'public organs' (as opposed to mere 'agents' or 'diplomats') representing IOs themselves,[46] and not only their Member States

39 See Viola, fn. 1.
40 See Dingwerth and Nanz, fn. 16.
41 See Louis, Chapter 7 in this volume.
42 On the WHO and the missed opportunity of FENSA, see Besson, 'Pour une représentation démocratique multiple au sein de l'Organisation mondiale de la Santé', fn. 11; Besson, 'We the Peoples of the United Nations', fn. 11. See also Durkee, Chapter 8 in this volume; Peters, Chapter 9 in this volume.
43 See von Bernstorff, fn. 17; von Bernstorff, Chapter 10 in this volume.
44 See Macdonald, Chapter 11 in this volume.
45 See Besson and Martí, Chapter 12 in this volume.
46 On the separation of powers in IOs, see Joana Mendes and Ingo Venzke (eds.), *Allocating Authority: Who Should Do What in European and International Law?* (Oxford: Hart, 2018); Miriam Cullen, 'Separation of Powers in the United Nations System? Institutional Structure and the Rule of Law' (2020) 17(3) *International Organizations Law Review* 492–530.

and/or other public and private institutions inside those IOs as discussed under the first set of issues.

As examples of democratic representation by IOs, one may think here of the debates surrounding the ways to ensure the dual democratic representation of States' peoples and EU citizens by the European Parliament in the EU.[47] Another more recent example is that of the democratic representation by the Council of the EU in the negotiation of international agreements by the EU or by the European External Action Service in other IOs.[48]

## 1.3 THE AIMS OF THE VOLUME

In light of the important current international and domestic stakes of the topic of democratic representation in, through, and by IOs in international law, both in practice and in theory, and the many issues it raises, there are at least two contributions of the discussion proposed in this volume.

First, and as I explained before, representation in, through, and by IOs has only been addressed in the form of a handful of articles and chapters to date, and without a focus on democratic representation itself in any case.[49] There have been, quite surprisingly for such a central topic in international IO law and in global democratic theory, no monograph and no edited volume dedicated to the issue of democratic representation in, through, or by IOs in English. In response to this identified gap in the literature, the best specialists of representation in both IO law and in democratic theory have been invited to contribute to this volume. They have been asked to explore the issues identified earlier and many others they deem pressing and interesting. They do so from the dual interdisciplinary perspective of international law and global democratic theory.

Second, and precisely on this last point, this volume is the first to open a dialogue, and hopefully a fruitful one, between international lawyers and global democratic theorists on the topic of democratic representation in, through, and by IOs specifically. Such issues are not usually addressed together and in all their philosophical complexity by existing accounts of the international law of representation. Those accounts tend indeed to oppose

47 See Bellamy, 'Representing the Peoples of Europe', fn. 10; Jürgen Habermas, 'European Citizens and European Peoples: The Problem of Transnationalizing Democracy', in Jürgen Habermas, *The Lure of Technocracy*, translated by Ciaran Cronin (Malden, MA: Polity Press, 2015), pp. 29–45. See also Dubout and Ritleng, Chapter 13 in this volume.

48 See Bouvier, fn. 28.

49 See the references in fn. 19 and fn. 28. See for my own publications on the topic, the references in fn. 30.

democratic participation (and deliberation) to democratic representation and to reduce democratic representation to electoral representation and, generally, are not attuned to the latest debates on representation in democratic theory. Those issues cannot, conversely, be solved in an informed way by democratic theorists alone either. The latter often tend to overgeneralize and fail to grasp the sheer institutional complexity of IOs and international law-making in their midst. As a result, the volume should be of interest to both international lawyers and democratic theorists, but also well beyond and especially in international relations theory circles where most discussions of the legitimacy of IOs have actually taken place to date. More generally, it could also be a valuable resource to all international lawyers working on IOs and the ways to make them more legitimate, on the one hand, and to all political theorists interested in international democratic legitimacy, on the other.

In light of those two contributions to the debate, the volume has three aims. Its primary aim is, of course, to discuss the three issues identified in the previous section. Those three issues give the volume its tripartite structure. True, those issues often overlap, and actually should overlap to ensure full democratic representation by IOs.[50] They are only identified and distinguished here to help understand the many layers of the problem and, eventually, of the institutional reforms that could help address it more effectively.

So-doing, the volume's second aim is to contribute to the more general debate about the concepts and conceptions of representation in contemporary democratic theory, by extending that debate to the international plane. It purports to explore what 'representation' itself, and especially 'political' and 'democratic representation' should amount to and how they differ from 'legal' or other forms of non-democratic representation.[51] This includes clarifying, for instance, what should be the exact relationship between democratic legitimacy and democratic representation,[52] on the one hand, and what should be democratic representation's subjects,[53] objects,[54] relations,[55] and characteristics, on the other.

[50] See Besson and Martí, Chapter 12 in this volume.

[51] See Peters, Chapter 9 in this volume; Cogan, Chapter 4 in this volume.

[52] See Macdonald, Chapter 11 in this volume; Besson and Martí, Chapter 12 in this volume; Rosanvallon, Chapter 2 in this volume; von Bernstorff, Chapter 10 in this volume.

[53] See Pettit, Chapter 3 in this volume; Cheneval, Chapter 5 in this volume; Besson and Martí, Chapter 12 in this volume; Dubout and Ritleng, Chapter 13 in this volume; Peters, Chapter 9 in this volume.

[54] See Peters, Chapter 9 in this volume.

[55] See Besson and Martí, Chapter 12 in this volume; Macdonald, Chapter 11 in this volume; Peters, Chapter 9 in this volume; Runavot, Chapter 6 in this volume.

For this essential discussion in a volume on democratic theory to take place and to extend fully and freely to the international plane, I have deliberately refrained from imposing not only a single conception of democracy and democratic legitimacy, but also a single conception of representation in general and of democratic representation in particular (such as the ones presented in my chapter in this volume).[56] The various contributions therefore exhibit different understandings of international democratic representation which they have been asked to explain at the outset of their argument and justify by reference to or by opposition to others, including other accounts of democratic representation at work in the volume. This also implies for them to draw delineations from related widespread concepts in international law that are often used interchangeably and not sufficiently rigorously, such as, for instance, 'participation', and 'deliberation',[57] but also from 'expertise' and 'lobbying' in IOs.[58]

This should actually be done in light of the continuum between domestic and international public law and institutions and between comparative foreign relations law and the international law of representation,[59] and hence, more generally, between domestic and international democracy.[60] To the extent that the conference took place at the College of France, the volume features many French-speaking specialists. Given the importance of French-speaking discussions of representation in democratic theory, both past and recent,[61] and their questioning of the influence of Hanna Pitkin's theory of

56 See Besson and Martí, Chapter 12 in this volume.

57 See Lagrange, Chapter 14 in this volume; Dubout and Ritleng, Chapter 13 in this volume; Runavot, Chapter 6 in this volume; de Frouville, Chapter 15 in this volume.

58 See Durkee, Chapter 8 in this volume; Louis, Chapter 7 in this volume.

59 On the latter and the international democratic representation by States, see Jenny S. Martinez, 'The Constitutional Allocation of Executive and Legislative Power over Foreign Relations', in Curtis A. Bradley (ed.), *The Oxford Handbook of Comparative Foreign Relations Law* (Oxford: Oxford University Press, 2019), pp. 97–114; Edward T. Swaine, 'International Foreign Relations Law: Executive Authority in Entering and Exiting Treaties', in Helmut P. Aust and Thomas Kleinlein (eds.), *Encounters between Foreign Relations Law and International Law: Bridges and Boundaries* (Cambridge: Cambridge University Press, 2021), pp. 46–59; Helmut P. Aust, 'The Democratic Challenge to Foreign Relations Law in Transatlantic Perspective', in Jacco Bomhoff, David Dyzenhaus and Thomas Poole (eds.), *The Double-Facing Constitution* (Cambridge: Cambridge University Press, 2020), pp. 345–375.

60 See Besson, 'Democratic Representation within International Organizations', fn. 19.

61 See e.g. Pierre Bourdieu, 'La représentation politique: Éléments pour une théorie du champ politique' (1981) 36–37 *Actes de la Recherche en Sciences Sociales* 3–24; Roger Chartier, 'Le monde comme représentation' (1989) 44(6) *Annales. Économies, sociétés, civilisations* 1505–1520; Marcel Gauchet, *La révolution des pouvoirs: La souveraineté, le peuple et la représentation* (Paris: Gallimard, 1995); Manin, fn. 18; Pierre Brunet, *Vouloir pour la nation: le concept de représentation et la théorie de l'État* (Paris: LGDJ, 2004); Rosanvallon, fn. 18;

representation[62] in Anglo-American circles,[63] their inclusion may contribute to diversify some of the recent discussions in global democratic theory, but also, by extension, in the philosophy of international law. Of course, for that theory to be truly global, such comparisons should be pursued beyond the boundaries of European and Western political and democratic theory. One may actually hope that international democracy law and especially the international law of democratic representation discussed in this volume will contribute to launching such comparative discussions in the future.

The volume's third and broader, albeit more distant, goal is to examine how IOs could be re-designed and re-organized under international law so as to ensure sufficient democratic representation of all those they claim to bind legally, either directly or through their Member States.

While the organizational diversity of IOs may be in the way of institutional design and amounts to part of the problem in this respect, it is this volume's premise that diversity has to be part of our debates about potential solutions. To that extent, the exploration of democratic representation in, through, and by IOs should also contribute to the larger discussion pertaining to a common international public status of those organizations and about their re-institution under public international law.[64] Again, I have deliberately refrained from imposing to all contributors a single and unified understanding of IOs (such as the one presented in my chapter in this volume).[65] The various contributions therefore exhibit different understandings of IOs which they have been asked to spell out and defend as part of their argument.

## 1.4 THE STRUCTURE OF THE VOLUME

The volume is divided into three parts that correspond to the three sets of issues identified earlier and that are addressed in the respective chapters: democratic representation *in*, *through*, and *by* IOs.

Louis Marin, *Politiques de la représentation* (Paris: Kimé, 2005); Claude Lefort, 'Démocratie et représentation', in Claude Lefort, *Le temps présent: Écrits 1945–2005* (Paris: Belin, 2007), pp. 611–624; Sintomer, 'Le sens de la représentation politique', fn. 18; Samuel Hayat, 'La représentation inclusive' (2013) 50 *Raisons Politiques* 115–135; Hayat and Sintomer, 'Repenser la représentation politique', fn. 18; Myriam Revault d'Allonnes, *Le miroir et la scène: Ce que peut la représentation politique* (Paris: Seuil, 2016); Hayat *et al.*, fn. 18; Albertone and Troper, fn. 18.

62 Pitkin, fn. 18.

63 See Sintomer, 'Le sens de la représentation politique', fn. 18.

64 See Besson, 'Democratic Representation within International Organizations', fn. 19. See also Besson and Martí, Chapter 12 in this volume; Lagrange, Chapter 14 in this volume.

65 See Besson and Martí, Chapter 12 in this volume.

Each of those three parts comprises four chapters. In each part, both international lawyers and democratic theorists (some authors qualify, and consider themselves, as both) have been asked to address what they take to be the most interesting questions raised by democratic representation in, through, and by IOs. This mixed authorship in each part avoids a common but fake opposition between the 'theory' and 'practice' of international law, and makes the exchanges more fluid between the two groups of authors.

Coming back to the tripartite structure of the volume, there may be overlaps between some of the issues discussed in the chapters in each part and some of those discussed in the other two parts, as it is often the case when addressing complex democratic theory principles. This is also how it should be. As mentioned before, indeed, it is difficult to classify any given argument about representation as pertaining only to representation in, through, or by IOs as the former two are necessary to the latter. Importantly, moreover, those overlaps have been addressed in the relevant chapters. The idea has not been to ask contributors in the later parts of the volume to endorse what was said in earlier ones, but to ask them to refer to the relevant arguments provided their own argument requires them to do so and to explain how they agree or disagree with what was said earlier in the volume. Finally, the concluding chapter does not only close the volume by drawing the main conclusions of the overlapping claims made therein, but it also identifies remaining open questions and some directions for future research and, of course, for future reforms of IOs and their international law. To that extent, it should also be read as a self-standing chapter.

Last but not least: while certain contributions in the volume have opted for a theoretical, either general or comparative approach to the topic, others have chosen to focus on specific types of representative institutions only (such as States, cities, NGOs, Affected Peoples' Organizations [APOs], refugees' associations, trade unions, employers' associations, business associations, the International Chamber of Commerce [ICC], the Interparliamentary Union [IPU], or the IOE); on particular types of represented subjects only (such as individuals, peoples including indigenous peoples, populaces, publics, polities, citizenries, public institutions, refugees, civil society, 'affected peoples', business entities, or animals and other non-human living beings); and in and by specific IOs only (such as the EU, the ILO, the UN, the WHO, the FAO, the UNHCR, international financial institutions [IFIs], or the World Organization for Animal Health [WOAH]).

The volume does not, therefore, aim to provide an exhaustive coverage of IOs, of the multiple representative public and private institutions in their midst (including of all the different types of CSOs), or of the multiple subjects to represent therein. Nor does the structure of the volume aim at reflecting that multiplicity in any systematic way. This would go beyond the scope of what is, as I explained earlier, a first foray into the topic of democratic representation in, through, and by IOs. Conducting a more exhaustive and systematic study would certainly be worthwhile and this will hopefully be done by other researchers in the future.

## 1.5 THE CONTENTS OF THE VOLUME

The volume is divided in three parts: the first part pertains to democratic representation *in* IOs; the second part to democratic representation *through* IOs; and the third part to democratic representation *by* IOs. It starts with a general opening chapter on the state of discussions of representation in democratic theory in general and their relevance for international representation, and closes with a concluding chapter that also maps directions for future research.

In the opening Chapter 2, 'The Dawn or Dusk of Democratic Representation', Pierre Rosanvallon argues that, historically, democratic progress has been widely understood as correlated to the representative quality of institutions. Representativeness has been seen as essential for the social appropriation of institutions in societies analysed as having a class structure. In the national political order, parties were intended to represent the different social interests, and in the particular context of labour, the recognition of trade unions played this role. It is in this spirit that the ILO included trade unions in its various bodies when it was created a century ago, and, since then, the ILO has served as a reference point for representation at the international level. While this conception of representativeness remains relevant, the author argues that the scope of its application has become more limited. A growing number of essential issues, such as the conservation of the environment or the protection of privacy, are, in fact, directly political: they structure our common world. In this context, authority and legitimacy carry weight in the public debate. Representativeness, by which we can 'measure' the social weight of a speaker, is only secondary. 'Public voices' have come to have greater relevance, due to their ability to resonate with, and thereby focus and shape, public opinion. These 'public voices' are expressed by expert groups with specific subject-area knowledge, or by individuals who have benefited from the haphazard nature of media coverage. As a result, their integration into international life can no longer be institutionalized in the 'old fashioned' way.

The first part of the book is comprised of four chapters and pertains to democratic representation *in* IOs. Those chapters discuss different aspects of the question. The first and third chapters address the identity of the subjects represented in IOs, be they a populace or sum of individuals, a State or public institution, or a people or citizenry, and reflect on whether there should be a single subject represented or many of those. The second and fourth chapters take a closer look at the different modes of representation in IOs, some being more democratic than others and, among the latter, some being clearly parliamentary, albeit in different shades of parliamentary representation.

In Chapter 3, 'International Representation by State-Independent Bodies', Philip Pettit discusses what might entitle agents or agencies that are not sponsored by the State, only by some other social group or organization, to represent their people in an international forum. A State-centred approach would deny that they ever have a title to such a role, while an individual-centred approach would hold that they have as good a title as the State. Both approaches have problems and the chapter presents a third, more satisfying alternative. On this approach, such bodies may claim to represent their people insofar as the State enjoys standby control over their proposals, being able to oppose them, should it wish to do so, with a radical veto or a moderate refusal to be bound. Ideally, however, the State with such standby control will be required to allow the proposals to be publicized domestically and to provide reasons for opposing them, if that is what it chooses to do. Under the arrangement proposed, State-independent representatives will be able to explore innovative ideas collaboratively with their counterparts from elsewhere, to identify imaginative solutions to common problems, and to have the opportunity to persuade their own States, under domestic pressure, to fall in line.

In Chapter 4, 'The Four Modes of Representation in International Organizations and the Challenge of Democratic Legitimacy', Jacob Katz Cogan describes four modes of representation in IOs – formal, operational, aspirational, and alternative. They are separate yet intertwined; they contend with yet depend on each other. Together they form the international system of representation. This is not simply descriptively true. The resort to, and the use of, the four modes is also optimal, under current conditions. All four are necessary, as for any successful system to evolve and maintain equilibrium there needs to be a variety of mechanisms available that allow for the balancing of competing values and the reconciliation of formal rules with the actualities of power and expectations of legitimacy, as the alignment will never be perfect. Importantly, the four modes allow a range of entry points for democratic legitimacy in the representative practices of IOs, creating the possibility of change going forward and meeting that challenge. The international representational system of the four modes is thus second best.

Yet second best is better than any of the possible alternatives while the process of change slowly proceeds.

In Chapter 5, '*Demoi*cratic Representation in and by International Organizations', Francis Cheneval proposes that we approach *demoi*cratic representation as a subtype of representation in international organizational practice. The chapter develops a social ontology of the People and theory of representation which underpins the thesis that the People is represented only by all the different types of representative persons who act within different types of governmental institutions and procedures of the People. A further important tenet of the chapter is that democratic Peoples are accountable to each other as Peoples and to each other's citizens. In a union of Peoples whose representatives act under any decision rule there is a possible second-order consent deficit about the decision rule. Consequently, in *demoi*cratic representation, IOs ought to embody all the representative institutions of the People in their organization or be part of a system of mutual accountability and thereby assure *demoi*cratic representation by IOs. *Demoi*cratic representation ought not to be understood as working exclusively under the principle of consent. Rather it is the representational space in which the consent deficit about the decision rule of inter-People relations is addressed and calibration sought.

In Chapter 6, 'Democratic Representation and Parliamentarization of International Organizations: Between False Friends and False Pretences', Marie-Clotilde Runavot argues that IOs are instances of international governance, that is, places where international (normative) power is exercised. As such, they are subject to requirements for democratization, among which is the need for democratic representation. The meaning of democratic representation varies. When applied to IOs in the context of globalization, democratic representation is understood as the set of mechanisms and techniques that make individuals present in their functioning, particularly in the making of international norms, including soft law. Among these mechanisms and techniques, parliamentarization is supposed to involve national parliaments to a greater extent, either as such, through their members, or through the institutions that bring them together: the international parliamentary institutions. Notwithstanding their diversity, these institutions appear to be the preferred vehicle for the parliamentarization of IOs because they institutionalize international parliamentary representation. Yet, the extent to which this parliamentarization effectively serves democratic representation in IOs is open to discussion. First, representation *within* international parliamentary institutions reveals that the parliamentary representative can be a false friend of IOs as democratic representatives. Moreover, representation *by* international parliamentary institutions or their members is often a false pretence of democratic representation within IOs, despite clear democratic virtues for their functioning.

The second part of the book is comprised of four chapters and pertains to democratic representation *through* IOs. Those chapters address different aspects of the question. They focus either on specific representatives within IOs or on specific IOs. The first two chapters focus on the democratic credentials of the representation of and by business entities in IOs and how IOs contribute to making those entities more democratically representative, while a fourth chapter addresses the democratic representativeness of APOs and their status in IOs. A third chapter looks at a specific IO's contribution to the democratic representation of animals, that is, the WOAH.

In Chapter 7, 'Differentiated Representation and Cross-Legitimization of Business in International Organizations: Comparing the International Organization of Employers with the International Chamber of Commerce', Marieke Louis proposes a socio-historical and comparative contribution to the controversy arousing around business participation and the democratization of global governance through a comparison between the ICC and the IOE in the twentieth and twenty-first centuries. While these two organizations have claimed to represent business and private enterprises at the global level, and have benefited from the legitimization of intergovernmental organizations themselves (the ILO and the UN) for more than a century now, they have done so in a quite differentiated way, both in their external relationships with intergovernmental organizations as in the definition of their internal representativeness. This chapter first delves into the process of institutionalization of the representation of the ICC and IOE. It then reveals the logic of their internal organization, particularly in their relations with their members, employers' associations, and multinational corporations. It insists on their selection process and the way they have built a collective entity that is now referred to as 'business'. By doing so, the chapter distinguishes the representation *of* the ICC and the IOE within IOs from the representation of business within and *by* the ICC and the IOE, insisting on the need for a more differentiated and historically grounded perspective on business actors in global governance institutions.

In Chapter 8, 'The Ambivalent Logics of Business Representation in International Organizations', Melissa J. Durkee begins by observing that the UN and its bodies have 'opened up' to a broad range of non-State actors over the last three decades, including for-profit actors and their representatives. The shift is reflected in the UN's Sustainable Development Goals and the Global Compact, emphasizing public-private partnerships; in greater participation of corporations at treaty conferences; in trade group roles as observers at organizations; and in multi-stakeholder projects. Yet, IOs have generally not developed robust responses to legitimacy concerns about businesses becoming closely involved in lawmaking and governance projects. These concerns focus on interest group capture, entrenchment of Western economic elites, creeping privatization, and erasure of public deliberation. Indeed, the participation of for-profit actors and their representatives has largely been a 'silent revolution': under-heralded and under-examined. This chapter argues that responses to for-profit roles in the work of IOs tend to express one of two logics, not yet reconciled. The logic of 'representation' values public authority, interest representation, transparency, and accountability. The logic of 'expedience' values pragmatic problem-solving, efficiency, knowledge, and progress. Each has different priorities and blind spots, encompasses an array of theoretical approaches, and would push the international system in a different direction.

In Chapter 9, 'Representation and Consideration of Animals in International Organizations', Anne Peters starts by observing that decisions by IOs typically neglect the interests of non-human animals. The chapter investigates whether and how animal interests can and should be brought to bear on the decision-making of IOs. It works through cognate concepts ranging from animal citizenship over animal representation to animal consideration and animal deliberation. The physical limits of human-animal communication foreclose responsiveness and accountability to the animals themselves. The chapter therefore prefers the term animal 'consideration' rather than animal 'representation'. After this groundwork, the chapter briefly canvasses some proposals for bringing animal interests to bear in democratic political processes. With due modifications, some schemes could be applied to the work of IOs. These range from animal ombudspersons, strengthening the voice of pro-animal CSOs through compulsory notice-and-comment procedures and extended speaking rights in the organizations, mandatory animal welfare impact assessment, and more. All attempts at upgrading the existing rudimentary schemes in the direction of a better and stronger consideration of animal interests in human politics, including in IOs, will require deep cultural and social change, including some which are to a large extent beyond the purview of existing law.

In Chapter 10, 'Democratic Representation in International Institutions: From Great Power Hegemony to Rebellions by the Most Affected', Jochen von Bernstorff observes that within and through international institutions, public and private, international, transnational, and national actors have reacted to recent crisis-phenomena in the field of international health, nuclear disarmament, and climate change by launching new political and legal initiatives. Broad coalitions of small and middle-sized States, including

CSOs are currently pushing for major institutional reforms in and outside certain international institutions such as IOs through complementary treaties reacting rather creatively to a perceived institutional stand-still often caused by great powers defending the legal and political status quo. The new treaty projects claim a specific legitimacy due to a stronger focus on those actors who are negatively affected by the existing regimes and their perceived deficiencies. The contribution describes these recent initiatives as a form of 'rebellious treaty-making' promoted by coalitions of 'the most affected' analysing their legal and theoretical repercussions in the context of broader legitimation-narratives in the law of IOs.

The third and final part of the book is comprised of four chapters and pertains to democratic representation *by* IOs. Those chapters discuss various dimensions of the question. The first two chapters address the institutional or constitutive dimension of democratic representation by IOs that contributes to the international re-institution of the world's peoples. They do so in the specific context of the constitution of a new refugee constituency through representation by the UN in the first chapter, or more generally by questioning the a-political private law analogies prevalent in the international law of incorporation-based or agency-based representation by IOs in the second chapter. The third chapter takes a fresh look at the democratic representation of European peoples and citizens by the EU, while the fourth chapter explores the role of subsidiary organs and of deliberation in their midst as an alternative to the democratic representativeness of IOs in general.

In Chapter 11, 'International Organizations as Orchestrators of Represented Constituencies: The Case of the Global Compact on Refugees', Terry Macdonald examines how IOs can contribute to the development of representative practices that strengthen global institutional legitimacy. More specifically, the chapter argues that global representative practice can contribute to democratic legitimacy through a distinct set of constitutive representative activities, which function to cultivate – within socially and institutionally emergent groups holding democratic representative claims – those ties of political recognition, integration, and commitment required to constitute them as active and legitimizing democratic constituencies. IOs can engage in this constitutive representation through the orchestration of represented constituencies: intervening in relationships among representatives and their emergent constituents in ways that cultivate their collective legitimating qualities of political recognition, integration, and commitment. These claims are illustrated through an examination of the roles of the UNHCR and the UN General Assembly (UNGA) as orchestrators of a transnational represented constituency of refugees, via their work in supporting a range of democratic commitments within the Global Compact on Refugees. Overall, this analysis shows how concepts of representation can be brought into closer alignment with the functional demands of democratic legitimation in the complex and dynamic political circumstances of contemporary global politics.

In Chapter 12, 'No International Democratic Representation without Institution: Lifting the Democratic Veil of Functionalist, Incorporation, and Agency Theories of Representation by International Organizations', Samantha Besson and José Luis Martí build upon their previous work on international democratic representation *in* and *through* IOs, and bring their argument in favour of IOs as 'multiple international representation systems' one step further to democratic representation *by* IOs. Their argument is three-pronged. The first section sets the conceptual framework for the argument by presenting what is meant by international 'democratic legitimacy' and 'representation' in the chapter. The second section specifies the subjects of democratic representation by IOs. It argues against an approach, now common both in international democratic theory and in the international law of IOs, that considers States to be the subjects of international representation as opposed to peoples, on the one hand, and to be States' peoples only as opposed to the multiple publics which those peoples, but also others, are re-instituted into by different public institutions now involved in international lawmaking, on the other. In the third and final section, the chapter turns to the relation of democratic representation by IOs. It criticizes three existing accounts of that relation, prevalent in theory and practice, for their lack of democratic legitimacy: functionalism, incorporation, and agency.

In Chapter 13, 'Democratic Representation in the European Union: Democratizing Democracy?', Édouard Dubout and Dominique Ritleng question the reality and possibility of the claim that the EU is founded on 'representative democracy'. In the absence of a European *demos*, three consecutive difficulties are analysed: the question of the unity of the represented, the representation of citizens as EU citizens, and, finally, the quest for representativeness of the European society. The reflection's conclusion points towards the complementarity and inseparability of the representative and participatory forms of democracy in a transnational context, with the participatory forms adding a transnational dimension to European representative democracy.

In Chapter 14, 'Extending the Sphere of Deliberation in Universal International Organizations: An Alternative to the Elusive Democratic Representation in/by International Organizations', Évelyne Lagrange argues that 'democratic representation' seems to have no explanatory power for the current structure and operation of universal IOs and a weak justificatory value for upcoming political reforms of these IOs. However, under the benefit of a renewed approach to universal IOs' functions and deliberation, which is one of their meta-functions, the creation of new subsidiary bodies designed to accommodate delegates from non-State actors and enable, or even compel, intergovernmental bodies to take into account other interests and perspectives appears to be both necessary and feasible, without any reference to contentious criteria of representativeness based on a fragile principle of democratic legitimacy in international law. The alternative to 'democratic representation' consists in amplifying diffuse attempts to redesign the institutional architecture of universal IOs and harnessing the potential of international institutional law, implied powers and privileges and immunities regimes for the sake of a genuinely international, transnational, and transgenerational deliberation. Concretely, people speaking for sub-State communities (for example from the Global South), future generations or natural entities for instance should be given an institutional role within consultative subsidiary bodies, in combination with State representatives or scientific experts, or not – depending on what is necessary for the fulfilment of the IOs' functions. The current context of exacerbated competition between more and less democratic States, some of them obviously being authoritarian, also pleads for a modest approach to IOs political reform leaving the concept of democracy unaltered.

In Chapter 15, 'Conclusions', Olivier de Frouville does not intend to summarize and even less to close the debate launched by the volume, but instead to revert to the main issues addressed therein so as to identify further issues for research. All contributors agree that not only a discussion on democracy and representation in and by IOs is not purely speculative or theoretical, but that it seems necessary today. Still, contributors are not all in agreement on the need to use the concept of representation when addressing the democratization of IOs. Some question the link between democracy and representation, or whether developing representative systems is even feasible in IOs. This, in turn, leads to various definitions of the concept of representation. The multiple international representation system (MIRS) as proposed by Besson and Martí is based on a strict concept of democratic representation and contrasts with other more flexible concepts such as 'descriptive' or 'mimetic' representation. In the end, the various chapters in the volume address the merits of various concepts of representation, including those used in existing processes of global governance, when further democratizing IOs.

2

# The Dawn or Dusk of Democratic Representation

Pierre Rosanvallon

I wish to thank Samantha Besson for inviting me to participate in this volume. This invitation has allowed me to reflect on my work, or, should I say, my former work, as a look at the conference's programme made me feel that the entire reflection on the question of representation that had been mine in the 1980–90s has changed dramatically. I recognized that this theme of representation and the demand for representativeness in institutions was a legacy to be preserved, maybe even developed in certain respects, but that it is perhaps no longer the engine of democratic progress that it had long been.

As a historian, I would like to recall that the notion of representation was historically linked to the creation of assemblies which were soon known as 'parliaments'. Representation was aimed at shaping and envisioning the constitution and role of these assemblies. It seems to have fulfilled this function successively through *archaism* and *utopia*. Archaism characterizes the old assemblies that were conceived of as the expression of a society of corporate bodies (*corps*). A society comprised of such *corps* had an obvious consistency because there is no separation between these societies' legal constitution and their social existence. Social *corps* can be defined as social forms that are legally constituted. In such a case, representation refers to the process of imagining and shaping these legally constituted parts. These social forms have evolved based on the purpose assigned to these assemblies, in order to organize the relationships to the royal power (levying taxes, defining margins of autonomy, etc.). To better understand this history, one should refer to the research performed over more than forty years by the International Commission for the History of Representative and Parliamentary Institutions, which published fifty volumes during the 1970s and many additional seminal works since. In these cases,

This chapter was transcribed by Sylvie Sportouch, and then translated from French by Sévrine Knuchel, thanks to the financial support of the College of France's Foundation.

representation is figurative. Its function is to offer a condensed yet faithful image of the social world. Hanna Pitkin spoke in this sense of a 'microcosmic' conception of representation.[1] Honoré-Gabriel de Mirabeau, in the context of France's *Ancien Régime* and a few months before the beginning of the French Revolution, wrote that an assembly 'must be constituted in such a way that it is for the nation what a map is for a physical land; either in part or in large, the copy must always have the same proportions as the original'.[2] And indeed, in order to be able to reduce scale, it is necessary to distinguish the constitutive principles of what the figure represents. This is why we have long spoken in this sense of *state assemblies* (states with a lower case, meaning social states). In this case, the assemblies had to reproduce the social structure, such as the *Ancien Régime*'s division into three social groups – those who prayed, those who fought, and those who worked – or its corporate organization into trades, or its territorial divisions into cities, provinces, and so on. This is the reason why Jean-Jacques Rousseau rejected the notion of representation by calling it 'medieval'. Karl Marx would say a century later in his *Critique of Hegel's Philosophy of Right* that this gave civil society an immediately political, not separate, dimension. Social states, he famously wrote, 'acquired no [additional] significance in the political world, but signified only themselves'.[3] 'The Middle Ages was the democracy of nonfreedom', concluded Marx.[4] For Marx, democracy means the complete identification of the political with the social, which took place in medieval societies, but in a context of non-freedom. This is why Marx used this seemingly paradoxical expression of democracy of non-freedom, to emphasize that the goal of modern democracy should always be to achieve a melding of the political and the social, and no longer return to the notion of representation.

The French Revolution endeavoured to break free from archaism. Triggered by Louis XVI's summoning of the Estates General (a typical form of ancient parliament), the Revolution resulted in the transmutation of this 'old' parliament into a modern National Assembly. Instituted in a society of (still exclusively male) individuals equal in civil and political rights, the French National Assembly was characterized first of all by its function to

[1] Hanna F. Pitkin, *The Concept of Representation* (Berkeley: University of California Press, 1967).

[2] Honoré-Gabriel Riqueti de Mirabeau, 'Discours sur la représentation illégale de la Nation Provençale dans les États actuels, et sur la nécessité de convoquer une Assemblée générale des trois Ordres, prononcé dans la quatrième séance des États actuels de Provence', Speech delivered on 30 January 1789.

[3] Karl Marx, *Critique of Hegel's Philosophy of Right*, edited by Joseph O'Malley, translated by Joseph O'Malley and Annette Jolin (Cambridge: Cambridge University Press, 1970), Part 5, remark on para. 304.

[4] Ibid., Part 2, remark on para. 279.

express the general will and guide the life of the nation accordingly. At the time, the legislature was considered the only real power and the executive was subordinate. Many ignore that one of the major innovations of the French Revolution in 1794 was the suppression of the executive power: ministers and ministries were abolished and replaced with commissions of the parliamentary assembly. The parliament and the enactment of laws were considered essential. The law's enforcement was the responsibility of parliamentary committees and, as a result, the executive power as such no longer existed.

Under such a configuration, the assembly not only represents the nation, it *is* the nation. The assembly is the nation because its members are not conceived of as delegates, but are elected in the French departments as 'representatives' (a formulation that has been retained in the current French constitution). These representatives – and here lies the utopia – are the embodiment of the qualities deemed constitutive of the process of elaborating the general will: a combination of intellectual capacity (*talent*) and moral qualities (*virtue*). The power of the general will expresses itself through an election-selection, with the 'aristocratic' dimension that this entails.[5] The utopia even appears twofold, as it not only relates to the elaboration of the general will, but also to the election itself. The election was not understood as a selection in the sense of a choice made after conducting an open competition between candidates. Rather, it was understood merely as a procedure for identifying 'representatives' who embodied *qualities of generality* (talent and virtue). This explains why, during the French Revolution, standing as a candidate in elections would be forbidden: there would never be competitive elections. The question then arises as to how to proceed with an election if there are no candidates. The voting techniques used during the French Revolution involved extremely time-consuming procedures because the voting was conducted in so-called primary assemblies composed of about a thousand people. Rounds of voting took place without candidates, and, indeed, in the first round, it was possible to have 200 different names written on the ballot papers. At least one to two days were necessary to finish with only one name, although the absence of official candidates did not preclude behind-the-scenes effects. In 1791, which is one of the most active voting times during the French Revolution, second-degree Parisian voters voted nearly 200 days a year. Without candidates, it took 200 days simply to

[5] On this point, see Bernard Manin, *Principes du gouvernement représentatif* (Paris: Calmann-Lévy, 1995) and Pierre Rosanvallon, *Le Sacre du citoyen: Histoire du suffrage universel en France* (Paris: Gallimard, 1992) and *Le Peuple introuvable: Histoire de la représentation démocratique en France* (Paris: Gallimard, 1998).

accomplish these appointments. This process was gradually seen as problematic, but it was not questioned until 1800. There was a firm belief that democracy was not a competition of ambitions but the discernment of the general will.

In this framework, the utopia is a kind of *direct government of the general will*. It must be distinguished from *direct democracy*, which was perceived as a power of the street. It is important to keep in mind that the word 'democracy' was absent from the vocabulary of French revolutionaries. Emmanuel-Joseph Sieyès often repeated that France – a country with twenty-five million inhabitants (ten times the American population at the time) – could not be a democracy in the strict and technical sense of the term. Such a view combined unspoken practical arguments and a form of implicit social contempt. Conversely, the distinction between democracy and representative government would be explicitly formulated in the United States. While the term democracy was considered 'archaic' in France,[6] the American founding fathers rejected direct democracy as an immediate threat and compared it to mobocracy.[7]

Archaism and utopia, the 'old' and the 'new', would eventually overlap in the nineteenth century. At that time, the two dimensions merged to give rise to 'representative democracies'. A 'neo-corporate' vision of society inspired that evolution in Europe, as traditionalist and socialist perspectives de facto overlapped.[8] The former envisioned a 'corps society' and the latter a 'class society' in similar terms. Pierre-Joseph Proudhon, for instance, regarded socialism as a kind of modernization of the corporate world. The 'old' and the 'new' combined in the development of a pluralism of parties that reflects, for some, class struggle, and, for others, the social world's diversity. This vision is the antithesis of the first conceptions of democratic unanimity in the American townships, and of what the 'spirit of 1848' would still signify in France. The 'good composition' of assemblies would also be evaluated in relation to all of the other characteristics considered to be structural in the society. This conception would feed into many electoral reform projects. In the nineteenth century, the movement advocating for 'proportional representation', which was first conceived in sociological terms,[9] offers an example.

6 See Pierre Rosanvallon, 'Histoire du mot démocratie en France', in Marcel Gauchet, Pierre Manent and Pierre Rosanvallon (eds.), *La Pensée politique* (Paris: Le Seuil/Gallimard, 1993), pp. 11–17.

7 See Bertlinde Laniel, *Le mot 'democracy' et son histoire aux États-Unis de 1790 à 1856* (Saint-Étienne: Publications de l'Université de Saint-Étienne, 1998).

8 See the important literature of the 1970s and 1980s on neo-corporatism and the use of this notion to conceptualize social democracy as a specific political regime.

9 Rosanvallon, *Le Peuple introuvable*, fn. 5, pp. 113–164.

Yet, in time, archaism will dissipate and utopia will turn against itself. Proudhon marked a turning point by publishing a famous pamphlet entitled 'For New Corporations'.[10] The intuition that Proudhon expressed in this pamphlet served as an inspiration for a new way to redefine representative democracy. This way included both the weight of the past, which was modernized through the vision of a class society, and a renewal of the electoral utopia, albeit in a much more restricted form. From that time forwards, the understanding of an assembly's good composition would be linked to all of the other characteristics considered to be structural in the society. In Europe, it is possible to make a double history of political representation with the two structuring dimensions of social representation and religious representation. Obviously, some political parties have an ideological dimension, but most important political parties were born as parties of a social class, whether among farm workers, the industrial working class, or in the form of religious parties (the Christian democracies were structuring parties).

The creation of international organizations (IOs) was approached on this basis. While IOs were initially considered through the sole lens of State representation, they gradually opened to the idea of complementing the representation of civil societies when they were dedicated to the study of, and the intervention in, specific areas. The example of the International Labour Organization (ILO), set up in the aftermath of the First World War, stands out.[11] The ILO has served as a model for a whole range of other IOs. There was, however, a practical difficulty of implementation: that of the determination of how the institutions of civil society could be considered as 'representative'. This question had been straightforward in the field of labour because trade unions and employers' organizations are institutionalized and universally recognized.

At this point, it may be interesting to draw a parallel with the contemporary reflections on the *economic and social councils* that have been set up in many countries, especially in Europe. There even is a European Economic and Social Committee that can be considered as an example of an IO. The French case is typical.[12] Considered as the third constitutional assembly of the State (after the Senate and the National Assembly), the French economic and social council was first a Labour Council and is now an Economic, Social, and

[10] Pierre-Joseph Proudhon, *Du Principe Fédératif et de la nécessité de reconstituer le parti de la Révolution* (Paris : E. Dentu, 1863).

[11] See Marieke Louis' seminal work, *Qu'est-ce qu'une bonne représentation? L'Organisation internationale du travail de 1919 à nos jours* (Paris: Dalloz, 2016).

[12] See Alain Chatriot, *La démocratie sociale à la française: l'expérience du Conseil national économique 1924–1940* (Paris: La Découverte, 2002).

Environmental Council (ESEC) that includes, in addition to unions and union representatives, social organizations, specifically those active in the field of ecology. The French ESEC now claims to see itself as an assembly of 'organized civil society'. But how to define its contours? This question is all the more difficult as the world of civil society organizations develops and becomes more complex. In specialized fields such as health, it is possible to envision a *multiple representation* model, to use the terms of Samantha Besson, because there are indisputable major players from civil society that are organized at the international level.[13] But such cases are difficult to generalize. At the same time, the perspective of the classical representative model also seems structurally problematic.

There are two reasons for this. First, the praise of civil society that marked the 1970s has waned.[14] It was linked to the presupposition that the structuring of civil society would be readily discerned. By contrast, today, in the age of social networks and the mutations of contemporary capitalism, civil society appears fragmented, even radically unrepresentable, in the sense that it imposes itself in the form of a 'direct opinion' that has de facto replaced 'direct democracy' in the public imagination. The weakening of the sociological substratum of the old representative ideal goes hand in hand with the second evolution, which is the tendency towards 'secondarizing', or reducing the centrality of, parliamentary institutions. While parliamentary institutions used to be at the heart of democratic life, it is now the executive power that imposes itself and dominates parliamentary power almost everywhere. Debates take place in the press and on social networks (which revives the old competing claims to representation between the pen and the tribune). The electoral procedure has also lost its representative monopoly, as seen, for example, in the development of 'citizens' conferences' constituted by drawing lots.

The new pre-eminence of the executive branch is reflected in a redefinition of democratic expectations. A 'good government' will henceforth be defined by criteria other than that of representativeness.[15] The way of assessing the 'democratic performance' of European institutions also testifies to this shift

13 Samantha Besson, 'Pour une représentation démocratique multiple au sein de l'Organisation mondiale de la Santé', in Olivier de Frouville and Dominique Rousseau (eds.), *Démocratiser l'Espace-Monde* (Le Kremlin Bicêtre: Mare & Martin, 2024), pp. 199–218; Samantha Besson and José Luis Martí, 'From Equal State Consent to Equal Public Participation in International Organizations: Institutionalizing Multiple International Representation', in Samantha Besson (ed.), *Consenting to International Law* (Cambridge: Cambridge University Press, 2023), pp. 314–346.

14 See Pierre Rosanvallon, *Le bon gouvernement* (Paris: Seuil, 2015).

15 See ibid.

from an 'input legitimacy' (representativeness) to an 'output legitimacy' (the nature of the decisions taken), to use a noted conceptualization.

In this context, one should highlight five major developments that traverse democratic regimes and call for a reassessment of the analytical framework of representation. The first element is the attention shift from the quality of representativeness to its legitimacy. Representativeness is always difficult to define because its relationship to social generality presupposes a vision of the division of society into different segments, that, once pieced together, comprise the collectivity. By contrast, legitimacy claims to directly define the common good. In the context of representation, the common good has a cooperative function: it is the cooperation between differentiated interests. In the context of legitimacy, the common good proceeds from the ability to articulate principles of justice and the meaning of the common good in terms that make them recognizable as such.

This sense of recognizing the common good applies across domains. For example, in France (as in other countries), there is a National Consultative Ethics Committee, whose important function is to give its opinion on ethical issues. This committee recently hosted a celebratory event to mark its fortieth anniversary, to which I was invited. At this occasion, one of its founding members stated: Fortunately, we have never been representative because if we had been representative, we could have been criticized on the ground that we did not cover the full spectrum of the different organizations that deserve to be consulted. We are strong because we are not representative. Quite the reverse: we are able to embrace this non-representativeness because it makes it possible to put forward another quality: the fact of being recognized as legitimate.[16]

This legitimacy is the product of social recognition. It is equivalent to the constitution of authority in the Roman sense of the term, that is, the exercise or possession of qualities that directly link an institution or a person to the foundations of collective existence. It is neither a power nor a status, but a quality. Today's world is saturated with competition for authority and legitimacy. The social movements that are the most important are not representative movements. To be representative requires giving proof of representativeness in the form of members, publications, budgets, or affiliations. However, the proof of legitimacy – the constitution of authority – is achieved differently: it is made in the public opinion. This explains why the contemporary emphasis on legitimacy over representativeness gives rise to new types of organizations and new forms of action. Nowadays, multiple emerging forms

16 Oral remark of a founding member of the French National Consultative Ethics Committee.

of direct action are developing as counter-powers: they begin as trial balloons and eventually become recognized as legitimate. The organization Extinction Rebellion does not have many members, but it has come to be recognized as a legitimate organization because of the compelling nature of the themes it highlights and its ability to carry out spectacular actions. The number of its members has become a secondary consideration.

This has led to heads of State becoming more willing to receive symbolic figures who appear legitimate than leaders of organizations. Greta Thunberg has been received by many heads of State in the world, even though, from a certain point of view, she represents only herself. But she has acquired a status of authority and is able to lead public opinion. While one can currently see a renewal of the idea of direct democracy, it is not infused by the idea of a direct exercise of power, but rather, by the idea of a hard-charging legitimacy that is external to the notion of representativeness. In such a framework, representativeness can even come to be perceived as a burden or an insurmountable constraint. Admittedly, there is always space for representative institutions, and IOs still need representativeness, but it is no longer the only way of expressing the social world.

When it comes to organizations, it is therefore crucial to distinguish between organizations of representativeness and organizations of legitimacy. These two different fields have come to impose themselves with their specific modes of operation, their different relationships to public opinion, and their own modes of recognition. Moreover, we increasingly see governments that are themselves able to play on both fields, which is also a decisive evolution.

Yet, another element impacts this assessment: the greater importance of the interstate level. Interstate meetings are increasingly important given the globalization of many issues and the fact that these issues are solved by agreements between nations. Diplomatic activity remains extremely important at the international level, and today maybe more important, from a certain point of view, than in the days when we anticipated a transition from the centrality of diplomacy to IOs. To illustrate this point, it seems that Samantha Besson's reference to the classic opposition between 'input and output legitimacy' amounts, at its core, to the opposition between representativeness and legitimacy.[17]

The third element that deserves emphasis is the creation of new arenas for international action or cooperation following the increasing number of truly global issues affecting humanity and the planet, which IOs can no longer handle alone. International organizations make functional distinctions between

[17] See Besson and Martí, Chapter 12 in this volume.

different regimes or sectors of activity. The whole variety of international organizations reproduces the variety of human activity or public activity, such as public policy. But when an increasing pre-eminence is given to a whole set of issues that are global, this functioning based on specialization no longer works, which explains why these new authorities become more important and, in a way, arbiters of legitimacy.

Representation remains essential in societies, but perhaps in a different sense than in the past. It appears to be gradually taking a figurative meaning: it is becoming representation in the sense of the need to explain and shed light on a complex world, a world in which, for example, the question is not simply to represent social classes, but to try to understand a whole world of social invisibility. Such a world is no longer a world of organized groups, but the world of those left behind, the forgotten. This corresponds to a narrative function of representation, which appears bound to play an increasingly important role at all levels, whether national or international. But who will be the actors of this narrative democracy? These actors of this narrative democracy can be multiple, and in the future, they will have an increasingly influential role because they are those who have the ability to impose a narrative on what constitutes society and to define its vital problems. From this intellectual power, they can draw a real social power. Social power has become inseparable from intellectual power, and this intellectual power is largely emerging or redrawn today through the different modalities of narrative representation.

The purpose of this reflection is not to say that we will move from one world to another, but to show that several democratic worlds now coexist, that there is a growing number of democratic forms and arenas, and that it is important to keep this in mind for a very simple reason: a single democratic modality will not suffice to advance our democracy.

For a long time, we believed that the imperative was for democracy to find the right representation, the ideal parliament, and the miracle election. Of course, procedures have been put in place to make politics or elections more moral, but the idea that a single modality of shaping democracy is enough seems a profound mistake.

Democracy can only exist to the extent that multiple institutions and experiences bring it to life: only a multiple vision may answer this call. In such a vision, IOs obviously have a role to play, but they must now contend with what we may call the new 'international voices'. Voices have become as important as organizations.

# PART I

# DEMOCRATIC REPRESENTATION IN INTERNATIONAL ORGANIZATIONS

# 3

# International Representation by State-Independent Bodies

Philip Pettit

## 3.1 INTRODUCTION

This volume is organized around the assumption that apart from Member States – in effect, member governments – there are other 'public or private institutions' that often play a part in international organizations.[1] In illustrating the range of such participants, Samantha Besson cites 'NGOs, multinational corporations, employer's associations, trade unions, or patients' associations'.[2] And she also makes the point that international organizations (IOs) may themselves constitute non-governmental participants in higher-level organizations.

The focus of my chapter, like that of the present volume, is on how far things can be organized within IOs 'to ensure sufficient democratic representation of all those they claim to bind legally, either directly or through their Member States'.[3] Those they bind in this way include most prominently the peoples of Member States. So how far can such peoples be democratically represented in IOs by bodies that form independently of the State or States from which their membership is drawn? I shall describe such agents or agencies as State-independent, or sometimes just as independent, bodies.

Peoples may exercise democratic control over an organization in a variety of ways that do not directly involve representation: for example, by constitutionally or otherwise requiring that it operate under certain constraints, that appointments be made according to strict procedures, that it offer broadly public-interest reasons for its decisions, and that it be subject to monitoring and auditing

[1] Besson, Chapter 1 in this volume.

[2] Ibid. For a good discussion of cities in such a role, see Samantha Besson and José Luis Martí, 'Cities as Democratic Representatives in International Law-Making', in Helmut P. Aust and Janne E. Nijman (eds.), *Research Handbook on International Law and Cities* (London: Edward Elgar, 2021), pp. 341–353.

[3] Besson, Chapter 1 in this volume.

by an independent body. But the focus in this chapter is on representation only and I shall ignore the democratizing role of other factors like these.

The chapter is in three sections. It begins with an account and critique of two extreme views of how IOs may relate to the peoples they involve, where the difference turns on the part that State-independent actors should be able to play (Section 3.2). In a third, long section, it then presents and defends a series of general principles governing representation, arguing that they undermine each of these two views (Section 3.3). And then in the final section it shows that the principles support a distinct, third model of the role that independent actors might play in representing their peoples within IOs (Section 3.4).[4]

## 3.2 TWO EXTREME VIEWS

There are two extreme views of how IOs may meet representative constraints on their relationship to the peoples supporting them, one State-centred, the other individual-centred. Each agrees that the people of every Member State may be represented by those State-independent agents or agencies that participate in an IO but they take diverging views of how this can be achieved.

The first, State-centred view holds that it is only States that have the standing to represent their peoples within IOs and that any independent parties that operate there must play a role assigned to them by their respective States. They must be commissioned in that role by State authorities such as the legislature or executive. And they must be required to act on the terms laid down for them by such authorities.[5]

The second, individual-centred view argues that while a people may certainly be represented by State appointees or authorities in an IO, it may also be represented, without State appointment or authorization, by independent actors. The idea is that IOs create networks of communication and collaboration across diverse peoples and that those networks should be allowed to vary in how they ensure the representation of peoples. One organization may recruit a people to its network by giving a place to appointees or authorities of their State, another by giving places to independent actors. The ideal projected is one in which States may rule over their peoples domestically – subject, presumably, to constraints of international law and the like – but those

[4] The paper draws on general propositions about the nature and function of a functional State – even a patently unjust functional State – defended in Philip Pettit, *The State* (Princeton: Princeton University Press, 2023).

[5] I set aside the possibility that they might be selected themselves under an independent, constitutionally licensed procedure, because in that case they would cease to be State-independent representatives.

peoples may connect and order things in the global sphere within a variety of State-independent, decision-making networks.

These contrasting views may reflect different images of how to understand what a people amounts to: that is, the people of any particular State.[6] Thus, the picture that supports the second individual-centred approach, each people is just the population of those who live – presumably, on a relatively permanent, legally ratified basis – within a political territory. It is a collection of those individuals, considered in their separate identities, with their particular interests, not a body of individuals organized to perform via incorporation in a State, where the State is taken to be a corporate entity like a corporation or church or whatever. This picture of the peoples that IOs would serve makes perfect sense of why they may be represented by a variety of State and other agencies in the different domains of common interest engaged by such organizations.

According to the rival image that supports the State-centred approach to international representation, a people is not just an amalgam of individuals. The people is a set of agents organized within the corporate agency of the State, so that State authorities – executive, legislative, or judicial – speak for them on a range of fronts: in framing and applying the law; in pursuing those policies, including international policies, that are determined in accordance with the law; and in appointing the actors charged with implementing such policies. This picture is embraced on the State-centred view, regardless of whether the State is democratically structured or not. All that counts is that it be a matter of common awareness among the membership – and common acceptance, however reluctant – that the State authorities should play this role. According to the view envisaged, members of a non-democratic State will recognize that in order to enjoy the order and benefits of law-governed relationships among themselves, and with other peoples, they must be organized under a State and have no feasible choice but to live within the established regime.[7]

6 The two images of the people are nicely and famously distinguished by Thomas Hobbes, *Leviathan*, edited by Edwin Curley (Indianapolis: Hackett, 1994). See Philip Pettit, *Made with Word: Hobbes on Language, Mind and Politics* (Princeton: Princeton University Press, 2008).

7 Such a government may be required to meet Bernard Williams's basic legitimacy demand, although it may not be legitimate by richer criteria such as those endorsed by John Rawls. My own less demanding view is that a regime will count as a proper State, representative of its people, if individuals in general see a benefit in the order established that motivates compliance independently of the fear of sanction; if the regime does not rule by terror alone. The issue comes up later in a discussion of Rousseau's distinction 'between subjugating a multitude and ruling a society'. See Bernard Williams, *In the Beginning was the Deed: Realism and Moralism in Political Argument* (Princeton: Princeton University Press, 2005); John Rawls, *Political Liberalism* (New York: Columbia University Press, 2005); Pettit, *The State*, fn. 4; Jean-Jacques Rousseau, *The Social Contract and Other Later Political Writings*, edited and translated by Victor Gourevitch (Cambridge: Cambridge University Press, 1997), I.5.1.

Whatever the merits of these motivating images of the people of a State, neither of the competing views of international representation is particularly appealing. The State-centred view suggests that nothing may be determined by representatives beyond the boundaries of the State that has not been pre-authorized at home or that is not in line with fairly strict pre-authorized instructions. Thus, it would make the forum of an international organization into what Edmund Burke casts as merely 'a congress of ambassadors'.[8] In such a congress, as Burke envisages it, participants would bargain with each other on the basis of their pre-existing, partisan interests, making only the minimal concessions to one another that are needed to get what they want. This is very different from the sort of organization in which members would focus on common problems and be willing to innovate in their search for solutions; it would fail to resemble anything like a deliberative assembly.[9]

While that makes the State-centred view unappealing, quite a different flaw detracts from the appeal of the individual-centred rival. If there is nothing to enforce unity across the commitments of each people, then the corresponding State is liable to find itself obliged to answer to rival and conflicting demands. The State will be the only agency, representative of its people, that operates in different forums and if it is at the mercy of what other representatives of the people agree in one or another domain, there is no guarantee that it will be able to implement all the commitments made in the name of the people. It may be required to pursue a policy on the relaxation of border controls, for example, that is at odds with a policy of international cooperation in policing; or to adopt a commitment to lifting tariffs on certain goods that competes with a domestic commitment to support local industry.

These observations should lead us to think again about how to model the representative role that State-independent members of IOs may play. I think there is a third model that ought to attract us more and in order to motivate it I propose to return to some basic principles of representation – this unfortunately requires a resort to rather abstract theory – and show how they combine to give salience to the possibility that that model represents.

8 Edmund Burke, 'Speech to the Electors of Bristol', in Edmund Burke, *Select Works of Edmund Burke*, Vol. 4 (Indianapolis: Liberty Fund, 1999), pp. 5–13.

9 Joshua Cohen, 'Deliberation and Democratic Legitimacy', in Alan Hamlin and Philip Pettit (eds.), *The Good Polity* (Oxford/New York: Basil Blackwell, 1989), pp. 17–34; Jürgen Habermas, *Between Facts and Norms: Contributions to a Discourse Theory of Law and Democracy* (Cambridge, MA: MIT Press, 1998).

## 3.3 SOME GENERAL PRINCIPLES OF REPRESENTATION

It may be useful to begin by setting out the principles addressed here and to display the argumentative connections between them. We can then discuss each principle in somewhat more detail. The fifth principle, as we shall see, argues against the individual-centred of how a people can be represented in an IO but the sixth supports the claim that this does not commit us necessarily to adopting the State-centred alternative. In the final section, we show that it directs us rather to a third and more appealing model.

The principles I defend are these:

i) An agent or agency may represent individuals in a responsive or indicative mode;
ii) Whatever the mode, the represented must authorize the representative system;
iii) In any domain, the represented can authorize only one representative voice;
iv) A people must authorize their State as an all-domains, sovereign spokesperson;
v) And so the State must be their only representative, with control over other voices;
vi) But the State need not exercise this control actively, only in a standby manner.

### 3.3.1 *One Agent or Agency May Represent Another in a Responsive or Indicative Mode*

In order to introduce this distinction, think of the different relationships I may seek with someone I am invited to nominate as my representative on the governing board of a company or association: the invitation, for example, might reflect my role as a founder of the body.[10] I may nominate someone on condition that they report to me weekly about upcoming decisions and respond to my specific or general instructions on how they should vote. Or, without requiring them to be responsive to me in any such manner, I may appoint someone whose views and values are generally indicative of my own, relying on their similar cast of mind to vote in general as I would vote.

10 Philip Pettit, 'Varieties of Public Representation', in Ian Shapiro, Susan C. Stokes, Elisabeth Jean Wood and Alexander S. Kirshner (eds.), *Representation and Popular Rule* (Cambridge: Cambridge University Press, 2009), pp. 61–89.

Where the agent appointed on the first basis would be a responsive representative, the agent appointed on the second would be an indicative representative. The responsive representative would vote in causal sensitivity to my advice, the indicative would vote independently of any such input from me but their votes would be generally likely to indicate how I would have voted, had I been on the board.

This distinction can apply regardless of a range of variations in the representation involved. The representer may be an individual or corporate agent. The represented may be an agent of either kind or just a collection of people who are not organized to perform as an agent: say, a collection as disunified as the individuals who live in a given postcode. And whether the representation is responsive or indicative, it may vary also in ways specific to those modes.

To take the responsive case, the representer may be required to respond to episodic, issue-by-issue instructions, to more general recommendations, or just to electoral constraints. The electoral case is the most familiar, of course: the represented elect the representer over rivals but are enabled to elect another in their place, should they not be satisfied with the original representer's performance.

The indicative relationship may also vary enormously. It may depend on a similarity that pre-exists appointment between the represented and representer, as in our simple example above. Or it may depend on pressures to which the representer will be subject after appointment, where these are designed to lead them to vote on a general pattern that the represented might be expected to approve.

Thus, to introduce the first possibility, if a government selects a citizen assembly that is statistically representative of the population, they will have a similarity-based reason to take it to represent the people as a whole. And, to introduce the second, if a government appoints an electoral commission under constraints of impartiality and expertise, requires them to endorse popularly accepted criteria for the fairness of districting and balloting, and exposes them to surveillance and critique, the commission will have a pressure-based reason to decide as the people as a whole would presumably want them to decide.[11]

[11] Democratic theorists often favour a system of proportional representation that is designed to make those elected into a body that most accurately models the population as whole. It may be, however, that selecting candidates on an electoral basis undermines the role that proportionality might have been expected to play. Benjamin Constant made the crucial point in 1810: 'You choose a man to represent you because he has the same interests as you. By the very fact of your choosing him, however, your choice of placing him in a different situation from yours gives him a different interest from the one he is charged with representing', see Benjamin Constant, *Principles of Politics Applicable to All Governments* (Indianapolis: Liberty Fund, 2003), p. 387.

### 3.3.2 *Whatever the Mode, the Represented Must Authorize the Representative System*

A random sample of the population in a certain area or profession or whatever is going to be statistically representative of the group as a whole; I put aside issues of stratification. And in order to be representative in that sense, those represented need not authorize the choice of the sample for whatever purpose it is then used. That marks a sharp difference from representation in the sense in which we are invoking it here.

In our sense of representation, those identified as representers must be selected under a system that is authorized by the represented. The reason is that the point of representation is to compensate for the inability of the represented to speak for themselves, whatever the source of that inability, and to identify a spokesperson – this may be a body constituted by different representers – to speak for them instead: to speak in their name, making them present in a domain of decision-making where they cannot participate.

For someone to claim to speak for another in this sense would be an affront to the other's independence or autonomy, if they did not speak with the authorization of the individual they claimed to represent. Thus, we would rightly object to the idea, widely endorsed in the nineteenth century, that it was fine for the electorate to be composed only of men, on the grounds that those men would identify with the interests of their womenfolk and represent them virtually.[12] Thus, most of us in liberal democracies today would reject the claim that James Mill makes in 1819 when he says of women in relation to men that being 'individuals whose interests are indisputably included in those other individuals', they 'may be struck off without inconvenience'.[13]

That the represented must authorize the representative system, however, does not mean that each individual agent or agency selected as representer will be entitled to speak on their own for those they represent. When different electoral constituencies select their legislative representers, for example, the assumption may be that they do so as part of a system for electing a legislature, and that it is only the legislative body as a whole that speaks for the people. In that case, the individual representers will help to constitute that representative voice but their own voices will not be representative in their own right.[14]

12 Anne Phillips, *The Politics of Presence* (Oxford: Oxford University Press, 1998).

13 James Mill, 'An Essay on Government', in Jack Lively and John Rees (eds.), *Utilitarian Logic and Politics: James Mill's 'Essay on Government', Macaulay's Critique, and the Ensuing Debate* (Oxford: Oxford University Press, 1978), pp. 53–96.

14 In the single-seat constituency, where the representer is strictly independent of the representers of other constituencies – this in a presidential but not a parliamentary system – that

To anticipate a point made later, however, it may not even be the legislature that constitutes this popular spokesperson. Suppose that the people directly or indirectly appoint judges – say, as presumptively indicative representers – and give them the power under the constitution to check the legislature. In that case the voice that speaks for them will be the emergent voice established in the interaction of the legislature and the judiciary, not the voice of either body on its own.[15]

### 3.3.3 *In Any Domain, the Represented Can Authorize Only One Representative Voice*

Insofar as representation establishes a voice that can claim to speak for the represented in a domain of connected issues, there can be only one voice that is entitled under the system of representation to speak for those represented. There is no sense to the idea that different voices might equally claim this spokesperson status, as we might describe it. Or at least there is no sense to the idea when they claim to speak for the represented within the same domain of issues. Even a federal system with different levels of representation satisfies this constraint, since it will have to operate under a constitution where the final authority on any issue is allocated to the representatives at just one level.

This means that within any single domain of issues there can only be one spokesperson recognized by the represented. But of course different voices might speak for the same individual, or body, or collection, in distinct, unconnected domains. In a small city one and the same group of people might constitute both the local tourist board and the board of the local hospital. And under those different aspects, addressed to different domains, that group might authorize a different individual to speak for them. Indeed those different individuals might even debate with one another quite sensibly about some common enterprise. They would each speak for a different group agent – the tourist or hospital board – although the same collection of people is involved in each.

Where a single individual or corporate agent is to be represented, or a collection represented as a whole, there is no room for two voices to be given such a spokesperson status: such final authority. The unity associated with individual or corporate agency, or with the collection considered as whole, will be betrayed in the act of representation, giving rise to conflicting authorities. The represented entity will be a hydra with as many heads and as many voices as it has rival representers.

individual may also claim to speak for their own constituency, making the legislature into something like Burke's 'congress of ambassadors'.

[15] Pettit, *The State*, fn. 4, chapter 3.

### 3.3.4 *A People Must Authorize Their State as an All-Domains, Sovereign Spokesperson*

The State in this principle is not to be identified just with the government, whether we identify the government with those in legislative or executive office, or also with those in judicial office. For example, it will encompass others insofar as the constitution is subject to amendment in a referendum involving all; insofar as that constitution gives citizens a role in electing or contesting those in formal office; or insofar as the constitution, or at least the accepted framework of public decision-making, gives fairly independent roles to unelected bodies like an election commission, a bureau of statistics, or a central bank. The State is an entity that may act via any such agents or agencies: when they play their parts they enable the State to act through them.

The people who live under a given regime will not authorize it as a sovereign spokesperson, we may assume, if those in office rely on force alone to elicit the compliance of others; as Rousseau says, there is 'a great difference between subjugating a multitude and ruling a society'.[16] By this assumption, such a regime will not count in a proper sense as a State. A State must be authorized in some sense as the people's sovereign spokesperson. But what does it mean for a people to authorize their State? And, more specifically, what does it mean for them to authorize it as a sovereign spokesperson?

Authorization, to take up the first question, cannot require the people to consent to the regime. Even the finest democracy will not enable citizens to consent or refuse to consent to the State; they will usually have no choice in the matter.[17] My own preference is to take a people to authorize a State when they see a suitably motivating merit in the laws and institutions it lays down. More specifically, what is required is that the State should give them a motive to acquiesce in the status quo that is independent of their fear of the retaliation that a refusal might trigger. Of course, they will be partially motivated to acquiesce by the fear of coercion, as is true even in a democratic State. But they will not acquiesce just because of that fear. Seeing the general merits of

16 Rousseau, fn. 7.

17 What democracy ideally ensures, by my own 'neo-republican' way of thinking, is that the people have a degree of more or less equally shared control over the doings of the State. See Philip Pettit, *On the People's Terms: A Republican Theory and Model of Democracy* (Cambridge: Cambridge University Press, 2013); Philip Pettit, *Just Freedom: A Moral Compass for a Complex World* (New York: W. W. Norton and Co, 2014). If the people have that form of control, however, they will be able to protest without danger about how the State is organized, even do so extra-constitutionally but peacefully. And so they may be said to consent, not to going alone with the State, but to going along unprotestingly, thereby authorizing it in a distinctive fashion. See Pettit, *The State*, fn. 4, chapter 4.

what the State does for its subjects, they will each acquiesce more or less willingly. They will accept the State for the benefits it provides and in that sense authorize it.

By this criterion, the authorized State need not be a democracy. But such a State must presumably operate by law, so that subjects will have some stable sense, however inadequate, of how they may and may not act in relation to others and in relation to the authorities. Consistently with counting as an authorized State in this minimal sense, of course, a given polity may fail in many ways. Although we are effectively excluding that possibility in this context, it may fail to extend full membership to all residents. And it may certainly fail, as the most inclusionary of States often fail, to deliver a law that gives people a congenially determinate sense of where they stand in relation to others and in relation to officials.

But, turning to the more specific question we raised, what does it mean for a people to authorize their State as an entity that speaks for them in a sovereign way? It is in the nature of the State as a body that it lays down the laws of the society, that it does so of its own will and, more particularly, that it need not have the permission of any other domestic entity in order to do so. In short, it must have the high or final authority that has been associated with sovereignty, since the idea was first introduced by Jean Bodin in the sixteenth century.[18] This high authority means that the State will also have a wide authority: an authority over many domains. It will have power over whatever it is that its subjects do, displaying that power in coercing people to act in certain determinate ways – say, to avoid violence – and, where it does not choose to coerce its subjects, in allowing them to act on their own choices – say, to marry or remain single – although perhaps only under certain procedural constraints.

One softening comment on sovereignty. Traditional sovereigntists like Bodin or Thomas Hobbes or even Rousseau assumed that the sovereign spokesperson in a State has to be a particular individual or a particular committee within it, whether the committee of an elite or – as Rousseau actually required – a committee of the whole. They thereby suggested that the sovereign would be a threatening presence, and made the idea of sovereignty uncongenial to many. But the voice that speaks with the high and wide authority of the sovereign may be a voice, as we noted earlier, that emerges from the interaction of the legislature with the judiciary or, more plausibly – at least in democracies – a voice that emerges from a pattern of interaction that also involves further parties, including people in an

[18] Jean Bodin, *Six Books of the Commonwealth*, translated by Marian J. Tooley (Oxford: Basil Blackwell, 1967).

electoral or contestatory role.[19] Thus, the sovereign need not be an unconstrained power from the point of view of those who live under a State.

### 3.3.5 *And So the State Must Be Their Only Representative, with Control Over Other Voices*

Whether the form taken by the sovereign spokesperson is emergent or not, that spokesperson can be identified with the State itself. There can be no representation of the people, then, that is not subject to the high and wide authority of the State. The State will be automatically in control of any representatives that are constitutionally designed to act in its name, as with the legislature that interacts with other bodies to determine the voice of the State. But what of other would-be representatives? The fifth principle holds that they too must be subject to the authority and control of the State, and should not constitute competitors.

This principle seems to support the State-centred view that we mentioned in the second section. It offers ground for thinking that if independent actors are to be taken as representatives of their people, acting together in any IO to speak for those people, then they must be deputed by their State to play that role, whether on an indicative or responsive basis. Some recognized State authority such as the executive must act in the name of the State, with constitutional licence, to assign the job to them. Or they must be selected under some independent, constitutionally established procedure – say, a form of election – to assume that role as official authorities in their own right. And in either case they must be constrained to act in a way that allows the sovereign voice of the State to display coherence in its decisions and instructions.

We mentioned earlier that this State-centred view is liable to turn an IO into a congress of ambassadors, with members being enjoined by their States to cleave to certain lines in advance of hearing the other sides. That would mean that members would bargain with one another in the hope of finding a compromise between pre-existing interests and opinions, rather than being motivated to explore new interests and ideas together in the hope of finding innovative solutions to common problems.

### 3.3.6 *But the State Need Not Exercise This Control Actively, Only in a Standby Manner*

The fifth principle just considered offers support for the State-centred view of international representation only on the following, active-control

[19] Pettit, *The State*, fn. 4.

assumption: that the only way for a State or a group of States to control the different independent actors within any IO is by causal intervention in selecting or de-selecting them; or by dictating ex ante the terms to which they must be responsive in their representation; or, to allow for the indicative case, by dictating the constraints under which they must operate. On this approach, States will have to deprive independent representatives of the capacity to exercise discretion – to innovate or improvise – on the grounds that otherwise those representatives might undermine the capacity of the State to exercise its sovereign authority, speaking clearly, unambiguously, and coherently for its people.

But the active-control assumption is false. There are broadly two ways in which one agent can control others and they direct us to two ways in which the State might exercise control over independent representatives in IOs. Consider the simple example of how a horse-rider might control the direction taken by a herd of cattle or a flock of sheep across open country. The rider might keep them moving with suitable calls and shouts and seek at the same time to drive them in the appropriate direction. Or, if the animals are inclined independently to move in that direction, the rider might simply let them follow their heads and intervene only when that is needed to put an errant animal back on track.

In the first case, the rider will be there actively urging the animals to keep to the track. In the second, the rider may relax, rely on the evidence of an errant animal to raise a red flag, and be poised to act in such a case to put that animal back on track with the others. As we say in the case of cattle, the rider in that case would ride herd on the animals, letting them do most of the work, and would maintain control by being there on standby to ensure that the efforts of the animals lead them in the desired direction. The rider may have to do little or nothing in that standby position but this lack of action does not entail a lack of control.

Generalizing from this rather remote analogue, we can see that if State authorities need to control what independent representatives within an IO say in the name of the people, that does not require them to assume the stance endorsed in the State-centred view. It does not require them even to dictate the instructions or terms on which the representatives are to act, or to establish the constraints under which they operate. They may assume a form of control over such representatives – a form of control, as we shall see, that may come in different varieties – that has a standby rather than an active character.

This observation raises a serious question for the State-centred view of international representation that our fifth principle seemed to support. But of course it does not provide support either for the individual-centred view. We suggest in the final section that it motivates a third alternative: a model of international representation that I describe, for reasons explained later, as citizen-centred rather than State- or individual-centred.

## 3.4 AN ALTERNATIVE VIEW OF INTERNATIONAL REPRESENTATION

### 3.4.1 *Sketching a Third Model*

The model of international representation that the sixth principle supports is one in which the members of an IO, in particular those who are not commissioned by their State, can take the initiative in proposing, debating, and deciding on a variety of arrangements. They may be responsively representative of one or another sector among the people or they may represent that sector on an indicative basis. But in either case they may commit finally to a certain arrangement only if their Member States go along.

This requirement may take different forms. Assuming that the IO is required to make its decisions unanimously, a Member State might be able to veto what the organization decides by not going along with the independent representatives who act for its people. Or, if it does not agree with what the organization decides, it might only be able to ensure that while the organization's decision binds supporting States, it is not itself bound by that decision: it might be able to refuse to be bound by any decision it does not support. Or, if it is committed to the organization operating without unanimity – this is a condition unlikely to be met – it might just be able to direct the votes of those representatives, ensuring that they do not help to constitute the required majority or super-majority.

This model would not differ much from the State-centred alternative if it made room only for such forms of State opposition. But I add one further feature to the model: that prior to opposing the independent representatives of its people, a Member State should be required to lodge objections to any proposal made and seek a response from its independent representatives, or from the organization as a whole. Amended in this way, the model begins to look very different from the State-centred one.

The amendment envisaged is not ad hoc, for there are reasons why it might emerge spontaneously, without having to be explicitly mandated. If the representatives on the organization have proposed an arrangement that purports to be in the interest of all, it will naturally back the proposal with considerations that are meant to argue for its implementation by all the relevant States. And in that case, any State that raises an objection will be expected by the same logic to identify the considerations that give it pause. The State will thereby be drawn into the debates of the representatives themselves rather than pronouncing from without on whether or not their deliverances are acceptable.

This effect will be reinforced by the addition of a second feature to the model: that Member States should allow the organization as a whole, and their representatives in particular, to publicize the proposals they are making in the relevant worldwide community, prior to gaining the approval of those States. This feature will put pressure on the States to go into the deliberative, debating space of the organization in suggesting amendments of any kind. It will guard against States resorting to familiar postures of bargaining with one another in search of the concessions that, as each wishes, will give them a result as satisfactory as possible from the point of view of their antecedent self-interest.

Not only will Member States be motivated under the arrangement proposed to enter deliberative space, downplaying the habit of bargaining. If the proposals have won general support within the larger community – this may involve member populations or a network of relevant experts across the world – then States will also be pressured to respond favourably to those proposals. That pressure will come from their home population, if the proposal has majority backing: this, at any rate, if there is a modicum of democratization in the society. And it will come from the experts in the area if the proposal wins the backing of those individuals and their professional bodies.

Think of matters on which relevant proposals are likely to bear. They may involve standardizing regulations in some area of commerce or industry, from the financial sector to the manufacture of automobiles. Or agreeing on worldwide fishing practices or on licences to put satellites into orbit around the earth. Or providing access to employment in richer countries for those from poorer regions. Or establishing standards for reducing reliance on fossil fuels. Or just facilitating exchanges between the residents of cities that wish to twin with one another.

In some of these areas, it may be essential to assign the issues to forums of discussion and negotiation between States. But in others it will be possible to establish a place for discussion within organizations where representatives are State-independent actors. And clearly those organizations can have a powerful effect on what arrangements come to be accepted if the representatives in the organization are given the freedom to debate the issues before them in a deliberative way and to publicize their proposals before winning the support of their respective States.

The third model sketched in these remarks contrasts sharply with the State-centred and individual-centred models. Like the individual-centred model it would grant independent actors a great deal of initiative in the exchanges they open with one another and the ideas they explore. But unlike that model, and like the State-centred alternative, it would give the State ultimate control, albeit control of the standby sort not envisaged in that alternative. The State would ride herd on those who represent its people responsively or indicatively, being positioned to challenge any proposal they support and if it is not satisfied with the responses those independent actors make, to oppose the proposal in a manner appropriate under the rules of the organization: that is, by vetoing the proposal, refusing to be party to it, or directing the votes that its independent representatives cast.

### 3.4.2 *Defending the Third Model*

The main thing to be said in favour of the model just sketched is that it ensures the benefits, and avoids the dangers, associated with the two rivals described. It ensures that there is State control and coherence, like the State-centred model, but it allows like the individual-centred model for the emergence of international arenas of debate and agreement in which participants operate with relative autonomy, and do not just channel the existing priorities of their States. But there is also more to be said.

In sketching the model, and in earlier discussions, we drew on an intuitive and familiar contrast between a deliberative and bargaining forum. The model, as we said, would facilitate deliberation and downplay bargaining. It is unlikely to eliminate bargaining altogether, of course, since deliberation may well leave States with different arrangements to negotiate about. And it is certainly unlikely to eliminate the partisan motives that are liable to influence the representatives of any people, State-sponsored or not. But it can discipline those motives in a way that may be to the benefit of all.

For purposes of this chapter, I take it as given that in any IO where State-independent representatives are gathered to resolve problems that their peoples face in common, there will be a working assumption that in making or supporting a proposal, each will cite considerations that they take to be relevant on all sides.[20] The claim is that it would make little sense for any representative to back a proposal on the grounds, for example, that it would benefit their home country in particular, or give it a certain advantage over others, or advance a special interest in which it is manifestly invested. That this would make little sense, and even expose the representative to a degree of mockery or ostracism, testifies to the endorsement of the working assumption mentioned.

20 That such a working assumption is likely to appear in suitable public forums has long been a theme in the work of Jürgen Habermas, as emphasized with great clarity by Jon Elster. See Jürgen Habermas, *The Theory of Communicative Action*, Vols. 1 and 2 (Cambridge: Polity Press, 1984 and 1989); Jon Elster, 'The Market and the Forum: Three Variety of Political Theory', in Jon Elster and Aanund Hylland (eds.), *Foundations of Social Choice Theory* (Cambridge: Cambridge University Press, 1990), pp. 103–132.

Working with that assumption, the members of the organization will naturally be disciplined into valorizing considerations of the common good or, less romantically, considerations that can be expected to pass muster on all sides. Passing muster in this way, the considerations will constitute reasons that everyone, regardless of their home country, will see as relevant to the issue on hand, even if some weight a given consideration differently from others. The considerations may include the observation that the proposal under discussion is a plausible bargaining solution – it requires only minimal concessions from each – but they may also include others that highlight common benefits without separating out the return to each individual people. These might consist in the ease or efficiency or stability that the arrangement would introduce in one or another system, the effect it is likely to have in guarding against a future war or some other global bad, or indeed its anticipated effect in promoting some global benefit.

Why does the deliberative character of the likely debates between them argue in favour of letting State-independent representatives operate under our third model? Deliberative debate may give rise to polarization when it is focused on determining the relative merits of the antecedent position of each side.[21] But it is more likely to build a culture of cooperation and solidarity among participants when they are charged with finding agreed solutions to common problems.

That is already a benefit that the third model promises to generate but there is also a further, related bonus to register. This is that the proposed arrangement would recruit participants in a common search for solutions to the problems raised. It would thereby energize them to identify the immediate goals they should prioritize, to seek further information they may require on feasible means of pursuit, and to explore all possible avenues of resolution in a process of generating and testing hypotheses. It would build them into a research team that is going to be better equipped than any bargaining forum between States to form new ideas and find new ground for international cooperation.[22]

### 3.4.3 *A Citizen-Centred Model*

Let me conclude by explaining why I cast this as a citizen-centred model of international representation: specifically, of the representation of peoples by State-independent actors.

[21] Cass R. Sustein, 'The Law of Group Polarization' (2002) 10(2) *Journal of Political Philosophy* 175–195.

[22] Anne-Marie Slaughter, A *New World Order* (Princeton: Princeton University Press, 2005).

In a tradition exemplified by Hobbes[23] and Rousseau,[24] 'the people' can be understood in either of two distinct ways. It may refer to the people taken in the aggregative sense of the population of the country – in Hobbes' phrase 'the multitude' – or to the people incorporated as a polity: the people proper as both Hobbes and Rousseau take the idea. These two figures take the incorporated people to constitute a single agent that acts through its sovereign: in Hobbes' picture, the sovereign may be a monarch or a popular or elite committee; in Rousseau's, it may only be a popular committee. And both assume that the people in the unincorporated sense are effectively incapable of acting together for any end, never again achieving the unanimity with which the State was established.

The Abbé Sieyès endorses a similar dichotomous conception of the people, while framing it in other terms.[25] He describes the people in the unincorporated sense as the constituting people and he too ascribes little capacity for action to them. The constituting people form and act on a will only by grace of an assembly of representatives: this is able to act by virtue of being incorporated under procedural rules – majority voting as he, like the others, proposes – and is authorized by members of the constituting people to act in its name.[26] He describes this incorporated body, in a manner that loosely parallels that of Hobbes and Rousseau, as the constituted people.

The dichotomous understanding of the people is unfortunate, as it ignores the fact that in every State, but especially in a democratic regime, there is a third way in which the people may be understood. In this sense, the people are those who sustain the State – as we assume, the authorized State – insofar as most obey the law, discharge any tasks legally allotted to them, and do not object to the presumption of the authorities in enacting and enforcing the law. In a democratic order, the tasks allotted will be particularly numerous, requiring or allowing individuals to vote, to sit on juries, to interrogate government proposals, to contest what government does, and so on.

The people in this sense are not incorporated as an agent in the polity but are merely a part – albeit a crucial part – of the polity. But neither are they just

23 Hobbes, fn. 6.

24 Rousseau, fn. 7.

25 Emmanuel J. Sieyès, *Political Writings*, edited by Michael Sonenscher (Indianapolis: Hackett, 2003).

26 For an argument that majority voting won't work – or indeed any similar bottom-up procedure – see Philip Pettit, *A Theory of Freedom: From the Psychology to the Politics of Agency* (Cambridge: Polity Press, 2001); Christian List and Philip Pettit, 'Aggregating Sets of Judgments: An Impossibility Result' (2002) 18 *Economics and Philosophy* 89–110; Christian List and Philip Pettit, *Group Agency: The Possibility, Design and Status of Corporate Agents* (Oxford: Oxford University Press, 2011).

the aggregate population of individual agents who are incapable of joint action. They are the citizens who each act as they do on the assumption that others will act in complementary ways and who thereby have the collective effect of keeping the State in existence. Unlike the people qua polity, they are not a corporate agent that is organized to act for different ends across different situations. The citizenry is that body of individuals who participate, as occasion requires, in joint State-sustaining activities.

On the third model of international representation that we have been sketching, those State-independent actors who assume positions in the representation of their people act on this front precisely in the role of citizens. Giving life to the model of a State that depends for its very existence and operation on the actions of its citizens, they assume their part in internationally representing their people. Or at least they do so, as our general principles of representation require, when existing authorities within the State do not object to what they propose. In that case, we may say that the State speaks and acts through them in the domain where they operate. But it speaks and acts through them by endorsing their independently generated proposals, not by giving them directions from on high. What they manage to do, imaginative and innovative as it may be, will constitute the growing tip of the State on the international front.

The State-independent citizens who act within IOs for their different peoples constitute a global form of civil society, as it is often put. They will come to the international forum by the nomination of one or another sector of their societies: a professional body, an industrial association, an organization of trade unions, a region within or across countries, a city or complex of cities, or an ethnic group from one or many places. But they won't gain the authority to represent their peoples by virtue of such an origin alone. They will achieve it only by winning support at home: only by becoming an integrated part of a State they help to constitute and sustain.

# 4

# The Four Modes of Representation in International Organizations and the Challenge of Democratic Legitimacy

Jacob Katz Cogan

## 4.1 INTRODUCTION

Two myths of statehood are foundational to the international system of representation as it is formally constituted. The first is that only States are international actors. The second is that all States are equal and should be treated accordingly. Both are obviously false. Many non-State actors – private organizations of all types, including non-governmental organizations (NGOs) and corporations, and sub-State and super-State governmental entities – clearly act internationally in important ways, leveraging their authority and power, making decisions and entering into agreements of consequence. And obviously as well States are unequal in any number of respects, including their economic wealth, military power, and technological capabilities. Nevertheless, the rules, processes, and institutions of the international system are designed as if these two assumptions and their corollaries were valid, as if States could be counted on to effectively govern their own territories and represent the diversity of their peoples, as if States alone ruled the world, and as if States participated equally in global governance. It is not surprising that a system built by States and for States would mythologize statehood and strictly and all-but-exclusively incorporate State-centric beliefs into its core formal rules, acting as if States are and should be the sole representatives at the international level.

What is true of the international system generally is true in particular of international organizations (IOs). IOs are created by, and composed of, States and, with rare exceptions (particularly the European Union in its areas of competence and employers and workers in organs of the International Labour Organization) only States. And those States are, with very rare exceptions, treated as equals in the founding documents of organizations. It follows that the rules of IOs, again with rare exceptions (such as voting in the Security

Council and international financial institutions (IFIs)), put States on an equal footing when it comes to decision-making: one State, one vote, with all members eligible to vote in the organization's plenary. It follows as well, in this statist framework, that all States should have an equal opportunity to take part in the organization's activities: to participate and vote in the organization's main committees, to be elected to non-plenary bodies within the organization, to have its nationals chosen for high-level positions, and to influence the organization's agenda and policies. Like the primary myths of international representation, these understandings are untrue. Some States and certain NGOs have heightened influence within organizations that belies the statist paradigm. Nonetheless, it is not surprising that IOs, as the creatures of States, adhere to statist myths and so reserve actual decision-making to States, and regional groups composed of States, and purport on the whole to treat States equally.

Though the myths are well-known as myths, and have been since their creation, that does not diminish their strength in the formal systems of IOs. Indeed, it is a testament to the power and resilience of these myths, and to the control that States still retain, and insist on retaining, at the international level, that their evident falsity has not yet led to any significant changes in blackletter international institutional law and its formal mode of representation.

Even so, the myths are problematic if they are strictly adhered to in practice. Systems cannot operate effectively unless they are recognized as authoritative and unless they can achieve their desired results. The absence of non-State representation and democratic legitimacy in IOs undercuts the authority of organizations because it does not permit the incorporation of a broad range of voices. And the notion that all States are equal undercuts the ability of organizations to achieve results as it fails to recognize the role of power in international society. There is thus a gap – an 'operational gap' – between the myth world of IOs and the real world in which IOs exist. It is understood by those who work in, with, and around IOs that there need to be ways to bridge this gap if organizations are to succeed and retain legitimacy and authority.

The operational gap inherent in the formal mode of representation can be, and has been, elided in three distinct ways in order to enhance and achieve both the democratic legitimacy and functionality of organizations. One is through informal adaptations in the operation of organizations – the operational mode – that seek to reconcile the needs for authoritativeness, legitimacy, and effectiveness with a formal system that falls short. A second – the aspirational mode of representation – aims to do the same but through changes in the formal and operational modes. A space for advocacy and critique, not a method of representation itself, the aspirational mode is liminal, for success formalizes or operationalizes the reform's content. And a third – the alternative mode – closes the operational gap by creating substitutes for IOs, such as informal groupings of States and organizations established under national law, that are not bound by the paradigmatic statist myths of the formal international system and, having been freed of those constraints, provide representation, including forms of democratic representation, in ways that are not fully possible within traditional IOs. Including the formal mode, which is the international system's default, the practice of representation, as it has evolved, encompasses four distinct forms. From the standpoint of democratic legitimacy, the formal and operational modes are generally weak in their current manifestations, as they most often reflect international law's State-centric assumptions and the influence of power. Those who advocate for greater democratic legitimacy in IOs therefore work most often within the aspirational frame as they attempt to promote and institute reforms.

This chapter reviews the four modes of representation – formal (Section 4.2), operational (Section 4.3), aspirational (Section 4.4), and alternative (Section 4.5). They are separate yet intertwined; they contend with yet depend on each other. Together they form the international system of representation. This is not simply descriptively true. The resort to, and the use of, the four modes is also optimal. All four are necessary, as for any successful system to evolve and maintain equilibrium there needs to be a variety of mechanisms available that allow for the balancing of competing values and the reconciliation of formal rules with the actualities of power and expectations of legitimacy, since alignment will never be perfect.[1] Importantly, the four modes allow a range of entry points for democratic legitimacy in the representative practices of IOs, creating the possibility of change going forward (Section 4.6).

## 4.2 THE FORMAL MODE

The formal mode of representation, with limited exceptions, codifies statist values through rules written into the constitutive treaties and resolutions of IOs and thus represents the greatest challenge to democratic legitimacy.[2]

[1] See Meir Dan-Cohen, 'Decision Rules and Conduct Rules: On Acoustic Separation in Criminal Law' (1984) 97(3) *Harvard Law Review* 625–637.

[2] Sections 4.2 and 4.3 are based on Jacob Katz Cogan, 'Representation and Power in International Organization: The Operational Constitution and Its Critics' (2009) 103(2) *American Journal of International Law* 209–263. I have mostly not included the citations here, since they can easily be found in the published article.

Representative principles in treaties appear in two ways: (1) in rules regarding the participation of States in decision-making bodies and (2) in rules regarding the election and appointment of individuals to formally non-political bodies, such as secretariats, courts, and expert panels. For the former, the principles largely arrange themselves by subject matter – political organizations, where sovereign equality is mostly paramount, and IFIs, commodities organizations, and similar subject matter specific institutions, where differential responsibilities are highlighted. For the latter, individuals are largely treated equally as to their nationality, but other personal characteristics or qualifications sometimes come into play explicitly, depending on the post.

In the constitutive documents of political organizations, such as the United Nations (UN) and regional institutions like the Organization of American States, the theory of the sovereign equality of States usually dominates. States are considered the electors, each one equal with the other, and all States (or, depending on the position, their individual nominees) are free to run for office. If one reviewed the documents of these organizations, as well as the plenary bodies of many non-political organizations, one would find much evidence to support this representational norm. The UN General Assembly (UNGA), where each Member State has a single vote regardless of the size of its population, territory, military, or economy, is the most obvious example, but there are many others.

Other principles appear in treaty form when the parties strongly agree on their relevance – most often in specialized organizations. For example, under the articles of agreement of IFIs, the members quotas, which are not equally distributed, (roughly) determine the number of votes allocated to each one. International commodities agreements divide votes equally between exporting and importing nations and allocate in the councils of such organizations individual States a subset of votes based upon the volume of their exports or imports. The Montreal Protocol requires that decisions of the Executive Committee of the Multilateral Fund be approved (in the absence of consensus) by two-thirds majorities of both developing and industrial countries.[3] The Convention on the Intergovernmental Maritime Consultative Organization (now the International Maritime Organization) allocates seats in the Organization's Council according to the 'interests' of its members (for example, international shipping services or seaborne trade),[4] and the Convention on International Civil Aviation sets aside seats in the Council to

[3] Art. 2(9)(c) of the Montreal Protocol on Substances that Deplete the Ozone Layer, 1522 UNTS 3 (adopted 16 September 1987, entered into force 1 January 1989).

[4] Art. 17 of the Convention on the International Maritime Organization, 289 UNTS 3 (adopted 6 March 1948, entered into force 17 March 1958).

'States of chief importance in air transport' and States with the 'largest contribution to the provision of facilities for international civil air navigation'.[5] In the Constitution of the International Labour Organization, 'members of chief industrial importance' are given representational preference over other States in the organization's Governing Body,[6] and the Chemical Weapons Convention allocates seats in the Executive Council by region, designating a certain number for 'States Parties with the most significant national chemical industry in the region'.[7] Some other agreements, such as the Statute of the International Tribunal of the Law of the Sea, provide regions with minimum representation in certain bodies.[8] Still others encourage, but do not require, electors to 'give consideration' to, pay 'due regard' to, or 'bear in mind' 'equitable geographic distribution'. In all these organizations, the negotiators of the agreements decided that the representative principle in question (differential responsibilities or regionalism) was essential to the success of the institutions they were building and that the institution itself could not operate unless this principle was incorporated into the organization's most fundamental document.

Ironically, what all these formal rules have in common is their flexibility. On the surface, they appear rigid – one State, one vote; the allocation of greater power to certain groups of States or regions; the requirement that candidates have certain qualities – but, in fact, these rules are designed as much to allow States to implement, or even avoid, their principles through lower-level decision-making.[9]

IOs thus often establish rules regarding representation through resolutions and decisions. These resolutions usually pertain to appointments to other bodies (both subsidiary and coordinate) or to the election of the organization's officers (such as chairs and presidents of sessions and committees). These rules

5 Art. 50 of the Convention on International Civil Aviation, 15 UNTS 295 (adopted 7 December 1944, entered into force 4 April 1974).

6 Art. 7 of the International Labour Organization Constitution. www.ilo.org/dyn/normlex/en/f?p=1000:62:0::NO:62:P62_LIST_ENTRIE_ID:2453907:NO, last accessed 9 December 2023.

7 Art. VIII(C)(23) of the Convention on the Prohibition of the Development, Production, Stockpiling and Use of Chemical Weapons and on their Destruction, 1974–1975 UNTS 45 (adopted 3 September 1992, entered into force 29 April 1997).

8 See Arts. 2, 3, and 35 of the Statute of the International Tribunal for the Law of the Sea, annex VI to the United Nations Convention on the Law of the Sea, 1833–1835 UNTS 31363 (adopted 10 December 1982, entered into force 16 November 1994).

9 The one great exception to this rule against the inflexible fixing of power allocations in formal agreements is permanent membership in the Security Council. In the Council, certain specified States – the Permanent Five (P-5), which are designated by name in the Charter – are accorded greater say as a result of their (immediate post-War) relative power through permanent membership, co-decision-making rules, and veto authority.

implement and supplement provisions that appear in constituent documents, filling in their intended gaps and ambiguities.

Resolutions are often used to establish regional representation. Thus, the resolutions of the UNGA rigidly allocate the Assembly's officers by region, including its presidency, vice presidency, and committee chairs. The General Assembly's resolutions also divide, by region, positions on subsidiary bodies, funds, and programmes, such as the International Law Commission (ILC), the United Nations Commission on International Trade Law (UNCITRAL), the United Nations Environment Programme (UNEP), the United Nations Children's Fund (UNICEF), the United Nations Development Programme (UNDP), and the World Food Programme (WFP), as well as positions on other principal UN organs, such as the Security Council and the Economic and Social Council (ECOSOC). ECOSOC resolutions allocate positions by region on its subsidiary bodies, the now defunct Human Rights Commission, the Commission for Social Development, and the Commission on the Status of Women, among others. In the Food and Agriculture Organization (FAO), resolutions distribute council seats by region. The General Conference Rules of Procedure of the United Nations Educational, Scientific and Cultural Organization, divide Member States into groups and give each group a set number of seats on the Executive Board. In the International Criminal Court, a resolution established a requirement that States Parties vote for a minimum number of judicial candidates per region, which number will vary according to judges from the region already sitting or elected.[10] A 1994 decision of the Congress of the Universal Postal Union distributed seats in the Council of Administration by region.[11] And by resolution the States Parties to the UN Convention on the Law of the Sea have allocated seats on the Commission on the Limits of the Continental Shelf and the International Tribunal for the Law of the Sea by region as well.[12]

The prevalence of regionalism at this level of decision-making should not surprise. As a representational principle, regionalism has (and has had for some time, particularly since decolonization) a level of legitimacy second only to the notion of sovereign equality. That stems, in part, from regionalism's

[10] International Criminal Court 6th plenary meeting, 'Procedure for the nomination and election of judges, the Prosecutor and Deputy Prosecutors of the International Criminal Court' (10 September 2004), ICC-ASP/3/Res.6, para. 20 b).

[11] Universal Postal Union, 'General Regulations of the Universal Postal Union' (1994), Art. 102(7).

[12] United Nations Convention on the Law of the Sea Meeting of State Parties, 'Arrangement for the allocation of seats on the International Tribunal for the Law of the Sea and the Commission on the Limits of the Continental Shelf' (26 June 2009), SPLOS/201.

guarantee that all (not just some) parts of the world will be represented. But the attractiveness of regionalism results from its effect of decreasing the number of States in the pool for elections and appointments, hence increasing the likelihood of election for States that might not otherwise be able to compete. This dynamic is enhanced by the common practice among regional groups of putting forward agreed slates of candidates that are often based on an informal rotational system among their members. The latter phenomenon points to other features of regionalism: efficiency and compromise. Regionalism 'reduces the potential for conflict in the selection of Members and gives all groups a more secure sense of representation'.[13] For these reasons, the regionalism principle is relatively easy to adopt in multilateral forums.

Democratic inroads in the formal mode manifest, albeit weakly, through techniques such as observer status that allow the access of non-State actors to IOs without providing them the decision rights accorded to States.[14] The UN Charter, for example, authorizes the 'Economic and Social Council [to] make suitable arrangements for consultation with non-governmental organizations which are concerned with matters within its competence'.[15] Accordingly, ECOSOC has established principles for consultative relations, most recently in resolution 1996/31, that outline the criteria for consultative status and the forms of consultation with the Council and its subsidiary organs, including (with some limitations) the ability to propose agenda items, attendance at meetings, written statements, and oral presentations.[16] The World Health Organization (WHO) has adopted a 'Framework of Engagement with Non-State Actors' that establishes rules for 'private sector entities' and 'international business associations', and others for 'nongovernmental organizations'.[17] The extent to which such participation can be understood as enhancing the democratic legitimacy of IOs will depend upon how these NGOs are characterized, the access they are provided, and the influence they wield in practice.[18]

[13] Christoph Schreuer, 'Regionalism v. Universalism' (1995) 6(3) *European Journal of International Law* 477–499, at 481.

[14] See generally Melissa J. Durkee, 'International Lobbying Law' (2018) 127(7) *Yale Law Journal* 1742–2203.

[15] Art. 71 of the Charter of the United Nations, 1 UNTS XVI (adopted 26 June 1945, entered into force 24 October 1945).

[16] See ECOSOC Res. 1996/31, 'Consultative relationship between the United Nations and non-governmental organizations' (25 July 1996), paras. 28–32.

[17] See WHO, 'Framework of Engagement with Non-state Actors' (28 May 2016), WHA69.10; see also Arts. 18(h) and 71 of the Constitution of the World Health Organization, 14 UNTS 185 (adopted 22 July 1946, entered into force 7 April 1948).

[18] Among many other examples, see International Monetary Fund, '2015 Guidelines on the IMF Staff Engagement with Civil Society Organizations' (2015); FAO, 'FAO Strategy for Private Sector Engagement, 2021–2025' (2021).

Altogether, the formal mode reflects State-centred international law at its apogee. The limited participation of non-State actors through formal mechanisms demonstrates simultaneously both the recognition of the need for a broader, more democratic representation and the strong impediments that exist for the achievement of that goal.

## 4.3 THE OPERATIONAL MODE

Formal rules of representation, because they are based on a statist myth, can only rarely recognize the differential power of States and the authority of non-State actors. The operational mode provides informal means that allow IOs to do both – but off the record and only in part. Representational practices in this mode take the form of informal agreements (that give greater say to powerful States), financing mechanisms (that give informal control over IO programmes to wealthy States and private foundations), and consultative processes such as meetings and conferences (that provide voice to non-governmental and sub-State actors).[19]

Much of international decision-making is done through informal processes, particularly informal agreements, either one-off or long-term. In no area is this more apparent than in the realm of agreements concerning international representation. Because of their unofficial, typically unpublicized, all but hidden, and often evolving nature, such agreements are inherently difficult to identify and ascertain. Unsurprisingly, a search of official records uncovers little, if any, explicit mention of their existence, let alone a comprehensive compilation. But only with an understanding of the entire scope of these informal rules can one comprehend not only international representation as it is currently constructed.

The obvious place to begin an examination of informal agreements concerning representational issues is with IFIs. The most well-known is the agreement between the United States and the Europeans regarding the leadership of the International Monetary Fund (IMF) and the World Bank. But the two flagship IFIs are not alone in allocating posts by custom. The four major regional IFIs exhibit the same pattern of informal delegation of leadership selection to a particular country or countries. Thus, the President of the Asian Development Bank has always been a Japanese national, the presidency

[19] As Ian Hurd notes in the context of the Security Council, the 'institutionalized practice of consultation' with certain States or groups of States can be just as significant and may amount to 'a kind of de facto membership'. Ian Hurd, 'Security Council Reform: Informal Membership and Practice', in Bruce Russet (ed.), *The Once and Future Security Council* (New York: St Martin's Press, 1997), pp. 135–152, p. 136.

of the European Bank for Reconstruction and Development has always alternated between French and German nationals, the President of the Inter-American Development Bank has always been a Latin American national, and the presidency of the African Development Bank has rotated among 'various [African] linguistic and geographic groups'.[20] Further, related institutions, such as the Multilateral Investment Guarantee Agency (MIGA), where only Japanese nationals have occupied the highest post, have also informally specified the nationality of their top officials.

Though scholars and the media have focused on the top positions in the IFIs, the allocation of posts goes deeper. For instance, IFI vice presidencies are frequently slotted as well. Adding this layer to the analysis shows that the designation of top posts cannot be seen in isolation – they are often part of a package deal. Thus, while the Managing Director of the IMF is always a European national, the IMF's First Deputy Managing Director is always a US national, chosen by the United States.

The pattern holds for the regional banks. Here, the designations are usually component parts of informal deals that allocate the top position to one State or group of States from the region the bank serves and the bank's deputy position or positions to another State or group of States that is located outside the region but contributes significantly to the organization's coffers. Consistently, whereas the Asian, European, and Inter-American Banks are headed by nationals from their respective regions, a US national has always served as the First Vice President of the European Bank and the Executive Vice President of the Inter-American Bank, and since 1978 has served as a Vice President of the Asian Bank.

US nationals are not the only ones who benefit from these arrangements. In 1983, a third vice presidency was added at the Asian Development Bank so that the Europeans would have a designated senior official there. And in 2003, a fourth vice presidency was added to give the Chinese representation. In the African Development Bank, vice presidencies are allocated informally as well. From the Bank's founding until 1985, the four vice presidents were distributed regionally within Africa – one to North Africa, one to Anglophone Africa, another to Francophone Africa, and one to Nigeria. In 1986, a fifth vice presidency was added for a non-African.

The patterns of high-level appointments in IFIs demonstrate a series of interlocking agreements, all off the books, that allocate positions among the institutions' major contributors and the world's financial powers – the US, the

[20] E. Philip English and Harris M. Mule, *Multilateral Development Banks, Volume 1, The African Development Bank* (Boulder, CO: Lynne Rienner Publishers, 1996), p. 45.

European Union, and Japan. These three take advantage of their positions as levers of influence within the IFIs, often seeking to staff their posts with individuals who previously served in their respective national finance ministries. Thus, for example, the US nationals who have held regional development bank vice presidencies have frequently been former US Government officials, usually from the Department of the Treasury.

The informal allocation of appointments and positions is also prevalent outside the context of the IFIs, particularly in the UN. Among the foremost beneficiaries in the UN are the P-5 – China, France, Russia, the United Kingdom, and the US. By a rule, nowhere codified and only occasionally breached, each of the members of the P-5 (or one of its nationals) can sit on any UN body, if the country so chooses. The only significant exceptions to this 'P-5 Convention' were considerable gaps in China's representation because of the long-running dispute over whether Taiwan or the People's Republic properly represented China in the UN.

This informal agreement has applied regardless of the nature of the institution or position, courts included. Thus, until recently, with one notable exception, a judge from each P-5 member, except for China, has had, by 'tradition' (the word used in a 1956 Department of State memo),[21] on the International Court of Justice (ICJ) since the Court's inception, even though its Statute does not provide for such preferences. Similarly, each of the P-5 countries continuously had a judge on one of the two ad hoc criminal tribunals, the International Criminal Tribunal for the Former Yugoslavia or the International Criminal Tribunal for Rwanda.

The P-5's prerogatives extend to other UN bodies as well. All of the P-5 States, again with the exception of China and some other minor, occasional interruptions, have continuously been members of the ECOSOC and its subsidiary bodies, such as the Commission on Human Rights, the Commission on Narcotic Drugs, the Commission on Population and Development, the Committee for Program and Coordination, the Commission on Social Development, the Commission on Sustainable Development, the Commission on the Status of Women, and the Statistical Commission. With few exceptions, they (or their nationals) have also served, when they have chosen to run, on the subsidiary bodies of the General Assembly – such as the Advisory Committee on Administrative and Budgetary Questions and the ILC – as well as on the executive boards and councils of UN Funds and Program – such as

[21] 'Instruction from the Department of State to Certain Diplomatic Missions, 17 October 1956' (1988) 11 *Foreign Relations of the United States, 1955–1957, United Nations and General International Matters* 118–128, at 119.

UNDP, UNEP, UNICEF, and the United Nations Human Settlements Programme. Furthermore, they have effectively held permanent seats on the councils and boards of UN specialized agencies, such as the FAO, the International Atomic Energy Agency, the International Civil Aviation Organization, the International Maritime Organization, the International Telecommunications Union, the Organization for the Prohibition of Chemical Weapons, and the World Meteorological Organization.

Finally, the P-5's preferential treatment extends to the top levels of the UN Secretariat. At least one of its nationals from each member of the P-5 has been appointed to the Under-Secretary-General level (the rank just below the Secretary-General and the Deputy Secretary-General) since the founding of the organization. The purpose is evident. As Marrack Goulding, himself a former British Under-Secretary-General, has written, '[a] senior UN official nominated by his or her government was ... assumed to be in the Secretariat to do that government's bidding'.[22] The P-5 Under-Secretaries-General are assigned the most significant portfolios, each one reflecting the country's particular interests at that moment. From 1992 until 2007, for instance, the US insisted on the post of Under-Secretary-General for Administration and Management, reflecting the US concern with those topics during this period.

The P-5 Convention is far from the only informal rule operating at the UN in the area of representation. Some positions informally rotate by region. For instance, upon Kofi Annan's resignation, it was widely said that it was 'Asia's turn' to have one of its own as Secretary-General – and so it was. Predictably, a European national – António Guterres – succeeded Secretary-General Ban Ki-moon. UNCITRAL informally rotates positions in the Commission's bureau among regional groups, and the ILC does the same for its officers. Further, judgeships at the ICJ are informally allocated by region, and even sub-region. Of the ten ICJ seats not set aside for the P-5, two are from the Western European and Other Group (WEOG), one is from the Group of Eastern European States, two are from the Group of Latin American and Caribbean States, three are from the Group of African States (including one from Arab North Africa, one from Francophone sub-Saharan Africa, and one from Anglophone sub-Saharan Africa), and two are from the Group of Asian States. This distribution mimics the formal distribution of the ten non-permanent seats on the Security Council. Regional groups choose their own candidates for 'their' seats, when they can agree, sometimes on the basis of region-specific informal agreements that allocate nominations among sub-regional groups.

[22] Marrack Goulding, *Peacemonger* (London: John Murray Publishers, 2002), p. 6.

Other positions are allocated exclusively to a specific region or country. Thus, the UN Legal Counsel (the Under-Secretary-General for Legal Affairs) is always a WEOG national (from a non-P-5 country). The US has been given the top job at UNICEF and the WFP (since the early 1990s) and the second-ranking job at the FAO. Since the 1970s, Japan, a major funder of the UN, has held a permanent slot at the Under-Secretary-General level and a judgeship on the ICJ for its nationals.

In addition to informal agreements, which privilege powerful States, the operational mode manifests in two other ways: in budgeting practices and informal consultation processes. When an organization depends on voluntary contributions, either for its general budget or for the support of specific programmes, the organization becomes particularly dependent on its donors. And with their contributions, donors expect to exert influence on the operation of the organization. Organizations themselves – and other Member States of the organization – understand this and provide donors with an outsized influence on the organization's operation. Sometimes, in the case of restricted contributions, this is recognized explicitly by the contracts entered into by organizations and their donors that establish reporting and monitoring frameworks. Sometimes it is done implicitly by giving donors special privileges within the organization.

Organizations that primarily rely on voluntary contributions therefore no longer act as true multilateral institutions with collective principals but rather in significant respects as the delegated agents of multiple principals. In this form of funding, the 'IO agent is guided by and held accountable through its bilateral relationships with individual donors, rather than through a single relationship with the intergovernmental body'.[23] Though the assessed contribution regime is not perfectly multilateral because of the greater sway of high-contributing States, in comparison the funding of IOs through voluntary contributions significantly decreases the role of collective decision-making on the critical issues that pertain to budgetary matters, including the size of the budget, burden sharing among Member States, the organization's priorities, and its accountability.[24] Depending on the type of voluntary contribution (restricted or unrestricted), some or all of those issues will be determined not by the organization's collective principal but by the aggregation of decentralized choices made by individual donors, including non-State actors such as the Bill & Melinda Gates Foundation. Effectively and informally, then,

23 Erin R. Graham, 'Money and Multilateralism: How Funding Rules Constitute IO Governance' (2015) 7 *International Theory* 162–194, at 163.

24 Ibid., at 164.

wealthy states and non-profit organizations control IO decision-making through their ability to control the funding of IO budgets.

The operational mode also manifests in informal influence arrangements. As an example, cities, networks of cities, and groups of networks have convened on the margins or sidelines of intergovernmental meetings and diplomatic conferences hosted by IOs, and mayors have testified at committees before and during negotiations. These efforts have had influence. In 2015, the Global Taskforce of Local and Regional Governments, together with others, worked with sympathetic States to ensure the inclusion of Goal 11 Sustainable Cities and Communities in the Sustainable Development Goals.[25] That same year, city networks were crucial in the run-up to the Paris Agreement and also had influence in the creation of the Sendai Framework for Disaster Risk Reduction 2015–2030. As part of the Habitat III process that generated the New Urban Agenda in 2016, the Global Taskforce advocated through the production of policy papers, the organization of informal hearings for the benefit of the Habitat III Secretariat and the Bureau of the Preparatory Committee, and the coordination of the second World Assembly of Local and Regional Governments.[26] The New Urban Agenda's Quito Declaration on Sustainable Cities and Human Settlements for All 'acknowledge[d] … the contributions of subnational and local governments, in the definition of the New Urban Agenda and [took] note of the second World Assembly of Local and Regional Governments'.[27] And the Quito Implementation Plan for the New Urban Agenda 'note[d] the importance of continuing to engage in the follow-up to and review of the New Urban Agenda with subnational and local government associations represented at the World Assembly of Local and Regional Governments'.[28] Following Quito, the 9th Global Conference on Health Promotion, held in Shanghai, included a Mayors Forum in recognition of the role mayors in urban health. Over 100 mayors adopted the Shanghai Consensus on Healthy Cities. Subsequently, cities had similar influence in the creation of the Global Compact for Safe, Orderly and Regular Migration and the Global Compact on Refugees.

[25] Noora Arajärvi, 'Including Cities in the 2030 Agenda: A Review of The Post-2015 Process', in Helmut P. Aust and Anél du Plessis (eds.), *The Globalisation of Urban Governance: Legal Perspectives on Sustainable Development Goal 11* (New York: Routledge, 2018), pp. 17–38, pp. 19–20.

[26] Habitat III, 'Global Taskforce of Local and Regional Governments'. http://habitat3.org/engagement/global-taskforce-of-local-and-regional-governments, last accessed 9 December 2023.

[27] UNGA Res. 71/256, 'New Urban Agenda' (23 December 2016), Annex, para. 8.

[28] Ibid., para. 169.

Policy communication between cities and IOs also takes place in forms and spaces specifically designed for that purpose. IOs have organized conferences, such as the World Urban Forum, for the exchange of information and perspectives with representatives of cities and city networks, and IOs have entered into memoranda of understanding and partnership agreements. Since 2014, the Global Partnership for Effective Development Co-operation, a 'multi-stakeholder vehicle for driving development effectiveness' that IOs participate in, has included a representative of local governments on its steering committee.[29] The Global Forum on Migration and Development (GFMD), an intergovernmental venue that works closely with the UN and the International Organization for Migration, has a Mayors Mechanism, which 'is a means to formalize the relationship between the government-led GFMD process and the local authorities' and 'establishes a platform to interact with States ... [and] aims to add depth to the GFMD deliberations by bridging existing divides between local realities and global policy discussions, and between migrants, civil society, and States'.[30] Similarly, local authorities, as a 'major group', are provided significant participatory rights in the High-Level Political Forum on Sustainable Development and previously in the Forum's predecessor, the Commission on Sustainable Development. IOs participate in or have strong links to these dialogic processes where cities have some form of participation.

This is not to exaggerate the role of cities in IOs, which varies significantly by organization and topic, but those in the know appreciate how and when the system works, how it differs from the official narrative (the formal mode), and where the fault lines are located. It is a silent compromise among those involved.

The operational mode works to enhance the influence of powerful actors – States and NGOs – and incorporate the voices of the less influential and those that are not recognized as formal participants at the international level, like cities. There are thus democratic aspects to the operational mode and anti-democratic characteristics in the mode's current practice.

29 Global Partnership for Effective Development Co-operation, 'Development Effectiveness and the 2030 Agenda'. www.effectivecooperation.org/landing-page/about-partnership, last accessed 9 December 2023; Global Partnership for Effective Development Co-operation, 'First High-Level Meeting of the Global Partnership for Effective Development Co-operation: Building Towards an Inclusive Post-2015 Development Agenda' (Mexico High Level Meeting Communiqué, 16 April 2014). Annex 2. www.mzv.cz/file/1755457/Development_Effectiveness_HLM_Mexico_2014_Communique.pdf, last accessed 9 December 2023.

30 Global Forum on Migration & Development, 'The GFMD Mayors Mechanism'. www.gfmd.org/process/gfmd-mayors-mechanism, last accessed 9 December 2023.

## 4.4 THE ASPIRATIONAL MODE

The operational mode incorporates and gives priority to voices and policies that are not countenanced by formal rules of IOs. In the aspirational mode, States, IO officials, politicians, activists, and scholars advocate for changes in the formal and operational modes. The aspirational mode is thus reformist in nature, though it can be revolutionary as well. Either way, it is necessarily a technique of advocacy, not of governance. It is an attempt to change the status quo, its rules and techniques. If successful, the results will be incorporated into the formal and operational modes. Its content, thus, can be transitory.

Contemporarily, broad calls for 'democratic representation within international organizations' dominate the aspirational mode,[31] as do more narrow proposals to change IMF quota formulas and decision-making rules[32] and 'calls for merit-based, open and transparent . . . selection process[es]' for high-level IO staff appointments, such as the World Bank president.[33] These critiques of the formal and operational modes of representation seek to change the rules to bring IOs more in line with the representational principles of democratic legitimacy propounded by their advocates.

In this way, the aspirational mode operates outside of the rules of IOs as they are currently constituted, though its policies can be advocated both inside and outside organizations by their supporters. The aspirational mode, therefore, is a position from which to reform IOs. It serves, in this way, as a great value for organizations, since it provides an opportunity to think through, suggest, and lobby for change and improvement. IOs need to maintain their democratic legitimacy, and therefore organizations require reformers to push for change. The aspirational mode serves that function by providing a space for bringing IOs into line with new and evolving expectations.

31 See Samantha Besson, 'Democratic Representation within International Organizations: From International Good Governance to International Good Government' (2022) 19(4) *International Organizations Law Review* 489–527.

32 See UN, 'Our Common Agenda Policy Brief 6: Reforms to the International Financial Architecture' (May 2023).

33 See Bretton Woods Project, 'Civil Society Demands the End of the "Gentleman's Agreement" and Calls for Merit-Based, Open and Transparent World Bank Presidential Selection Process' (29 March 2023). www.brettonwoodsproject.org/2023/03/civil-society-demands-the-end-of-the-gentlemans-agreement-and-calls-for-merit-based-open-and-transparent-world-bank-presidential-selection-process, last accessed 9 December 2023.

## 4.5 THE ALTERNATIVE MODE

The aspirational mode can lead to changes in IOs and their formal or operational modes, but sometimes the desired change will not be possible or will not occur soon enough. Under these circumstances, actors may resort to alternatives to IOs as a means of allowing representational practices that the formal and operational modes do not permit. In the alternative mode, States and non-State actors establish either groups or NGOs that are not constituted within international law's formalist framework, thereby allowing them to create representational systems that are not available under current international law.

Perhaps the best examples of IO alternatives are the Global Fund to Fight AIDS, Tuberculosis and Malaria and Gavi, the Vaccine Alliance, both organized under Swiss domestic law. The Global Fund's board includes twenty voting and eight non-voting members.[34] Of the voting members, seven represent developing countries (with regional distribution among them), eight represent donors, and five represent civil society and the private sector (including one person living with HIV/AIDS or from a community living with tuberculosis or malaria). The non-voting members represent additional constituencies or Fund officials (the Board Chair and Vice-Chair, the Executive Director). Similarly, the Gavi Alliance board is divided into 'Representative Board Members' (representatives from partner institutions and stakeholders, including permanent seats for UNICEF, WHO, the World Bank, and the Bill & Melinda Gates Foundation) and 'Unaffiliated Board Members' (individuals appointed in their personal capacity on the basis of their skills and networks).[35] Both organizations are established as foundations under the Swiss Civil Code and are provided a significant degree of independence that they generally would not have under most countries' domestic law. Further, under its Host State Act, and previously under other domestic authority, Switzerland has entered into headquarters agreements with both organizations because they 'carry[] out tasks which are normally the responsibility of those intergovernmental organizations, international institutions or States; [and] play[] a key role in an important area of international relations'.[36]

34 The Global Fund, 'Bylaws of the Global Fund to Fight Aids, Tuberculosis & Malaria' (2016, last amended 12 May 2022), Art. 7.

35 Gavi Alliance, 'Statutes of 29 October 2008', Art. 9. www.gavi.org/sites/default/files/document/2020/Gavi-Alliance-Statutes–June-2020.pdf, last accessed 9 December 2023.

36 Federal Act on the Privileges, Immunities and Facilities and the Financial Subsidies granted by Switzerland as a Host State, 22 June 2007 (Status as of 1 November 2022), Art. 14. www.fedlex.admin.ch/eli/cc/2007/860/en, last accessed 9 December 2023.

Such agreements grant them privileges and immunities, including tax exemptions, distinct from those that would otherwise apply under Swiss law.[37] Other States have also provided privileges and immunities to the Global Fund by amending their domestic law[38] or entering into a multilateral privileges and immunities treaty for their benefit.[39] Effectively, these States have recognized these NGOs (foundations) as IOs.

Groups, like the G7 and G20, are another alternative to IOs. These meetings allow States to meet together and with representatives of IOs, such as the African Union, the European Union, the IMF, and the Word Bank. Recently, for example, the heads of the IMF, World Bank Group, Organisation for Economic Co-operation and Development, and Financial Stability Board met with the G7 finance ministers and central bank governors.[40] In September 2023, the African Union was made a permanent member of the G20.[41] These types of State-IO interactions would generally be difficult within the formal confines of IOs.

The alternative mode provides opportunities for the representational assumptions of the formal mode to be bypassed. It is not a perfect solution to the challenge of democratic legitimacy, however. There is nothing inherent in the alternative mode that leads to that outcome. The alternative mode is used primarily by States when it is convenient for them to do so: when States find that they want to operate outside of the formal and operational modes because those modes do not allow them to achieve their desired goals. The alternative mode therefore is an opportunity to achieve democratic legitimacy, but as with change to the other modes, there must be political commitment and an openness to innovative thinking to realize that goal.

37 See e.g. Agreement between the Swiss Federal Council and the Global Fund to Fight AIDS, Tuberculosis and Malaria in view of determining the legal status of the Global Fund in Switzerland (13 December 2004).

38 The United States, pursuant to the International Organizations Immunities Act, provides IO immunities to a select few NGOs.

39 See Agreement on Privileges and Immunities of the Global Fund to Fight AIDS, Tuberculosis and Malaria, 3300 UNTS 1 (adopted 14 December 2009, entered into force 17 April 2019).

40 See US Department of the Treasury, 'G7 Finance Ministers and Central Bank Governors' Statement' (Press release, 1 October 2023). https://home.treasury.gov/news/press-releases/jy1800, last accessed 9 December 2023.

41 'African Union made permanent member of G20 at Delhi summit', *The Guardian*, 9 September 2023. www.theguardian.com/world/2023/sep/09/african-union-made-permanent-member-of-g20-at-delhi-summit, last accessed 9 December 2023.

## 4.6 A SECOND-BEST SYSTEM OF REPRESENTATION AND DEMOCRATIC LEGITIMACY

Each of the four modes of representation reflects different inclinations: the positivist, the functionalist, the principled, and the practical. The positivist prefers the formal mode; the functionalist employs the operational mode; the principled advocates through the aspirational mode; and the practical looks to the alternative mode. All four have their advantages, and all four have their limits.

Where an actor (a State, a sub-State actor, an NGO, a corporation) falls along the representational spectrum will depend on particular circumstances, not who they are. For some issues, a State will act within the formal and operational modes, while at other times and for other issues they will use the alternative mode. Similarly, an NGO may be satisfied with the formal mode in some instances but resort to the alternative mode in other situations. Many actors thus work in multiple modes simultaneously, often doubling up with the aspirational mode as they operate within established rules and attempt to reform them at the same time. The four modes are different techniques of representation, used by participants to achieve desired goals within the State-centric framework of international law and IOs.

From the perspective of minimum public order, the co-existence of all four is essential. Each mode does separate work. Together, they allow for change and provide processes to achieve an equilibrium among competing values.[42] Within the statist paradigm that defines the international system, a system of multiple modes of representation is thus not only descriptively accurate, it is also necessary because of the challenge of democratic legitimacy that is most prominently manifested in the aspirational mode. Optimally, the formal system would fully adapt to that challenge. But there are limits to the formal system's ability to change because of the unwillingness of certain actors to accede to that change. In the meantime, there need to be methods and spaces to advocate and implement change. The international representational system of the four modes is thus second best. Yet, second best is better than any of the possible alternatives while the process of change slowly proceeds.

[42] On the notion of equilibrium, see Monica Hakimi and Jacob Katz Cogan, 'The Two Codes on the Use of Force' (2016) 27(2) *European Journal of International Law* 257–291.

# 5

# *Demoi*cratic Representation in and by International Organizations

Francis Cheneval

## 5.1 INTRODUCTION

This chapter proposes *demoi*cratic representation as a subtype of representation in international organizational practice. While the regime-neutral representation of States remains prudent for legitimate international organization of States with different and conflicting regime types, *demoi*cratic representation ought to guide international law- and policy-making among democratic Peoples.

The tenets of the chapter's argument are the following:

P1: The People is constituted by rules that create a set of interconnected statuses, institutions, and procedures which jointly exercise highest political authority, i.e. govern sovereignly.

P2: The People is composed of citizens. The democratic People is composed of citizens who hold specific deontic powers that enable them to govern via the institutions of the People, directly and by representatives whom they authorize and hold accountable.

P3: Political representing is either standing for the People as a whole or its institutions, or it is the acting of representatives in the stead of and for the citizens in governmental institutions of the People.

P4: The People is represented only by all the different types of representative persons who act within different types of governmental institutions and procedures of the People. These types of governmental institutions are determined by essentially different and jointly complete types of governmental actions, such as law-giving, executive government, and jurisprudence.

P5: Democratic Peoples are accountable to each other as Peoples and to each other's citizens.

P6: Under any decision rule, even consent, there is a possible consent deficit about the decision rule even in case of unanimity on a substantive issue.
C1: Towards each other, the Peoples are adequately represented and held accountable only via the systemic interaction of all the different types of highest governmental institutions.
C2: *Demoi*cratic representation needs to be designed in common institutions of the Peoples that unite its highest governmental intuitions, i.e. in the Peoples' councils of parliaments, the Peoples' councils of executives, the Peoples' councils of high courts.
C3: *Demoi*cratic representation ought not to be understood as working exclusively under the principle of Peoples consent (unanimity rule). Rather it is the representational space in which the consent deficit about the decision rule of inter-People relations is addressed and calibration sought by seeking a balance between different decision rules.
C4: Political international organizations (IOs) ought to conform to the principle that all institutional manifestations of the People be represented in the corresponding common governmental institutions. They need to embody *demoi*cratic representation within their organization. The less comprehensive, economic, legal, technical intergovernmental organizations (IGOs) ought to be part of a system of mutual accountability and thereby assure *demoi*cratic representation by IOs.

The goal of this chapter is to sketch out a conception, justification, and some basic guidelines of an institutional design of *demoi*cratic representation.[1] It aims to contribute to further joining the fields of philosophy of democracy and philosophy of international law.[2] Given the plurality and interdependence of

[1] I subscribe to Hart's view that principles are different from rules, first, because the former are always general, broad, and rather unspecific and secondly because principles, in their reference to some goal, entitlement, purpose or value, are always regarded as desirable and justificatory from some point of 'view'. For principles of multilateral democracy or *demoi*cracy, see Francis Cheneval, *The Government of the Peoples: On The Idea and Principles of Multilateral Democracy* (New York: Palgrave Macmillan, 2011).

[2] Samantha Besson, 'State Consent and Disagreement in International Law-Making: Dissolving the Paradox' (2016) 29(2) *Leiden Journal of International Law* 289–316; Samantha Besson, *Reconstruire l'ordre institutionnel international* (Paris: College of France/Fayard, 2021); Samantha Besson, 'Democratic Representation within International Organizations: From International Good Governance to International Good Government' (2022) 19(4) *International Organizations Law Review* 489–527; Samantha Besson, 'Investment Citizenship and Democracy in a Global Age: Towards a Democratic Interpretation of International Nationality Law' (2019) 29(4) *Swiss Review of International and European Law* 525–547; Samantha Besson and José Luis Martí, 'From Equal State Consent to Equal Public

Peoples, philosophy of democracy ought not to remain fixated on the monadic *demos* and exclude the dimension of the relation among governing Peoples from the core of its normative and empirical inquiries. Alternatively, it ought not to dissolve the *demos* by conceiving democracy as 'subject-less' and 'unbounded' deliberation[3] as this disregards the capacity of Peoples to act effectively and responsibly which is necessary for any meaningful realization of democracy.[4] Philosophy of international law, for its part, ought not to remain largely a philosophy of States, of will and consent of States, and of law of States, the legal possibility of treaty-making by IOs in their area of competence notwithstanding.[5] Important ground has been broken by the thesis of the exception of democratic State consent in international law at large.[6] This chapter proposes that the forging of consent and addressing of reasonable disagreement among democratic States in international relations and in IOs ought to be realized by *demoi*cratic representation. It thereby goes beyond but not against the thesis of exception of democratic State consent.

## 5.2 *DEMOI*CRATIC THEORY

European law theory has been the primary meeting ground of philosophy of democracy and of international law.[7] Kalypso Nicolaïdis, who coined the term

Participation in International Organizations: Institutionalizing Multiple International Representation', in Samantha Besson (ed.), *Consenting to International Law* (Cambridge: Cambridge University Press, 2023), pp. 314–346; Samantha Besson and José Luis Martí, 'Legitimate Actors of International Law-Making: Towards a Theory of International Democratic Representation' (2018) 9(3) *Jurisprudence* 504–540; Samantha Besson and José Luis Martí, 'Cities as Democratic Representatives in International Law-Making', in Helmut P. Aust and Janne E. Nijman (eds.), *Research Handbook on International Law and Cities* (London: Edward Elgar, 2021), pp. 341–353; Francis Cheneval, *La cité des peuples: mémoires de cosmopolitismes* (Paris: Cerf, 2005); Cheneval, *The Government of the Peoples*, fn. 1.

3 William E. Scheuerman, *Frankfurt School Perspectives on Globalization, Democracy, and the Law* (New York: Routledge, 2008); Arash Abizadeh, 'Democratic Theory and Border Coercion: No Right to Unilaterally Control Your Own Borders' (2008) 36(1) *Political Theory* 37–65.

4 Mark E. Warren, 'Democracy and the State', in John S. Dryzek, Bonnie Honig and Anne Philips (eds.), *The Oxford Handbook of Political Theory* (Oxford: Oxford University Press, 2006), pp. 382–399.

5 Henry G. Schermers and Niels Blokker, *International Institutional Law: Unity within Diversity*, 6th ed. (Leiden/Boston: Brill/Nijoff, 2018), p. 1097.

6 Besson, 'State Consent and Disagreement in International Law-Making', fn. 2; Besson, 'Democratic Representation within International Organizations', fn. 2.

7 Robert Schütze, *Foreign Affairs and the EU Constitution* (Cambridge: Cambridge University Press, 2014), pp. 26ff; Matthias Oesch, *Europarecht. Band 1: Grundlagen, Institutionen, Verhältnis Schweis-EU* (Zürich: Stämpfli Verlag, 2019), p. 309; Samantha Besson, 'Deliberative *Demoi*-Cracy in the European Union: Towards the Deterritorialization of Democracy', in

*demoi*cracy[8] succinctly defines it as 'a Union of peoples who govern together, but not as one'.[9] In the version of Pavlos Eleftheriadis, the European Union as 'Union of Peoples' is a dual system, based on reciprocity and equality of Peoples.[10] The assumption is that a multitude of democratically governed Peoples relate to each other horizontally based on shared principles. A *demoi*cratic union is a plurality of concordant members. A democratic unit, on the other hand, is a whole without vetoes, opt-outs, or exit rights for the subunits.[11] The debate on *demoi*cracy has gained momentum.[12] The recent publications remain confined to EU studies, but the normative core includes claims that go beyond contingent voluntary association: mutual non-domination and mutual recognition of Peoples.[13]

Samantha Besson and José Luis Martí (eds.), *Deliberative Democracy and Its Discontents* (Ashgate: Aldershot, 2006), pp. 181–214; Cheneval, *The Government of the Peoples*, fn. 1.

8 Kalypso Nicolaïdis, 'Our European Demoi-Cracy: Is This Constitution a Third Way for Europe?', in Kalypso Nicolaïdis and Stephen Weatherill (eds.), *Whose Europe? National Models and the Constitution of the European Union* (Oxford: Oxford University Press, 2003), pp. 137–152; Kalypso Nicolaïdis, 'The New Constitution as European "Demoicracy"?' (2004) 7(1) *Critical Review of International Social and Political Philosophy* 76–93.

9 Nicolaïdis, 'Our European Demoi-Cracy', fn. 8, p. 351.

10 Pavlos Elftheriadis, *A Union of Peoples: Europe as a Community of Principle* (Oxford: Oxford University Press, 2020).

11 Nicolaïdis, 'The New Constitution as European "Demoicracy"?', fn. 8; Kalypso Nicolaïdis, 'European Demoicracy and Its Crisis' (2013) 51(2) *JCMS: Journal of Common Market Studies* 351–369; Francis Cheneval and Kalypso Nicolaïdis, 'The Social Construction of Demoicracy in the European Union' (2016) 16(2) *European Journal of Political Theory* 235–260; Kalypso Nicolaïdis and Juri Viehoff, 'Just Boundaries for Demoicrats' (2017) 39 *Journal of European Integration* 591; Joseph Lacey, *Centripetral Democracy: Democratic Legitimacy and Political Identity in Belgium, Switzerland, and the European Union* (Oxford: Oxford University Press, 2017).

12 Philippe Van Parijs, 'Should the EU Become More Democratic?', in Andreas Føllesdal and Peter Koslowski (eds.), *Democracy and the European Union* (Berlin/Heidelberg: Springer Verlag, 1998), pp. 287–301; Nicolaïdis, 'Our European Demoi-Cracy', fn. 8; Nicolaïdis, 'European Demoicracy and Its Crisis', fn. 11; Cheneval and Nicolaïdis, fn. 11; Francis Cheneval and Frank Schimmelfennig, 'The Case for Demoicracy in the European Union' (2013) 51(2) *JCMS: Journal of Common Market Studies* 334–350; Francis Cheneval, Sandra Lavenex, and Frank Schimmelfennig (eds.), *European Democracy as Demoi-Cracy* (London/New York: Routledge, 2015); Richard Bellamy and Joseph Lacey, 'Balancing the Rights and Duties of European and National Citizens: A Demoicratic Approach' (2018) 25(10) *Journal of European Public Policy* 1403–1421; Besson, 'Deliberative *Demoi*-Cracy in the European Union', fn. 7; Sergio Fabbrini, 'Which Democracy for a Union of States? A Comparative Perspective of the European Union' (2017) 8(S6) *Global Policy* 14–22.

13 Kalypso Nicolaïdis, 'The Peoples Imagined. Constitution a Demoicratic European Polity', in Jan Komárek (ed.), *European Constitutional Imagineries Between Ideology and Utopia* (Oxford: Oxford University Press, 2023), pp. 231–258; Kalypso Nicolaïdis and Ulrike Liebert, 'Demoicratic Theory: Bridging Positive, Critical and Normative Approaches to European Studies', in Samuel B. H. Faure and Christian Lequesne (eds.), *Elgar Companion to the European Union* (Cheltenham/Northampton, MA: Edward Elgar Publishing, 2023), pp. 48–66.

The concept and theory of *demoi*cracy have been criticized in three ways: (1) *Demoi*cracy as the *finalité* of European integration.[14] (2) *Demoi*cracy as justification of the actual EU.[15] (3) Miriam Ronzoni criticized Nicolaïdis' 'third way'-conception of *demoi*cracy, stating that it conceptually collapses either into intergovernmentalism or statist federalism.[16] Ad (1) and (2): The present chapter is committed to an ideal-typical and general justificatory theory of *demoi*cracy, not a philosophy of history about the perfect end-state of the EU, and not a legitimation of the actual EU. The legitimation of the instantiation of *demoi*cracy in a concrete political entity such as the EU cannot be directly deduced from a general concept and justification of *demoi*cracy. Ad (3): First, Ronzoni's position neglects the possibility of the existence of a rule of recognition among *demoi* who want to act together but not as one. The existence of such a rule would mark a qualitative difference between *demoi*cracy and intergovernmentalism as well as State federalism. Second, if *demoi*, as popular sovereigns, are understood to have legal disabilities, multiple institutional modes of being, and guarantee transnational fundamental rights, the reduction of *demoi*cracy to either statist federalism or executive intergovernmentalism is inadequate. Third, intergovernmental rule-making limited to executives violates the separation of powers principle and sidelines representational bodies through which citizens can authorize and control legislation.[17] Federalism, for its part, is a theory that predates liberal democracy.[18]

## 5.3 THE SOCIAL ONTOLOGY OF THE DEMOS

At the basis of a theory of *demoi*cratic representation lies the question how the citizen, the People, and a group of Peoples can be understood ontologically as social entities, and what modes of representation are possible and normatively

[14] Thorsten Hüller, 'Out of Time? The Democratic Limits of EU Demoicracy' (2015) 23(10) *Journal of European Public Policy* 1407–1424; Fabio Wolkenstein, 'Demoicracy, Transnational Partisanship and the EU' (2017) 56(2) *JCMS: Journal of Common Market Studies* 284–299.

[15] Fritz W. Scharpf, 'After the Crash: A Perspective on Multilevel European Democracy' (2015) 21(3) *European Law Journal* 384–405, at 400.

[16] Miriam Ronzoni, 'The European Union as a Demoicracy: Really a Third Way?' (2016) 16(2) *European Journal of Political Theory* 210–234.

[17] Daniel Innerarity, 'Transnational Self-Determination. Resetting Self-Government in the Age of Interdependence' (2015) 53(5) *JCMS: Journal of Common Market Studies* 1061–1076.

[18] Kalypso Nicolaïdis, 'Conclusion: The Federal Vision Beyond the Federal State', in Kalypso Nicolaïdis and Robert Howse (eds.), *The Federal Vision: Legitimacy and Levels of Governance in the US and the EU* (Oxford: Oxford University Press, 2001), pp. 439–482.

necessary from the democratic standpoint. I avoid the dichotomy between a substantialist and interactionalist ontology of democracy[19] by assuming that social beings are constituted by social speech and document *acts*.[20] If we assume that (1) 'people' denotes the same social entity in all three descriptions of democracy as government of, by, and for the people; if we further assume that (2) the people are the sovereign person in democracy, then there occurs:

(i) a circularity problem concerning the people as *pouvoir constituant* ('of the people') and *pouvoir constitué* ('by the people'; *demos* problem);
(ii) a paradox of popular sovereignty: the sovereign and the subject are identical (transitivity problem).

We must be able to show that 'people' does not refer to the same entity in the three nominal descriptions of democracy. The People as origin or ground of the exercise of governmental powers (*pouvoir constituant*) cannot be the same as the People that rules via institutions (*pouvoir constitué*). Furthermore, the People that rules cannot be the same as the People that is ruled. I will not address the *demos* problem. As I have tried to show, *demoi*cracy might be the closest shot we can get at solving the *demos* problem.[21] I will also not further pursue the question what the people is, for which rule is exercised (population). I assume it is the group of agents under the obligation to follow the laws and orders of the *demos* and the group of agents to whom the governing People is supposed to give priority in serving. It is important to understand the ontological difference between the People as *pouvoir constituant*, the People as *pouvoir constitué*, and the population to be served. To understand the term in the middle that is of interest here, the People that rules, I follow and complement the Ciceronian, jural position, and circumscribe the People in the following terms.

The democratic People is a group that is constituted by the common recognition of a coherent set of primary and secondary rules, which establish statuses, institutions, and procedures through which status holders, first and

[19] Roberto Frega, 'The Social Ontology of Democracy' (2018) 4(2) *Journal of Social Ontology* 157–185.

[20] Adolf Reinach, 'The Apriori Foundations of the Civil Law', translated by John F. Crosby (1983) 3 *Alethia* 1–142; John R. Searle, 'Social Ontology and Political Power', in Barry Smith, David M. Mark and Isaac Elrich (eds.), *The Mystery of Capital and the Construction of Social Reality* (Chicago/La Salle: Open Court, 2008), pp. 19–34; John R. Searle, *Making the Social World: The Structure of Human Civilization* (Oxford: Oxford University Press, 2010); Barry Smith, 'Document Acts', in Anita Konzelmann Ziv and Hans Bernhard Schmid (eds.), *Institutions, Emotions and Group Agents. Contributions to Social Ontology* (New York: Springer, 2014), pp. 19–31.

[21] Cheneval, *The Government of the Peoples*, fn. 1, pp. 62–69.

foremost citizens, exercise highest lawmaking and law-enforcing authority (deontic power) in view of providing the service of government, that is to say, of public goods and public services within a territory, to a population.[22]

The democratic People has ownership of and priority over the State and not vice versa. A State controlled by the People deserves the name '*res publica*', as opposed to a State that is the instrument of self-serving rulers. It is important to determine what constitutes a People (*demos*) as a specific social entity in distinction to what constitutes a State, and how the two are related. The ontology of the State is beyond the remit of this chapter. I consider the State an apparatus of epistemic and coercive administrative instruments and procedures that are purely rational from an ideal-typical point of view (as opposed to reasonable). In a democracy, the State apparatus is controlled by the democratic People. In virtue of this control and constraint of the State by the People via reasonable debate on the yielding of rational State power, the State becomes *res publica*. 'Est res publica … res populi' as Cicero wrote. Whoever officiates in the State or represents the State as *res publica*, must act under the control of the People in the service of the Population. The representation of the People vis-à-vis other Peoples might, and most likely must pass through the State, but the latter has only an instrumental value for the People. For *demoi*cratic IOs this means that the core social entity that is to be represented is the People, not the State.[23] From a democratic point of view, international relations are inter-People relations. The term *ius gentium* can be reinterpreted in this jural and republican sense, that is, as *ius populorum*. To conceive international law as a law of States can be accepted as a shorthand that indicates that only Peoples disposing of certain State-like capacities and instruments to give credible assurance to other Peoples can honour justice among Peoples.[24] Second, international representation as representation of States can be understood as compromise that one must consider to avoid severe conflict with and to allow for constructive peaceful relations with non-democratic States. But among governing *populi*, the system of representation needs to be conceived and designed as a representation of Peoples.

[22] 'Est igitur … res publica res populi, populus autem non omnis hominum coetus quoquo modo congregatus, sed coetus multitudinis iuris consensu et utilitatis communione sociatus'. See Cicero, *De Re Publica*, edited by James E. G. Zetzel (Cambridge: Cambridge University Press, 2008).

[23] See John Rawls, *The Law of Peoples* (Cambridge, MA: Harvard University Press, 2001), pp. 23–30. Rawls of course does not go so far as to conceive a *demoi*cracy, but according to him already a just international law is conceived as law of peoples (liberal and decent in his terminology), and not of States.

[24] Anna Stilz, 'Why Do States Have Territorial Rights?' (2009) 1(2) *International Theory* 185–213.

I cannot go through the full set of rules that constitute a governing People. Nor can I fully explain my approach to social ontology, which draws on Adolf Reinach, Herbert L. A. Hart, John Searle, and Barry Smith. However, I can aim for completeness regarding the types of secondary rules that constitute a democratic People: (1) a fundamental act of recognition of a union claim of the People as constitutional unit under one system of law. This enactment of the claim to constitute a coherent system of law is the rule of recognition;[25] (2) constitutive and regulative rules that establish statuses, institutions, and procedures and regulate them.[26] The regulative rules include rules of change and adjudication; (3) rules conferring deontic rights, powers, and duties to office holders and institutions, but first and foremost to citizens.[27]

Here, I skip over the rule type (1). It is identical in content for democratic and non-democratic peoples. Peoples under any type of government require a rule of recognition, a recognized union claim, to exist as a constituted people or union of Peoples. To (2) and (3): a democratic People is distinguished from other legally constituted non-democratic Peoples by the content of specific secondary, formalized rules. Also by informal rules and social norms, but these cannot be the object of my analysis here and require a historical and empirical method of analysis. Furthermore, I cannot do justice to the concrete instantiations of the formal rules. I hold that the distinctive formal rules of a democratic People concern mainly the status (office) and deontic powers of citizenship, and the procedures that citizens are involved in when making authoritative decisions themselves or via representatives, when governing together as People.

These rules, first, determine freedom rights that are necessary elements of democratic procedures.[28] These freedoms do not conceptually depend on the status of citizenship. Freedom of speech and association, essential conditions of the deliberative *demos* in any democracy, are not specifically citizen-freedoms, they are fundamental freedoms of humans. It necessarily follows that the deliberative People (as type) and the formally governing People (as type) are not constituted by the same set of statuses of individuals, and they are potentially composed by different individuals *de re*.[29] This means that liberal democratic Peoples, in which citizens and non-citizens have freedom of expression of

25 Herbert L. A. Hart, *The Concept of Law: With a Postscript Edited by Penelope A. Bulloch and Joseph Raz*, 2nd ed. (Oxford: Clarendon Press, 1994).

26 Frank Hindriks, 'Constitutive Rules, Language, and Ontology' (2009) 71(2) *Erkenntnis* 253–275.

27 Hart, fn. 25; Searle, 'Social Ontology and Political Power', fn. 20; Searle, *Making the Social World*, fn. 20.

28 Robert A. Dahl, *Democracy and Its Critics* (New Haven: Yale University Press, 1989).

29 Cheneval, *The Government of the Peoples*, fn. 1, pp. 69–79.

opinion and association, are essentially open towards each other as deliberative Peoples. In this sense, deliberative *demoi*cracy is a fact as soon as contiguous liberal democratic Peoples exist. The fact that domestic publics are stronger than transnational publics and the individual ability and structural conditions to participate in deliberation are different empirically[30] does not change this ontological fact of reciprocal openness of liberal democratic *demoi*. The existence of 'echo chambers' and 'filter bubbles' in cyber space would reinforce the point, because they do not only fragment the deliberative *demos* within the borders of the formal *demos* but also cut across formal *demoi*. The formal governing People as *demos* type is composed by members constituted by rules that define the status of citizenship and regulate accession and exit to this status. Following Searle, the status is a term in a rule holding: **X** counts as **Y** in **C**. Meaning, **X** counts as citizen in **C**. The **C**-term refers to the entity established by the recognition of the union claim. The status-term, the **Y**-term (the status of citizen in our example), is established by a rule that enacts something like 'members of **C** have the status of citizens of **C**'. This is then further substantiated by deontic powers given to individuals with this status, and by the rules of accession to and exit from the status, as well as the rules how to document identification of a person as holder of a status, and so on. The conceivable deontic powers of the democratic citizen are the power to vote and stand in elections of political representatives, to vote in issue-specific votes (referenda or initiatives) as well as to be active in bringing them about. The status of citizens and of office holders of the institutions of the People also comes with a right over duties, duties that only the status-holder can claim to be under an obligation to fulfil and that persons who do not hold the status are not allowed to fulfil. Examples are jury duties, military service, and civil service.

The status rules just mentioned are not sufficient to constitute the People. When citizens sleep in bed, gather informally, gather to protest, and so on, they are, and they might even be acting specifically as citizens, but they are not the People that rules with democratic authority. Their acts (e.g. of protesting, of making representative claims, deliberating, etc.) are not acts that directly yield the deontic powers of the People. The ruling *demos* needs what Jean-Jacques Rousseau called 'lois fondamentales'. Minimally, they consist in rules of assembly and decision-making procedure.[31] But more are necessary,

30 Nancy Fraser, 'Rethinking the Public Sphere: A Contribution to the Critique of Actually Existing Democracy' (1990) 25/26 *Social Text* 56–80; Nancy Fraser and Kate Nash (eds.), *Transnationalizing the Public Sphere* (Malden, MA: Polity Press, 2014).

31 Jean-Jacques Rousseau, *Du contrat social. Écrits politiques*, edited by François Bouchargy, Bernard Gagnebin and Marcel Raymond (Paris: Gallimard, 1996) Œuvres Complètes III, pp. 393–394.

because the People need executive and juridical institutions, and a functional legislative assembly in most cases is an assembly of representatives, not of all citizens. Direct democracy is not assembly democracy, it is the existence of direct democratic devices within fundamentally representative democratic systems.[32] The People is thus further constituted by rules setting up an ensemble of governmental institutions and procedures with office holders who are social persons: representatives; and by rules conferring deontic powers to the citizens and office holders. Democratic authority is yielded by the citizens and representatives just in case they act within specified institutional procedures.

As ruling collective, the People need to perform many different types of acts at the same time and hence delegate these tasks to various institutions. This seems clear, independent of any (inadequate) conception of direct versus representative democracy and independent of any conception of group agency one might subscribe to.[33] The people will delegate control to institutions, who control each other. The consequence is that vertical accountability is complemented by horizontal accountability and that the realization of democracy is best understood not by looking at the individual institutions of the People in isolation but as a democratic system solving certain problems.[34] Any form of horizontal accountability necessarily implies representation in some form and shape.[35] Overall, the exercise of the deontic powers of citizens happens via institutions which necessarily demand the existence of the status of representative in different institutional instantiations. It is these institutions through which the People is to be represented toward other Peoples in *demoi*cratic representation.

## 5.4 REPRESENTATION

Political representation is a broad concept, widely debated, multidimensional, and complex in different contexts.[36] Nevertheless, I hold that the analytical

[32] Alice el-Wakil and Francis Cheneval, 'Designing Popular Vote Processes to Enhance Democratic Systems' (2018) 24(3) *Swiss Political Science Review* 348–358.

[33] Christian List and Philip Pettit, 'Group Agency and Supervenience', in Jacob Hohwy and Jesper Kallestrup (eds.), *Being Reduced: New Essays on Reduction, Explanation, and Causation* (Oxford: Oxford University Press, 2008), pp. 75–92.

[34] John Parkinson and Jane Mansbridge (eds.), *Deliberative Systems. Deliberative Democracy at the Large Scale* (Cambridge: Cambridge University Press, 2012); Mark E. Warren, 'A Problem-Based Approach to Democratic Theory' (2017) 111(1) *American Political Science Review* 39–53.

[35] Bernard Manin, *Principes du gouvernement représentatif* (Paris: Flammarion, 1996).

[36] Hanna F. Pitkin, *The Concept of Representation* (Berkeley: University of California Press, 1967); Anne Phillips, *The Politics of Presence* (Oxford: Oxford University Press, 1998);

structure of political representation is simple, and it is the following. Political representation of ***x*** is either standing for ***x*** or acting for ***x***.[37] The former can be attributed to many sorts of beings including agents, the latter is enacted only by social persons, which I call representatives. '**X** is a social person, if and only if **X** is the subject of social acts'.[38] Social acts are acts that a person addresses to another person and that have as their success-condition that the other person grasps it. Political representation is a social act. If **A** (or a group $\mathbf{A_{1\text{-}n}}$)[39] represents **B** (or a group $\mathbf{B_{1\text{-}n}}$) in the mere sense of standing for, then **A** embodies, depicts, or symbolizes **B**. It can also be that **A** carries essential traits of **B** (descriptive representation). Examples are a head of State who stands for the union of the People under a constitution. The fish represents the Christian community in coded form.[40] The half-moon stands for Islamic community. The star of David stands for Judaism. A flag symbolizes the nation, and so on. These entities (fish-image, half-moon image, flags, etc.) are not social persons. Unlike promising, commanding, requesting, agreeing with, symbolizing is not a social act. A 'mini-public', created by semi-random sortition, depicts the people as image of the public at large, that is why it is called a mini-public in distinction to an elected assembly, which is not an image of the people but an elite or group of interest representatives under some criterion of choice. An image does not perform social acts, a 'mini-public' *as such* is not a social person. Women can be understood to represent women in the sense that they share their essential descriptive features and life-perspectives (descriptive representation). A descriptive representative *as such* is not a social person. An attorney defending a serial killer sharing no descriptive traits with the serial killer is a social person, they act for the serial killer in court. The representational *action for* can only be

Jane Mansbridge, 'Rethinking Representation' (2003) 97(4) *American Political Review* 515–528; Michael Saward, *The Representative Claim* (Oxford: Oxford University Press, 2010); Sonia Alonso, John Keane and Wolfgang Merkel (eds.), *The Future of Representative Democracy* (Cambridge: Cambridge University Press, 2011); Richard Bellamy, '"An Ever Closer Union Among the Peoples of Europe": Republican Intergovernmentalism and *Demoi*cratic Representation within the EU' (2013) 35(5) *Journal of European Integration* 499–516; Dario Castiglione and Mark E. Warren, 'Rethinking Democratic Representation: Eight Theoretical Issues', in Lisa Disch, Mathijs van de Sande and Nadia Urbinati (eds.), *The Constructivist Turn in Political Representation* (Edinburgh: Edinburgh University Press, 2019), pp. 21–47.

37 Pitkin, fn. 36.

38 Kevin Mulligan, 'Conservatism, Value and Social Philosophy' (2019) 6 *Cosmos + Taxis* 15–20, at 16; Kevin Mulligan, 'Persons and Acts: Collective and Social. From Ontology to Politics', in Alessandro Salice and Hans Bernhard Schmid (eds.), *The Phenomenological Approach to Social Reality* (Cham: Springer, 2016), pp. 17–45, p. 36.

39 In what follows, **A** or **B** can stand for an individual or a group.

40 Pitkin, fn. 36, p. 69.

tied to descriptive representation under the empirical assumption that people who share features of other people can be expected to act in their interest because the descriptive features have led them to certain experiences and perspectives which will allow them to act for others. They thus draw trust in view of acting for. But this is not a necessary dependence. The lawyer representing the serial killer does not have to share the experience of this practice to be a good representative of the serial killer at court. *Pro tanto*, **B** does nothing for **A** or vis-à-vis **A** by simply sharing features of or symbolizing **A**. This aspect merits a lot more analysis, but I will leave it at this because I think democratic legitimacy depends on social action much more than symbolic action. It is a feature of fascist theory of representation to misrepresent the symbolic standing for the People as a whole of one leader as the acting for the People as a whole.[41] Authorization and accountability that are part of an a priori theory of social acts of representation are cut out.

If **A** represents **B** in the sense of acting for, this comes in two forms: (1) **B** puts an obligation or a rule on **A** to carry out an act on its behalf or in its stead (delegation); (2) **B** creates representative powers in **A**, that is, powers to act freely in their name and best interest and thereby commit **B** to certain positions, or even to put **B** (and themselves *de re*) under rules and obligations. Who puts a rule and obligation on whom is the opposite in the two figures of representation: (1) **B** puts an obligation on **A**; (2) **A** puts an obligation on **B** (or on **B** and **A**). Both cannot be the case at the same time regarding the same content of obligation. One collides with the other. Furthermore, both figures can be conditional or unconditional. Ad (1): **B** can give **A** a conditional command (obligation) with unconditional content (**B** commands **A** to do *y* just in case *x* occurs) or an unconditional command with conditional content (**B** commands **A** to do *y* or *z* in case *x* occurs).[42]

The *democratic* representative government adopts both counter-directional forms of representation (1) and (2), and this in respect to the same legislative or executive body of representatives. The system of democratic representation is like a two-way street with no clear rule on which side to drive on. Representatives have a mandate in the sense that they are elected by the represented based on promises and programmes of what they will do on their behalf or interest, or in what they see as the public interest, with different conditionalities. The election is the acceptance of a promise by the represented that puts an obligation on the representatives. When they get elected, there is a sense in which the represented rightly see the representatives as being

41 Ibid., pp. 107–109.
42 Reinach, fn. 20.

under the obligation to carry out the programme for which they were sent to parliament, the executive, or the judiciary. The representative promises 'if elected, I will do x'.

The counterargument to this thesis would be to say that the representatives put the obligation on themselves by making the electoral promises. There is thus no bidirectionality. But that is not what happens in an election, and it does not cover the election of the representatives in the judiciary. The promise, as any social act, is '*vernehmungsbedürftig*'.[43] Some act of grasping, reception, or acceptance is necessarily part of its success conditions. If you promise to help me move next weekend that promise does not put any obligation on you if I do not acknowledge your promise. Representatives make all sorts of promises before the election. By casting a vote, the voter chooses between different promises of different representatives and parties. The winner of the election is under a *pro tanto* obligation to carry out a promise only because their promises of the promisor have been accepted by the promisees in the electorate and their votes have been aggregated according to the rules. It is thus the represented who choose (under a decision rule) which promises count and thereby confirm a mandate of the representatives to do ***x*** in the representative assembly. Besides, offices also come with preset duties *ex ante*. There is always a non-promissory mandate implied in the office of a representative.

However, in many cases representative government implies that the political representatives impose obligations on the represented in a way not foreseen in the mandate they voted for. Representatives have a mandate and their promissory obligations are only *pro tanto* obligation. Additionally, they have representative powers to put binding obligations on all in ways their voters did not foresee or in an interpretation of the public interest that is not necessarily shared by their constituents. In all this, the representatives still claim to act for the represented, but not in a narrow sense of responsiveness to mandates. The represented, on the other hand, still expect the representatives they voted for to stay as close to the mandate as possible, or to have a reasonable explanation for why they moved away from the mandate, or even did something completely not foreseen in the mandate. One should not misconceive this situation with a simple citizen-bourgeois dichotomy ascribing the mandate to narrow interests of a constituency and the going past the mandate to a citizen perspective of common interest or best overall solutions. The mandate can be understood in terms of best overall solution and the compromise going beyond the mandate can be the result of interest bargaining. Be that as it may, it is inconceivable to ascribe only a mandate to representatives who have powers to put obligations

43 Ibid., at 19.

on all (legislative, executive orders). They operate in a normative space that is characterized by the countervailing normative figures of mandate and representative power. The creative granting of deontic powers authorizes the representative to act in the name of the represented when putting obligations upon them. The election is the clearest and most certain form of authorization, albeit not the only one.[44] On the other hand, it is also a priori possible that **A** act in the interest of **B** and according to the intention of **B** without representing **B** and even without making a claim to represent **B**.[45]

The 'puzzle' of the two necessary, but counter-directional figures of democratic representation has no definite solution in purely representative systems. It is only manageable over time in a cycle of authorization and accountability. One should not expect this to change in *demoi*cratic representation in and by IOs. Elections are moments of authorization of representatives with both a mandate and with representative powers for cases in which it is not possible or not reasonable to narrowly adhere to the mandate. What is possible and reasonable must be judged by the represented and the representatives and renegotiated at each election. By the formal periodic repetition of elections (and informal critique and debate), the electoral cycle also assures accountability. Representatives explain their choices, or the choices of their predecessors in the same party in case they are not incumbents. Voters judge if the representatives they voted for kept their promises and programmes, for which the represented gave them a mandate via their vote. They also judge whether the representatives have used their representative power in a reasonable way given their original programme and promises. The right to vote is a normative power, an instrument of authorization and accountability, meaning also of sanction or confirmation of the representatives or their party, in the hand of the represented, the citizens. Be that as it may, the tension and possible confusion between delegation of a mandate and representative power always remains present in democratic systems.[46] The representative democratic system that includes the facultative referendum is a close shot at solving the 'puzzle' of democratic representation. For one, it puts additional normative powers of accountability in the hands of citizens (and non-elected representatives such as action committees) and increases deliberative qualities.[47] This

44 Saward, fn. 36, pp. 81–110.

45 Reinach, fn. 20, at 84.

46 Pitkin, fn. 36; Nadia Urbinati, 'Representative Democracy and Its Critics', in Sonia Alonso, John Keane and Wolfgang Merkel (eds.), *The Future of Representative Democracy* (Cambridge: Cambridge University Press, 2011), pp. 23–49.

47 Alice el-Wakil, 'Supporting Deliberative Systems with Referendum and Initiatives' (2020) 16(1) *Journal of Deliberative Democracy* 37–45.

make for a reasonable justification of facultative referenda.[48] But here I mean something more fundamental. The facultative referendum implies that representative powers are given to the representatives conditionally, and that the direction of command can be reversed by the represented in the framework of a democratic procedure (e.g. collecting a certain amount of signatures that trigger a vote the result of which is legally binding and can annul an obligation the representatives wanted to put on the represented). A representative democratic system with the facultative referendum has an instrument that allows for the possibility to avoid bidirectionality in case the countervailing forces of the latter cause an issue-specific gap between responsiveness to preferences of the represented and the decisions of the representatives, and in case this gap is judged too large by a majority of the represented. This is especially important in international *demoi*cratic representation where the long chains of representation can make the gap between the represented and the representatives particularly large. A representative system with facultative referendum is a bidirectional system of obligation-imposition that can switch back to a unidirectional system of command with the possibility to avoid negative or confusing effects of bidirectionality. I say closest shot to solving the problem and not total solution to the problem because in the facultative referendum the command remains one of editing and not authoring the obligation (law). The facultative referendum gives citizens the right to refuse an obligation put upon them by representatives in the exercise of their representative powers. It does not give them the right to statute, to be the authors of the laws.

## 5.5 *DEMOI*CRATIC REPRESENTATION

The People as governing entity is a semi-abstract entity and as such a composite of real human individuals under documents and representations that constitute offices and institutional entities and institutional procedures by document acts. This is important to understand democratic and *demoi*cratic representation. It might be the case that a single institution of the *demos* alone is understood to stand for the People as if it were the whole or as if it were to encapsulate the whole, for example, the flag, the head of State, the citizen assembly. But this should not be misconceived as representative acting for the People. No single human or social status person, no single party, no single institution of the People alone, no single branch of government, not even the assembly of all the citizens, can act solely for the People as a whole. The People can only act via the institutional constellation of *all* interconnected offices, institutions, and

48 el-Wakil and Cheneval, fn. 32.

procedures. Hence, if the People is to be represented adequately vis-à-vis other Peoples, all these institutions need to be involved and several different IOs together might be understood to represent the Peoples. The representative acting for needs to be performed by the corresponding highest institution of the People, that is, of lawmaking, law enforcement, and jurisprudence. Consequently, *demoi*cratic representation ought to be understood systemically, as horizontal and vertical interplay of checks and balances of several institutions (IOs) commonly created and upheld by the Peoples.

In what follows, I try to show that the democratic representation is unfinished if there is no *demoi*cratic representation and that *demoi*cratic representation needs to be designed as representation of the Peoples via all their highest governing institutions, that is, legislative, executive, and judicial. In other words, the law of Peoples should be drafted by lawmaking representatives of the Peoples, the execution of the law overseen by representatives from the executive, the judiciary of Peoples by representative from the highest judiciary powers of the Peoples, and these institutions ought to respond to each other in a representative system. Part of this are also referenda of the Peoples.

(1) Only in a *demoi*cracy, the governing People is accountable to other governing Peoples. In international relations in general, the People is accountable to other States or IOs of States overseeing international law, but not to other Peoples. Within a democracy, the popular sovereign might have restricted domain via legal disabilities, but in such a setting the popular sovereign is ultimately accountable to no one. It does not matter whether popular sovereignty is enacted as parliamentary sovereignty, in a system of checks and balances with constitutional jurisprudence, or direct democracy, or any other mode or combination of the above. The People, as a whole, is accountable to no one if we conceive democracy as an enclosed system of a singular *demos*. If the place of the sovereign is considered empty and the democratic sovereign replaced by the constant struggle for hegemony[49] we can no longer distinguish the legitimate electorate or legitimate voice of the people from usurpation. But in a democracy, the place of the sovereign is not empty. It is occupied by a set of interconnected institutions that represent the legitimate expression and authoritative voice of the People. A group of demonstrators is a legitimate form of voicing demands in democratic politics, but it is not an authoritatively binding voice of the People that replaces or empties the seat of sovereign People. The first *raison d'être* of *demoi*cratic representation is the necessity of accountability of the Peoples towards each other. In international law, States are accountable

[49] Claude Lefort, *Democracy and Political Theory*, translated by David Macey (Cambridge/Oxford: Polity Press in association with Basil Blackwell, 1988).

to each other and that is of course a good thing and not to be replaced but complemented by the mutual accountability of Peoples. If we agree that the State, as a rational administrative and coercive apparatus is only an instrument of the People under its control in democracy, and if we hold that many States are not controlled by the People via corresponding institutions, then if follows that a democratic People is accountable to other democratic Peoples, not States. Second, all the democratic Peoples together cannot form a sovereign democratic People because this People would be an entity that is again accountable to no one.[50] The overarching union of democratic Peoples[51] is a union of sovereigns, not a sovereign unit.

(2) In a constellation of interdependence, democratic Peoples face (minimally) the following challenge: It is possible that People $\mathbf{P_1}$ take a domestic decision **d**, that would not be accepted by either all or a majority of the citizens of Peoples $\mathbf{P_{2\text{-}n}}$, a majority of the citizens $\mathbf{P_{2\text{-}n}}$, a minority of the citizens $\mathbf{P_{2\text{-}n}}$, or any combination of the three possibilities, i.e. a majority of **P2**, a majority of **P3**, a minority in **P4**, and so forth. The unacceptability of expected consequences $C_{exp}$ in case they would affect **P1** constitute the reason why the majority of $\mathbf{P_1}$ take decision **d.** The citizens of **P1** thus take a decision they would possibly have reason to reject were they the citizens of **P2**, and so on, but they have no idea if it is really the case and if it were the case how they could justify their decision to the citizens of other peoples or their corresponding representatives. Suppose that to create accountability among democratic Peoples, international institutions are created as we know them. In the classic form this happens by giving the executives representative powers in common international institutions. Suppose this institution of $\mathbf{P_{1\text{-}n}}$ discusses decision **d.** This can give the citizens of $\mathbf{P_1}$ important guidance. They will know how many and which States do (not) accept their decision **d,** and for what reasons. But the citizens of $\mathbf{P_1}$ still have at least the following epistemic problems:

(i) The citizens of $\mathbf{P_1}$ have no way of knowing if the executives of $\mathbf{P_{2\text{-}n}}$ represented the majority or minority will of their citizens regarding decision **d**;

(ii) The citizens of $\mathbf{P_1}$ have no way of knowing if decision **d** would be accepted by a majority of all citizens of $\mathbf{P_{1\text{-}n}}$, albeit not by all the executives of the States, due to the fact that majorities and minorities will occur in **Ps** of unequal size;

[50] Cheneval, *La cité des peuples*, fn. 2.

[51] Francis Cheneval, 'Demoicracy. A Democracy of Democracies', in Hanspeter Kriesi and Lars Müller (eds.), *Democracy: An Ongoing Challenge* (Zürich: Lars Müller Publishers, 2013), pp. 492–496.

(iii) The citizens of $\mathbf{P}_1$ have no way of knowing the reasons why the majorities and minorities of the citizens of $\mathbf{P}_{2\text{-}n}$ reject (accept) their decision **d**.

*Demoi*cratic representative institutions, in which the domestic political constituencies are represented vis-à-vis other Peoples have an epistemic and normative function. They can produce the knowledge about what other Peoples want when confronted with decisions of common concern. 'People' here refers to all the essential institutions that constitute the People as a collective actor, as opposed to only the executive. Such common institutions create a knowledge that central international bureaucracies, State executives, or domestic institutions that only debate internally cannot produce. Common *demoi*cratic institutions in form of IOs can further serve the normative function to address mutual accountability issues of popular sovereigns in a manner that fulfils normative principles of the relation of sovereign Peoples.[52] If the citizens of $\mathbf{P}_1$ or any $\mathbf{P}_{2\text{-}n}$ assume that being a citizen is accepting accountability to citizens acting in legitimate democratic institutions, they will accept *demoi*cratic institutions that serve an epistemic function of knowing how other majorities and minorities of other Peoples view decisions of common concern, and that serve the minimal normative function to calibrate decisions while taking into account the information produced by common institutions.

(3) In a democracy, the decision process is based on the majority rule in some form and shape. In a *demoi*cracy, it is assumed that decisions are based on unanimity and that individual Peoples have veto rights and exit options. I will show that, fundamentally, *demoi*cracy at the core is about dealing with reasonable disagreement among democratic Peoples about the adequate decision rule.[53]

As opposed to legal representation where one to one representation is possible, in political representation a representative represents not only one individual, always a group's interests, opinions, perspectives. That is the whole point of political representation. This means that no individual's particular interests are represented entirely by one single representative, as is the case when an attorney represents a client. The largest group in a constitutional unit are the group of the represented (all the citizens) and the group of the

[52] Cheneval, *The Government of the Peoples*, fn. 1.

[53] For a critical discussion of the consent principle in international relations and an original proposal to replace it see Besson and Martí, 'From Equal State Consent to Equal Public Participation in International Organizations', fn. 2. My proposal of *demoi*cratic representation is different from and goes beyond the principle of equal State participation but not against it in case States are democratic.

representatives (the government in various institutional forms and instantiations). The collective action of the group becomes possible by a collective decision rule. The decision so taken is considered as the decision of the group in virtue of the correct application of the decision rule (and further fairness conditions). In that case, the representative assembly (as group) acts in the name of the represented (as group), the disagreement of individual representatives and represented notwithstanding.

The consent of the group as such is established by a collective decision rule and only applies to the group.[54] If the group adopts a unanimity rule, the difference between the number of vetoes and the majority votes is called a majority deficit.[55] If a decision is rejected because three out of five persons vote against, the majority deficit is two, meaning that the majority of two who would have decided the vote under a majority rule are disregarded under the unanimity rule. If the group adopts a majority rule, the number of minority votes can be called the consent deficit. The consent deficit is the absolute number of minority votes under a majority rule, not to be confused with the minority–majority quota. If four out of five vote against a decision, the consent deficit is four meaning that the decision was adopted against four who would have been necessary to change their vote to reach consent, or who would have each been decisive in rejecting the decision under the unanimity rule. In this case the majority-superavit is one as an absolute number and the minority–majority quota (*mi/maj*) is 80 per cent. The *mi/maj* is one in case of a tie (a non-decision) and decreases the higher the number of the minority–majority difference gets. The higher the *mi/maj*, the less voters are disregarded in proportion to the total number of voters under a majority rule. The *mi/maj* thus puts the consent deficit in relation to the number of voters the veto-rule would disregard.

If the *mi/maj* ratio is repeatedly very low under the unanimity rule, the unanimity rule gets charged with increasing burdens of justification because a minority is constantly vetoing decisions. If the *mi/maj* ratio is repeatedly high under a majority rule, the majority rule gets charged with increasing burdens of justification because only a small majority is deciding the outcome. It is thus important to notice that the decision about the decision rule is subject to the same formal relations as the decision on material issues. It is not the case that under a unanimity rule everybody gets their way due to everybody's veto

54 John P. Plamenatz, *Consent, Freedom and Political Obligation*, 2nd ed. (Oxford: Oxford University Press, 1968).

55 Arash Abizadeh, 'Counter-Majoritarian Democracy: Persistent Minorities, Federalism, and the Power of Numbers' (2021) 115(3) *American Political Science Review* 742–756.

position. There can be a second-order consent deficit, including a very large one, about the application of the unanimity rule even if the decisions that are taken under this rule are unanimous, that is, even when there is first-order unanimity about content. The application of the unanimity rule is in that case 'pseudo-libertarian', because under full libertarianism there would be no second-order consent deficit about the unanimity rule. But regarding the majority rule as well there can be a large consent deficit regarding its application even when the *min/maj* ratio is very low.

What does this mean for international relations' principle of State consent in relation to the idea of *demoi*cratic representation? First, international relations, based on free State consent, are possibly 'pseudo-libertarian' until proven otherwise. In the Vienna Convention on the Law of Treaties the 'principle of free consent' is voiced as 'universally recognized' but applied only to States, not citizens.[56] Granted, all States that sign the Vienna Convention on the Law of Treaties agree to the consent-rule. There is thus no second-order consent deficit regarding the general application of this rule as far as the States that signed the convention are concerned. Now, in international representation, the States are represented by their executive governments. In some States, freely and equitably elected parliaments have the right to refuse binding obligations by the right to ratification of treaties. If that is the case, we could say that the principle of State consent is realized as Peoples' consent in so far as the highest legislative institution of the People consents to an obligation. In the case of decision-making in the representative assembly of the People (parliament), the individual represented can assume that their representatives weigh in on the collective decision in deliberation and decision-making. If the assembly is elected by proportional representation that possible weight increases for minority positions. In international representation as it is currently practiced, the individual represented (citizen) is no longer represented by a representative of their constituency in an assembly, but only by a representative chosen by the assembly by majority rule or by direct election by majority rule, or by usurpation of the ruler. In other words, international representation means moving up the steps of a multilevel representation system whereby the possible consent deficit increases at each step, State consent notwithstanding. Furthermore, there is no voice in agenda-setting. In international relations where States have veto powers, there is no consent deficit regarding new decisions taken, but there is a possible large consent deficit among States regarding this decision procedure when it comes to certain issues, and this consent deficit will not be noticed from the inside of

[56] Preamble of the Vienna Convention on the Law of Treaties, 1155 UNTS 18232 (adopted 23 May 1969, entered into force 27 January 1980).

the system of State representation. What is more, from the point of view of the individual citizens, there might be a large first-order consent deficit regarding the decisions taken by State consent and regarding the unanimity rule of binding common State action. In brief, the problem of international representation is not only that international law is a set of primary rules and that IO lacks a single legislator adapting the law under a rule of change.[57] Arguably, by endorsing the universal principles of free consent, of good faith, and of *pacta sunt servanda* (this principle is grounded on the a priori rule that promises create obligations), international law is based on a rule of recognition: the States form a union by recognizing as law all law that is enacted under these principles. As Hart mentioned,[58] this is increasingly changing.[59]

The argument here is thus not about making consent and unanimity a direct source of international law by *demoi*cratic representation of Peoples with veto powers. The point is that *demoi*cratic representation can be understood as a way of institutionalizing a more adequate management of disagreement of international lawmaking, which, as Samantha Besson has pointed out, is arguably more pervasive in international than in domestic lawmaking, consent as constitutive element of international law notwithstanding.[60] If we assume that international representation ought to be the representation of Peoples at least among democratic Peoples, meaning of citizens governing via common representative institutions, the possible first-order consent deficit of decisions taken by States and the possible second-order consent deficit of citizens of Peoples acting together regarding the principle of State consent cannot be ignored.

For a representation of democratic Peoples, this means that first-order State consent in international lawmaking is too reductive. From the point of view of the citizens, State consent to international law is given with a possible (and highly probable) first-order consent deficit, but one that can be assumed to be accepted within a democratic constitutional order accepting majority decision rule. But citizens can arguably assume that:

(i) first-order State consent masks large first-order majority dissent in case the population-strong States' numerically large minorities who are discarded in the decision outnumber population-weak States' numerically weak majorities who are decisive in the decision;
(ii) there is a large second-order consent deficit of citizens regarding the principle of consent, at least on some issues.

57 Hart, fn. 25, p. 213.
58 Ibid., p. 230.
59 Besson, 'State Consent and Disagreement in International Law-Making', fn. 2, at 299.
60 Besson, 'State Consent and Disagreement in International Law-Making', fn. 2.

*Demoi*cratic representation therefore minimally implies a principle of free consent of Peoples as opposed to States. The free consent of the People needs to be given to international obligations (treaties) by the People's highest law-giving body, which can be a freely and equitably elected parliament or a direct vote of the citizens. But that is not where *demoi*cratic representation can stop. *Demoi*cratic representation needs common institutions in which representatives of Peoples address the second-order consent deficit about the principle of People-consent in relation to the positioning of the citizens regarding this decision rule when applied to specific laws and issues. *Demoi*cratic representation cannot be solely committed to the principle of State or People-consent, nor can it simply abandon the principle of People-consent in favour of a majority decision rule across the board. The latter is democratic representation. *Demoi*cratic representation needs to account for the citizens' possible second-order consent deficit regarding the principle of People-consent in common institutions, in which the decision which decision rule ought to be adapted for what decision is debated, settled, and constantly re-adapted. In other words, *demoi*cratic representation institutionalizes a rule of change that allows for switching from the decision rules of People-consent to majority voting in common institutions of the Peoples in international lawmaking.

(4) For IGOs the argument here presented has different normative implications depending on the type of IO. There is no room here for an in-depth typology of IOs. My normative argument proposes that the IOs of democratic Peoples ought to form a *demoi*cratic system of representation. Not all democratic IOs are as or need to be as comprehensive as the EU, that is, engage in lawmaking, executive transnational government, and jurisprudence.[61] Ideally, such a comprehensive political IO ought to embody *demoi*cratic representation within, that is to say, contain all the representative institutions of the Peoples. Less comprehensive IOs are not under this imperative of separation of power and completeness of representation. But they ought not to stand alone. They ought to be a complementary part of a representational system and thereby contribute to assuring *demoi*cratic representation by IOs. As I propose to understand democracy and *demoi*cratic representation systemically, there is thus no need that all IOs encompass all the institutions of the Peoples in one organization. *Demoi*cratic representation can be realized if IOs are integrated in a coherent and transparent institutional system of separation of power and checks and balances upheld by the member Peoples.

[61] See Dubout and Ritleng, Chapter 13 in this volume.

# 6

# Democratic Representation and Parliamentarization of International Organizations: Between False Friends and False Pretences

Marie-Clotilde Runavot

## 6.1 INTRODUCTION

Both the object and the approach of this chapter are thought-provoking and in need of clarifications, not only with regard to the general theory of democracy but also, and especially, with regard to their own meaning in international institutional law.[1] Applying the notions of 'democratic representation' and 'parliamentarization' to international organizations (IOs) is no small undertaking and carries its share of weighted connotations. To be precise, 'democratic representation' is not 'representative democracy', and, consequently, 'parliamentarization' is not a variation of democratic representation in the way that 'parliamentarism' is a variation of representative democracy.[2] One must be wary of false friends and false pretences.

First, democratic representation is not the same as representative democracy. Unlike what the latter notion seems to suggest, democratic representation is not about apprehending IOs as political systems or forms of government. Nor is it self-evident to associate democratic representation with the governance (rather than government) of IOs since governance refers to the way in which international (normative) power is exercised *in* or *through* IOs. In any event, this

The author wishes to thank Kareen Jabre (Director, Division of Programs, Inter-Parliamentary Union (IPU)) and Paddy Torsney, Permanent Observer of the IPU to the United Nations in New York for the interview they kindly granted her and the valuable information they provided. This chapter was translated from French by Sévrine Knuchel, thanks to the financial support of the College of France's Foundation.

[1] See Marie-Clotilde Runavot, 'Rapport introductif', in Marie-Clotilde Runavot (ed.), *La démocratie appliquée au droit international: de quoi parle-t-on?* (Paris: Pedone, 2018), pp. 7–42. The expression 'international institutional law' is preferred over 'law of international organizations', in order to mark a distance from the intergovernmental model upon which the latter is premised, and from which the former emancipates itself in the pursuit of, among other objectives, democratization.

[2] On the link between parliamentarism and representative democracy, see Bernard Manin, *Principes du gouvernement représentatif*, 3rd ed. (Paris: Flammarion, 2019), pp. 369, pp. 259ff.

association deserves further evaluation, and it is one of this chapter's objectives. The European Union (EU) is an exception worth mentioning: its functioning is uniquely 'founded on representative democracy',[3] even if it does not escape duality. In the EU, representative democracy is – at the risk of falling sometimes into oxymoron, sometimes into pleonasm – *direct* in the European Parliament, and *indirect* in the Council – through governments 'themselves democratically accountable, either to their national parliaments, or to their citizens'.[4]

As for democratic representation in relation to IOs, this notion appears in the discourses on the democratic deficit of which IOs are accused under the combined effect of two phenomena. On the one hand, the end of the Cold War led to the universalization of democracy as a form of government and political system suitable for States. While the promotion of democracy in the States by IOs is not the object of this contribution, the fact remains that the generalization and idealization of democracy in States has spread to the institutions they have created in the international order.[5] On the other hand, and correlatively, contemporary globalization has been accompanied by an internationalization of the exercise of public power. In other words, more and more decisions affecting individuals are now taken jointly by States within IOs and the IOs participate in the exercise of international public authority and establish themselves as international governance bodies.[6] As IOs have become the seat of a true international (normative) *power* (understood as the elaboration process of international norms, including soft norms as they can affect individuals), they are subjected to democratic requirements. Without pretending to entrust the exercise of such power to an untraceable international people, the 'democratization' of IOs aims at bringing the human component of States closer to international governance bodies so that individuals may 'understand' themselves as the authors of the international norms that affect them.[7] In that sense, international democracy is 'understood as an institutional form providing

3 Art. 10(1) of the Consolidated Version of the Treaty on the European Union (TEU), OJ 2012 No. C326, 26 October 2012, p. 13.

4 Art. 10(2) TEU. See also Dubout and Ritleng, Chapter 13 in this volume.

5 Péter Bajtay, 'Shaping and Controlling Foreign Policy: Parliamentary Diplomacy and Oversight, and the Role of the European Parliament' (European Parliament, 2015), p. 7.

6 Armin Bogdandy, Rüdiger Wolfrum, Jochen von Bernstorff, Philipp Dann, and Matthias Goldmann (eds.), *The Exercise of Public Authority by International Institutions: Advancing International Institutions Law* (Heidelberg: Springer, 2010), p. 100, and especially pp. 3–32 and 727–760; Évelyne Lagrange, 'La catégorie "organisations internationales"', in Évelyne Lagrange and Jean-Marc Sorel (eds.), *Traité de droit des organisations internationales* (Paris: LGDJ, 2013), pp. 35–70, pp. 63–65, paras. 110–112.

7 In the words of Jürgen Habermas, *Droit et démocratie, Entre faits et normes*, translated by Rainer Rochlitz and Christian Bouchindhomme (Paris: Gallimard, 1997), pp. 47–48.

accountable *channels of representation* between people and governments, and producing policies based on this interaction'.[8] Democratic representation is one of the tools for the 'democratization' of IOs. It is also one of the most classic, even if its modalities have evolved and taken different shapes.

Applied to IOs in the context of globalization, democratic representation can be defined as the legal mechanisms and techniques that make the voice of individuals heard and make individuals present in the functioning of IOs, particularly in the elaboration process of international norms (including soft norms) of which IOs are the crucibles. As a result, democratic representation is a driver in the movement to reform the law of IOs into a new law of international institutions.

Indeed, if IOs are 'ultimately, nothing more than the "personification of a representative system"', that system is inherently 'intergovernmental'.[9] Traditionally, IOs make (Member or non-Member) States present in their functioning – including in decision-making processes – through their governments. The fact that some IOs have extended membership to non-State entities has altered the principle of the governmental representation of States, but it did not call it into question, even if this principle has known some long-standing exceptions.[10] Traditionally, the governmental representation of States assured the legitimacy of the power exercised by IOs, including a form of indirect democratic legitimacy when State governments are democratically elected. This perception remains relevant, as evidenced by a report of the Swiss Federal Council on the 'democratization of the United Nations' and according to which '[d]emocratic UN member States, such as Switzerland, have a democratically legitimate government, and therefore also a *democratically legitimate representation* at the UN'.[11] After noting that the United Nations (UN) Charter leaves no room for

[8] Dawisson Belém Lopes and Guilherme Casarões, 'Can International Organizations Be Democratic? A Reassessment' (2019) 41(3) *Contexto Internacional* 481–499, at 490 (emphasis added).

[9] Jean-Pierre Queneudec, 'Préface', in Évelyne Lagrange, *La représentation institutionnelle dans l'ordre international: une contribution à la théorie de la personnalité morale des organisations internationales* (The Hague: Kluwer Law International, 2002), pp. V–VII (translation from French to English).

[10] Art. 3(1) of the International Labour Organization (ILO) Constitution confirms that the workers' and the employers' delegates to the International Labour Conference are as much Member State representatives as Governments' delegates; see ILO Constitution. www.ilo.org/dyn/normlex/en/f?p=1000:62:0::NO:62:P62_LIST_ENTRIE_ID:2453907:NO, last accessed 24 September 2023. On this point, see, more generally, Marie-Clotilde Runavot, 'La représentation de l'État au sein des Organisations internationales', in Julie Ferrero, Pierre-François Laval, and Kiara Neri (eds.), *Actualités de la participation aux organisations internationales* (Paris: Pedone, 2024), pp. 11–28.

[11] Swiss Federal Council, 'Démocratisation des Nations Unies. Rapport du Conseil fédéral en réponse au postulat 18.4111 Jositsch du 27 novembre 2018' (4 December 2020)

parliaments in the UN structure, the Standing Committee on United Nations Affairs of the Inter-Parliamentary Union (IPU) took a qualitative leap and concluded that the '"Peoples of the United Nations" are represented by governments, and not by the representatives they have elected'.[12] Beyond the *governmental* representation of *States*, there would also be *democratic* representation by *governments*.

In addition to the looseness of the representative link with individuals,[13] not all State governments enjoy democratic legitimacy. By introducing parliaments – 'the cornerstone of functioning democracies'[14] – into the machinery of IOs, parliamentarization aims precisely at correcting the democratic limits of the governmental representation of States ... without necessarily coinciding with democratic representation.

Next, the parliamentarization of IOs claims to involve national parliaments to a greater extent, whether as such, through their members, or through the institutions that convene them, first and foremost the IPU. The plural character of this parliamentarization is apparent from the outset, at the level of both its actors and its modalities, given that this 'involvement' covers a whole range of mechanisms, instruments, and techniques whose nature varies: representative, consultative, participatory. Understood like this, the parliamentarization of IOs gets closer to related notions without being confused with them.

First, the parliamentarization of IOs is distinct from the parliamentarism of political theory, which, as a form of representative government, is based on the elective principle. Because of the 'particularly great distance separating individuals from international governance institutions ... the electoral technique allowing the governed to directly choose their rulers remains logically marginal at the universal level, even if it is carried out for the appointment of MEPs [Members of the European Parliament] who share the exercise of

(translation from French to English). www.newsd.admin.ch/newsd/message/attachments/64264.pdf, last accessed 12 April 2023 (emphasis added).

12 Geert Versnick, 'Report on the Nature of the Relationship between the United Nations and the World of Parliaments' (Policy Paper approved by the 117th IPU Assembly, 10 October 2007), para. 4. http://archive.ipu.org/conf-e/117/117-un-rel.htm, last accessed 24 September 2023.

13 Similarly, '[w]hile the decisions of many international institutions have a discernable effect on the life of citizens, their only form of democratic legitimation available today is a highly indirect one derived from the (elected) national governments, rather than from the collectivity of world citizens', see Patrizia Nanz and Jens Steffek, 'Assessing the Democratic Quality of Deliberation in International Governance: Criteria and Research Strategies' (2005) 40 *Acta Politica* 368–383.

14 UN, 'International Day of Parliamentarism'. www.un.org/en/observances/parliamentarism-day, last accessed 12 April 2023.

legislative power with the EU Council'.[15] The parliamentarization of IOs largely ignores the elective principle, including when it rests upon the representative technique.

Second, the parliamentarization of IOs differs from parliamentary diplomacy by its modalities and actors, even if it also contributes to bridging the democratic deficit of international relations.[16] On the one hand, the parliamentarization of IOs only considers the involvement of parliaments within *IOs*, and not the role that these parliaments may play, *at the national level*, on their governments' international action. On the other hand, the parliamentarization of IOs encompasses the parliamentary world *lato sensu*, that is to say, beyond national parliaments. In addition to national parliaments and their members, the parliamentarization of IOs also concerns international parliamentary institutions, which include international parliamentary bodies – still known as international parliaments – and interparliamentary assemblies.[17] The former are organs of an IO, especially at the regional level; the latter are created by agreement outside any IO, but remain established in connection with and/or under the aegis of an IO, when they are not themselves constitutive of an IO. The IPU is an 'international organization *sui generis*, that is, it is an international *parliamentary*, *political* and *representative* organization'.[18] International parliamentary institutions appear to be a decisive instrument for the parliamentarization of IOs because they bring about the (sometimes personified) institutionalization of international parliamentary representation. Yet, with such definitions, they mostly feed the democratic ambivalence of the parliamentarization of IOs and the confusion between parliamentary presence and democratic representation.

Finally, although parliamentarization seeks the democratization of IOs, the extent to which parliamentarization advances democratic representation within these IOs deserves further discussion. In other words, while the parliamentarization of IOs may contribute to reducing the distance separating

15 Runavot, *La démocratie appliquée au droit international*, fn. 1 (translation from French to English).

16 On parliamentary democracy and its incidence in terms of democratization of international relations, see Mario Damen, 'Multilateralism and Democracy: A European Parliament Perspective' (European Parliament, 2022).

17 Laurence Dubin and Marie-Clotilde Runavot, 'Représentativité, légitimité, efficacité', in Lagrange and Sorel, fn. 6, p. 89, para. 169; Zlatko Šabič, 'Building Democracy and Responsible Global Governance: The Role of International Parliamentary Institutions' (2008) 61(2) *Parliamentary Affairs* 255–271.

18 Ian Brownlie and Guy S. Goodwin-Gill, 'Joint opinion prepared on the Instructions of Mr. Anders B. Johnsson, Secretary-General of the Inter-Parliamentary Union' (31 May 1999), Statement point 1 (emphasis added). http://archive.ipu.org/finance-e/opinion.pdf, last accessed 24 September 2023.

individuals from international governance bodies, it is not necessarily by making individuals or their interests present in the exercise of the international normative power of which such bodies are the seat. From this perspective, in the era of globalization, the parliamentarization of IOs feeds into the democratic illusion – 'to qualify this form of representation without reality'[19] – which ultimately excludes individuals from decision-making. In particular, the parliamentarization of representation does not necessarily mean the democratization of the representative link in IOs. False friends and false pretences reappear.

To better identify these false friends and false pretences, it is necessary to separate, on the one hand, the question of *who represents* and *how*, and, on the other, the question of *what is represented*, and *why*. Do the parliamentary modalities of representation (who represents and how) in IOs give them a democratic object (who is represented and why)? The plurality of the former precludes a clear-cut answer. The duality of international parliamentary institutions and the diversity of their relations with IOs are worthy of special attention and call for distinguishing what is represented *in* and *by* these different international parliamentary institutions and their members. The measure of democratic representation found in IOs is clearly not the same in these two hypotheses.

On the one hand, representation *in* international parliamentary institutions reveals that the parliamentary representative can be a false friend of the democratic representative *in* IOs (Section 6.2). On the other hand, representation *by* international parliamentary institutions or their members is often a mere false pretence of democratic representation in IOs despite some actual democratic virtues for their functioning (Section 6.3).

## 6.2 THE REALITIES REPRESENTED IN INTERNATIONAL PARLIAMENTARY INSTITUTIONS: THE PARLIAMENTARY REPRESENTATIVE, A FALSE FRIEND OF THE DEMOCRATIC REPRESENTATIVE?

This section focuses on what international parliamentary institutions members *ut singuli* make present within them. From this viewpoint, the very composition of international parliamentary institutions suggests that representation is double, if not dual. It stems from the statutory duality of their

[19] Anaisabel Prera Flores, 'La démocratie à l'aube du XXIe siècle: une fin ou un moyen? Un modèle ou une culture? Principes universels ou simples règles de conduite?', in *Boutros Boutros-Ghali Amicorum Disciplorumque Liber* (Brussels: Bruylant, 1998), pp. 1279–1294, p. 1279 (translation from French to English).

members due to their quality, but also to their designation modalities. In this respect, States' human component is obviously present in these institutions if their members are elected by direct universal suffrage. But in practice, this configuration remains exceptional for international parliamentary organs, and is never realized for interparliamentary assemblies, which can also admit parliaments as members (Section 6.2.1). Thus, the most frequent hypothesis remains that of the 'dual mandate' of the members of international parliamentary institutions, which raises questions about the entity on whose behalf they speak (Section 6.2.2).

### 6.2.1 *The Statutory Duality of the Parliamentary Representative*

Duality emerges, first, at the level of the modalities for designating the members of international parliamentary institutions. In addition to elections by direct universal suffrage (which guarantee the immediacy of the link of democratic representation), members can also come from national parliaments. International parliamentary bodies combine these two modalities, which can compromise the representative status of the individuals who compose them (ii). While interparliamentary assemblies exclude elections by direct universal suffrage, the representative function of the national parliamentarians within them remains dual depending on whether the members of such assemblies are the national parliamentarians directly or their national parliaments (i).

(i) An election by direct universal suffrage is completely and logically inapplicable to interparliamentary assemblies, the purpose of which is to bring together parliamentarians from different States on the basis of an agreement between them or possibly between their governments. At the regional level, the Nordic Council comprises eighty-seven members who 'are members of the national parliaments and are nominated by the party groups'.[20] Similarly, both the North Atlantic Treaty Organization (NATO) and the Organization for Security and Cooperation in Europe (OSCE) assemblies are a mere institutionalized form of parliamentary diplomacy. Created in 1955 by an interparliamentary initiative as the annual conference of NATO parliamentarians, the former 'consists of parliamentary delegates who are selected from the members of national parliaments of member countries of the Atlantic Alliance by the procedure best suited

[20] See the official website of the Nordic Council, www.norden.org/en/information/nordic-council, last accessed 24 September 2023, as well as Art. 2 of the Statute of the Nordic Council (adopted 22 February 1957, entered into force 1 January 1958). www.cvce.eu/obj/the_statute_of_the_nordic_council_helsinki_22_february_1957-en-d4904999-b567-42f8-bd25-5f9411c0097b.html, last accessed 12 April 2023.

to each country'.[21] The latter was created by the Charter of Paris for a New Europe and brings together 323 parliamentarians from fifty-seven European, Asian, and North American States.[22] Although the Charter of Paris is a non-conventional concerted act, its interstate character brings the OSCE Parliamentary Assembly closer to the Latin American and Caribbean Parliament, known as 'Parlatino'. Established by a 1987 treaty in which the States of that region gathered in an intergovernmental conference agreed 'on the Institutionalization of the regional, permanent and unique organization denominated the Latin American Parliament',[23] the Parlatino's membership has extended beyond parliamentarians themselves to include 'congresses or Legislative Assemblies of member States, which have been democratically constituted'.[24] On a universal scale, the IPU, that is, 'the global organization of national parliaments',[25] utilizes an identical schema even though it was established solely by parliamentarians in 1889.[26]

In any event, the internal representative logic seems to depart from that of the Parliamentary Assemblies of NATO or the OSCE which 'directly' bring together national delegations of parliamentarians. If parliamentarians participate in the functioning of the IPU or the Parlatino, is it then not to make member parliaments present within them? The IPU actually requires that the delegations of parliamentarians be accountable to the parliament from which they come.[27] Given that the Parlatino was created by an intergovernmental treaty, it is not

[21] NATO Parliamentary Assembly, 'Rules of Procedure' (October 2025), Art. 1. https://www.nato-pa.int/document/, last accessed 5 March 2026.

[22] OSCE, Charter of Paris for a New Europe (November 1990). www.osce.org/files/f/documents/0/6/39516.pdf, last accessed 24 September 2023. According to the Charter, Heads of State or Government participating in the Conference on Security and Co-operation in Europe (CSCE) 'call for greater parliamentary involvement in the CSCE, in particular through the creation of a CSCE parliamentary assembly, involving members of parliaments from all participating States'. See also OSCE Parliamentary Assembly, 'Rules of Procedure' (21 March 2020), Arts. 3(1) and 3(4). www.oscepa.org/en/documents/rules-of-procedure/1832-rules-of-procedure-english/file, last accessed 24 September 2023.

[23] Art. 1 of the Treaty on the institutionalization of the Latin American Parliament, UNTS 57830 (adopted 16 November 1987, entered into force 10 November 1988).

[24] Ibid., Art. 4.

[25] To borrow the terms of the official presentation on the IPU's website. www.ipu.org/, last accessed 13 September 2023.

[26] The same applies to the Inter-Parliamentary Assembly of the Association of South-East Asian Nations (AIPA), whose statutes were adopted in 1977 and revised several times since then. See ASEAN Inter-Parliamentary Assembly, 'AIPA Statutes' (last updated in October 2021), especially Art. 4. https://aipasecretariat.org/statutes/, last accessed 24 September 2023.

[27] See Art. 7 of the IPU Statutes and Art. 39(2) of the Rules of the Assembly. See IPU, *Statutes and Rules* (March 2023). www.ipu.org/about-ipu/structure-and-governance, last accessed 13 September 2023.

incongruous to consider that the parliament is apprehended as a State organ, which questions the democratic object of parliamentary representation.[28] Only the election of members of international parliamentary institutions by direct universal suffrage sweeps away any doubt as to their status as democratic representatives. Yet, in that respect, the European Parliament remains an exception.

(ii) International parliaments can also be distinguished by their composition. On the one hand, several of them merely draw their members from the pool of parliaments of the Member States of the IO of which they are an organ. The Assembly of the Council of Europe,[29] or the Benelux Inter-Parliamentary Assembly, for example, do not seek to elect their members by direct universal suffrage. It is also significant that the latter recently replaced the Benelux Inter-Parliamentary Consultative Council that had been established in 1955 without at any time raising the question of a change in its composition.[30] It should be noted, however, that members of the Pan-African Parliament (which is intended to become an organ of the African Union beyond the African Economic Community) should be elected by the parliaments or any deliberative body of the Member States, but outside their own members.[31]

On the other hand, with the exception of the European Parliament, only the members of the Central American Parliament (PARLACEN, an organ of the Central American Integration System)[32] are elected by direct universal

[28] See Section 6.2.2 (i).

[29] The presentation of the Parliamentary Assembly on the Council of Europe's website leaves no doubt in this regard. Council of Europe, 'Parliamentary Assembly'. www.coe.int/fr/web/no-hate-campaign/parliamentary-assembly1, last accessed 24 September 2023.

[30] Pursuant to Art. 2(2) of the Agreement regarding the Benelux Inter-Parliamentary Assembly, the Assembly remains comprised of '49 members, of which: (a) 21 shall be chosen and appointed by the Federal Parliament and the community and regional parliaments of the Kingdom of Belgium from among their members; (b) 7 shall be chosen and appointed by the Luxembourg Parliament from among its members; (c) 21 shall be chosen and appointed by the Netherlands Parliament from among its members'. See Convention between the Kingdom of Belgium, the Grand Duchy of Luxembourg and the Kingdom of the Netherlands regarding the Benelux Inter-Parliamentary, 3309 UNTS 55870 (adopted 20 January 2015, entered into force 1 August 2019). Compare with Art. 1 of the Agreement between Belgium, the Grand Duchy of Luxembourg and the Netherlands setting up a Benelux Inter-Parliamentary Advisory Council, 250 UNTS 3524 (adopted 5 November 1955, entered into force 9 September 1956).

[31] Art. 5(1)(a) of the Protocol to the Constitutive Act of the African Union relating to the Pan-African Parliament (adopted 27 June 2014). Currently, the Pan-African parliamentarians are 'elected or designated by their respective National Parliaments or any other deliberative organ of the Member States, *from among their members*', Art. 5(1) of the Protocol to the Treaty Establishing the African Economic Community Relating to the Pan-African Parliament, 3269 UNTS 55375 (adopted 2 March 2001, entered into force 14 December 2003) (emphasis added).

[32] The Central American Integration System (SICA) was created in 1991 by a protocol to the Charter of the Organization of Central American States signed by Costa Rica, El Salvador,

suffrage.[33] Several parliamentary bodies of regional integration organizations aspire to have their members elected by direct universal suffrage.[34] However, this objective is not yet (or not yet fully) effective despite claims to that effect in existing legal provisions. The Parliament of the Southern Common Market (MERCOSUR), that is, PARLASUR, and the Parliament of the Andean Community (Andean Parliament) offer an illustration, as the designation of their members by direct universal suffrage remains partial and variable. The 2005 Protocol that established the PARLASUR and replaced the previous Joint Parliamentary Committee (which was composed of delegates from national parliaments)[35] provides for the election of its members by direct universal suffrage.[36] While this requires legislative adjustments in the MERCOSUR Member States, Argentina is the only State to have introduced direct universal suffrage for the election of PARLASUR members. Moreover, a decision of the Council of the Common Market has postponed until 2030 the transitional phase to direct universal suffrage elections.[37] Although the founding texts of the Andean Parliament are old,[38] in 2021 only three States had organized elections specifically for the appointment of its members,[39] while Chile and

Guatemala, Honduras, Nicaragua, and Panama. See Tegucigalpa Protocol to the Charter of the Organization of Central American States (OCAS) of 12 December 1962, 1695 UNTS 8048 (adopted 13 December 1991, entered into force 23 July 1992). Whether SICA or MERCOSUR qualify as IOs is open to discussion, but that question lies beyond the scope of this chapter.

33 Art. 2 of the Treaty on the establishment of the Central American Parliament and other political organs, of the PARLACEN and other political entities, 1777 UNTS 30999 (adopted 2 October 1987, entered into force 1 May 1990).

34 On the link between parliamentarization and the integration of IOs, see Martin Quesnel, 'Les parlements internationaux et l'exercice du pouvoir international', in Runavot, *La démocratie appliquée au droit international*, fn. 1, pp. 103–125, p. 105.

35 Protocol on the Establishment of the MERCOSUR Parliament, 2444 UNTS 37341 (adopted 9 December 2005, entered into force 24 February 2007).

36 Compare Art. 6 of the Protocol on the Establishment of the MERCOSUR Parliament, with Art. 24 of the Additional Protocol to the Treaty of Asunción on the Institutional Structure of MERCOSUR (Ouro Preto Protocol), 2145 UNTS 37341 (adopted 17 December 1994, entered into force 15 December 1995). While the former provides that '[P]arliamentarians will be elected by the citizens of the respective States Parties, through direct, universal and secret suffrage', the latter states that '[t]he members of the Joint Parliamentary Commission shall be appointed by the respective national parliaments, in accordance with their internal procedures'.

37 MERCOSUR, Council of the Common Market, 'Funcionamento del Parlamento del Mercosur' (4 December 2020), Decision 09/20. www.sice.oas.org/Trade/MRCSRS/Decisions/DEC_009_2020_s.pdf, last accessed 24 September 2023.

38 Art. 42 of the Acuerdo de integración subregional andino (adopted 26 May 1969, entered into force 16 October 1969); Tratado Constitutivo del Parlamento Andino (adopted 25 October 1979, entered into force 17 December 1979). These texts are available at: www.parlamentoandino.org, last accessed 24 September 2023.

39 Ecuador, Bolivia, and Peru.

Colombia continued to send national parliamentarians. As a result, there is a duality among the members of these parliaments in terms of their designation method.[40]

In the Parliament of the Economic Community of West African States (ECOWAS), the situation is homogeneous, but at the expense of elections by direct universal suffrage. More specifically, the Supplementary Act relating to the enhancement of the powers of the ECOWAS Parliament[41] provides for elections by direct universal suffrage in order for its members to be 'representing all the peoples of the Community'.[42] Yet, the same Act further provides for a transitional solution consisting in electing the deputies to the ECOWAS Parliament within each 'National Assemblies of Member States or their equivalent institutions or organs'.[43] To this day, the evolution towards an election by direct universal suffrage remains an objective of the current legislature, as well as the subject of reflection within an ad hoc committee set up in 2020 and which issued a report on this matter in 2021.[44] As with interparliamentary assemblies, the ECOWAS Parliament and almost all international parliamentary organs remain composed of delegations of national parliamentarians.[45] Consequently, in international parliamentary institutions, dual mandates seem to be the rule, which blurs the contours of the reality that their members make present within these institutions.

### 6.2.2 *Parliamentary Representatives: Between Duplication and Functional Ambivalence*

On whose behalf do the members of international parliamentary institutions speak? National peoples, regional populations, the States of which they are an organ, or the national parliament? The answer provided by regulatory texts is not obvious. In this respect, it is necessary to distinguish, based on the quality of the members of these institutions, the parliamentarians (ii) and the parliaments to which they belong (i).

40 'Elecciones al Parlamento Andino'. https://elecciones.larepublica.pe/parlamento-andino/, last accessed 24 September 2023.

41 Art. 18(1)(a) of the Supplementary Act relating to the enhancement of the powers of the EC OWAS Parliament (17 December 2016), A/SA.1/12/16.

42 Ibid., Art. 1(14).

43 Ibid., Art. 18(1)(g).

44 See the ECOWAS Parliament's press release, 'ECOWAS Parliament calls for Election of its Members by Direct Universal Suffrage'. https://parl.ecowas.int/ecowas-parliament-calls-for-election-of-its-members-by-direct-universal-suffrage/, last accessed 24 September 2023.

45 Lagrange, *La représentation institutionnelle dans l'ordre international*, fn. 9, p. 172.

(i) When the members of international parliamentary institutions are national parliamentary institutions, the statutory ambiguity of the latter in the internal order – national parliaments are both the representative institution of the citizens and an organ of the State – has repercussions on the representation that they can ensure in international institutions and, more specifically, in interparliamentary assemblies. The ambiguity is all the greater since member parliaments are represented in the organs of the interparliamentary assembly by some of their own members. Pursuant to the IPU Statutes, its Assembly is composed 'of parliamentarians designated as delegates by the Members of the IPU'.[46] Such a multiplication of the representative link obscures the reality that is represented. Moreover, despite the emphasis placed on reinforcing the participation of peoples or populations, the normative origin of an assembly of national parliaments will influence the way in which its members are perceived. As mentioned above, this is particularly clear for the Parlatino, whose constitutive act is an interstate treaty. Its preamble acknowledges 'that the participation of *the Latin American countries* through the diversity of their political and ideological inclinations, *represented* in their national Parliaments, ensure the democratic foundation for integration'.[47] Is it then not the State, rather than its citizens, that each national parliament makes present within the Parlatino? Conversely, the preamble to the ASEAN Inter-Parliamentary Assembly (AIPA) Statutes, which is of interparliamentary origin, brings to fore the democratic dimension of member parliaments by affirming their conviction 'that the strength of ASEAN emanates from the roots of our societies and that closer cooperation among the *respective legislatures* would result in *greater participation by the peoples of* ASEAN Member States'.[48]

(ii) The direct participation of national parliamentarians in international parliamentary institutions is also not without ambivalence.

On the one hand, they can appear, at times, as representatives of their national parliament or of a human component, whether national or transnational,

[46] IPU members are the national parliaments; see Art. 10(1) IPU Statutes. See also, Art. 9(1) AIPA Statutes which provides that: '[t]here shall be a General Assembly of AIPA consisting of delegations from each member Parliament comprising not more than fifteen (15) members, headed by the Speaker or his representative. At least three (3) of the members shall be women parliamentarians'. Similarly, Art. 4 of the Treaty on the institutionalization of the Latin American Parliament stipulates that within the Parlatino, the participation of member parliaments 'will be by representatives of plurally constituted delegations'.

[47] Ibid. (emphasis added).

[48] See Preamble of the AIPA Statutes (emphasis added).

singular or plural. For instance, the parliamentarians who compose the OSCE Parliamentary Assembly are 'representing their national parliaments',[49] in the same way as the NATO Parliamentary Assembly 'by virtue of its membership drawn from the various national parliaments, provides a link between the NATO authorities and these parliaments'.[50] However, in the transitional composition which is still that of the ECOWAS Parliament,[51] its members 'represent *all* the peoples of the Community'.[52] Similarly, the 'Pan African parliamentarians shall represent *all* the peoples of Africa and the interests of the African diaspora',[53] while the Andean Parliament brings together 'representatives of the peoples of *each* of the contracting parties'.[54] Yet, the interstate normative origin of these two regional parliaments paradoxically suggests that their members also make present the States to which they belong.[55] The wording of Article 25(a) of the Statute of the Council of Europe used to convey the same incongruity with regard to the Consultative Assembly of this organization, which was said to 'consist of Representatives of each Member, elected by its Parliament from among the members thereof, or appointed from among the members of that Parliament, in such manner as it shall decide'.[56]

On the other hand, and correlatively, the trouble stems from the 'dual mandate' with which members of international parliamentary institutions are deemed to be invested as soon as they are chosen from among national parliamentarians, 'thus serving both at the national and the international level'.[57] Their provenance can certainly help to establish their legitimacy,

[49] See the official presentation of the OSCE Parliamentary Assembly. OSCE Parliamentary Assembly, 'The OSCE Parliamentary'. www.oscepa.org/en/documents/factsheets/669-factsheet-english/file, last accessed 24 September 2023.

[50] Art. 2 of NATO Parliamentary Assembly's Rules of Procedure.

[51] That is, an assembly of national parliamentarians. See Section 6.2.1.

[52] See Art. 2(2) of the Supplementary Act relating to the enhancement of the powers of the ECOWAS Parliament (emphasis added).

[53] Art. 2(2) of the Protocol to the Constitutive Act of the African Union relating to the Pan-African Parliament (emphasis added).

[54] Art. 2 of the Treaty Constituting the Andean Parliament, 19 ILM 269 (adopted 25 October 1979) (emphasis added).

[55] Art. 4(1) of the Protocol to the Constitutive Act of the African Union relating to the Pan-African Parliament on the composition of the Pan-African Parliament is very explicit: 'each State Party shall be represented in the Pan African Parliament by an equal number of parliamentarians'. Art. 4 of the Treaty Constituting the Andean Parliament provides that: 'the representatives shall act in function of the common objectives and interests of the contracting parties'.

[56] Statute of the Council of Europe, 87 UNTS 1168 (adopted 5 May 1949, entered into force 3 August 1949).

[57] Beat Habegger, 'Democratic Accountability of International Organizations: Parliamentary Control Within the Council of Europe and the OSCE and the Prospects for the United Nations' (2010) 45(2) *Cooperation and Conflict* 186–204, at 190.

but it also has disadvantages if they 'consider themselves primarily as representative of home parliaments and look at the priorities of IPIs [International Parliamentary Institutions] exclusively through the prism of national priorities'.[58] As Martin Quesnel aptly underscores, one must also add to this:

> the competition that may exist between national parliamentarians of a geographical area and international parliamentarians elected to represent that group. It is not easy to determine who has the legitimacy of representation on a question that is both of national and international interest ... This type of competition for democratic representation is likely to push international parliaments to seek both the careful defense of the interests of a defined community, and to account for the national public opinion.[59]

But this then slides from the issue of representation *in* international parliaments to the issue of representation *by* international parliaments, all the more so since they have the characteristic of being an integral part of the organic architecture of an IO.

## 6.3 THE REALITIES REPRESENTED BY INTERNATIONAL PARLIAMENTARY INSTITUTIONS: FALSE PRETENCES OF DEMOCRATIC REPRESENTATION IN IOS?

On whose behalf do IPIs speak? And, consequently, whom do they make present in the IOs to which they are functionally linked, when they are not an organ thereof? The answer to this question overlaps, at least in part, with that of representation *in* the international parliamentary institution when the international parliamentary institution is a component of the organic apparatus of an IO.[60] But it is not perfectly identical, *a fortiori* when the relationship with the IO is only functional. In any event, the representative link with individuals is significantly loosened, and the gap widens even further in the hypothesis of interparliamentary assemblies jointly established by some of these organizations. The IPU and its various relationships with intergovernmental organizations (first among them the UN) illustrate the distention and the multiplication of the relationship with individuals, a relationship which then has only the appearances of a representative link (Section 6.3.1). It therefore seems that parliamentary involvement in IOs allows for the adjustment of democratic principles to these organizations, rather than a true democratic representation. In other words, IPIs

58 Šabič, fn. 17, at 266.
59 Quesnel, fn. 34, p. 112 (translation from French to English).
60 See Section 6.2.1 (ii).

encourage and promote a more inclusive, transparent, and accountable functioning of IOs, but without necessarily making the voice of individuals heard (Section 6.3.2).

### 6.3.1 *Between Multiplication and Distension: An 'en Trompe l'Œil' Representative Link with the Individuals*

'In a world that increasingly suffers from the lack of legitimacy and transparency, and where the creation of a global parliament is an unlikely scenario in a foreseeable future, IPIs can establish themselves as a contributor to a more democratic ... global governance'.[61] International parliamentary institutions can do so through their representative function. Still, it remains necessary to specify the terms of such a function and to clarify its holder before assessing its democratic nature, that is, the extent to which the representative function can make the voice of individuals heard in the functioning of international governance bodies such as IOs. On the one hand, the distribution of the representative function in IOs between IPIs and their members is ambiguous (i). On the other hand, and correspondingly, the distance is widening between the place of representation – the IOs – and the reality represented – the individuals (ii).

(i) The representative function of international parliamentary organs in their respective IO doubles, if not replicates, that of their member parliamentarians when they are, or are entitled to be, elected by direct universal suffrage. The ECOWAS Parliament does not seem to add any representative value in relation to its members within the Community, since both are meant to represent 'all the peoples of the Community'.[62] Currently, the Treaty on European Union provides that MEPs are also 'representatives of Union's citizens', who are thus 'directly represented at Union level in the European Parliament'.[63] But this has not always been the case within the EU, and, including for international parliamentary bodies, the representative function in the IO to which they belong may not exactly overlap with that which their own members perform within them. The networking of parliamentarians and its institutionalization seem to allow for the *transnationalization of representation*. In other words, the international parliamentary institution

[61] Šabič, fn. 17, at 255.

[62] Art. 2 of the Supplementary Act relating to the enhancement of the powers of the ECOWAS Parliament.

[63] See, respectively, Arts. 14(2) and 10(2) of the Treaty on the European Union. See also Dubout and Ritleng, Chapter 13 in this volume.

> accumulates and transcends the representation of the national human component that each of its members individually ensures, in order to mediate a representation of the human as a whole. PARLASUR parliamentarians are thus representatives of the citizens of the States parties to the Treaty establishing the PARLASUR in which they were respectively elected, while the PARLASUR is the organ representing all the peoples of MERCOSUR.[64] The same applies to the representation in the Andean Community by the Andean Parliament or its members.[65] The representative function is then no longer doubled, but *double* in the IO, depending on whether one considers the international parliamentary organ or its member components. In all these cases, its object nevertheless remains democratic, which is doubtful in the case of the Parliamentary Assembly of the Council of Europe and its members, who, in addition to government representation in the Committee of Ministers, seem to mediate a parliamentary presence of Member States in the Council of Europe.[66]

The logic is somewhat different for interparliamentary assemblies that are not formally integrated into an IO with which they may nevertheless maintain close functional relations. Interparliamentary assemblies are intended to bring a parliamentary dimension to the work of one or more IOs and are rarely expressly endowed with a representative function. This is obvious with the OSCE Parliamentary Assembly, whose purpose is simply to support and strengthen OSCE missions alongside it.[67] In many respects, the same applies to the Parliamentary Conference on the World Trade Organization (PCWTO), established jointly by the IPU and the European Parliament in 2003.[68] While it is true that the NATO Parliamentary Assembly 'provides

64 Compare, in the Protocol on the Establishment of the MERCOSUR Parliament, Art. 6 (representation by the parliamentarians) with Art. 1(1) and 2(2) (representation by the PARLASUR).

65 Art. 2 and 12 d) of the Treaty Constituting the Andean Parliament.

66 In that respect, see Parliamentary Assembly of the Council of Europe, 'Parliamentary representation'. https://pace.coe.int/en/pages/representation, last accessed 24 September 2023.

67 See Rule 2 of OSCE Parliamentary Assembly's Rules of Procedure: 'The Parliamentary Assembly of the OSCE shall: (a) assess the implementation of the objectives of the OSCE; (b) discuss subjects addressed during meetings of the Ministerial Council and the summits of Heads of State or Government; (c) develop and promote mechanisms for the prevention and resolution of conflicts; (d) support the strengthening and consolidation of democratic institutions in the OSCE participating States; (e) contribute to the development of the institutional structures of the OSCE and of relations and cooperation between the existing OSCE institutions'.

68 On the composition and functions of the PCWTO, see IPU, 'Parliamentary Conference on the World Trade Organization'. www.ipu.org/about-ipu/strategic-partnerships/parliamentary-conference-world-trade-organization, last accessed 24 September 2023.

a *link* between the NATO authorities and these parliaments',[69] like the previous ones, it does not enjoy any representative status in NATO.[70] From this point of view, the IPU is taking a qualitative leap forward at the UN.

Created in 1889 (much earlier than the UN), the IPU has, for a long time, enjoyed only a consultative status with the Economic and Social Council, in accordance with Article 71 of the UN Charter.[71] Beyond the fact that such a status did not seem adapted to the nature of the IPU, which was endowed with international legal personality by its Statutes,[72] it did not entail any right to participate in the work of the UN. Yet, it was only fifty years after its creation that the UN considered changing this status. The initiative came from its General Assembly (UNGA), which, in 1995, expressed its desire to 'strengthen … existing cooperation between the United Nations and the Inter-Parliamentary Union and … giv[e] it a new and adequate framework'.[73] This framework was first established by a cooperation agreement concluded less than a year later in order to provide the IPU with an 'appropriate representation' within the UN and allow it to attend the plenary sessions of the UNGA, and to participate in the meetings of the subsidiary organs and in the work of the conferences held under the auspices of the UN when matters falling within the mandate, activities, and competences of the IPU are considered.[74] This framework was expanded in 2002 with the granting of observer status within the UNGA,[75] which then led to the reformation of the cooperation relationship into a new agreement signed during the summer of 2016.[76] Each time, the evolution of the representative status of the IPU was motivated by the UN's observation

69 Art. 2 of its Rules of Procedure (emphasis added).

70 Conversely, it is important to note that Member States of the organization may send government representatives as observers to these parliamentary assemblies. This is the case in the PCWTO, for instance.

71 ECOSOC, 'Decision conferring consultative status on certain organizations' (28 March 1947), E/435/57(IV).

72 Art. 1(4) of the IPU Statutes provides that '[t]he IPU has legal personality and has the authority to enter into international agreements, including cooperation agreements with national parliaments and inter-parliamentary organizations, as well as with international intergovernmental and non-governmental organizations'.

73 UNGA Res. 50/15, 'Cooperation between the UN and the Inter-Parliamentary Union' (15 November 1995).

74 UNGA Res. 51/402, 'Cooperation Agreement between the United Nations and the Inter-parliamentary Union' (24 July 1996), Annex, Art. III.

75 UNGA Res. 57/32, 'Observer status for the Inter-Parliamentary Union in the General Assembly' (19 November 2002).

76 IPU, 'Draft Cooperation Agreement between the United Nations and the IPU' (27 February 2015), CL/196/9-R.2.

that the IPU is a 'world organization of parliaments'.[77] At the same time, the First World Conference of Speakers of Parliament, held in New York in 2000, took note of the transformation of international relations and called for consolidating not only the role of the IPU 'as a world organization for inter-parliamentary cooperation and for relaying the vision and will of its members to intergovernmental organizations', but also 'the role of parliament and its members as intermediaries between a complex international decision-making process and citizens'.[78] What emerges here is the multiplication of the links of representation established by the IPU, by the national parliaments that are members of that organization, and by the parliamentarians who compose these national parliaments. It is not certain that this effectively contributes to making the voice of individuals heard in international governance bodies.[79]

(ii) Of the IPU or its members, who makes the other present in IOs, especially the UN, and in whose name does each speak? The reports on 'Interaction between the United Nations, national parliaments and the Inter-Parliamentary Union' issued to date by the UN Secretary-General and the corresponding UNGA Resolutions do not answer this question because they simultaneously address the international role of the IPU and of the national parliaments.[80] With regard to the IPU's representative function in the UN, a 2022 UNGA resolution on this subject recalls, like the previous ones that, in the Outcome Document of the 2005 World Summit, 'Heads of State and Government resolved to strengthen further cooperation between the United Nations and national parliaments *through their world organization*, the Inter-Parliamentary Union, in all fields of the work of the United Nations'.[81] As observed by Ian Brownlie and Guy S. Goodwin-Gill, there is, on the part of State governments, an 'implied recognition of

[77] See Art. 1(1) of the 1996 Agreement; preamble of UNGA Res. 57/32, fn. 75; preamble to the Cooperation Agreement of 2016.

[78] Conference of Presiding Officers of National Parliaments, 'The parliamentary vision for international cooperation at the dawn of the third millennium' Declaration adopted by consensus (UN Headquarters, 30 August–1 September 2000). http://archive.ipu.org/splz-e/sp-dclr.htm, last accessed 24 September 2023.

[79] The following developments draw from, and update, a previous contribution: Marie-Clotilde Runavot, 'L'Union interparlementaire et la parlementarisation de l'ONU', in Runavot, *La démocratie appliquée au droit international*, fn. 1, pp. 87–102.

[80] All these reports can be found on the IPU's website. www.ipu.org/about-ipu/strategic-partnerships/un-resolutions-and-reports-linked-ipu, last accessed 24 September 2023.

[81] UNGA Res. 76/270, 'Interaction between the United Nations, national parliaments and the Inter-Parliamentary Union' (24 June 2022), preamble (emphasis added).

the IPU as an organization that *represents* the parliaments as *representatives* of the peoples'.[82]

For its part, the IPU seems to see itself as the relay, in IOs in general and in the UN in particular, of the representative democracy embodied by its members. In this sense, its 2022–2026 Strategy commits 'to further strengthen the parliamentary dimension of multilateralism and global governance *including the voice of parliaments at the United Nations and other multilateral organizations*'.[83] The IPU Governing Council, at its 210th session in October 2022, considered and approved the report on the IPU Policy Project at the UN which 'provides a roadmap to intensify the IPU's work with the United Nations *on behalf of parliaments*'.[84]

In the UN as in other IOs, the IPU would thus be the representative of representatives democratically elected at the national level. In other words, there would be a form of cascading parliamentary representation of citizens and peoples, which remain defined within the framework of the State. Admittedly, there is a practical explanation for this multilayered democratic representation: the particularly large distance that separates the human component of States and IOs would call for such a superimposing of links of representation. And the mandatory nature of the IPU's representative function could moderate the stretching of democratic representation that it performs in IOs. But there are two reservations to that.

First, with regard to the nature of the representative relationship between the IPU and its members, the recent analysis of the IPU's political project at the UN notes with a certain disenchantment that 'too many [members of parliament] around the world – including those engaged with the IPU – are not fully aware of or do not fully understand the IPU's mission at the UN. One significant reason for this is that much of the IPU's political work at the UN is not reaching national parliaments'.[85] In these conditions, how can 'all of this [be] done by the IPU at the request of parliaments'?[86] Second, the technical argument of distancing is short-lived when, alongside the IPU, the direct involvement of national parliaments and/or their members is maintained, and even encouraged, at the UN, which regularly praises 'the practice of including parliamentarians as members of national delegations to major

82 Brownlie and Goodwin-Gill, fn. 18, para. 13 (emphasis added).
83 IPU, 'IPU 2022–2026 strategy. For democracy. For everyone' (2022) (emphasis added).
84 IPU, 'Results of the 145th IPU Assembly' (11–15 October 2022), p. 17, pt. 8 (emphasis added).
85 IPU, 'The IPU political project at the United Nations. Implementation Roadmap' (15 October 2022), p. 2.
86 Versnick, fn. 12, respectively paras. 21 and 24.

United Nations meetings and events ... and invites Member States to continue this practice in a more regular and systematic manner'.[87] As a result, the ways of bringing *the voice of parliamentarians* to the UN have diversified: there is not only the inclusion of parliamentarians in Member States' delegations, but also parliamentary hearings and the organization of meetings and conferences as adjuncts to major intergovernmental meetings.[88] Does this allow for *the voice of individuals* to be heard? The diversity of parliamentary involvement in IOs may contribute to their democratization, but without necessarily conveying democratic representation.

### 6.3.2 *Parliamentary Involvement and the Democratic Acculturation of IOs*

The involvement of national parliaments and their members in the functioning of IOs, whether through IPIs or directly, promotes and encourages the acclimatization of democratic principles traditionally associated with deliberative democracy and centred on the principle of Habermasian discussion. In truth, such a democratic acculturation of IOs does not exclude any representative mechanism and often accompanies it. According to Patrizia Nanz and Jens Steffek:

> In a nutshell, deliberative democracy must ensure that citizens' concerns feed into the policymaking process and are taken into account when it comes to a decision on binding rules. What is important to the notion of public reasoning is not so much that everyone participates but more that ... the process of (political) deliberation within international governance is open both to *public scrutiny* and to *the input of stakeholders' concerns*.[89]

On these last two aspects, the focus is then generally placed on the international civil society, embodied in particular by NGOs. However, national and international parliamentary institutions are also relevant. Some techniques for the parliamentarization of IOs make it possible to control the (inter)governmental action within IOs (i), while others tend to increase the transparency and inclusiveness of normative processes (ii).

(i) In its 2022 resolution on the interaction between the UN, national parliaments and the IPU, the UNGA acknowledges 'the role and responsibility of national parliaments in regard to ... ensuring greater

[87] UNGA 'Interaction between the United Nations, national parliaments and the Inter-Parliamentary Union' (13 June 2022), A/76/L.63, para. 10, but also paras. 11–12.
[88] For an enumeration of these techniques, see UNGA Res. 76/270, fn. 81, preamble.
[89] Nanz and Steffek, fn. 13, at 370 (emphasis added).

transparency and accountability at both the national and the global levels'.[90] Yet, the parliamentary oversight of governmental action within IOs generally takes place at the national level and parliamentary accountability mechanisms remain marginal at the international level. The IPU's political project at the UN confirms this 'renationalization' of parliamentary control over institutionalized international action of governments.[91] Further, according to the UN Secretary-General, '[p]arliaments, given their legislative and oversight mandates and their role in translating international instruments into national legislation, can make a unique contribution to United Nations processes'.[92] The implementation and monitoring of the Sustainable Development Goals (SDGs) and related instruments offer an excellent example.[93] However, the situation is different and parliamentary scrutiny becomes more international both in its form and its object when the IPU's Standing Committee on UN Affairs conducts its work to 'review implementation of international commitments'.[94] Created within the IPU in 2007 and made permanent in 2013, this Committee received a mandate from the IPU Governing Council to 'examin[e] the overall working of the United Nations and its reform, in particular in terms of system-wide coherence, institutional effectiveness and the use of public funds'.[95] It is therefore not absurd to consider that, through this Committee, the IPU exercises, with regard to the universal intergovernmental organization, the equivalent of the traditional parliamentary function of governmental control. However, the representative logic endures, since the IPU considers that its Committee 'helps to close the

90 UNGA Res. 76/270, fn. 81. For a similar formulation, see also UNGA Res. 77/159 (20 December 2022), preamble.

91 IPU, 'The IPU political project at the United Nations. Implementation Roadmap', fn. 85, pp. 3–7.

92 UNGA, Report to the Secretary-General 'Interaction between the United Nations, national parliaments and the Inter-Parliamentary Union' (31 March 2022), A/76/780, para. 92.

93 UNGA Res. 77/159, fn. 90, paras. 2–3. See also the declaration of Duarte Pacheco, President of the IPU, during the first global parliamentary meeting on achieving the SDGs jointly organized by the IPU and the House of Representatives of Indonesia (28–30 September 2021), according to which 'Parliamentarians are instrumental in the realization of the SDGs through their ability to turn the voluntary commitment to the SDGs into enforceable laws, to hold governments to account on development policy choices and strategies, and the adoption of national budgets.' IPU, 'First global parliamentary meeting on achieving the SDGs' (1 October 2021). www.ipu.org/, last accessed 10 April 2023.

94 UNGA Res. 76/270, fn. 81, preamble.

95 IPU, 'IPU Cooperation with the United Nations – Standing Committee on United Nations Affairs'. http://archive.ipu.org/un-f/un-cmt.htm, last accessed 24 September 2023.

"democracy gap" between citizens' voices and global decision-making. Its meetings ensure the voice of "we the people" is communicated to UN policy-makers'.[96] The Standing Committee then joins the mechanism of parliamentary hearings which 'make it possible for parliamentarians to convey to UN Member States their views based on their own national and local experiences'.[97] Generally organized on a common theme at an upcoming intergovernmental conference,[98] these hearings contribute more to the inclusiveness of the normative process within the UN than to its control, by enriching it with a parliamentary perspective.

(ii) The parliamentarization of IOs undoubtedly helps to diversify the interests taken into account and the points of view expressed, particularly in the normative process of which they may be the seat. Parliamentarization, in essence, makes it possible to overcome the intergovernmentalism that traditionally characterizes such a process. International parliamentary institutions are therefore doubly conducive to fostering greater inclusion in IOs.

First, attention is placed on the composition of delegations of parliamentarians brought together by IPIs when they are themselves constitutive or an organ of an IO. Indeed, such delegations are often encouraged or compelled to be inclusive and, thus, contribute to diversifying, 'from within', the interests represented in IOs. In addition to the diversity of political opinions, the delegations participating in IPIs must also represent societal diversity. For instance, while the AIPA General Assembly is an interparliamentary assembly, it brings together delegations from each member parliament, and at least three of the fifteen members of each delegation are women parliamentarians.[99] Among international parliamentary organs, EU Member States must also ensure gender equality when electing MEPs.[100] Finally, Article 4 of the

96 According to the terms used on the IPU's official website to introduce the standing Committee; see IPU, 'Committee on United Nations Affairs'. www.ipu.org/about-ipu/structure-and-governance/assemblies/committee-united-nations-affairs, last accessed 24 September 2023.

97 According to the terms used on the IPU's official website to introduce the parliamentary hearings; see IPU, 'Annual Parliamentary Hearings at the UN'. www.ipu.org/about-ipu/strategic-partnerships/annual-parliamentary-hearings-un, last accessed 24 September 2023.

98 It is the case, for example, of the last parliamentary hearing held on 13 and 14 February 2023 in anticipation of the UN 2023 Water Conference and entitled 'Water for People and Planet: Stop the waste, change the game, invest in future'.

99 Art. 9(1) AIPA Statutes.

100 European Parliament, 'The Members of the European Parliament'. www.europarl.europa.eu/about-parliament/en/organisation-and-rules/organisation/members/, last accessed 24 September 2023; European Parliament, 'Ethics and Transparency'. www.europarl.europa.eu/meps/en/about/meps, last accessed 24 September 2023.

Protocol to the Constitutive Act of the African Union on the Pan-African Parliament will tighten the requirement of parity. In addition to the requirement that the delegations of five parliamentarians from each State party must include at least two women (and no longer just one), a failure to respect this quota is sanctioned by a loss of accreditation.[101] From this point of view, this international parliamentary body joins the world organization of parliaments, whose Statutes promote under Article 10 both gender equality and youth representation in parliamentary delegations, and sanction a member parliament whose delegation comprises only parliamentarians of the same sex during two consecutive sessions of the IPU Assembly.[102] Other IOs have emulated this internal policy of the IPU.

Second, this time 'from the outside', the IPU has been able to export its 'best practices' on inclusiveness in the functioning of other IOs. The 2022 report of the Secretary-General on the interaction between the UN, national parliaments, and the IPU reaffirms that '[p]arliaments play a critical role in this regard, by helping to ensure that United Nations decision-making is informed by a wide range of views and opinions'.[103] In its subsequent resolution, the UNGA encouraged 'the Secretary-General to include members of parliament,

[101] Currently, Art. 4(2) and (3) of the Protocol to the Treaty Establishing the African Economic Community Relating to the Pan-African Parliament provide that '[t]he representation of each Member State must reflect the diversity of political opinions in each National Parliament' and that State delegations must include 'five (5) members, at least one of whom must be a woman'. Similarly, the representation of each Member State in the ECOWAS parliament 'shall reflect, as much as possible, the political configuration in the State' and parliamentary delegations must include 'at least 30% female representation', see Art. 18(1)(b) and (c) of the Supplementary Act relating to the enhancement of the powers of the ECOWAS Parliament.

[102] Art. 10 of the IPU Statutes: '1. The Assembly shall be composed of parliamentarians designated as delegates by the Members of the IPU. Members shall include men and women parliamentarians in their delegation and shall strive to ensure their equal representation.... 3. A Member Parliament may register one additional delegate if at least one young parliamentarian is part of the delegation, on condition that the delegation is composed of both sexes and the Member is not in arrears in the payment of its assessed contributions. 4. Any delegation that for two consecutive sessions of the Assembly is composed exclusively of parliamentarians of the same sex shall automatically be reduced by one person'. See also IPU, 'Gender-equal IPU'. www.ipu.org/about-ipu/gender-equal-ipu, last accessed 24 September 2024.

[103] UNGA, Report to the Secretary-General 'Interaction between the United Nations, national parliaments and the Inter-Parliamentary Union', fn. 92, para. 4; UNGA Res. 77/159, fn. 90, para. 4: 'Welcomes the practice of including parliamentarians as members of national delegations to major United Nations meetings and events, as appropriate, including the high-level political forum on sustainable development, and invites Member States to continue this practice in a more regular and systematic manner, and with due consideration given to achieving gender balance within such delegations'.

particularly from the developing countries, in multi-stakeholder high-level advisory groups as well as in mediation teams and other such exercises where a multiplicity of perspectives can help to ensure fair and lasting solutions to specific challenges'.[104] Finally, since COP 18, the functioning of the IPU has led the UN Conferences on Climate Change to a positive evolution in parity in the composition of their structures, as well as in that of the national delegations of the participating States. After generally encouraging the inclusion of women in the institutions established by the Climate Change Convention and its related texts, COP 18 adopted a 'gender balance goal' that participating States are invited to pursue in their national delegations and instructed the secretariat to ensure its follow-up.[105]

While this is still just the representation of States, parliamentarization nonetheless directly influences its modalities in order to make it more 'inclusive', and therefore . . . more democratic!

[104] UNGA Res. 76/270, fn. 81, para. 24.

[105] UNFCCC, Decision 36/CP.7 (adopted 9 November 2001), FCCC/CP/2001/13/Add.4. The follow-up report by the Secretariat reveals that States' efforts remain very insufficient: UNFCCC 'Report by the Secretariat "Gender composition"' (20 August 2021), FCCC/CP/2021/4.

# PART II

# DEMOCRATIC REPRESENTATION THROUGH INTERNATIONAL ORGANIZATIONS

# 7

# Differentiated Representation and Cross-Legitimization of Business in International Organizations: Comparing the International Organization of Employers with the International Chamber of Commerce

Marieke Louis

## 7.1 INTRODUCTION

The participation of business in the public sphere in general, and in the institutions of global governance in particular, especially in intergovernmental organizations, remains an unrelenting source of indignation, as manifested in the alter-globalist movements during the World Trade Organization (WTO) summit in Seattle in 1999 and their contemporary analogues,[1] or by today's massive demonstrations to address climate change. Yet, this phenomenon is nonetheless historically firmly anchored, normalized, and increasingly documented by academic research.[2]

There is a robust academic literature addressing these questions. On the one hand, analyses from the fields of international relations, business history, economic sociology, public policies, international political economy, international law, or political theory tend to place emphasis on the lobbying practices of the private sector, the logic of influence and power, and the capture of public interests by private commercial actors at the expense of public institutions.[3] These works resonate that much more strongly today

This chapter was translated from French by Sévrine Knuchel, thanks to the financial support of the College of France's Foundation.

[1] See for example Hélène Baillot, 'Hiérarchies militantes et pratiques de participation aux sommets annuels des institutions financières internationales: le cas de Jubilee 2000', in Delphine Lagrange, Marieke Louis and Olivier Nay (eds.), *Le tournant social de l'international: Les organisations internationales face aux sociétés civiles* (Rennes: Presses Universitaires de Rennes, 2021), pp. 127–141.

[2] Melissa J. Durkee, 'Industry Groups in International Governance: A Framework for Reform' (2023) 14(1) *Journal of Human Rights and the Environment* 4–26.

[3] The introduction to the special edition of 'Critique internationale' on transnational business actors features a literature review highlighting some works from each of these disciplines. See

when the debates on the various responsibilities of 'business' and of the capitalist system in relation to climate change are highly politicized.[4]

On the other hand, academic reflection on the democratic deficit,[5] the lack of accountability,[6] and the lack of transparency[7] of global governance institutions, as well as on the legitimacy crisis of multilateralism,[8] has inspired recommendations for the 'democratization' of global governance institutions in order to make them more legitimate. The reform proposals brought by this thirty-year-old debate are at times expressed in a 'utopian' mode symptomatic of cosmopolitan democracy, and at other times in the 'realistic' mode of stakeholders' participation.[9]

Marieke Louis and Yohann Morival, 'Au-delà de l'unité. Penser les conflits dans l'étude des acteurs économiques privés transnationaux' (2022) 97(4) *Critique internationale* 9–22. On capture, see also Melissa J. Durkee, 'Welcoming Participation, Avoiding Capture: A Five-Part Framework' (2020) 114 *Proceedings of the ASIL Annual Meeting* 39–42.

4 See for example Sarah Benabou and Birgit Müller, 'De l'autojustification du capitalisme. Les ambitions du secteur privé à Rio+20', in Jean Foyer (ed.), *Regards croisés sur Rio+20. La modernisation écologique à l'épreuve* (Paris: CNRS Éditions, 2015), pp. 163–184 and, with a more activist bent, Édouard Morena, *Fin du monde et petits fours. Les ultra-riches face à la crise climatique* (Paris: La Découverte, 2023).

5 Jens Steffek and Kristina Hahn (eds.), *Evaluating Transnational NGOs: Legitimacy, Accountability, Representation* (Basingstoke: Palgrave Macmillan 2010); Jan Aart Scholte (ed.), *Building Global Democracy? Civil Society and Accountable Global Governance* (Cambridge: Cambridge University Press, 2011); Lagrange, Louis and Nay, fn. 1.

6 Steve Charnovitz, 'Accountability of Non-governmental Organizations in Global Governance', in Lisa Jordan and Peter von Tujil (eds.), *NGO Accountability: Politics, Principles and Innovations* (London: Earthscan, 2006), pp. 21–42; Mathias Koenig-Archibugi, 'Accountability', in Jacob Katz Cogan, Ian Hurd, and Ian Johnstone (eds.), *The Oxford Handbook of International Organizations* (Oxford: Oxford University Press, 2016), pp. 1146–1169.

7 Alexandru Grigorescu, 'Transparency of Intergovernmental Organizations: The Roles of Member States, International Bureaucracies and Nongovernmental Organizations' (2007) 51(3) *International Studies Quarterly* 625–648.

8 Jonas Tallberg, Karin Bäckstrand, and Jan Aart Scholte (eds.), *Legitimacy in Global Governance: Sources, Processes, and Consequences* (Oxford: Oxford University Press, 2018); Lisa Dellmuth, Jan Aart Scholte, Jonas Tallberg, and Soetkin Verhaegen, *Citizens, Elites, and the Legitimacy of Global Governance* (Oxford: Oxford University Press, 2022).

9 Daniele Archibugi and David Held (eds.), *Cosmopolitan Democracy: An Agenda for a New World Order* (Cambridge: Polity Press, 1995); Hans Agné, Lisa Dellmuth, and Jonas Tallberg, 'Does Stakeholder Involvement Foster Democratic Legitimacy in International Organizations? An Empirical Assessment of a Normative Theory' (2015) 10 *Review of International Organizations* 465–488. This distinction between 'utopian' and 'realistic' approaches grew out of a discussion with Jens Steffek in the context of a presentation at the Marc Bloch Center in which he presented alternative approaches for reforming international institutions: the 'reactionary' approach (return to Nation-States), the 'revolutionary' approach (World State and Global Democracy) and the 'evolutionist' approach (convergence of international institutions and organized interests), see Jens Steffek, 'Technocracy and Democracy in International Governance' (Presentation at the Marc Bloch Center, delivered on 4 May 2023).

In the absence of explicit dialogue between these two segments of academic literature, the impression that emerges from their cross-reading, especially in the present context, is that of a problematic, conflicting, or even incompatible, relationship between, on the one hand, the participation of business within the institutions of global governance, and, on the other hand, the democratization of these institutions. This chapter does not seek to provide a list of the democratic objections raised against business' participation, particularly within international organizations (IOs) explicitly mandated by their statutes to advance the general interest. On that issue, readers may consult Melissa J. Durkee's chapter in this volume and, for more specific case studies related to health and food, the analyses of the relationship between the World Health Organization and pharmaceutical companies,[10] as well as between the Food and Agriculture Organization and agri-food companies.[11]

The present chapter wishes to make a socio-historical and comparative contribution to these debates, as well as to the more general reflection on the challenges faced by IOs in their relationship to democracy, and on the stakes of their democratic representativeness. It aims at contextualizing this gap between the persistent concerns about the state of democracy in IOs and the historical process of normalization of the representation of private companies by a number of established and authorized spokespersons and their active participation in global governance institutions. This contextualization will build upon a comparison between the International Chamber of Commerce (ICC) and the International Organization of Employers (IOE) in the twentieth and twenty-first centuries. For more than a century (since 1919 for the ICC and since 1920 for the IOE),[12] these two organizations have claimed to represent business, a term that they most often translate into French as *'l'entreprise'* or, more precisely, as *'l'entreprise privée'*. While both organizations claim to be representative of private companies,[13] their areas of focus differ. The IOE specializes in so-called 'social' issues,[14] including

[10] Auriane Guilbaud, *Business Partners: Firmes privées et gouvernance mondiale de la santé* (Paris: Presses de Sciences Po, 2015).

[11] Birgit Müller, *The Gloss of Harmony: The Politics of Policy-Making in Multilateral Organisations* (London: Pluto Press, 2013).

[12] Which was then called International Organization of Industrial Employers.

[13] They make a 'representative claim', in the sense described in Michael Saward, *The Representative Claim* (Oxford: Oxford University Press, 2010); Samuel Hayat and Virginie Dutoya, 'Prétendre représenter: la construction sociale de la représentation politique' (2016) 66 *Revue française de science politique* 7–25.

[14] The use of quotation marks indicates the historically constructed character of the distinction between economic and social issues, which was partly constructed by these same organizations.

employment-related issues within the International Labour Organization (ILO), and, as such, represents the employers' dimension of the representation of business. The ICC specializes, although not exclusively, in 'economic' issues related to trade and, its historical role, as a forum for arbitration of international disputes, particularly in connection with the League of Nations (LN) and the United Nations (UN). Today, the IOE introduces itself as 'a powerful and balanced voice for business', while the ICC claims to be '[t]he bold, inclusive voice of business'.[15]

This chapter does not intend to verify the accuracy of these two organizations' claims to represent the interests of business by means of a quantitative analysis of their members or their perceived legitimacy, for example. Instead, the objective is to study the actors, the ICC and the IOE, understood as institutional, established, and authorized[16] spokespersons that endorse these claims and defend the private commercial sector's interests. This chapter will also examine the processes by which these claims and the defence of these interests have developed, by outlining the contexts in which they are socially accepted (mainly in the LN, the ILO, and the UN).

Moreover, the terminology used by the ICC and IOE will serve as the starting point of our analysis, keeping in mind that using these terms (which further varied over the course of history) can be confusing in a reflection on the links between the private sector (in the sense of market institutions) and democracy, because they sometimes refer to business, company, private compan(ies), trade, or employers' organizations. The confusion seems only heightened by the fact that, while 'civil society' is an entity that is, in theory, dissociated from the market, and, in particular, from for-profit organizations,[17] it is not necessarily the case in practice within IOs, where 'civil society' rather refers to an unstable nebula of social and economic actors who may use this concept as a label for strategic purposes of legitimization and representation within international institutions. The goal of this chapter is not so much to discuss, from a normative or democratic theory perspective, the soundness or the unsoundness of these distinctions; rather, it is to analyse what these categories refer to in practice when they are used by organizations such as the ICC or the IOE.

[15] See the slogans on these organizations' respective websites, last accessed 15 May 2023.

[16] Samuel Hayat, Nicolas Kaciaf, and Cédric Passard (eds.), *Le porte-parole. Fondements et métamorphoses d'un rôle politique* (Villeneuve d'Asq: Presses Universitaires du Septentrion, 2022).

[17] Olivier Nay, 'Introduction: Le tournant social des organisations internationales: dynamiques d'ouverture et jeux de frontière', in Lagrange *et al.*, fn. 1, pp. 11–33.

Although research on international business organizations is not new,[18] it remains marginal in the constellation of works that focus either on international non-governmental organizations (and favour those issued from civil society and trade unions), or on interest groups.[19] This chapter's socio-historical perspective seeks to reveal the role of these organizations in the more global process of legitimization and normalization of the representation and participation of business in general, and 'private enterprise' in particular within global governance institutions, uncovering the different meanings of these terms. One point should be specified upfront: while representation and participation ought not to be confused, these two dimensions are intrinsically linked in the context of IOs because, most often, these organizations' representation is a precondition for their participation. If representation and participation were to be distinguished, representation would rather refer to processes of authorization, accreditation, and justification of representativeness, as discussed below, whereas participation would rather refer to advocacy and lobbying practices and the negotiation of international norms.

The use of a socio-historical perspective, together with a comparison between the IOE and the ICC – two false twin organizations in the representation of the private commercial sector – is especially interesting because it questions the now commonly admitted view that business ought to be part of global governance institutions. Moreover, it also qualifies the view according to which the 1970s and 1990s would have marked a break from the point of view of the legitimation of private companies as political actors, a break that is often swiftly assimilated to the neo-liberal turn of the 1970s and to the end of the Cold War twenty years later.[20] As is well known, the participation of the private commercial sector occurred at least concomitantly with the

[18] See for example Dominic Kelly, 'The International Chamber of Commerce' (2005) 10(2) *New Political Economy* 259–271; Claire Lemercier and Jérôme Sgard, *Arbitrage privé international et globalisation(s)* (Paris: CNRS/Sciences Po, 2015); Karsten Ronit, *Global Business Associations* (London: Routledge, 2018); Thomas David and Pierre Eichenberger, '"A World Parliament of Business"? The International Chamber of Commerce and Its Presidents in the Twentieth Century' (2023) 65(2) *Business History* 260–283; Pierre Eichenberger, Neil Rollings and Janick Marina Schaufelbuehl, 'The Brokers of Globalization: Towards a History of Business Associations in the International Arena' (2023) 65(2) *Business History* 217–234.

[19] Marieke Louis and Yohann Morival, 'Les groupes d'intérêt patronaux français et la scène internationale. XXe-XXIe siècles', in Guillaume Courty and Marc Milet (eds.), *Les groupes d'intérêt en France* (Paris: Classiques Garnier, 2023), pp. 253–278.

[20] On this point, see the work of Robert Fitzgerald who aptly demonstrates the historicity and the precedence of that question. Robert Fitzgerald, *The Rise of the Global Company. Multinationals and the Making of the Modern World* (Cambridge: Cambridge University Press, 2015).

institutionalization of IOs in the mid/end of the nineteenth century,[21] even though the modes of legitimization and the institutional forms have evolved, also thanks to a clearer distinction, in the category of non-State actors, between non-governmental organizations (NGOs), civil society, and the market.[22] As for the market, attempts to create what would eventually become the ICC and IOE in 1919 and 1920 even preceded the First World War.[23]

This chapter aims at problematizing and characterizing the links between the representation and participation of the ICC and the IOE within IOs, as well as the issue of democracy from an empirical-inductive perspective, mostly relying upon institutional documentation, archival work, semi-structured interviews, and participant-observation. The analysis identifies discussions and controversial debates at different times in these organizations' history that either squarely address the question of democratic representation, contend with it, or touch upon it, mainly through questions about the legitimacy of these organizations' representation and participation in the development of global governance. For greater clarity, we distinguish two dimensions that refer to two distinct levels of analysis: the process of institutionalization of the representation of these two international employers' organizations in IOs (Section 7.2, or external dimension); and their internal organization, particularly in their relations with their members, the way in which they select them and build a collective entity that is now referred to as 'business' (Section 7.3, or internal dimension). By doing so, we distinguish the representation *of* the ICC and the IOE *within* international organizations from the representation *of* business *within* and *by* the ICC and the IOE.

## 7.2 THE ICC AND THE IOE: DISTINCT TRACKS FOR THE REPRESENTATION OF BUSINESS IN INTERNATIONAL ORGANIZATIONS

### 7.2.1 *Building an Institutionalized Representation*

The ICC and the IOE are two international employers' organizations that took root in a common ground, the (very European) 'matrix' of the First World

[21] According to certain analyses, the creation of IOs dates back even further. See Steve Charnovitz, 'Two Centuries of Participation: NGOs and International Governance' (1997) 18(2) *Michigan Journal of International Law* 183–286.

[22] Nay, fn. 17.

[23] Pierre Eichenberger '"Employers of the World, Unite!" The International Organization of Industrial Employers (1900–1950)', in Matteo Millan and Alessandro Saluppo (eds.), *Corporate Policing, Yellow Unionism, and Strikebreaking, 1890–1930* (London: Routledge, 2021), pp. 97–114.

War.[24] They are composed of (often common) organizations and of individuals who maintain more or less close ties through international conferences and their membership in national employers' organizations and networks. Yet, the institutional positions of these two organizations are relatively distinct. While the IOE occupies a secure position, it remains largely confined to the ILO. In contrast, the ICC progressively developed (if unofficially, at first), a privileged relationship with the LN, and later with the UN but without exclusivity.

In beginning our examination of the IOE and the meaning of business representation at the ILO, it is important to keep in mind that the ILO is the only truly tripartite intergovernmental organization where governments, trade unions, and employer representatives are represented on an almost equal footing. According to constitutional and regulatory provisions, the IOE had no institutional existence at the time of the ILO's creation because the official members of the ILO are *national* employers' organizations. Much has already been written about the selection and conditions of participation of national employers' organizations at the ILO.[25] Much of the debate relates to the national representativeness of employers' organizations for participating in the International Labour Conference (ILC),[26] a condition set out in Article 3 of the ILO Constitution. At this level, the IOE does not play a decisive role, except maybe before the ILO Credentials Committee in order to challenge the representativeness of an employers' organization and prevent it from participating in the ILC and for coordinating the employers' group as a whole, to better oppose governments and trade unions.[27] It is more at the level of the ILO's restricted and executive body, the Governing Body[28] and of certain strategic committees such as the Committee on Freedom of Association that the IOE may influence the policy of the ILO. It does it successfully by controlling the composition of the employers' group at the

[24] Clotilde Druelle-Korn, 'The Great War: Matrix of the International Chamber of Commerce, a Fortunate Business League of Nations', in Andrew Smith, Simon Mollan, and Kevin D. Tennent (eds.), *The Impact of the First World War on International Business* (New York: Routledge, 2017), pp. 103–120.

[25] For a recent synthesis, see Marieke Louis, *Qu'est-ce qu'une bonne représentation? L'Organisation internationale du travail de 1919 à nos jours* (Paris: Dalloz, 2016).

[26] The ILC is the general assembly of members, a functional equivalent of the UN General Assembly.

[27] On the role of this organ, see Faina Milman Sivan, 'Labor Rights and Globalization: An Institutional Analysis of the International Labor Organization', PhD thesis, Columbia University, 2006; Éliane Vogel-Polsky, *Du tripartisme à l'Organisation internationale du travail* (Brussels: Éditions de l'institut de sociologie de l'ULB, 1966).

[28] The Governing Body would be the functional equivalent of the UN Security Council.

Governing Body (which is far more restricted than the employers' group of the ILC). Since 1948, the IOE has obtained a general consultative status. This status further formalized the role and participation of the IOE, but it is comparable, at least on paper, to that of other NGOs such as (at the time) the International Confederation of Free Trade Unions (ICFTU) now the International Confederation of Trade Unions (ITUC), or the International Cooperative Alliance to name a few. Yet, labelling the IOE as an ordinary NGO within the ILO would be misleading. In practice, and mostly because of the tripartite structure of the organization, the IOE's relations and influence exceed that of other NGOs with that same status at the ILO. The place of the IOE extends to the ILO's bureaucracy through a specific service devoted to private companies (the Bureau for Employers' Activities, ACT/EMP) with which it maintains close ties, even though ACT/EMP is not subordinated to the IOE. Within the ILO, the IOE can only truly be compared to its trade union 'counterpart', the ITUC (previously the ICFTU and before it the International Federation of Trade Unions (IFTU)). While the IOE is not mentioned as such in the ILO's Constitution, it de facto operated the secretariat and federated the Employers' group within that organization without interruption, if not without contestation, since 1920.

The institutional configuration of the ICC, which also claims to be the most representative organization of business at the international level, is quite different. As highlighted above,[29] the ICC likewise established very early on a lasting relationship both official and unofficial with the LN in order to exert influence on commercial, financial, and monetary issues. The formalization and institutionalization of this privileged relationship were strengthened in the aftermath of the Second World War, since the ICC was one of the very first NGOs to obtain general consultative status with the Economic and Social Council (ECOSOC) pursuant to Article 71 of the UN Charter. Moreover, if we move to the contemporary period, it is currently the only organization representing the private sector to have obtained, in 2016, a permanent observer status with the UNGA, following a long negotiation process that benefited from significant political support, including that of France.[30] But contrary to

[29] Druelle-Korn, fn. 24; Monika Rosengarten, *Die Internationale Handelskammer: Wirtschaftspolitische Empfehlungen in der Zeit der Weltwirtschaftskrise* 1929–1939 (Berlin: Duncker & Humblot, 2001).

[30] Auriane Guilbaud and Marieke Louis, 'L'Assemblée et la gouvernance économique et sociale. Une marginalisation inéluctable?', in Guillaume Devin, Franck Petiteville and Simon Tordjman (eds.), *L'Assemblée générale de l'ONU. Là où le monde se parle depuis 75 ans* (Paris: Presses de Sciences Po, 2020), pp. 241–261. The list of organizations with that same status in 2019 is available at: https://documents-dds-ny.un.org/doc/UNDOC/GEN//254/21/PDF/.pdf?OpenElement, last accessed 27 June 2023.

the IOE, the ICC does not control the composition of strategic organs and its influence over the negotiation process is more diffuse.

A comparative perspective reveals that the IOE and the ICC hold different positions in terms of institutional representation. To ground its position as spokesperson, the IOE can rely on the *constitutive* link that binds national employers' organizations to the ILO, a link which derives both from the constitutional texts and from its bureaucratic structure. The IOE is a kind of 'proxy member' of the ILO towards business, a role which was sanctioned a posteriori when it was granted consultative status. The ICC, however, remained outside the LN treaty system, before moving constitutionally closer to the UN, owing to its consultative status with ECOSOC and then to its observer status with the General Assembly. The ICC strived to develop, through other channels than institutionalized representation, a privileged relationship as *adviser*, rather than *negotiator* as would be the case for the IOE, vis-à-vis the UN and other organizations.

Despite its a priori more certain and secured position within the ILO, the IOE remained, in the early years of the ILO at least, very hesitant as to its ability to be a true spokesperson for the interests of business, and oscillated between functions of information and expertise, of facilitation, and of representation. It was not until the Cold War that the IOE fully endorsed its spokesperson role, especially by popularizing the idea of a group of 'free' employers[31] and the representation of the 'free enterprise', while defending itself from being a 'propaganda' or 'combat' institution.[32] The ICC, however, embraced much more quickly, as early as the interwar period and without a specific institutional basis, its role as 'spokesman for economic information in its broadest sense, and the intelligent, unofficial but effective guide to international action'[33] and 'spokesperson of the business world to the League of Nations',[34] which is in line with the 'Merchants of Peace' slogan popularized in particular by the 1938 book of George Ridgeway and constantly repeated by the ICC.[35]

[31] The term 'free' also appears in the name of its trade union counterpart, the ICFTU. Moreover, since 1961, the IOE has called its newsletter 'The Free Employer'.

[32] IOE Archives, 'Meeting of the Executive Committee' (File 1.03 Comex PV 1945–1947, doc no 371, 30 November 1945).

[33] Following the expression of the French representative to the ICC Council, de Peyerimhoff. See, ICC Archives, '17$^{e}$ session du Conseil' (Recueil Conseil March 1926–November 1928, 6 February 1925).

[34] ICC Archives, '15$^{e}$ session du Comité exécutif' (Recueil Conseil March 1926–November 1928, 16 September 1928).

[35] George Ridgeway, *Merchants of Peace. Twenty Years of Business Diplomacy through the ICC. 1919–1938* (New York: Columbia University Press, 1938).

Moreover, the IOE's a priori privileged position only applies to the ILO, despite a strategy clearly pursued by the IOE since the early 2000s to broaden its field of competence and make its relationship with the ILO 'one among others', somewhat on the model of the ICC, which also developed privileged links with the General Agreement on Tariffs and Trade (GATT) and then the WTO. Despite its openness to other organizations, the IOE is clearly struggling to expand beyond its organic relationship with the ILO. It is on that basis that the IOE believes it has legitimacy to be represented in the UN. Indeed, notwithstanding its consultative status with ECOSOC since 1948 (which it obtained two years after the ICC), the IOE does not have, like the ICC, observer status with the UNGA. In its still pending application for the same status, the IOE places particular emphasis on its link with the ILO, and highlights the support given to its application by the ILO Director-General.[36] Even in arenas relatively far from UN multilateralism and the ILO, such as the Business7 or Business20 (i.e. the employers' counterpart of the G7 and G20 summits), the IOE most often justifies its participation by highlighting its relationship with the ILO.[37] In this respect, while the ICC remains quite independent from the LN and UN system, one could discuss whether the IOE belongs to the category of 'IO-sponsored NGOs' developed in particular by the political scientist Jens Steffek in order to better characterize the interdependency between intergovernmental organizations and NGOs.[38]

### 7.2.2 *An Ambivalent Process of Cross-Legitimization*

As a counterpoint to the research on lobbying, which most often sees the relationship between business and employers interest groups as a unilateral logic of pressure exerted by the private sector on the public sector, the elements highlighted above point to a more ambivalent process of cross-legitimization between international employers' organizations and intergovernmental organizations, even if it may vary depending on the historical context. We now suggest moving to the end of the 1990s until today to show

36 UN, 'Request for the inclusion of an additional item in the agenda of the seventy-fourth session. Observer status for the International Organization of Employers in the General Assembly' (19 August 2019), A/74/291.

37 Marieke Louis, 'The ILO, the Social Partners and the G20. New Prospects for Social Dialogue at the Global Level?' (2016) 16(3) *Global Social Policy* 235–252.

38 Jens Steffek, 'Les organisations internationales et la construction politique de la société civile: le cas des "ONG parrainées"', in Lagrange *et al.*, fn. 1, pp. 55–67.

the dynamic through which intergovernmental organizations seem to welcome the participation of the business organizations.

A press conference held in 1999 in the UN at the behest of the then Secretary-General Kofi Annan offers an interesting illustration. This event was convened for the launching of what would become the Global Compact, an initiative that supports private companies in upholding principles on human rights, labour rights, and the environment. Juan Somavia, then Director-General of the ILO, highlighted the ILO's experience in cooperating with what he sometimes calls 'business', and 'the private sector', and which refers, in the case of the ILO, to national employers' organizations, to the IOE, but also to the links cultivated by ACT/EMP with companies of various natures – in the following words:

> [S]een from *an institution in which business is part of the company*, I am saying now that we are in the presence of private sectors. I believe that a greater engagement of the United Nations system as a whole is good for the United Nations and it is also good for business. One thing that I think is clear is that good values in the end are good business, and this is about how we see and how we develop that really basic notion that good values are good for business *and business is necessary for creation of employment through investment in other fields* in order to be able to bring development solutions to many countries. We just want to make sure that it is done in a way that responds to what the United Nations represents, which is basically a value institution.[39]

These words do not convey unbridled enthusiasm for business participation in the work of the ILO, but a rather pragmatic posture justified by a logical imperative (employment and development) and supported by a relatively vague reference to 'values'. They are also interesting from the point of view of the institutional logic (tactics, almost) by which the ILO sets itself up as an example, or, at least, as a forerunner and reference organization for the inclusion of non-State actors, in the present case, business. Now more than a hundred years old, the ILO continues to relentlessly draw attention to its tripartite structure and negotiating system as a key element of its legitimacy, both in terms of processes and results. As shown in a previous analysis where we define representativeness as a 'practical value',[40] the way in which the notion of representativeness is codified in legal texts but also performed by relevant actors in their capacity of delegates and representatives, does not

39 UN Secretary-General, 'Transcript of press conference by Secretary-General Kofi Annan and leadership of International Chamber of Commerce at Geneva on 5 July' (6 July 1999), UN [ST/DPI/PRESS/]SG/SM/7062/Rev.1 (emphasis added).

40 Louis, *Qu'est-ce qu'une bonne représentation?*, fn. 25.

allow for a clear delineation as to what would fall under 'input' legitimacy (legitimacy through procedures) or 'output' legitimacy (legitimacy through results).[41] The representativeness resulting from tripartism is based both on a logic of efficiency linked to the representation of the interests and forces involved, and on a democratic logic. Here, this democratic logic is essentially understood in terms of social democracy, which (among other characteristics) transposes the mechanisms of collective bargaining tested at the national level to the international level. These two logics (efficiency and democracy) make it possible to justify the presence of employers' organizations, trade unions, and governments by presenting it as both desirable (in terms of norms and values) and beneficial (in terms of results).

Yet, this difference in status and institutional positioning does not necessarily mean that the IOE has been able to exert a stronger influence at the ILO than the ICC within the LN and later the UN, nor that its relationship is always well accepted by members of these organizations. On this point, it is always interesting to come back to the 'mythology', that is, to the stories passed down by generations of employers' representatives, within these same international employers' organizations.[42] Within the IOE for instance, there is a recurring theme of the IOE's perception as the ILO's 'unloved' partner. This narrative goes back to the time when Albert Thomas, the first Director of the ILO, would have compared the organization to a train in which the unions are the engine and the employers the brake, a metaphor to which the Employers' group itself keeps referring.[43] The defensive organizational culture of the IOE, the virulence of the debates, and the recurrent crises of social dialogue (most recently with regard to the right to strike)[44] also temper the impression of harmonious cooperation, including at the level of the relations between Secretaries General and Presidents. The IOE fosters a culture of social dialogue which is made possible by a guaranteed representation and a participation on a (quasi) equal footing with States and trade union organizations, as well as by the recognition of conflicting interests. This culture of social dialogue prevails within the framework of the ILO and is framed not

[41] Fritz W. Scharpf, among others, crafted this distinction; see Fritz W. Scharpf, *Governing in Europe: Effective and Democratic?* (Oxford: Oxford University Press, 1999).

[42] See e.g. the IOE narrative as told by an original pillar of the organization, Jean-Jacques Oechslin, *L'Organisation internationale des employeurs: trois quarts de siècle au service de l'entreprise* (1920–1998) (Geneva: IOE, 2001).

[43] Ibid.

[44] See Claire La Hovary, 'The ILO's Employers' Group and the Right to Strike' (2016) 22(3) *Transfer: European Review of Labour and Research* 401–404; Julien Louis, 'La "crise" du droit de grève à l'OIT: genèse d'une mobilisation patronale transnationale' (2022) 94(1) *Critique internationale* 147–168.

only by the ILO Constitution but also by the negotiation practices that have crystallized over time.

In contrast, the ICC's relationship with the UN borrows more from the flexible channels of economic diplomacy, even though it is sustained by institutional arrangements. The ICC has participated in many UN initiatives, starting with the Global Compact in 1999–2000 or the Paris Agreement in 2015, thus developing its reputation as a responsible partner rather than an adversary. Indeed, even if the Global Compact mainly focuses on individual companies and not on international employers' organizations, it was primarily from the ICC that the then UN Secretary-General Kofi Annan sought and obtained political support, through Maria Livanos Cattaui (ICC Secretary-General) and Adnan Kassar (ICC President). This is exemplified in Adnan Kassar's declaration at the aforementioned 1999 press conference:

> The ICC business delegation appreciates the exceptional leadership, determination and vision that Secretary-General Kofi Annan has shown over the past few years in establishing the fruitful new relationship that now exists between business and the United Nations. *Today, on behalf of the private sector, we welcome his call for business to join with the United Nations in a Global Compact to promote shared values in the area of human rights, labour standards and environmental protection. Business takes up the challenge. Business, by creating wealth, makes a powerful contribution to further humanitarian values.* That contribution, through the market economy system, is immensely strengthened if accompanied by good governance, labour – neither business nor Government can do it alone. For the Global Compact to succeed all of us – Governments, the United Nations system and business – must be realistic in our expectations. Companies cannot be expected to take on responsibilities beyond their own sphere of activity that are the proper preserve of Governments.[45]

This is also exemplified in Maria Livanos Cattaui's following words:

> The starting point for Mr Annan's compact must be a clear understanding of roles. Business cannot meet demands and expectations for which governments are primarily responsible – ensuring the rule of law, universal access to education, freedom of speech, fair distribution of wealth and an adequate safety net for the old, the sick and the jobless. *What companies can do is to be good corporate citizens* in their relations with the community in which they operate and in their treatment of employees, suppliers, sub-contractors,

[45] UN Secretary-General, 'Transcript of press conference by Secretary-General Kofi Annan and leadership of International Chamber of Commerce at Geneva on 5 July', fn. 39 (emphasis added).

> customers and business associates. They can conduct their business fairly, and resist corruption. The continued spread of high corporate standards in all these areas is a powerful combination for progress towards a world which, in Mr Annan's words 'offers everyone at least a chance of prosperity, in a healthy environment'.[46]

While both insist on a strict delineation between the public and private spheres in order to avoid too many responsibilities and public interference, they began to sketch a narrative of their participation that is more compatible with democratic values and articulated around the idea that companies could be 'good citizens', in particular by doing their part in abiding by international law.

One could think that the context of the 1990s, which was marked by a generally business friendly atmosphere offers an explanation for these statements. However, this was only the beginning of a more deeply rooted trend. For instance, twenty years later, in 2019, in a context already much more critical of business and multinational corporations, we could hear a political figure like Laurent Fabius, in his capacity as former Minister of Foreign Affairs of France, declare on the occasion of the Centenary of the ICC: '[I] hope that ICC will use all its authority to convince governments … *obviously you are realistic men and women because you are in business*, interested in short term issues but you never forget long term issues … *I appreciate very much the way you tackle problems: realistic, humanistic, with your heart.*'[47]

This brief comparison of the IOE and the ICC in their relationships with the ILO, the LN, and the UN, reveals, first of all, the different trajectories taken by the institutionalization of the representation of business. Such a finding resists a homogenizing view on the channels of influence of the private sector on the public sphere. This comparison further highlights a movement of interdependence and cross-legitimization between international and intergovernmental employers' organizations based on arguments that sometimes draw on a form of pragmatism very close to the functionalist reading grid,[48] sometimes in a (neo)corporatist culture of social dialogue, sometimes in a more classically liberal register of the necessity and desirability of a pluralist representation of interests. As a result, this process of cross-

46 Maria Livanos Cattaui, 'Letters to the Editor: Making Companies Good Citizens', *Financial Times*, 24 March 1999 (emphasis added).

47 ICC Centenary, 'Fieldnotes' (May 2019) (emphasis added).

48 On the similarities between functionalist theory and pragmatism, see Marieke Louis and Lucile Maertens, *Why International Organizations Hate Politics: Depoliticizing the World* (London: Routledge, 2021), Chapter 4.

legitimization must be described as ambivalent, because it does not pursue the same type of purposes or rest on the same foundations.

The third part of this contribution now leaves the analysis of the relationship between the IOE and the ICC and intergovernmental organizations and moves to a closer examination of their internal organization and the way they deal with the issue of representativeness.

## 7.3 WHEN THE ICC AND THE IOE CONFRONT THEIR REPRESENTATIVE CLAIMS

### 7.3.1 *The Political Limits of a 'Universal' Representation*

Accessing the documents governing the internal organization of employers' organizations is undoubtedly more difficult than accessing those of trade unions and NGOs. Yet, a journey through the archives of the IOE and the ICC evidences a concern to codify the rules of representation and the statutes of the organization, ranging from the admission criteria for membership to the rules governing the delegation of the authority to speak to the international employers' organization on behalf of private companies, but also to exchanges on the evolution of the political context. Without necessarily interpreting these discussions as signs of a democratic vitality on the part of the ICC and the IOE, they show, at the very least, a concern for demonstrating their representativeness, as a way to ground their legitimacy and safeguard their authority in representing a rather heterogeneous collective, in a twofold concern for inter-*sectoral* and inter-*national* universality.

As explained in the first part of this contribution, whereas the ICC seems to quickly embrace the role of 'spokesperson' or even 'parliament' of the business world,[49] the first years of the IOE were marked by its initial difficulty in assuming a representative function and speaking on behalf of a collective. This is especially visible when the IOE urges to respect the voting autonomy of its members, but also in its emphasis on the diversity of national contexts, as well as in vivid discussions about the possibility, for a member of the IOE or the employers' group at the ILO, to speak on behalf of a wider collective. As for the ICC, while this consideration for the autonomy of the members is more likely driven by considerations of institutional survival – aimed above all at not alienating the support of large employers' organizations which pay larger contributions – rather than by a concern for internal democracy, there remains a certain attachment to issues of procedure and authority delegation,

49 David and Eichenberger, fn. 18.

most often aimed at preserving this autonomy. Both the IOE and the ICC are searching for a compromise that is classically sought by any IO, governmental or not: a compromise between the affirmation of their role as representative institutions with their own voice, and the recognition of the autonomy of their members. This quest leads them to constantly insist on the diversity and heterogeneity of the collective they represent.

With regard to the selection of their members, the common choice made by the IOE and the ICC to represent the entire private sector[50] results in a preference given to 'umbrella organizations' or 'peak organizations', as opposed to sectoral professional associations. Although the IOE has long been more restrictive than the ICC by only accepting employers' organizations and not individual companies (this restriction has been loosened since the 2010s) and insisting on the need for a single interlocutor per State,[51] the two international employers' organizations share a concern for geographical representativeness on a national basis (by country), while also encouraging regional groupings. They both ground part of their legitimacy on their ability to 'universalize' representation and speak on behalf of the 'greatest number'. This concern to *increase the number* of their members, whether employers' organizations in the case of the IOE, or national committees in the case of the ICC, manifests itself at different key moments in the history of these two organizations, which more or less overlap (creation phase, Second World War which caused the loss of many members, decolonization, end of the Cold War), but towards which they will at times adopt different attitudes. This is again where distinct trajectories are observable in the representation of business.

While the ICC places greater emphasis on the number and the diversity of the companies it represents, the IOE mostly insists on the number of States in which it has members (i.e. employers' organizations), and even more on the fact that its members come from States in which employers' organizations are *independent from public authorities*. Without necessarily raising the argument of democratic representation, the condition of representativeness in the sense of the independence and autonomy of employers' organizations from State authorities, is a more decisive criterion for admission within the IOE than the ICC. The 'borderline' case of communist countries, of which both the IOE and the ICC are, unsurprisingly, open adversaries, offers an illustration which

50 See the ambitious slogans quoted in the introduction of this chapter.

51 There are, until today, some exceptions to that principle, as exemplified by India (three employers' associations), Morocco, China (because of Taïwan), etc. See IOE, 'Annual Report 2022–2023' (2023). www.ioe-emp.org/index.php?eID=dumpFile&t=f&f=159166&token=24e538126778a663613015dca1e3ae6824a3feb7, last accessed 31 May 2023.

can be studied from the interwar period until (at least) the end of the Cold War and even afterwards. The relationships between the IOE and the ICC and Soviet and then Russian organizations and companies are generally non-existent until the end of the 1990s. The rejection was more pronounced on the side of the IOE which spearheaded the fight against communist 'employers', to whom it denied any representativeness. The treatment of China, however, is slightly different. As for the IOE, there was no question, until the end of the 1990s, of making room for Chinese representatives within the IOE and the ILO Governing Body (see Section 7.1).[52] Infringements of the principle of freedom of association and suspicions about the lack of independence of employers' organizations continue to be considered as obstacles, if not fully prohibitive impediments, to the genuine integration of Chinese organizations into the IOE for instance. No Chinese national holds a leadership position within the IOE's internal structures or in the employers' group of the ILO Governing Body. To this day, the Chinese delegate in the ILO Governing Body only has a deputy member status and plays a rather marginal role in the employers' group dynamic.[53]

Quite to the contrary, as early as the interwar period, the ICC adopted a much more depoliticized and open attitude towards China, prompted by the need to maintain links with Chinese trading circles and the observation of China's dynamic trade and development.

In 1995, the ICC publicly supported China's (and Russia's) accession to the newly created WTO pointing to the supposed benefits of socialization into multilateral institutions and to the gradual normalization of these countries in the economic and commercial system. ICC Secretary-General Maria Cattaui then declared: 'ICC wants to deliver a very important message that as Asia – especially China – develops, there is a growing need for Asian economies to be integrated into the rule-based, multilateral system for international business transactions'.[54] Moreover, the ICC includes a large number of Chinese chambers and organizations among its members,[55] and among its most senior

[52] In the accessible minutes of the IOE Management Board, there are traces of the first steps towards rapprochement beginning in 1999 and continuing through subsequent exchanges with Chinese employers' organizations and the formalization of the accession of the China Enterprise Confederation (CEC). This reconciliation is nevertheless complicated by the presence of the Taiwanese organization and the non-payment by the CEC of its contributions.

[53] On the different status of titular and deputy members, see Louis, *Qu'est-ce qu'une bonne représentation*, fn. 25.

[54] Lu Hongyong, 'Trade official optimistic about China's WTO Bid', *China Daily*, 9 April 1997.

[55] ICC, 'List of the World Chambers Federation members as of March 2023'. https://iccwbo.org/wp-content/uploads/sites/3/2023/03/Final-list-of-Chambers-2.pdf, last accessed 31 May 2023.

representatives (presidents and secretaries-general) are many individuals who have developed privileged interests and connections with Chinese companies.

This type of borderline case highlights the two different conceptions of representativeness of the IOE and the ICC. The IOE seems to rely more on a neo-corporatist paradigm, grounded in the recognition of the autonomy of interest groups as a prerequisite for the institutionalization of negotiations and any form of democratization. In contrast, the ICC seems to follow a liberal paradigm of 'gentle commerce' ('*doux commerce*'), which bets on the democratization resulting from the development of trade and liberalization, in line with its historical slogan of 'Merchants of Peace' mentioned above. Such a slogan allows it to display a posture apparently less political and restrictive than the IOE in its relationships with its members.

### 7.3.2 *The 'Diversity' Argument in Light of the Growing Importance of Multinational Companies*

This last section addresses the dilemmas raised by the growing place of multinational corporations in the public debate. It examines how the IOE and the ICC have tried to reconcile their claim of representation of all companies with the need to intervene in the specific field of regulation of multinational corporations to defend their interests. Since the 1970s, when the debates on the regulation of multinational corporations became increasingly politicized[56] and the number of arenas and forums speaking in the name of business like the Davos Forum multiplied, the question of members' representativeness and of the type of companies represented (multinational or not) became more and more pressing. In order to understand the place of multinational corporations in the organizational structures of the IOE and the ICC, it is necessary to review their respective membership admissions procedures.

As mentioned above, the IOE's statutes have long reserved membership to employers' organizations (with a preference for a single interlocutor per State), whereas the ICC established a system of national committees which oversee multiple entities and to which companies can adhere directly. In the case of the ICC, employers' organizations, chambers of commerce, and businesses are also eligible for membership status, and the ICC tries to federate them

[56] Samuel Beroud and Thomas Hajduk, 'L'OCDE et les bonnes pratiques. Une histoire inséparable', in Camille Laporte, Asmara Klein, and Marie Saiget (eds.), *Les bonnes pratiques des organisations internationales* (Paris: Presses de Sciences Po, 2015), pp. 61–77; Marieke Louis, 'La diplomatie sociale des multinationales', in Christian Chavagneux and Marieke Louis (eds.), *Le pouvoir des multinationales* (Paris: Presses Universitaires de France/ Vie des idées, 2018), pp. 79–93.

through its national committees. In the case of IOE, the national member is the employers' organization (in principle the largest organization, even if this is not systematic),[57] which results in the indirect representation of companies, including those that are multinational. In addition, the ICC brings to the fore at the level of its presidency the *leaders* of large companies, including multinational corporations; for a long time, this was not the case at the IOE, where preference is given sometimes to leaders, sometimes to 'permanent employers', thus making the presence of multinational corporations within this organization even less visible.

In addition, the architecture of the ICC tends to layer on levels of representation by adding new structures such as the World Chambers Federation which was created in 1951 and currently claims to convene some 12,000 chambers of commerce.[58]

As a result, the ICC at least seems to benefit from a kind of a 'critical mass' effect, from a diversity of companies, and from an institutional flexibility that seems to be greater than the IOE. Because of its network structure, the ICC has a varying membership which should be analysed in greater depth, but such an analysis goes beyond the scope of this chapter. According to a report on its relationship with the UN, the ICC represented, in 2015, 6.5 million companies in more than 130 countries.[59] In 2023, the ICC claims in the membership section of its website to be bringing together more than forty-five million companies from more than 170 countries 'ranging from the world's largest companies, to SMEs, business associations, banks, law firms and local chambers of commerce'.[60] Again in 2023, the World Chambers Federation section of the ICC's website claims that the ICC has members in 116 countries/territories.[61] The IOE, which also claims to be 'the largest network of the private sector in the world', lists 150 employers'

57 In France, the UIMM, and not the CNPF (today, the Medef), was the reference interlocutor to the IOE and the ILO until the 1970s. See Louis and Morival, fn 19.

58 Ronit, fn. 18, pp. 36–37. While the World Chambers Federation is formally independent of the ICC, it remains one of its emanations.

59 ICC, 'The United Nations and the World Business Organization, A Partnership for People, Planet and Prosperity' (24 October 2016). https://iccwbo.org/news-publications/news/icc-and-the-un-a-partnership-for-people-planet-and-prosperity/, last accessed 31 May 2023.

60 ICC, 'Become a member'. https://iccwbo.org/become-a-member/#:~:text=Companies%2C%20banks%2C%20law%20firms%2C,the%20international%20and%20national%20level, last accessed 31 May 2023.

61 ICC, 'Our members'. https://iccwbo.org/world-chambers-federation/our-members/#:~:text=Our%20members%20are%20in%20116,of%20ICC%20World%20Chambers%20Federation, last accessed 31 May 2023.

organizations,[62] representing fifty million companies worldwide,[63] in about 140 States and territories.[64]

Yet, these competing claims of representativeness result in different strategies of positioning and justification on the question of multinational corporations. The ICC defends the idea according to which the organization, while directly including multinational corporations and powerful actors from the international trade among its members, also represents small and medium-sized enterprises, regardless of their degree of integration into the world market. Hence the emphasis placed on national committees, which are (in principle) a privileged liaison body with the local companies:

> I would like to clarify one point which is the prevailing idea about ICC that it is composed only of the very important multinationals and that we, in the ICC, are just taking care of these multinationals. This is not true. The ICC is representing business and in business, there are plenty of middle and small-sized enterprises. We are represented in 137 countries and most of these countries are developing countries. For instance, I come from a very small country, from Lebanon, and I have been elected as President of the ICC. This shows that we are concerned with the business in general, and the marriage with the United Nations according to us, coming from a small country, will yield good benefits.[65] (Adnan Kassar, ICC President)

The IOE resorts to the same type of arguments, especially when it finds itself caught up in debates on the regulation of multinational corporations. It is also because of the intense lobbying exercised by the IOE during the negotiations on the 1977 ILO Tripartite Declaration of Principles concerning Multinational Enterprises and Social Policy that the definition of a multinational enterprise adopted in that Declaration is so broad.[66] However, the IOE is subject, especially within the ILO, to a different criticism

62 IOE, 'Annual Report 2022–2023', fn. 51.

63 IOE, 'World business community launches IOE Manifesto' (2 September 2020). https://www.ioe-emp.org/news/details/world-business-community-launches-ioe-manifesto, last accessed 31 May 2023.

64 This figure is not officially given by the IOE but calculated based on the list of its members since its last annual report.

65 UN Secretary-General, 'Transcript of press conference by Secretary-General Kofi Annan and leadership of International Chamber of Commerce at Geneva on 5 July', fn. 39.

66 According to para. 6 of the Declaration, 'Multinational enterprises include enterprises – whether fully or partially state-owned or privately owned – which own or control production, distribution, services or other facilities outside the country in which they are based. They may be large or small; and can have their headquarters in any part of the world. The degree of autonomy of entities within multinational enterprises in relation to each other varies widely from one such enterprise to another, depending on the nature of the links between such entities and their fields of activity and having regard to the great diversity in the form of

than the ICC. Indeed, the employers' group and the IOE are regularly accused by trade unions and other civil society NGOs of not being representative of any companies, multinational or not. This criticism points to the 'lawyers',[67] working for the law firms defending the employers' interests, to the employer civil servants or to the 'permanent employers' who hold the main representative functions within the Employers' group and the IOE. Although this criticism is only partially justified and is part of the much broader phenomenon of bureaucratization of professional representation and the NGO world,[68] it is worth noticing that, in 2008, the IOE decided to make explicit room for multinational corporations within the framework of specific mechanisms such as the Global Industrial Relations Network (GIRN). The GIRN aims to offer a small group of multinational corporations, in exchange for a specific fee, a space for confidential discussion on the problems they encounter in terms of labour law, as well as information and advice on existing international regulations pertaining to social matters.

In a context where the representation of business is becoming increasingly competitive, and where debates are becoming politicized – whether about the responsibility of multinational corporations or the issue of conflicts of interest, as exemplified by the progressive exclusion of the tobacco sector from the UN public-private partnerships or the negotiation since 2014 of a UN treaty to regulate the activities of transnational corporations – the question of the representativeness of organizations such as the ICC and the IOE is no longer only an issue of internal legitimacy, that is, vis-à-vis their members, but also, of external legitimacy, that is, vis-à-vis their trade union interlocutors and civil society, as well as the IOs in which they have institutionalized and established their representation.

## 7.4 CONCLUSION

To conclude, this comparative analysis of the representation and participation in IOs of the ICC and the IOE as spokespersons for business has shown that

ownership, in the size, in the nature and location of the operations of the enterprises concerned. Unless otherwise specified, the term "multinational enterprise" is used in this Declaration to designate the various entities (parent companies or local entities or both or the organization as a whole) according to the distribution of responsibilities among them, in the expectation that they will cooperate and provide assistance to one another as necessary to facilitate observance of the principles laid down in this Declaration'.

67 Louis, 'La "crise" du droit de grève à l'OIT', fn. 44.

68 On the bureaucratization of NGOs, see for example Kerstin Martens, *NGOs and the United Nations: Institutionalization, Professionalization and Adaptation* (Basingstoke: Palgrave Macmillan, 2005).

questions and tensions have not so much focused on the legitimacy of such representation as on its modalities, confirming the argument of a 'non-problematic'[69] participation of business in the institutions of global governance. The absence of representation has never really been envisioned and representation has not been the subject of any particular dilemma, since these two organizations were created for the very purpose of representing the interests of private companies within IOs and accepted as such by the latter. However what must result from, this representation, is a more open question. But whether this place has been reserved and guaranteed for them (as for the IOE at the ILO), or whether it has been achieved through the establishment and maintenance of diplomatic relations (as for ICC with the UN), the representation and participation of private companies through these two organizations has not been fundamentally questioned.

Criticism against the place of the private sector addressed by the current protest movement, which is undoubtedly more pressing in the context of the climate crisis and in the aftermath of the 2008 financial crisis, raises the issue of whether to challenge this historical process of normalization of relations between the private and the public sectors at the international level. Because this debate seems formulated with reference to democratic concerns (denunciation of conflicts of interest, strengthening of the general interest), the question also arises of what 'defence' strategy organizations such as the ICC and the IOE can adopt if they want to stick to a democratic mode of legitimization. A first strategy precisely consists of reverting to this historical dynamic of convergence, based on the institutionalization of the relations between the private and the public, their codification in texts or in diplomatic practices. Another strategy is to question the legitimacy of their opponents, for example by denying their representativeness and highlighting the fundamental principles of their own.

For instance, in 2000, ICC Secretary-General Maria Livanos Cattaui spoke in response to the mobilizations of civil society, aiming to deny any representative legitimacy to these movements and accusing them of running counter to 'true' democratic processes:

> It is quite natural that people flail out. But there's a tendency when you're flailing out and looking for a cause to say, I represent the world. And that is simply not true. Nobody voted for these protesters. We have to be very careful to listen and understand the causes for uncertainty. But we must also understand that this cannot undermine proper democratic processes. When I go around the world and I see developing countries, there is only one thing they

[69] Durkee, 'Industry Groups in International Governance', fn. 2.

> want and that is to be more a part of this world, to be more integrated into the economy, have better access to our markets, to our knowledge and to our technology. The last thing they want is to stop the world and get off.[70]

The IOE uses the same rhetoric, but less so in its relations with trade unions, which it considers to be negotiating partners, than with NGOs.[71]

If the two organizations now share this assumed position of representative spokesperson of business[72] by taking part in the creation of international norms and taking on a historical function of 'responsible partner', the socio-historical perspective allows us to see a less linear process, or, at least, a less obvious and more differentiated one than it may seem. The institutionalization of the relations between the ICC and the IOE and intergovernmental organizations, as well as their positioning as spokespersons for business at the international level, occurs without the democratic question being central in the discussions, but with a constant concern to secure their place and legitimize their representative claims that can lead them to reveal, or even to take on, positions that are more political than they may initially appear. Finally, it is unclear that this strategy, which is essentially based on the demonstration of external and internal representativeness, will achieve its goal of defending against the claims of lack of legitimacy that seem to currently face business organizations.

70 Clive Mathieson, 'Tireless evangelist spreads the gospel of globalization – Analysis – Maria Livanos Cattaui', *The Times*, 21 April 2000.

71 Louis, *Qu'est-ce qu'une bonne représentation?*, fn. 25.

72 At times, they are competing for it, but this is another issue.

# 8

# The Ambivalent Logics of Business Representation in International Organizations

Melissa J. Durkee

## 8.1 INTRODUCTION

This chapter considers how for-profit actors participate in the work of international organizations (IOs), and how this relates to democratic representation in and through those organizations. Specifically, I want to focus attention on *perspectives* on inclusion of these for-profit actors in the work of IOs. What are the rationalities that animate movements to include or exclude business entities and groups, which in turn produce regulatory and institutional design choices?

By 'for-profit actors', I mean non-State actors that are business organizations, such as corporations and other business entities. I am also focusing on groups that represent business interests, such as industry and trade associations. While those industry and trade associations are usually formally organized as non-profit entities, I am grouping them together with for-profit actors because they participate in international governance fora for the purpose of advancing the agendas of the business sector[1] – for shorthand, I will also refer to both for-profit entities and their non-profit representatives as 'business'. Together, these various business actors interact with IOs to advance and represent a particular kind of interest: investor profits.

The animating question of this chapter is thus whether those who advance the profit interests of investors should participate in the work of international

[1] Incidentally, because trade and industry associations are usually organized as non-profit entities, they formally fall within the larger umbrella of non-governmental organizations (NGOs) for the purposes of many IO access rules, and thus gain access on equal terms with groups advancing other missions. Melissa J. Durkee, 'Industry Lobbying and "Interest Blind" Access Norms at International Organizations' (2017) 111 *American Journal of International Law Unbound* 119–124. For the purposes of this chapter, I am carving out the subset of NGOs that represent for-profit actors and considering them as a unified group with the for-profit businesses they represent.

governance. The question is live because for-profit actors and their representatives now take very significant roles in many aspects of global governance, serving as commentators, consultants, funders, partners, stakeholders, experts, delegates, and lobbyists, as well as rule generators, interpreters, and enforcers. To a large extent, IOs have not developed regulatory frameworks or whole-of-organization approaches to these forms of engagement by for-profit actors and their representatives, though there are some outliers.[2] The regulatory gap flows in part from a legal gap, as business groups have no formal legal status under international law, unlike States, IOs, and, nascently, civil society. Somewhere between the regulatory gap and the legal status gap lies a conceptual gap: scholars and organizations have not yet developed adequate frameworks to conceptualize how for-profit representatives should participate in international governance or what the ideal form of this participation should be.

So now the question is framed: should for-profit actors and their representatives participate in the work of IOs, and if so on what terms? Rather than addressing that question in a normative sense, this chapter offers a conceptual scaffold for it. Specifically, my claim is that it is possible to elicit answers to this question in the ways that IOs have welcomed or excluded a broader range of non-State actors over time. These answers reveal an ambivalence that centres on the *value* of representation versus other agendas. That is, there are two basic logics animating the ways that IOs organize themselves with respect to for-profit actors and their representatives.[3] One of these is a status-based logic, and the other is functional. Let us call the first a logic of 'representation', and the second a logic of 'expedience'.

The logic of *representation* is concerned with participation, processes, and participants. Concerns about representation prompt a certain set of questions about for-profit participation in the work of IOs. For example, is for-profit participation balanced with the participation of other groups or is the presence of for-profit groups (e.g. trade lobbyists) preventing, outweighing, or drowning out other interests that should be represented (e.g. labour, environment, health, or other groups)? Are the for-profit representatives speaking for the relevant interests or groups in a particular process?

[2] OECD, *Compendium of International Organisations' Practices: Working Towards More Effective International Instruments* (Paris: OECD Publishing, 2021); see also Ayelet Berman, 'Between Participation and Capture in International Rule-Making: The WHO Framework of Engagement with Non-State Actors' (2021) 32(1) *European Journal of International Law* 227–254, at 228 (noting the regulatory gap).

[3] It is also likely true that for-profit groups may organize their relationships with IOs according to these two logics, justifying their participation according to one or the other. While this analysis is beyond the scope of this brief chapter, the reader may consider Louis' Chapter 7 in this volume as a starting point for the inquiry.

The logic of *expedience* is concerned with effectiveness. Concerns about expedience prompts a separate set of questions about for-profit participation in the work of IOs. Does for-profit participation improve or harm an organization's achievement of its agenda? Can for-profit groups offer useful things, like resources, knowledge, technical expertise, or domestic political support?

The logics of representation and expedience are not mutually exclusive. That is, I am not arguing that one logic does not value expedience or the other does not value representation. Rather, these labels are meant to highlight the emphases, or most core values, of each logic. These organizing logics have different priorities, agendas, blind spots, and potential consequences. Moreover, conversations about institutional design tend to focus on one or the other. The two logics can operate like parallel sliding doors, moving past each other without being in conversation.

Each logic has come to prominence at different moments during the last century of public-private relationships in international governance. Now, debates about the proper role of for-profit actors in governance are fuelled by these competing rationalities, and both narratives are intensifying in parallel as crises like climate change ratchet up demands on the international system. Conceiving of a way forward should involve bringing these narratives to the surface so they may be reconciled or the choice among them rendered explicit.

In this contribution I will proceed through three steps. First, I will outline the state of play in terms of public-private interactions in IOs, offering a taxonomy of some of the many roles for-profit actors now take (Section 8.2). The discussion focuses on the United Nations (UN). I will then introduce the two logics, illustrating them with a vignette about responses to for-profit participation in conferences of the parties (COP) of the United Nations Framework Convention on Climate Change (UNFCCC) (Section 8.3). Finally, I will illustrate the push and pull of these logics through several important moments in the history of engagement between UN entities and for-profit actors (Section 8.4).

## 8.2 PARTICIPATION OF PRIVATE ACTORS: THE STATE OF PLAY

First, let us frame the importance of this debate by considering the very significant roles business actors and groups now take in the work of IOs. There is nothing new about links between the public and private sectors at the international level. The International Chamber of Commerce (ICC), for example, has sought to counsel UN entities since the founding of that organization, and had significant roles in the earlier League of Nations system.[4] Since the turn of the twenty-first century, however, there has been a very significant 'opening up' of the UN to collaborations of many kinds with the private sector, including business.[5] For-profit actors and representatives are so embedded in many forms of IO governance, and so significant to some of them, that it is not possible to consider questions of democratic representation in and through IOs without evaluating that representation in context of these business roles.

This 'opening up' is reflected in the Sustainable Development Goals and the Global Compact, which heavily emphasize public-private partnerships, as well as a whole array of other modes of interaction.[6] Many organizations are 'updating their strategies and work programmes to collaborate through partnerships' with business groups.[7] Ayelet Berman describes this trend as a transformative move that 'spans all issue areas, policy functions, and world regions' and that is gaining momentum.[8] Projects celebrate synergies between the private sector's need for stable market conditions and the UN's peace imperative, which in the post–Cold War context has prompted the organization's attention to human rights and development.[9]

What follows is an array of examples of ways business groups now engage with IOs.[10] Because a complete account is beyond the scope of this chapter, the taxonomy is meant to be illustrative rather than comprehensive.

*Consultants and Observers.* Business entities and representatives serve as consultants and observers within IOs, often on the same terms as civil society organizations. For example, the Economic and Social Council (ECOSOC) non-governmental organization (NGO) accreditation procedure excludes for-profit entities (such as individual businesses) but accepts non-profit *representatives* of

4 Steve Charnovitz, 'Two Centuries of Participation: NGOs and International Governance' (1997) 18(2) *Michigan Journal of International Law* 183–286, at 223. See Louis, Chapter 7 in this volume.

5 George Kell, 'Relations with the Private Sector', in Jacob Katz Cogan, Ian Hurd and Ian Johnstone (eds.), *The Oxford Handbook on International Organizations* (Oxford: Oxford University Press, 2016) pp. 730–754, pp. 730, 743.

6 See e.g. UN, 'Transforming our World: the 2030 Agenda for Sustainable Development' (2015). https://sustainabledevelopment.un.org/post2015/transformingourworld, last accessed 31 May 2023.

7 Berman, fn. 2, at 3.

8 Ibid., at 228.

9 Kell, fn. 5.

10 I am using 'international organizations' capaciously to include IOs in the legal sense (including treaty-based organizations governed by international law and possessing legal personality) as well as other intergovernmental forums without separate legal personality but that engage in rulemaking, such as UNCITRAL and the UNFCCC COP process.

for-profit entities.[11] Since many trade and industry associations are organized as non-profit entities, they can become accredited consultants alongside other kinds of civil society organizations.[12] Approximately ten per cent of accredited groups are organized to advance business agendas.[13] Among these are representatives of multinational oil and gas companies, financial services, construction, lumber, automotive industries, railways, nuclear power, and coal.[14] Accreditation gives groups a variety of rights of access to the work of the UN, including access to agendas and working documents, grounds passes that give consultants access to delegates for informal lobbying, and sometimes the right to circulate information, speak from the floor in a proceeding, or raise an agenda item.[15]

Business representation among consultants and observers is significant enough that a number of organizations have developed separate tracks or pathways for these groups. Among these are the Food and Agriculture Organization (FAO), the World Health Organization (WHO), and the UNFCCC's COP process. The first two organizations have divided business groups from other civil society groups in order to protect the organization against capture or undue influence from those with profit motives.[16] Thus, these organizations have implemented more restrictive working methods for groups that have private sector links than for other groups. The UNFCCC COP process has not separated the groups to modulate levels of access for each but to streamline communication to and within the groups.[17]

[11] For descriptions of ECOSOC regulations codifying privileges and practices relating to NGOs, see Stephen Hobe, 'Article 71', in Bruno Simma, Hermann Mosler, Andreas Paulus, and Eleni Chaitidou (eds.), *The Charter of the United Nations: A Commentary*, 3rd ed., Vol. 2 (Oxford: Oxford University Press, 2012), pp. 1788–1815, pp. 1788, 1797.

[12] Melissa J. Durkee, 'Astroturf Activism' (2017) 69 *Stanford Law Review* 201–268.

[13] UN, 'Advanced Search for Civil Society Organizations, United Nationals Department of Social and Economic Affairs'. https://esango.un.org/civilsociety/displayAdvancedSearch.do?method=search&%20%20sessionCheck=false, last accessed 19 May 2023.

[14] Ibid.; see also Melissa J. Durkee, 'International Lobbying Law' (2018) 127 *Yale Law Journal* 1742–2203, at 1768–1769.

[15] See the UN Office at Geneva, 'Accreditation with the United Nations Office at Geneva (UNOG)'. www.ungeneva.org/en/faq/52, last accessed 31 May 2023; see ECOSOC Res. 1996/31, 'Consultative relationship between the United Nations and non-governmental organizations' (25 July 1996); see generally Kal Raustiala, 'NGOs in International Treaty-Making', in Duncan B. Hollis (ed.), *The Oxford Guide to Treaties*, 1st ed. (Oxford: Oxford University Press, 2012), pp. 173–199.

[16] WHO, 'Framework of Engagement with Non-state Actors' (28 May 2016), WHA69.10. https://apps.who.int/gb/ebwha/pdf_files/wha69/a69_r10-en.pdf, last accessed 31 May 2023; FAO, *Principles and Guidelines for FAO Cooperation with the Private Sector* (Rome: FAO, 2016). www.fao.org/3/a-x2215e.pdf, last accessed 31 May 2023.

[17] Stephen Tully, 'Commercial Contributions to the Climate Change Regime: Who's Regulating Whom?' (2005) 5(2) *Sustainable Development & Law Policy* 14–27, at 16.

*Delegates.* A second way business groups can engage in the work of IOs is through participating on a State delegation to an IO. This can be a somewhat invisible mode of participation as States are often not required to disclose the composition of their delegation. For example, a recent study of the International Maritime Organization (IMO) revealed that many delegations were staffed by industry representatives.[18] The report found that national delegations 'can have a mixture of government officials and industry representatives, with no established norm on composition'.[19] Indeed, the authors noted that many national delegations featured representatives of the shipping industry.[20] This representation supplements the shipping industry's official representation, which is through industry associations (NGOs) with observer status.[21]

*Participants in Multi-Stakeholder Institutions.* Private sector actors participate in multi-stakeholder organizations. The most prominent example here is the International Labour Organization (ILO), which features a tripartite governance structure including representatives of employers, labour, and States.[22] The ILO's founding predated the UN and this tripartite structure was not replicated when the UN system was developed.[23] Nevertheless, in the late twentieth and early twenty-first centuries, the UN began to establish new multi-stakeholder projects that also welcomed business groups as robust participants. The GAVI Alliance (founded by the Gates Foundation), and the Global Fund to Fight AIDS, Tuberculosis and Malaria are more recent examples of multi-stakeholder partnerships.[24]

*Funders and Sponsors.* Private sector actors fund the work of IOs. As Kristina Daugirdas has noted, voluntary contributions make up an increasingly large share of organizations' budgets, and private actors are increasingly significant contributors under this umbrella.[25] This includes landmark donations, such as the Bill & Melinda Gates Foundation's sponsorship of the WHO, as well as more pedestrian fundraising projects, like the 7.28 million the IMO's

[18] Harilaos N. Psaraftis and Christos A. Kontovas, 'Influence and Transparency at the IMO: The Name of the Game' (2020) 22 *Maritime Economics & Logistics* 151–172.

[19] Ibid., at 159.

[20] Ibid., at 159–160.

[21] Ibid., at 160.

[22] ILO, 'Structure' (2023). http://ilo.org/global/about-the-ilo/who-we-are, last accessed 19 May 2023.

[23] ILO, 'History of the ILO' (2023). http://ilo.org/global/about-the-ilo/history, last accessed 19 May 2023.

[24] See generally Kenneth W. Abbott and David Gartner, 'Reimagining Participation in International Institutions' (2012) 8 *Journal of International Law and International Relations* 1–35.

[25] Kristina Daugirdas, 'Funding Global Governance' (2021) 29(3) *NYU Environmental Law Journal* 639–658, at 641–642.

Department of Partnerships and Projects mobilized in 2021.[26] Daugirdas has observed that voluntary contributions make up more than eighty per cent of the WHO's funding and more than ninety-seven per cent of the funding of the International Organization for Migration (IOM).[27] The UN frequently issues 'calls for participation and assistance' to elicit support from philanthropic foundations.[28] These contributions affect IOs' governance choices as they often come with conditions and earmarks.[29]

*Other Forms of Partnership*. In addition to the four general categories of participation by business actors and their representatives outlined above (observers, delegates, participants, and funders), business actors engage in a variety of other forms of partnership, support, and engagement with IOs, sometimes in conjunction with one of the other categories. These can take many forms. For example, the United Nation's Children Fund (UNICEF) has developed 'strategic public-private partnerships to move populations up the sanitation ladder', such as a partnerships with Lixil, a global sanitation products company, which 'aims to increase the availability of affordable sanitation products and services'.[30] Microsoft launched a 'United Nations representation office' in New York, with an aim to engage in 'multi-stakeholder action', particularly 'enabling the UN and its agencies to achieve more using computer and data science'.[31] The Boeing- and Airbus-created Aviation Working Group developed a treaty on aviation equipment financing, which was ultimately taken up and finalized by UNIDROIT.[32] UN Women established a Private Sector Leadership Advisory Council, which invites business leaders, including chief executives of The Coca-Cola Company, L'Oréal, Goldman Sachs, Unilever, and others, to offer periodic strategic input.[33] Other multi-stakeholder efforts that include the

[26] IMO, 'Financial Report and Audited Financial Statements for the Year Ended 31 December 2021: Report of the External Auditors' (2021). https://wwwcdn.imo.org/localresources/en/OurWork/Documents/Financial%20Statements/IMO%20Financial%20Statements%202021.pdf, last accessed 31 May 2023.

[27] Daugirdas, fn. 25, at 642.

[28] Julia Emtseva, 'The Philanthropic Community and International Law' (2023) 116 *Proceedings of the ASIL Annual Meeting* 29–32, at 30.

[29] Daugirdas, fn. 25, at 642–643.

[30] UNICEF, 'Sanitation and Hygiene'. www.unicef.org/esa/sanitation-and-hygiene, last accessed 31 May 2023.

[31] John Frank, 'Our Interconnected World Requires Collective Action' (2020) *Microsoft on the Issues*. https://blogs.microsoft.com/on-the-issues/2020/09/17/microsoft-un-affairs-team-unga/, last accessed 31 May 2023.

[32] Melissa J. Durkee, 'The Business of Treaties' (2016) 63 *UCLA Law Review* 264–321.

[33] UN Women, 'UN Women Launches Private Sector Leadership Advisory Council' (2 June 2014). www.unwomen.org/en/news/stories/2014/6/private-sector-leadership-advisory-council-launched, last accessed 30 June 2020.

private sector are the CEO Water Mandate, Caring for Climate, Every Women Every Child, Sustainable Energy for All, and Education First, among others.[34] An Annual Private Sector Forum gathers 'CEOs and government officials in conjunction with the opening of each annual UN [General Assembly]' to 'ensure that private sector solutions garnered from an informal setting will inform subsequent Assembly debate'.[35] As may be gathered from this quite varied list of 'partnership' examples, the forms of engagement are varied and their number is extensive.

The bottom line is that for-profit actors and their representatives are now significant presences within IOs. Despite the UN's 'opening up', the participation of these actors in international governance is under theorized. Indeed, the breadth of this participation has largely been a 'silent revolution', drawing little scholarly analysis, popular attention, or regulatory response. Given the significance of business engagement in twenty-first century IOs, any consideration of the composition, legitimacy, or representativeness of those organizations should account for it.

## 8.3 THE LOGICS OF REPRESENTATION AND EXPEDIENCE

While for-profit participation in the work of IOs is undertheorized, the claim of this chapter is that it is possible to perceive two basic logics or rationalities that motivate responses to this participation: the logics of 'representation' and 'expedience'. These logics appear in responses to business participation and to animate institutional design and regulatory choices in relation to these business roles. A caveat at the outset: first, the titles are shorthand. Second, creating two categories requires lumping different movements and approaches together. Any such lumping exercise will inevitably gloss over differences that are significant in other contexts. Whether it is useful to overlook those differences depends on whether the categories produce useful insights. My argument is that in this case the categories help make sense of a persistent ambivalence towards for-profit participants in the work of IOs over the past century or so of experience, and thus offer structure for a principled approach to these actors in the future. Before describing these logics, let me begin with an anecdote that demonstrates their use in practice.

[34] Kell, fn. 5, p. 743.
[35] Ibid.

### 8.3.1 *Illustrating the Logics*

Each year, COPs to the UNFCCC draw droves of participants of every kind, and garner global attention. In recent years, these conferences have received particularly pointed critique for the presence of many oil and gas representatives.[36] Consider COP 26, in Glasgow, Scotland, in November of 2021. This COP was particularly notable for at least two reasons: it was delayed for a year due to the Covid-19 pandemic, and according to the five-year timetable set by the Paris Agreement, this was the first COP at which many parties were required to communicate new climate pledges that reflected more ambition than the pledges they had delivered when first joining the Paris Agreement.[37] Adding to the drama of the occasion, organizers had promised 'the most inclusive COP ever', specifically encouraging participation by traditionally marginalized groups.[38]

Consider the narratives emerging from this climate conference. The first was a narrative of failure, principally focused on failures of participation, representation, and access, but also noting substantive failures and linking those substantive failures to process failures. The second was a narrative of success, focusing neither on representation nor on the substantive content of the traditional interstate climate agreements (in this case the pledges made by State parties), but rather on innovative new agreements made by private sector entities.

*Narrative 1.* Many reports coming out of Glasgow focused on how, despite the organizers' claims that this would be the 'most inclusive COP ever', Glasgow was in fact not inclusive at all. The challenge mostly seemed to stem from pandemic restrictions, but reports in popular and social media communicated the sense that these restrictions excluded some groups more than others, and the privileged groups were private sector lobbyists.[39] Reports highlighted the fact that indigenous peoples' groups, groups from the Global South, and other civil society actors had borne the expense and burdens of pandemic travel, yet were not able to gain access to the conference.[40] They

36 See e.g. 350.org and others, 'Open Letter Calling for Rules to Protect the Integrity of Climate Policy-Making from Vested Corporate Interests' (2013) *Corporate Europe Observatory*. https://corporateeurope.org/en/blog/open-letter-calling-rules-protect-integrity-climate-policy-making-vested-corporate-interests, last accessed 31 May 2023.

37 UNFCCC, Decision 1/CP.21, 'Adoption of the Paris Agreement' (adopted 12 December 2015), FCCC/CP/2015/10/Add.1, paras. 23–24.

38 Alok Sharma, 'Questions to the President of COP26' (9 June 2021).

39 Center for International Environmental Law, 'Public Participation and COP26: A Report from Glasgow'. www.ciel.org/public-participation-and-cop26-a-report-from-glasgow/, last accessed 31 May 2023.

40 Ibid.

described prohibitively long lines and pandemic restrictions that kept participants from meaningful engagement with the conference. The result was rampant frustration, with civil society representatives being sent back to their expensive hotel rooms to view the proceedings over the internet – no different than if they had not made the effort to attend the COP at all. Juxtaposed against these access challenges were stories about fossil fuel representatives garnering privileged access.[41] According to one BBC headline, the '[f]ossil fuel industry has [the] largest delegation'.[42] Climate youth activist Greta Thunberg tweeted in response: 'I don't know about you, but I sure am not comfortable with having some of the world's biggest villains influencing and dictating the fate of the world.'[43] Others claimed that fossil fuel representatives were being 'ushered to the beginning of the line' and that they had access to otherwise closed-door negotiations between the delegates.[44] One story concerned Australia's pavilion being sponsored by a fossil fuel company, with the observation that the pavilion colouring and logos looked strikingly similar to those of the corporate sponsor.[45] This narrative juxtaposed the privileged access of fossil fuel groups with the disappointing substantive results of the conference, expressed memorably from outside the pavilion by the activist chant: 'blah blah blah'.[46] Indeed, State pledges made at that conference expressed insufficient ambition to avert disastrous global warming consequences, and often committed States to reductions far in the future, much past the tenure of current officeholders.[47]

*Narrative 2.* A second narrative emerging from the conference was a celebratory one. This report did not focus on representational disparities or

41 See generally Climate Investigations Center, 'Thousands of Fossil Fuel "Observers" Attended Climate Negotiations – UNFCCC Data 2005-2018 COP1-COP24' (21 June 2019). https://climateinvestigations.org/thousands-of-fossil-fuel-observers-attended-climate-negotiations-unfccc-data-2005-2018-cop1-cop24/, last accessed 31 May 2023.

42 https://www.bbc.com/news/science-environment-59199484 Matt McGrath, 'COP26: Fossil Fuel Industry Has Largest Delegation at Climate Summit', *BBC News*, 8 November 2021. www.bbc.com/news/science-environment-59199484, last accessed 31 May 2023.

43 Karla Adam and Harry Stevens, 'Who Has the Most Delegates at the COP26 Summit? The Fossil Fuel Industry', *The Washington Post*, 8 November 2021.

44 Alexandria Villaseñor, [Tweet] (*Twitter*, 2 November 2021). https://twitter.com/AlexandriaV2005/status/1455706039769186310, last accessed 31 May 2023.

45 Adam Morton, 'Australia Puts Fossil Fuel Company Front and Centre at Cop26', *The Guardian*, 2 November 2021. www.theguardian.com/australia-news/2021/nov/03/australia-puts-fossil-fuel-company-front-and-centre-at-cop26, last accessed 19 November 2021.

46 Alyssa Lukpat and Marc Santora, 'Greta Thunberg Joins a Protest in Glasgow', *New York Times*, 1 November 2021. www.nytimes.com/2021/11/01/world/europe/greta-thunberg-cop26-glasgow.html, last accessed 31 May 2023.

47 David Hunter, James Salzman and Durwood Zaelke, *International Environmental Law and Policy*, 6th ed. (New York: Foundation Press, 2022).

even the mediocre pledges by State parties, but rather celebrated non-State commitments. These reports focused on the newly launched Glasgow Financial Alliance for Net-Zero (GFANZ) project, a platform to coordinate climate pledges by the financial sector, which, by the end of the COP, had drawn membership from financial firms responsible for assets of over $130 trillion.[48] A November 2021 GFANZ press release delivered the message that ultimate climate success had essentially been achieved. Here is the headline: 'Amount of finance committed to achieving 1.5 °C now at scale needed to deliver the transition'.[49] According to Mark Carney, UN Special Envoy for Climate Action and Finance (and former head of the Bank of England), '[t]he rapid, and large-scale, increase in capital commitment to net zero, through GFANZ, makes the transition to a 1.5 °C world possible'.[50] In this narrative, governments are not sources of public authority or agenda-setters, but rather sources of 'help' for the private sector: 'Now we need governments to help get the job done, by setting the ambitious policies that can unlock, accelerate and help direct the investment to where it's needed most.'[51]

As these stories show, popular and social media reporting from the Glasgow climate conference offer a window into two narratives that can arise around the work of IOs.

The first centres public process values, representation, and input legitimacy. Those who decry the failures of the Glasgow conference are concerned not just about substantive failures but about public law values like representation, transparency, and equality in the processes of decision-making, and they link failures in substance to failures in process. Animating this narrative is an implicit claim that, without these process values, an international institution cannot effectively wield public authority.[52] There is a deontological claim here: indigenous people's groups, island nations, and other members of civil society *should* be heard. There is also a consequentialist claim: States' failure

[48] Liz Alderman and Eshe Nelson, 'Global Finance Industry Says It Has $130 Trillion to Invest in Efforts to Tackle Climate Change', *New York Times*, 3 November 2021. www.nytimes.com/2021/11/03/world/europe/cop26-climate-change-finance-industry.html, last accessed 31 May 2023.

[49] Glasgow Financial Alliance for Net Zero, 'Amount of Finance Committed to Achieving 1.5 °C Now at Scale Needed to Deliver the Transition' (3 November 2021). www.gfanzero.com/press/amount-of-finance-committed-to-achieving-1-5c-now-at-scale-needed-to-deliver-the-transition/, last accessed 31 May 2023.

[50] Ibid.

[51] Ibid.

[52] Armin von Bogdandy, Matthias Goldmann and Ingo Venzke, 'From Public International Law to International Public Law: Translating World Public Opinion into International Public Authority' (2017) 28(1) *European Journal of International Law* 115–145.

to take more ambitious action within the COP process could be related to the fact that the primary influences in that conference were those who have a stake in doing little, that is, fossil fuel representatives. Bad outcomes flow from a tainted, illegitimate process that includes undue influence or capture.

The second narrative shifts focus from the representativeness of the process to functional outcomes, no matter the source of those outcomes. It is laser-focused on consequences: which actors and which actions can best achieve the 1.5 °C goal? This narrative widens the lens beyond State action to celebrate productive contributions by any kind of actor. This is a functionalist, consequentialist, output legitimacy sort of account. Proponents of these successes celebrate the way that private actors can sometimes outstrip or bypass slow-moving States or interstate organizations.[53] IOs can be 'reinvented' by a process of opening up and welcoming input and participation from multiple stakeholders, which can bring fresh ideas and capacity to solve important problems.[54] According to this perspective, progress can be achieved outside of formal interstate commitments and all forms of progress are equally worth celebrating.

### 8.3.2 *Representation and Expedience As Ideal Types*

The two lenses on the Glasgow COP illustrate the two logics I am trying to crystallize. I will soon claim that these logics have animated various choices to open and close international institutions to private sector actors over time. Before getting there, let me sketch out the logics another way – as ideal types.

The *logic of representation* centres the values of democratic self-determination and interest representation. It views legitimacy through these lenses of democracy and representation. That is, an organization possesses democratic legitimacy when it can make a claim that its governance decisions are representative of populations, whether through State authority or a broader conception of public authority.[55] Because self-determination and representation are the touch points for the legitimacy of the organization's work, the organization seeks to ensure that the right actors are contributing to governance, however that 'rightness' is conceived. Indeed, different concepts of representation have gained prominence at different times.

Because, in this concept, self-determination and representation are key to an organization's legitimacy, organizations should care about democratic

[53] Kell, fn. 5.

[54] Ibid.

[55] Samantha Besson, 'The International Public: A Farewell to Functions in International Law' (2021) 115 *American Journal of International Law Unbound* 307–311.

values like the *accountability* of governance organizations to represented populations for actions taken in their interest. Governance acts should be constrained by notions of accountability to the public. Moreover, those purporting to take decisions or actions in the public interest must bear some sort of *authority* to do that, grounded in the principle of representation. Different theoretical strains within this logic will focus on different units of authority, whether those be national governments, smaller self-determining political communities, or perhaps interests, represented by civil society or others.

The key challenges for organizations, as this logic sees it, are to reconcile diverging interests and policy differences and to determine how to implement functional public structures at the global level without the many possible representation distortions that lead to legitimacy failures and effectiveness failures. Thus, the logic of representation sees many of the problems facing the international system as distortions of public authority and democratic process: rent-seeking, imperfect interest representation, and replication of entrenched power structures.

The logic of representation can be conceived as a deontological perspective rather than a consequentialist or teleological one. That is, democratic self-determination and interest representation are inherent goods. Decisions made, rules developed, and actions taken through a legitimate process are right and correct because they are products of that process.

The *logic of expedience* is defined by its embrace of consequentialist and teleological reasoning. An outcome is right and correct when it advances the mission of an organization. This position values efficiency, problem-solving, and progress on accomplishing public goals, whether those goals be public health, climate stabilization, sustainable development, and so on.

What is important, according to this logic, is ends-oriented progress. Therefore, participants in the process should be those who can help the organization accomplish these ends. Participants to be welcomed include those with expertise, capacity to develop meaningful rules or policy interventions, innovative new approaches, or ability to assist with implementation.

This perspective can see processes of public deliberation as draws on the resources of an organization, and civil society as an outside force to be answered by satisfactory resolutions to practical challenges. It sees the challenges facing the international system as information and capacity failures, and opportunities for innovation and new synergistic partnerships. An organization's incapacity to address a problem may arise out of a need for scientific and technical advancement, or it might be a result of bureaucratic dysfunction and too much deliberation without action.

TABLE 8.1 *Two Logics*

| | Logic of Representation | Logic of Expedience |
|---|---|---|
| *Values* | Self-determination, interest representation | Efficiency, problem-solving, faithfulness to mission |
| *Source of legitimacy* | Authority, representation | Progress, accomplishments |
| *Looks for* | Accountability, transparency, public authority | Capacity, expertise, effectiveness |
| *Sees as challenges* | Reconciling divergent interests, avoiding representation distortions like rent-seeking and over-representation of global elites | Information and capacity failures, bureaucracy, implementation problems |
| *Blinds spots* | Output legitimacy and effectiveness issues | Input legitimacy, deliberative failures, entrenchment of western economic elite |
| *Ethical orientation* | Deontological | Consequentialist |

The blind spots for this approach are legitimacy problems, particularly input legitimacy, and the entrenchment of the western economic elite. As with the logic of representation, the logic of expedience can encompass different conceptualizations of how to capture progress, such as technocracy or neoliberalism. See Table 8.1.

Of course, proponents of one logic or the other will have differences of opinion about some of the particulars. For example, theories falling within the 'representation' logic might be concerned with the authority of States in the international system, deriving public authority at the international level from the representative structures within the nation-State.[56] A more cosmopolitan approach to representation might note the realities of global interdependence and interconnectedness[57] and seek representation of populations, whether or not mediated by governments.[58] Armin von Bogdandy has called this

[56] A. Claire Cutler, 'Critical Reflections on Westphalian Assumptions of International Law and Organization: A Crisis of Legitimacy' (2001) 27(2) *Review of International Studies* 133–150, 138. For an extreme view, see Jack L. Goldsmith and Eric A. Posner, *The Limits of International Law* (Oxford: Oxford University Press, 2005).

[57] Eyal Benvenisti, 'Sovereigns as Trustees of Humanity: On the Accountability of States to Foreign Stakeholders' (2013) 107(2) *American Journal of International Law* 295–333.

[58] Samantha Besson has suggested 'the institutional continuum of the international public' that is, that the public 'institutes' itself in various ways at various scales. Besson, 'The International Public', fn. 55, at 310.

TABLE 8.2 *Logics of Participation*

| | Logic of Representation | Logic of Expedience |
|---|---|---|
| *Participation orientation* | Status | Function |
| *Welcomes participation by . . .* | Representatives of those affected by governance choices | Those with expertise, capacity, ideas |
| *Attitude towards for-profit participation in lawmaking & governance* | For-profit entities and their representatives can distort law- and policy-making process; should guard against undue influence and capture | For-profit entities and their representatives should be included to the extent they can present useful expertise, capacity, ideas |

a concept of 'international public' authority, and others have explored other extra-governmental perspectives on authority.[59] The logic of expedience could be more technocratic, taking a knowledge-based perspective, or it could be more neo-liberal, seeking synergies between the goals of the public and private sectors and advocating for market-based solutions to public problems.

The two positions do tend to lead to distinct perspectives about the participation of private sector actors in international governance, and it is this difference that concerns us for the purposes of this chapter. See Table 8.2.

## 8.4 MAPPING THE LOGICS OVER TIME

While the previous section set out some features of the two logics in an impressionistic way, these two rationalities are best illustrated in the context of significant moments in the history of for-profit engagements in international governance. This section reviews five such moments over the last century or so.

### 8.4.1 *The 'League Method': Expedience*

During the 1920s and 1930s, the League of Nations approach to non-State groups came to be known as the 'League Method'. The League Method

[59] von Bogdandy, Goldmann and Venzke, fn. 52; see also Terry Macdonald, *Global Stakeholder Democracy: Power and Representation Beyond Liberal States* (Oxford: Oxford University Press, 2008), p. 193; Gráinne de Búrca, 'Developing Democracy Beyond the State' (2008) 46(2) *Columbia Journal of Transnational Law* 221–278; Anne Peters, 'Membership in the Global Constitutional Community', in Jan Klabbers, Anne Peters, and Geir Ulfstein, *The Constitutionalization of International Law* (Oxford: Oxford University Press, 2009), pp. 153–262.

characterized a working relationship where 'voluntary associations' and IOs had very close collaborations. As Steve Charnovitz characterizes this, '[b]ehind many [early IOs] stood idealistic and active [associations]'.[60] These associations defined and presented issues for the League's consideration; served as 'insiders working directly with government officials and international civil servants to address' international problems, principally through policy conferences; and lobbied those in power.[61] These methods of cooperation had emerged by the end of the nineteenth century, when 'there was a pattern of private international cooperation evolving into public international action'.[62]

In the League era, there was no strong distinction made between voluntary associations that advanced business or commercial ends and those that lobbied for other causes. Rather, associations advancing business interests were among the influential early 'semi-public and private organizations', terms which correspond to the modern-day NGO.[63] In Charnovitz's assessment, during the League period, the ICC was among the top three most significant associations in its impact on international governance, together with the Red Cross and the Women's International League for Peace and Freedom.[64]

For example, at this time railway businesses helped form the International Railway Congress Association, which led to the creation of the intergovernmental Central Office for International Railway Transport. The International Telegraph Union invited private companies to participate in its meetings. The ICC had official roles in League-sponsored economic conferences. Business associations also participated in the League's work relating to finance, commercial law, transportation, pharmaceuticals, and other areas.[65]

With some exceptions, the League of Nations generally took an approach to engagement with private sector actors that aligns with the logic of expedience. Public-private relationships in this era were often characterized by function over status, looked for expertise, capacity, and ideas more than interest representation, and were open to associations representing the private sector whenever their participation was relevant to the matter under consideration. That said, even in the League of Nations, there was a status-function ambivalence. For example, the ILO was developed according to a tripartite structure that

60 Charnovitz, fn. 4, at 245. Charnovitz used the anachronistic term 'NGOs' here, which I substituted with the term 'associations', since the term 'non-governmental organization' was not coined until its use at the founding of the UN in Art. 71 of the Charter of the United Nations, 1 UNTS XVI (adopted 26 June 1945, entered into force 24 October 1945).

61 Ibid.

62 Ibid.

63 Ibid., at 221.

64 Ibid., at 12–13, 223, 245–246.

65 Ibid., at 222–227.

welcomed employers, labour organizations, and government representatives on equal, but status-based, terms.

### 8.4.2 *Article 71 of the UN Charter: Representation*

The pendulum swung in a different direction at the founding of the UN – towards status and away from function; towards authority and representation, and away from ends-based collaboration.

Consider Article 71 of the UN Charter, which contains the Charter's single reference to non-State actors and empowers ECOSOC to 'make suitable arrangements for consultation with non-governmental organizations which are concerned with matters within its competence'.[66] The 'League Method' of close working relationships between non-State groups and intergovernmental groups had been an informal practice, but non-State groups wanted to formalize this practice in the new UN Charter. About 1,200 of them travelled to San Francisco in 1945 to seek some sort of 'provision for NGOs in the UN Charter'.[67] They partly succeeded, as Article 71 did authorize the ECOSOC to 'consult' with NGOs. However, that provision formalized a clearly subordinate role for NGOs in comparison with IOs and State parties. NGOs did not obtain any voting privileges, rights to participate in treaty drafting, or any other formal rights of participation. Moreover, even the term 'consultation' was not defined in the Charter, and so the contours of this relationship were left to ECOSOC's later discretion. The Charter also failed to articulate or formalize relationships between NGOs and any other organ or instrumentality of the UN, such as the General Assembly or the Security Council.

Article 71's terms reflect the preoccupation of the drafters of the UN Charter, and this was to clarify the special status of intergovernmental organizations, like the UN itself. Even the term 'non-governmental organization', or 'NGO', was coined at the birth of the UN; its purpose was to distinguish these groups from *inter*governmental organizations, as well as government-sponsored groups. These are status-based distinctions, as groups are organized based on identity. If a group is governmental, it must be represented through a delegation and not through the consultation procedure. If it is non-governmental, it can participate, but only as an outsider to the organization: merely 'consulting', not contributing.

66 Art. 71 UN Charter.

67 See Bill Seary, 'The Early History: From the Congress of Vienna to the San Francisco Conference', in Peter Willets (ed.), *The Conscience of The World: The Influence of Non-Governmental Organisations in the UN System* (Washington, DC: Rowman & Littlefield Publishers/Brookings Institution Press, 1996), pp. 15–30, pp. 15, 25–26; see also Charnovitz, fn. 4, at 251.

Note, too, that Article 71 did not distinguish between groups advancing different kinds of agendas, such as business agendas versus other kinds. Rather, as Stephen Tully has tellingly observed, Article 71 lumped together all kinds of non-governmental groups, in order to obtain '*equality of status* for the purpose of counterbalancing competing perspectives' rather than 'differential access or treatment to exploit operational specialization'.[68]

Thus, the UN at its founding moved away from the League's largely function-based working relationships towards a largely status-based model that attempted to elevate governments and the new intergovernmental organizations by giving all *non*-governmental groups an equal and secondary status.

### 8.4.3 *ECOSOC Accreditation Reforms: Still Representation*

Another significant moment in the relationship between IOs and non-State actors came a half century later, when ECOSOC reformed its working relationships with NGOs in 1996. This moment featured a reaffirmation of the logic of representation, but in a more cosmopolitan and less sovereigntist form than at the UN's founding.

In the half century between the founding and the 1996 reforms, ECOSOC had wielded the authority granted to it by Article 71 to pass regulations establishing an accreditation procedure and consultation system.[69] However, by the early 1990s, the existing accreditation procedure had drawn various forms of criticism. There was a perception that the rules were too restrictive in that they allowed only 'international' groups, and allowed States to veto consultative status for NGOs from their own countries.[70] There was also a perception that there was 'unequal representation ... [of NGOs] from different regions of the world' and, in particular, over-representation of organizations from Western industrialized nations.[71]

The resulting reforms clearly spotlight the influence of the logic of representation in seeking a 'representative' composition of NGOs in the consultation system. ECOSOC Resolution 1996/31 noted that ECOSOC sought 'just, balanced, effective and genuine involvement of non-governmental

68 Stephen Tully, *Corporations and International Lawmaking* (Leiden: Martinus Nijhoff, 2007) (emphasis added).

69 See Hobe, fn. 11; and Rainer Lagoni, 'Article 71', in Bruno Simma and Hermann Mosler (eds.), *The Charter of the United Nations: A Commentary* (Oxford: Oxford University Press, 1995), pp. 902–915, pp. 902, 904–905.

70 See ECOSOC Res. 1996/31, fn. 15; see also Hobe, fn. 11, p. 1800.

71 Hobe, fn. 11, p. 1801.

organizations from all regions and areas of the world', and in particular, greater participation from developing countries and countries in transition.[72]

In addition to an increased representation of NGOs from developing countries, ECOSOC sought to ensure that accredited associations would be *accountable* representatives of the interests of their constituencies. The new rules therefore moved to criteria that evaluated the representativeness of the organization's governance structure. The criteria focus on how well an NGO seeking accreditation represents its members, whether it has internal governance mechanisms that make its representatives accountable to that membership, and whether it has governance documents that evidence and safeguard this representational character. For example, the new rules required:

> 10. The organization shall ... have a democratically adopted constitution, ... which shall provide for the determination of policy by a conference, congress or other representative body and for an executive organ responsible to the policy-making body[;]
>
> 11 ... shall have authority to speak for its members through its authorized representatives[;]
>
> 12 ... [and] shall have a representative structure and possess appropriate mechanisms of accountability to its members, who shall exercise effective control over its policies and actions through the exercise of voting rights or other appropriate democratic and transparent decision-making processes.[73]

Organizations must be non-profits and obtain their funding from 'national affiliates ... or from individual members'.[74] Finally, the organization must represent its particular field by 'be[ing] of recognized standing within the particular field of its competence or of a representative character'. ECOSOC moved to a three-tier access structure at this time, with NGOs representing the broadest constituencies receiving the most access, and those representing more narrow, specialized interests receiving the least. All of these reforms express a *representative* model, premised on the theory that what NGOs offer is representation of populations or interests.

Indeed, this representative function was explicitly celebrated at the time. UN Secretary-General Boutros Boutros-Ghali gave a speech in 1994 calling NGO participation in IOs a 'basic form of popular representation in the present-day world' and a 'guarantee ... of political legitimacy'.[75] A high-level panel of

72 ECOSOC Res. 1996/31, para. 5.
73 Ibid., paras. 10–12.
74 Ibid., para. 13.
75 Boutros Boutros-Ghali, UN Secretary-General, 'Keynote Address by Secretary-General Boutros Boutros-Ghali to the 47th DPI/NGO Conference', in 47th Annual DPI/NGO Conference, *We the People: Building Peace* (8–10 September 1994), [ST/]DPI/1670, para. 3.

experts a decade later observed that '[t]he growing participation and influence of non-State actors is enhancing democracy and reshaping multilateralism'.[76]

Several years after the 1996 reforms, ECOSOC commissioned a report known as the 'Cardoso Report', which organized then-prominent critiques of the existing consultation system and proposed reforms. This report, too, emphasized the representative function of the NGO consultation system. It advocated 'forging stronger links between [NGOs at] the local and global levels, which would help overcome democratic deficits in global governance'.[77] The Cardoso Report also collected concerns by national governments about the 'legitimacy, accountability and "hidden agendas"' of NGO consultants: 'Many of the accredited NGOs are perceived as lobbyists rather than "true" stakeholders. Most are seen as not accountable while demanding higher government accountability. Many governments feel they, being elected, are the legitimate representatives of society'.[78]

These concerns by national governments exhibit the prominence of the logic of representation in how the consultation system was conceived at the time. They reveal a fundamental normative assumption that it is NGOs' 'democratizing' and representational qualities that qualify them to participate as consultants to IOs. For example, if the principal concern were to gather sufficient expertise to develop an efficient or workable rule, the principal analysis would not be whether an NGO represents its members, but whether the organization offers expertise, local knowledge, implementation assistance, or some other benefit.

### 8.4.4 *Global Compact: Now Expedience*

As the latter half of the twentieth century brought longer supply chains and globally dispersed corporate families, IOs sought to engage multinationals directly, in a move that embraced functional contributions over representation of populations. UN Secretary-General Kofi Annan ushered in a new logic and created a major inflection point in the relationship between the UN and non-State entities just a few years after the 1996 ECOSOC reforms. In a landmark speech at the 1999 World Economic Forum in Davos, Switzerland, to an

76 UN, 'We the Peoples: Civil Society, the United Nations and Global Governance: Report of the Panel of Eminent Persons on United Nations-Civil Society Relations' (11 June 2004), A/58/817, para. 3.

77 UN, 'Press Briefing by Panel on UN – Civil Society Relations' (21 June 2004). www.un.org/press/en/2004/Cardoso062104.doc.htm, last accessed 31 May 2023.

78 UN System and Civil Society, An Inventory and Analysis of Practices, 'Background Paper for the Secretary-General's Panel of Eminent Persons on United Nations Relations with Civil Society' (May 2003). https://archive.globalpolicy.org/reform/initiatives/panels/cardoso/0503practices.htm, last accessed 31 May 2023.

audience of CEOs, Kofi Annan advocated for 'a creative partnership between the United Nations and the private sector'.[79] The speech, introducing the Global Compact, proposed a synergy of interests:

> [T]he everyday work of the United Nations – whether in peacekeeping, setting technical standards, protecting intellectual property or providing much-needed assistance to developing countries – helps to expand opportunities for business around the world. And . . . without your know-how and your resources, many of the objectives of the United Nations would remain elusive.[80]

Through the Global Compact initiative, Kofi Annan asked business entities to 'demonstrate their leadership roles as world citizens' by pledging to 'endors[e] and champion' the principles of the Global Compact and try to carry them out in corporate practice.[81] The Global Compact was an enormously successful initiative, claiming, as of this writing, membership from 'over 15,000 companies based in over 160 countries, both developed and developing, representing nearly every sector and size'.[82] Its participant database has nearly 20,000 entries.[83]

The impact of the Global Compact has stretched far beyond the four corners of that initiative. As George Kell has observed, in its wake, 'cooperation with the private sector became politically acceptable and institutionally supported'.[84] It 'enabl[ed] other UN entities to explore cooperation with the private sector. It gave strong impulse to the role of business in the work of the Organization.'[85]

The launch of the Global Compact coincided with several other significant movements in the relationship between the UN and private sector entities, including the Millennium Declaration and the creation of the Millennium Development goals, which advocated for lifting populations out of poverty and improving health, education, equality, and environmental sustainability while reducing hunger, lack of shelter, and disease. These were all goals to which the private sector was invited to contribute, and indeed, the Millennium

79 UN, 'Secretary-General Proposes Global Compact on Human Rights, Labour, Environment, in Address to World Economic Forum in Davos' (1 February 1999), SG/SM/6881. https://press.un.org/en/1999/19990201.sgsm6881.html, last accessed 31 May 2023.

80 Ibid.

81 Kathryn Gordon, 'The OECD Guidelines and Other Corporate Responsibility Instruments: A Comparison', *OECD Working Papers on International Investment*, No. 2001/05 (OECD Publishing, 2001), pp. 1–16.

82 United Nations Global Compact, 'The World's Largest Corporate Sustainability Initiative'. www.unglobalcompact.org/what-is-gc, last accessed 1 June 2023.

83 See United Nations Global Compact, 'See Who's Involved'. https://unglobalcompact.org/what-is-gc/participants, last accessed 1 June 2023.

84 Kell, fn. 5, p. 749.

85 Ibid., p. 740.

Declaration of 2000 noted explicitly that the private sector had an important role to play in carrying out these agendas. The year 2000 also saw the founding of the Global Fund to Fight AIDS, Tuberculosis and Malaria, a multi-stakeholder project that welcomed participation from the private sector. The next year, the General Assembly introduced UN-private sector relationships as a new agenda item.

In the years since that 2000 launch, the UN has seen a 'silent reform',[86] with the organization adopting private sector ideas like 'brand management, modern management formats, more effective use of technology, and ... opensourced, networked collaborations'.[87] The UN has developed a 'Private Sector Focal Point', the 'Annual Private Sector Forum' and numerous public–private partnerships.

By 2015, the orientation towards the private sector had changed such that UN Secretary-General Ban Ki-moon called for 'all hands on deck' when opening the Paris Climate conference.[88] In particular, he praised climate pledges by 'some of the world's largest' oil and gas companies and financial institutions and asked that others come on board.[89] The Paris Agreement adoption document contained meticulous provisions calling for efforts by non-State actors and launching the Non-State Actor Zone for Climate Action (NAZCA) platform and its Global Climate Action portal. Both called for non-State actors to 'display their commitments to act on climate change'.[90]

The narrative these events expose is an ends-oriented narrative. It is about encouraging progress on distinct goals, and enlisting contributions from all actors who can contribute to these goals. It is less concerned with self-determination, which requires representativeness of some sort, and more concerned with progress, which requires contributions. It is less about status – public versus private, international versus domestic – and more about function – less poverty, less disease, more renewable energy.

### 8.4.5 *Early Twenty-First Century: Unreconciled Narratives*

What has unfolded since the Global Compact turning point? In the first quarter of the twenty-first century, the two narratives are both prominent in

86 Georg Kell, Ann-Marie Slaughter and Thomas Hale, 'Silent Reform through the Global Compact' (2007) 44(1) *UN Chronicle* 26–31.

87 Kell, fn. 5, p. 749.

88 Ban Ki-moon, UN Secretary-General, 'Remarks to COP21 Presentation of Draft Outcome Document' (12 December 2015). www.un.org/sg/en/content/sg/speeches/2015-12-12/remarks-cop21-presentation-draft-outcome-document, last accessed 1 June 2023.

89 Ibid.

90 Decision 1/CP.21, fn. 37, para. 114.

the UN system. They animate debates about the practices and outcomes of IOs and, to the extent they conflict, this conflict is largely unresolved.

*United Nations Framework Convention on Climate Change.* For example, the reports from the COPs at UNFCCC show one area where the two logics produce entirely different perspectives on what happened and how to assess what happened. After the Glasgow COP, one narrative decried failures in inclusivity and linked these to failures in output. Better representation, according to this account, may have produced a better outcome. The presence of oil and gas interests – and perhaps their privileged access – was detrimental to progress on climate stabilization commitments. The failure to offer adequate access to those most affected by climate change could have affected the outcome, and tainted the conference regardless of the outcome. In sum, the conference was plagued with both input and output legitimacy problems. The second narrative from the Glasgow COP focused on an entirely different set of facts: rather than representation, participation, or access issues, this narrative focused instead on progress. Rather than progress by State actors on core climate commitments, which was limited, the narrative focused on commitments by non-State actors, celebrating the Glasgow Financial Alliance for Non-State Action.

*United Nations Commission on International Trade Law.* The United Nations Commission on International Trade Law (UNCITRAL), an organization focused on the harmonization and modernization of international trade law, offers another view of the competing, unreconciled narratives. In its working processes, UNCITRAL has come to embrace the logic of expedience. The organization is very open to outside observers. Its deliberations are open to both non-Member States and non-State actors, all of which are called 'observers', and which are admitted without distinction. Note the focus on function, rather than status, in UNCITRAL's description of its participatory structures: UNICTRAL 'maintains mailing lists of organizations whose expertise is relevant to issues addressed by the various working groups' and will send invitation letters to request expertise for a particular meeting. UNCITRAL will continue to send invitations to particular groups 'so long as their work remains relevant'. Moreover, these non-State actors can shape the consensus process, so the UNCITRAL working practices themselves minimize the status distinctions between State parties and non-State actors.

However, those UNCITRAL working methods have been subject to critique by those who would instead have the organization emphasize status and representation. France challenged current practices in a complaint lodged in 2007, calling for a review of the meaning of consensus and the level of nonmember participation. France noted that non-State actors were 'play[ing] a major role because of the expertise they possess in the areas under discussion'.[91] In particular, France observed that when UNCITRAL seeks to draft a new legal instrument, it is the non-State experts and the groups that they represent that initiate the process and provide much of the technical expertise. France expressed the concern that these non-State groups were neither representatives nor delegates, and that their number had expanded greatly, with a substantial effect on the ultimate UNCITRAL work product. France's principal complaints were identity based: many of the NGOs were not members of civil society but instead professional associations; distinction between Member States and observers was frequently blurred; and non-State groups had too much influence in the decision-making procedure. France sought to preserve the sovereign rights of States to exert control over the international lawmaking process.

This debate at UNCITRAL crystallizes the two narratives. UNCITRAL's working practices exhibit a functionalist, consequentialist, logic of expedience approach. France sought a status-based approach that preserved a special role for State authority.

*World Health Organization*. The WHO's recent activity also epitomizes the current century's representation/expedience ambivalence. The WHO reforms address a function problem by doubling down on status.

The WHO has long been plagued by concerted interest campaigns around tobacco, sugar, pharmaceuticals, and other public health issues, which have harmed its efforts on these issues. In response, the organization updated its working relationships with non-State entities in 2016 with a Framework of Engagement with Non-State Actors (FENSA).[92] FENSA distinguishes between 'private sector entities' and 'international business associations' on the one hand, and 'non-governmental organizations' on the other, with additional safeguards in place for engagement with the former group.[93] FENSA's safeguards are meant to guard against conflicts of interest that may have negative impacts on the 'WHO's integrity, independence, credibility and reputation; and public health mandate'.[94] Thus, the rules try to create separate influence pipelines for public interest NGOs on the one hand, and for-profit entities and groups on the other.

91 Claire Kelly, 'The Politics of Legitimacy in the UNCITRAL Working Methods', in Tomer Broude, Marc L. Busch and Amelia Porges (eds.), *The Politics of International Economic Law* (Cambridge: Cambridge University Press, 2011), pp. 106–130, pp. 106, 115.

92 WHO, 'Framework of Engagement with Non-State Actors' (28 May 2016), WHA69.10.

93 Ibid.

94 Ibid.

The WHO's reform flows from a functional concern about bad outcomes, but it addresses this concern by making a further set of distinctions based on status. Yet, this reform is not about representation. That is, this looks different than the prior examples of institutional design based on representation: the WHO reforms are not aimed at elevating the status of governmental representatives (as at the UN founding) or trying to generate a sense of popular democracy (as with the 1996 ECOSOC reforms). Rather, they flow from an *ex ante* normative judgement about the functional benefits and risks that attach to private sector participation. This is a functional concern channelled into a status-based distinction: private sector influences may taint a process seeking to develop public health regulations. Non-profit-oriented groups do not pose such a risk. What is to be regulated, then, are the *actors* that participate in the process.

The WHO reform suggests the possibility that IOs do not have adequate tools to conceive of the relationship between themselves and the for-profit sector. Even when organizations, like the WHO, think functionally about these relationships, the familiar tools are representational. But as I have argued elsewhere, those status-based tools will not likely address the problems they aim to solve. Nor will they necessarily deliver a process with more representation or more public authority because they are not optimized for that agenda, but rather aimed at a functional problem.

## 8.5 CONCLUSION

How should IOs compose themselves with respect to non-State actors, specifically for-profit entities and their representatives? The question is live because for-profit actors are now embedded in many aspects of international governance, and their participation is increasing. Trade and industry association representatives serve as members of civil society, usually on the same terms as other groups.[95] IOs increasingly lean on for-profit actors and their trade and industry association representatives for 'partnerships', financial sponsorship, technical expertise, and implementation of international agendas. At the same time, sharp criticism of these roles persists by those who believe that the

[95] See Samantha Besson and José Luis Martí, 'Legitimate Actors of International Law-Making: Towards a Theory of International Democratic Representation' (2018) 9(3) *Jurisprudence* 504–540 (noting that there is no clear way to distinguish between 'good' and 'bad' members of civil society, between 'democratic' and 'non-democratic' ones, or between those concerned with general or collective interests and those who are merely motivated by personal or partial agendas').

participation of business actors threatens something essential about the way IOs conduct their activities.

Resolving this tension requires greater clarity about what we expect of IOs. Do we require 'public' institutions?[96] That is, do we require institutions that instantiate and facilitate the self-determination of populations? Are IOs instruments of democratic representation at the supranational scale?[97] Their working practices should reflect some sort of ongoing responsiveness and fidelity to the interests of a 'public', however that public is constituted. Business groups might be a part of this if they, too, mediate public interests.[98] Or, do we instead have a teleological view: an IO exists to serve a particular purpose. It is a wound clock, so to speak, which carries out its time-telling with no additional inputs needed along the way to refine its goal. In this latter view, the agenda is supreme – climate stabilization, public health – and anyone who can contribute to that mission should be welcome to do so. 'All hands on deck', says Ban Ki-moon. Business groups come out well in this analysis, especially those that have been honed into efficiency machines by the forces of capitalism. Why shouldn't Microsoft teach the UN to better use technology? In this logic of expedience, public input can keep the actors honest; civil society can serve a 'watchdog' function.[99] But the true measure of an organization is not its responsiveness to these perspectives, but its capacity to take concrete action, or so this logic goes.

In an era when threats to international peace, equality, and environmental security seem increasingly insistent, the competition between these two visions for the institutional design and legitimacy of IOs is likely to persist and intensify. The best resolution will not be ever more detailed regulations governing non-State access to these institutions, but rather approaches aligning with our deeper purposes for them.

96 As Letizia Lo Giacco points out, even the question of how to imagine or evaluate the 'publicness' of international law is underexplored. See Letizia Lo Giacco, 'Private Entities Shaping Community Interests: (Re)Imagining the "Publicness" of Public International Law as an Epistemic Tool' (2023) 14(3) *Transnational Legal Theory* 270–306.

97 Samantha Besson, 'Democratic Representation within International Organizations: From International Good Governance to International Good Government' (2022) 19(4) *International Organizations Law Review* 489–527.

98 Lo Giacco, fn. 96.

99 Kell, fn. 5.

# 9

# Representation and Consideration of Animals in International Organizations

Anne Peters

## 9.1 INTRODUCTION

Decisions by international organizations (IOs), in all their legal and political dimensions, typically neglect the interests of non-human animals (in the following: animals). The animals moreover do not have a say in the political processes that lead to such decisions.[1] The chapter investigates whether and how animal interests can and should be brought to bear in the processes of decision-making, using the World Organisation for Animal Health (WOAH) as an example. I articulate this claim with the soft phrase 'bringing to bear' and 'consideration', and not in terms of 'representation', in order not to pre-empt the question whether non-democratic, symbolic, and paternalistic forms of speaking or standing 'for' should be properly qualified as representation.

The chapter first shows the need for a better consideration of animal interests in decision-making by IOs (Section 9.2), and contrasts this normative quest to the deficient reality of the neglect of animal interests in political processes (Section 9.3). It uses the WOAH as an illustration (Section 9.4). It then works through cognate concepts that have structured the debates so far, ranging from animal citizenship over animal representation to animal consideration and animal deliberation (Section 9.5). After this groundwork, the chapter briefly canvasses some proposals for animal 'representation' in democratic political processes, drawing on proposals for the representation of other absent actors such as 'extraterritorial' humans, future generations of humans,

[1] I understand decisions in a broad sense, including recommendations and rules or standards. These are mostly not formally binding, but they have some legal effects. They concern the common life in a given community (polity) and are thus political as opposed to 'private', in the sense of personal choices in the lives of individuals. They are also political as opposed to 'technical', because they rest, inter alia, on (controversial) value judgements. I will in the following use the words 'decision-making' and 'political process', interchangeably.

and nature (Section 9.6). With due modifications, some schemes could be applied to the work of IOs (Section 9.7).

## 9.2 THE NEED FOR CONSIDERING ANIMAL INTERESTS IN THE DECISION-MAKING BY INTERNATIONAL ORGANIZATIONS

The disregard of animals' interests in decision-making of IOs poses a problem of what has been called 'interspecies justice'[2] because animal interests and maybe even animal rights are at stake (Section 9.2.1) and because the political action concerning animals' lives and death is shaped by actors beyond the Nation-State (Section 9.2.2).

### 9.2.1 *Animal Interests or Rights*

The interspecies injustice[3] exists independently of the answer to the controversial question whether animals (or some animals such as sentient animals) have fundamental moral and/or legal rights (such as the right to life). I posit that animals have interests (stakes in something that concerns them). In many respects, their (presumable or discernible) interests significantly diverge and conflict with the typical human interests, also in areas that are regulated by the WOAH. For example, the WOAH has adopted standards on slaughter. The mitigation of suffering on their way to death is in the interest of the animals, but in the end, the animals certainly are even more interested in not being killed at all.

On the premise that sentient animals possess a set of fundamental rights, it can be argued that the proper protection of those rights requires political power and order. The political order best able to protect those rights is a democratic political order.[4] It follows that animals need to become part of (or must be better considered in) this democratic order.

Alternatively, on the contrary premise that non-human animals do not possess fundamental rights, the political process also needs to be changed. The reasoning along this line is that in liberal democracies, the legal sphere (the protection of fundamental rights) or the political sphere (democratic lawmaking procedures) are seen as complementary and even as communicating vessels. Mechanisms and safeguards in one sphere might (to some limited

[2] Alasdair Cochrane, *Sentientist Politics: A Theory of Global Inter-Species Justice* (Oxford: Oxford University Press, 2018).

[3] I do not dwell on distinctions between justice, legitimacy, and fairness in this chapter.

[4] This is Alasdair Cochrane's line of reasoning in favour of democratic representation of sentient animals, Cochrane, fn. 2, p. 13.

extent) compensate for the lack of mechanisms and safeguards in the other sphere. On this premise, it can be argued that as long as animals lack fundamental rights, their interests must all the more be brought to bear in political (democratic) processes.

### 9.2.2 *Relevant Decision-Making Beyond the Nation-State*

In a world of global capitalism and with global governance, animal interests are affected by (and subjected to) decision- and rule-making across State boundaries. Much of the human behaviour harming animals occurs in the context of global supply chains, and has manifold extraterritorial or global implications. This ranges from animal live transports to the global trade of animal derivatives, the transboundary transmission of zoonotic diseases (such as Covid-19), to deforestation, erosion, water scarcity, and global warming (caused inter alia by methane from cattle waste) as a result of animal overuse and abuse by humans.[5]

These global problems are being addressed by States, and by international, transnational, and hybrid actors. For illustration, this chapter describes in some detail one IO, the WOAH. Other IOs also make decisions that are often especially relevant for the well-being and flourishing of animals, for example, the World Trade Organization (WTO) and the Food and Agriculture Organization (FAO). Relatedly, activities by other bodies and programmes run by IOs, such as the International Conference on Population and Development (ICPD) and the Programme of Action and the Environmental Programme of the United Nations (UNEP), matter. The line between decision-making 'of' an organization and decision-making by States under its auspices may be blurry. For example, heads of States and governments have, under the aegis of the United Nations (UN), adopted the Sustainable Development Goals (SDGs) in 2015 which are highly relevant for animals. Also, in non-incorporated treaty regimes, conferences of the parties (COPs), such as committees under the Convention on International Trade in Endangered Species (CITES) or the International Whaling Commission (IWC) under the International Convention on the Regulation of Whaling (ICRW), take decisions without much consideration for animals' interests. Finally, transnational civil society organizations (such as People for the Ethical Treatment of Animals (PETA)) and hybrid actors (such as the International Conservation Union (ICU)) specifically deal with animals. Given the relevance of the said actors' activity for animal interests, these

[5] Anne Peters, *Animals in International Law* (Leiden: Brill/Nijhoff, 2021), pp. 37–56.

interests need to be brought to bear not only in national but also in international decision-making. In the end, political (democratic) processes need to be redesigned for a dual extension: beyond State boundaries and beyond species boundaries. This has been called 'a sentientist cosmopolitan democracy' by Alasdair Cochrane.[6]

## 9.3 NASCENT PRACTICES OF ANIMAL CONSIDERATION IN POLITICAL DECISION-MAKING

The preceding section has argued that animal interests should be brought to bear more in human political decision-making including in IOs. Practices of animal consideration are currently only rudimentary. This section will give some examples, on the domestic plane (Section 9.3.1) and on the international level (Section 9.3.2).

### 9.3.1 *Animal Consideration in National (Democratic) Lawmaking*

In some democratic States, political parties that stand for animals have been created, but their candidates have been gaining only exceedingly small numbers of votes.[7] In addition, several jurisdictions (national and local) have established ombudspersons, committees, commissioners, or advocates for animals. One example is the German *Tierschutzbeauftragte* (animal commissioner). The office was created in 2023. The first office holder espouses a broad and loose conception of representation, claiming 'to give animals a voice on the federal level and, for example, *represent* them in the legislative process'.[8] Typically, these institutions and offices do not possess lawmaking powers but are tasked to observe, make recommendations, or develop strategies. They are (despite the language used) not democratic representatives. If they are sufficiently independent from the executive and legislative branches, their work may help to mitigate the systematic neglect of the animal interests in national (or subnational) political processes.

6 Cochrane, fn. 2, p. 13. Also Anthony Burke and Stefanie Fishel, 'Across Species and Borders: Political Representation, Ecological Democracy and the Non-Human', in Joana Castro Pereira and André Saramago (eds.), *Non-Human Nature in World Politics: Theory and Practice* (Cham, Switzerland: Springer, 2020), 33–52.

7 cf Paul Lucardie, 'Animalism: a Nascent Ideology? Exploring the Ideas of Animal Advocacy Parties' (2020) 25(2) *Journal of Political Ideologies* 212–227.

8 German Federal Government's website, 'Interview of the Animal Commissioner' (12 June 2023). www.bundesregierung.de/breg-de/service/gesetzesvorhaben/interview-tierschutzbeauftragte-kari-2195612, last accessed 1 February 2026 (my translation and emphasis).

### 9.3.2 *Animal Consideration in International Forums*

In transnational and international political forums, including in formal IOs, various players have articulated representative claims in favour of animals. Several big transnational civil society organizations (CSOs) defend various aspects of animal-related causes on a global plane, ranging from animal species protection (such as the World Wildlife Fund (WWF)) to the welfare of agricultural animals (such as Compassion in World Farming).[9] These CSOs seek to bring animal interests to bear both in the domestic political processes of States and in IOs. Their voice and participation in decision-making processes can make a democratic contribution, but they are not democratic 'representatives' of animals.[10]

The European Union (EU) is a special IO, inter alia because its lawmaking process has (weak) democratic characteristics. In the EU Parliament, delegates of animalist political parties won three seats (out of 705) in the 2019 elections to the EU Parliament.[11] Moreover, several EU citizens' initiatives (ECIs) have been successfully launched under Article 11(4) TFEU[12] with regard to animal welfare, and have triggered political responses by the EU Commission. Recent examples are the ECI 'End the Cage Age'[13] and 'Save Cruelty-free Cosmetics – Commit to a Europe without Animal Testing'.[14] Such initiatives are one building block of what the EU calls democratic participation (Article 10(3) TFEU), and they do feed animal interests into EU decision-making. However, the citizens launching an initiative do not 'represent' animals, and unfortunately the legal effects of an ECI are very feeble by design because initiators cannot propose a concrete bill.

To conclude, the current practices of bringing animal interests to bear in political processes on the national and international level are very weak. They need to be stepped up for the reason given in Section 9.2.

9 Compassion in World Farming's website. www.ciwf.org.uk/, last accessed 1 February 2026.

10 But see Laura Montanaro, *Who Elected Oxfam? A Democratic Defense of Self-Appointed Representatives* (Cambridge: Cambridge University Press, 2017) and below Section 9.5.2.3.

11 The delegates belong to the group 'Animal Politics EU' which is composed of eleven political parties.

12 Art. 11(4) of the Consolidated Version of the Treaty on the Functioning of the European Union, OJ 2012 C326, 26 October 2012, p. 47.

13 European Citizens' Initiative, 'End the Cage Age'. https://europa.eu/citizens-initiative/initiatives/details/2018/000004/end-cage-age_en, last accessed 1 February 2026.

14 See the statement of the EU Commission of 23 July 2023: European Commission, 'Commission acts to accelerate phasing out of animal testing in response to a European Citizens' Initiative' (25 July 2023). https://ec.europa.eu/commission/presscorner/detail/en/ip_23_3993, last accessed 1 February 2026.

## 9.4 THE WOAH

This section singles out one particularly relevant organization, the WOAH. It describes the WOAH decision-making, especially standard-setting processes, to illustrate how animal interests are neglected here.

### 9.4.1 *Institutional Framework*

The WOAH has its main seat in Paris and a dozen regional representations in the entire world. It was founded as the Office International des Epizooties (OIE) in 1924, in response to a Rinderpest occurrence, by twenty-eight States. It now counts 183 Member States and is thus an almost universal intergovernmental organization.[15] Its English name was introduced in 2003, and its English acronym WOAH in 2023.

The legal bases of the organization are the International Agreement for the Creation at Paris of an International Office for Dealing with Contagious Diseases of Animals with annexed Organic Statutes forming an 'integral part' of the agreement.[16] Further key legal texts are the Organic Rules,[17] the General Rules,[18] and several headquarters agreements.

The WOAH's narrow original objectives are defined in Article 4 of the Organic Statutes.[19] On its current website, the WOAH formulates its 'vision' as follows: 'Provide leadership in global animal health governance. Improve animal health care and welfare worldwide and support global goals.' The guiding principles of the WOAH's animal health (and welfare) governance are, according to the former General Director, 'excellence [i.e. scientific expertise], transparency and solidarity'.[20] The website describes the organization's mission as: 'Promoting coordination of animal health and welfare; fostering transparency in the animal disease situation worldwide; support

[15] As of 1 October 2023.

[16] International Agreement for the Creation at Paris of an International Office for Dealing with Contagious Diseases of Animals, 57 LNTS 136 (adopted and entered into force 25 January 1924), with Annex (Organic Statutes of the International Office for Dealing with Contagious Diseases of Animals (hereafter Organic Statutes). See for the relationship of agreement (founding treaty) and organic statutes Art. 2 of the agreement.

[17] International Committee of the International Office for Dealing with Contagious Diseases of Animals (now 'Assembly'), 'Organic Rules of the Office International des Epizooties' (adopted 24 May 1973). https://www.woah.org/en/who-we-are/structure-and-governance/framework/basic-texts/organic-statutes/ last accessed 1 February 2026.

[18] WOAH Assembly, 'General Rules of the World Organisation for Animal Health (OIE)' (hereafter General Rules) (adopted in May 2011, last revised in May 2013).

[19] Organic Statutes of the International Office for Dealing with Contagious Diseases of Animals.

[20] Monique Éloit (Director General), 'Editorial' (2016) 1 *Bulletin OIE* 1–3, at 2.

Veterinary Services to strengthen the governance of animal health systems.' In order to fulfil its mission, two main activities of the WOAH are (1) the production, collection and dissemination of information on the global animal disease situation; and (2) standard-setting on animal health (and welfare).

The WOAH's main organs are listed in Article 3 of the Organic Rules.[21] For the purposes of 'representation', I shall mainly look at the plenary body, the World Assembly of Delegates (Assembly).[22] Similarly as in other IOs, this Assembly is neither democratically elected by (nor directly accountable to) any global citizenship, nor does it have the power to make binding laws. The Assembly meets at least once a year for the General Session in May in Paris.[23]

The WOAH's mandate, structure, working methods, and activities have evolved significantly during its near one hundred years' existence. Its bodies have been re-organized and its mandate has been extended. This practice of high dynamism should make further reforms that would strengthen the consideration of animal interests easier than in other organizations that have been more static.

### 9.4.2 *Standard-Setting*

One important task of the WOAH Assembly is the adoption of codes and standards and other rules. The standard-setting activity seeks to contribute to a worldwide regulatory harmonization whose twofold aim is (just like the purpose of the entire organization) to ensure a high level of protection of animal health and welfare and to remove undue sanitary obstacles to animal and animal product trade.[24]

Working for this dual purpose, the two major standards produced by the WOAH are the two Animal Health Codes: the Terrestrial Animal Health

[21] Besides the World Assembly of Delegates, the WOAH has a Council (the executive body), the Director General with a secretariat (i.e. the organization's management), five regional commissions (see Arts. 12–13 of the General Rules), and four standing specialist commissions (the Scientific Commission, the Code Commission, the Aquatic Animal Commission, and the Biological Standards Commission) (see Arts. 14–18 of the General Rules).

[22] The plenary body was called 'International Committee', in Art. 6 of the Organic Statutes, but was renamed in 2009 (WOAH International Committee Res. No 13, 'Modernisation of the Basic Texts: name of the International Committee' (24–29 May 2009)); see also Art. 1 of the General Rules.

[23] Arts. 2 and 39 of the General Rules.

[24] WOAH Assembly Res. No 36, 'Implementation of OIE standards by OIE Member Countries: state of play and specific capacity building needs' (24 May 2018), para. 1.

Code (TAHC)[25] and the Aquatic Animal Health Code (AAHC).[26] These Codes are updated and revised annually, under the responsibility of two code commissions which each comprise six elected members. The final code texts are adopted by decision of the Assembly.[27] The 2025 edition of the TAHC comprises sixteen sections, covering topics ranging from animal transport over slaughter and killing for disease control to the use of animals in research and education, plus chapters on agricultural animals (beef-cattle, broiler chicken, dairy cattle, and working equids).

All Member States are represented in the Assembly 'by one permanent technical Delegate' (who should belong to the Member State's official veterinary services). These delegates are appointed by the Members States in differing procedures, depending on the State. They act under the instruction of the State's bureaucracy. Each delegation has one vote in all matters that require voting and in all ballots.[28] In practice, many proposals are adopted by consensus (absence of a formal counting of votes).

The WOAH standard-setting activity is science-driven. All leading officials are veterinarians or scientists, and the elaboration of standards is based mainly on scientific input. This approach bears some guarantee of rationality and distance from political influence. However, the scientific approach cannot completely rule out capture by industrial interests (agro, food, and pharmaceutical) that are often harmful for animal welfare.

Given the importance of influencing (up to capturing) the organization through the 'golden reigns' of funding, it is laudable that the final reports formally acknowledge voluntary financial contributions by Member States, the EU, and animal friendly non-governmental organizations (NGOs). No direct industry donations are mentioned.[29] To conclude, the WOAH standard-setting does not enjoy any democratic legitimacy, but it enjoys some legitimacy through scientific expertise, participation of stakeholders (except the animals themselves), and a modest degree of transparency. Animal interests are hardly brought to bear in the processes.

25 WOAH, 'Terrestrial Animal Health Code' (TAHC) (33rd ed., WOAH 2025), reflecting the revisions at the 92th General Session (May 2025). www.oie.int/en/what-we-do/standards/codes-and-manuals/terrestrial-code-online-access/, last accessed 1 February 2026.

26 WOAH, 'Aquatic Animal Health Code' (AAHC) (27th ed., WOAH 2025), reflecting the revisions at the 92th General Session (May 2025). www.oie.int/en/what-we-do/standards/codes-and-manuals/aquatic-code-online-access/, last accessed 1 February 2026.

27 Art. 1 of the General Rules.

28 Arts. 4–6 and 11 of the Organic Rules, and Arts. 3(2) and 50(2) of the General Rules.

29 WOAH Assembly Res. No 4, 'Acknowledgements to the Members and Partners that made Voluntary Contributions or Subsidies to the WOAH, or contributed in the Organisation of WOAH Meetings and for the Provision of Personnel' (27 May 2021).

### 9.4.3 *Legal and Other Functions of the Standards*

The WOAH standards are not formally legally binding. Nevertheless, the animal *health* standards are, due to their solid scientific base and their institutional and legal link with the Agreement on Sanitary and Phytosanitary Measures (SPS), a crucial economic factor for States seeking to trade animals and animal products.[30] The reason is that conformity with these standards largely determine whether a State's sanitary measures constitutes an unlawful trade barrier or not under the WTO and under regional or bilateral regimes modelled on the WTO regime.

The WOAH animal *welfare* standards are a more novel output. The welfare chapters in the Codes are recommendatory in form, and vague in substance. As a general matter, such secondary law must be taken into account in good faith by the organization's Member States.[31] Moreover, the standards are referred to or otherwise incorporated into the national laws of most Member States, they are cited in international trade law agreements, they are a constant reference point in the work of other IOs (such as the WTO, the Organisation for Economic Co-operation and Development (OECD), and FAO), and they are also mentioned in business codes of conducts. Thereby, these standards, as shallow as they may be, affect and arguably even subject animals.[32]

### 9.4.4 *The Failed Laying Hen Welfare Standard*

To illustrate the abysmal failure of the standard-setting procedures to properly take into account animal interests, we might look at the defeated attempt to introduce a laying hen welfare standard in 2021. An ad hoc working group had worked five years (since 2016) on this topic. The Code Commission had proposed a new Chapter 7.Z. on animal welfare and laying hen production

30 The WOAH is (besides the Codex Alimentarius Commission) a sister organization to the SPS-Committee which manages the SPS. All three bodies are mentioned in Art. 12(3) of the WTO Agreement on the Application of Sanitary and Phytosanitary Measures (SPS Agreement) (adopted 15 April 1994, entered into force 1 January 1995). The WOAH is moreover mentioned in the preamble and in Art. 3(4) and in Annex A, 3(b) of the SPS.

31 ICJ, *Voting Procedure on Questions Relating to Reports and Petitions Concerning the Territory of South-West Africa*, (Advisory opinion) [1955] ICJ Rep. 67, Separate opinion of Judge Lauterpacht, p. 90, p. 119; Markus Benzing, 'International Organizations or Institutions, Secondary Law', in Anne Peters and Rüdiger Wolfrum (eds.), *Max Planck Encyclopedia of Public International Law* (Oxford: Oxford University Press, 2007), para. 17; Jan Klabbers, *An Introduction to International Organizations Law* (Cambridge: Cambridge University Press, 2022), p. 169.

32 See on affectation and subjection below Section 9.5.3.

systems. The drafts had been circulated five times to Member States.[33] The language of the final draft Chapter was very modest, saying that bathing areas, foraging areas, nesting areas, and perches were 'desirable' – not more.[34] Moreover, the chairman of the Code Commission stressed that the code was 'not a legal text' but a 'recommendation' and that the new chapter's implementation 'was not expected to be immediate'.[35]

The EU had already in 1999 started to legislate against laying hen batteries and prescribes 'enriched cages' since 2012. For the EU, the proposed standards were too weak and 'would not lead to any real improvements'.[36] The EU had requested that the word 'desirable' be replaced by 'should' in those points, 'as this would encourage countries to gradually converge with these international recommendations, leading to a progressive improvement in the welfare conditions of laying hens in the mid to long term'.[37]

But even the mere 'desirability' was too much for numerous southern States from all continents. They found the draft chapter too rigid and demanded 'more flexibility'. The USA (which does not ban battery cages itself) was ready to compromise with the Global South. It is noteworthy that the industry representative, the 'International Egg Commission' had a say in the plenary, but no animal protection organization.[38] In the end, the reluctance of States of the Global South to commit to enrichment of cages, not to speak of outdoor areas for laying hens, prevented the adoption of the new chapter.[39] This story illustrates how basic animal interests of billions of animals who suffer extreme harm (most painful leg disorders and broken bones during their entire life span) are neglected in the standard-setting of the WOAH.

In conclusion, the organization's decision-making, including its standard-setting activity, is not democratic. And although the standards (in combination with the domestic law of its Member States) affect and arguably even subject animals such as the laying hens, their interests in physical integrity, health, and well-being hardly come to bear in the standard-setting process. This situation should and could be changed. The following sections lay out the

33 WOAH, 'Final Report of the Sessions of May 2021' (2021), p. 18.

34 The full text of the proposed new chapter is reproduced in WOAH, 'Report of the Meeting of the WOAH Terrestrial Animal Health Standards Commission' (February 2021), Annex 15, pp. 93–113.

35 WOAH, 'Final Report 2021', fn. 33, pp. 18, 20.

36 Ibid., p. 19.

37 Ibid., pp. 18–19.

38 Ibid., pp. 19–20.

39 Ibid., pp. 18–21. The vote was fifty-three in favour against forty-one against, with twenty-two abstentions. Therefore, the necessary two thirds majority was not reached, see WOAH, 'Final Report 2021', fn. 33, pp. 21, 58–59.

complicated underlying concepts and some concrete proposals for procedural design.

## 9.5 CONCEPTUAL ISSUES

The exploration of practical possibilities for bringing animals to bear in the decision-making of IOs such as WOAH depends on some conceptual groundwork.

### 9.5.1 *Interspecies Democracy*

The neglect of animal interests in the political process has been picked up in interspecies democratic theory.[40] The problems are most discussed under the headings of animal citizenship and political agency. Various proposals have been made to define a new political status for at least some animals in politics.[41] They range from animal 'enfranchisement' without animal citizenship (Robert Garner)[42] up to 'animal citizenship' for domesticated animals (Sue Donaldson and Will Kymlicka).[43] An intermediate position which I find most convincing is to qualify animals as political patients and part of the *demos* with the 'passive political right' to have their interests considered in political processes (Janneke Vink).[44]

40 See for this term Janneke Vink, *The Open Society and Its Animals* (Cham: Palgrave Macmillan, 2020), p. 13. See also Eva Meijer, *When Animals Speak: Towards an Interspecies Democracy* (New York: New York University Press, 2019); Sue Donaldson, Janneke Vink and Jean-Paul Gagnon, 'Realizing Interspecies Democracy' (2021) 8 *Democratic Theory* 71–95.

41 This debate has concentrated on domestic political processes (Nation-States and subnational territorial entities). On the international plane, additional problems arise such as the very thin character of a putative global citizenship for humans and the thinness of proto-democratic procedures in IOs.

42 Robert Garner, 'Animals, Politics and Democracy', in Robert Garner and Siobhan O'Sullivan (eds.), *The Political Turn in Animal Ethics* (Lanham, MA: Rowman and Littlefield International, 2016), pp. 103–117, p. 114.

43 Sue Donaldson and Will Kymlicka, *Zoopolis* (Oxford: Oxford University Press, 2011); Sue Donaldson and Will Kymlicka, 'Unruly Beasts: Animal Citizens and the Threat of Tyranny' (2014) 47(1) *Canadian Journal of Political Science* 23–45; Sue Donaldson and Will Kymlicka, 'Rethinking Membership and Participation in an Inclusive Democracy: Cognitive Disability, Children, Animals', in Barbara Arneil and Nancy J. Hirschman (eds.), *Disability and Political Theory* (Cambridge: Cambridge University Press, 2016), pp. 168–197.

44 Vink, *The Open Society and Its Animals*, fn. 40, pp. 52–54. See also Dan Hooley, 'Political Agency, Citizenship, and Nonhuman Animals' (2017) 24 *Res Publica* 509–530.

### 9.5.1.1 Animal Citizenship

The most radical view of animal citizenship most straightforwardly leads to animal representation: when domesticated animals (such as dogs, cats, horses, and the like) are seen as fellow-citizens, it follows that they can and should also be democratically represented in politics.

The companion idea is the recognition of a political agency of animals. Democratic representation is normally reserved for political agents (i.e. those who possess the capacity to act politically, such as voting or deliberating). Applied to animals, Kimberly K. Smith has pointed out that animals have the 'ability to be'. She calls this ability 'a kind of agency', a socially constructed agency.[45]

Proponents of animal citizenship and political agency draw parallels to prior debates on the non-representation of other human groups or – put differently – their exclusion from the citizenry. In classic political theory, the democratic citizenry has been conceptualized as a group whose members are deemed to have concluded a (fictitious) social contract which grants some representatives the right to govern the others, which can be understood, due to the consent of the governed, to be 'self-government'. However, the legal capacity to conclude this social contract was historically seen to be lacking in, for example, women and humans with cognitive disabilities who were thought to want the necessary capabilities such as sufficient reasoning faculties. Such exclusions from being a party to the social contract and hence a full citizen are today considered unfair. This argument has been extended to domestic animals. The thresholds for membership are considered arbitrary, especially as they are defined by those who are inside the circle of citizens and benefit from the threshold.[46]

The consequence of animal citizenship would be that animals can and should participate in politics, and may also be 'represented' by humans. The assumption here is that animals can express their interests. They show humans through their behaviour what they like and what they do not like. If humans listen and watch properly, they can read the animals' 'facial expressions, body language, and vocalizations'.[47] Also animal acts of resistance, 'voting with their feet', and cooperation with humans are instances of animal speech to humans.

45 Kimberly K. Smith, *Governing Animals: Animal Welfare and the Liberal State* (Oxford: Oxford University Press, 2012), p. 108.

46 cf Donaldson in Donaldson, Vink and Gagnon, fn. 40, at 80.

47 Sue Donaldson, 'Animal Citizens and the Democratic Challenge' (2020) 46(4) *Social Theory and Practice* 709–735, at 723.

All this then leads to 'international communication'.[48] This communication is seen as being *political*, it is qualified as an 'interspecies political exchange'.[49] More even, when animals utter approval and disapproval, and when specially tasked humans respond, this would form a 'direct animal representation' (Sue Donaldson).[50] The animal behaviour could, according to Donaldson, count as animals *selecting* humans (who could then act as representatives) and also *redirect or sanction* humans who do not act according to the animal constituency's preferences: 'Animals would choose (authorize) their representatives through expressions of trust and affiliation.'[51]

#### 9.5.1.2 Against Animal Citizenship

In contrast, the majority of writers opine that the theory of animals' citizenship and political agency stretches the concepts too far and dilutes them so much that they risk becoming meaningless.

First, although animals have interests and express their preferences, they lack understanding of political processes, because they are not able to oversee the various interests that are at stake in shaping the rules of a society. Choosing a dog-food and a dog-walk is no political act. The animals' choices and their behaviour are private and not political.[52] Instead of dragging animals artificially into political agency, we should accept the reality that animals do not act politically.[53] Relatedly, animals cannot, not even in an ideal-typical way, be seen as the *co-authors* of the human laws that govern and subject them, and therefore do not qualify as 'self-governed' in the sense of (our human) democracy. Their social life is governed by their own social norms which we understand only imperfectly.

Second, places such as lawns and parks are not political forums but just public spaces. Animals cannot, or only with great difficulty, be brought into political forums such as parliaments and discussion rooms such as the WOAH standard-setting committee. As a weaker surrogate, animal films and images

48 Erica von Essen and Michael P. Allen, 'Solidarity between Human and Non-Human Animals: Representing Animal Voices in Policy Deliberations' (2017) 11(5) *Environmental Communication* 641–653.

49 Bernd Driessen, 'Animal Deliberation', in Marcel Wissenburg and David Schlosberg (eds.), *Political Animals and Animal Politics* (Basingstoke: Palgrave Macmillan, 2014), pp. 90–104, p. 102.

50 Donaldson, 'Animal Citizens and the Democratic Challenge', fn. 47, at 709.

51 Ibid., at 723.

52 Angie Pepper, 'Political Agency in Humans and Other Animals' (2021) 20 *Contemporary Political Theory* 296–317; Vink in Donaldson, Vink and Gagnon, fn. 40, at 82.

53 Vink in Donaldson, Vink and Gagnon, fn. 40, at 83.

could be shown in those chambers. Such images might generate the desired effect of consideration of animal interests and solidarity with them.

Third, even the increased presence of animals in the public domain and screenings in parliaments at best causally influence the debates *among humans*. The animals themselves cannot refer to such debates in an intentional way. They are also incapable of grasping the normative content of the relevant concepts. They are, as Bernd Ladwig points out, 'constitutively unable to see themselves as citizens of particular political communities and to take a responsible part in international relations'.[54] Therefore, their sheer presence or their affiliation expressed towards certain humans would constitute 'representation' only in a very loose way, to which we now turn.

### 9.5.2 *From Animal Representation to Animal Consideration*

This section argues that the difficulties of a systematic responsiveness to animals allow us to speak of animal representation only in the very broad and most literal sense of 'making present'. The job of political representatives is to render politically present to an audience those who are not physically present in the forum that takes political decisions.[55] Several aspects of the complex concept of representation are especially important for a (potential) political representation of animals.

#### 9.5.2.1 Animal Agoras?

At first blush, the idea of representing animals which are, according to most laws of the world, things (*res*) seems to benefit from the post-structuralist approaches to representation. However, when Bruno Latour speaks of an '*Assemblée des choses*', he understands representation in a very loose way that also blurs the (linguistic, pictorial, and narrative) meaning (speaking '*of*' an absent actor/entity) with the more typically *political* meaning (speaking '*for*' the absent).[56] The (post-structuralist) debates on the difficulties of representation will not be pursued here.

54 Bernd Ladwig, 'Against Wild Animal Sovereignty: An Interest-based Critique of Zoopolis' (2015) 23(3) *Journal of Political Philosophy* 282–301, at 301. See also ibid., at 296.

55 See for the meaning of 'political' above fn. 1.

56 Bruno Latour, *Politiques de la Nature: Comment faire entrer les sciences en démocratie* (Paris: La Découverte, 1999), esp. p. 57. In the representation theory of Michael Saward (Michael Saward, *The Representative Claim* (Oxford: Oxford University Press, 2010)), these two strands of meaning (the linguistic and the political meaning) flow into each other. See for a very helpful analysis Robert R. McKay, 'Representation', in Lori Gruen (ed.), *Critical Terms*

Another relevant point is the current attention paid to secure some degree of descriptive representation. It is now widely assumed that marginalized and neglected humans (minorities, migrants, indigenous, people with disabilities, and others) should be at least partly represented by others who share (physical or social) traits with those absent. Those present can then perform a 'politics of presence', inter alia by raising awareness, bringing life experience to bear, and serving as role-models for those who are absent and motivating them to engage in politics.[57] Again, Sue Donaldson's model seems to fit at first glance. The proposal to create 'multispecies commons' or an 'animal agora' such as lawns and parks[58] is reminiscent of the above-mentioned 'politics of presence', where some individuals depict those who are absent in the political forum and render them visible to the audience. The above-mentioned functions of descriptive representation such as awareness-raising can to some extent be delivered by the present animals. However, the animal individuals who are ostensibly rendering visible all other animals who are physically absent, have not been chosen as representatives by those other animals.

#### 9.5.2.2 Claim-Making and Trusteeship Over Animals

With a view to the animal question, non-democratic forms of representation are especially relevant. Historically, both the concept and practice of representation has little to do with democracy.[59] Today still, non-democratic representation is the normal form of representation of humans on the international plane. Humans are generally deemed to be 'represented' by their States in the decision-making bodies of IOs and when it comes to treaty-making. The governments (the executive agents) of non-democratic States (in which the largest share of the world's human population lives) regularly speak 'for' their nationals, without any democratic mandate.

Relatedly, the tasks of the representatives have been traditionally conceived as sitting on a spectrum. On the one end of this spectrum, representatives are seen as 'delegates', as mouthpieces of the electors, in the extreme even acting

*for Animal Studies* (Chicago: University of Chicago Press, 2018), pp. 307–319, pp. 311, 314–315. For a seminal application of Latour to animals as 'wild things': Steve Hinchliffe, Matthew B. Kearnes, Monica Degen and Sarah Whatmore, 'Urban Wild Things: A Cosmopolitical Experiment' (2005) 23(5) *Environment and Planning D: Society and Space* 643-658. Cf also Michael Hardt, 'Non Parlare a Nome d'Altri', in Massimo Filippi, Michael Hardt and Marco Maurizi (eds.), *Altre Specie di Politica* (Milano Udine: Mimesis, 2016), pp. 39-45, p. 42.

57 Seminally Anne Phillips, *The Politics of Presence* (Oxford: Oxford University Press, 1998).

58 Donaldson, 'Animal Citizens and the Democratic Challenge', fn. 47, at 714.

59 Hanna F. Pitkin, *The Concept of Representation* (Berkeley: University of California Press, 1967), p. 2.

upon the latter's mandatory instructions. This has been called the 'imperative mandate' given to the so-called councils in the socialist and communist tradition of a people's democracy. On the other end of the spectrum, 'representatives' exercise their own judgement to discover the best interests of those represented. These 'representatives' are not necessarily elected and recalled in democratic elections. It is then a matter of vocabulary whether these 'trustees' (or guardians or fiduciaries)[60] still fall under the umbrella of representation (as non-democratic representatives) or not.

The recent theory of representation has, in a 'constructivist turn', situated the typical task of representatives more on the latter end of the spectrum.[61] Michael Saward and others have elaborated that representatives in any case shape the interests that they claim to represent. Neither the interests nor the constituencies lie around ready for representation, but first have to be constituted in the very act of claiming to speak for them.[62] From this perspective, the representation of animals by humans does not look categorially different from interhuman representation, because in both constellations, a creative and proactive role is indispensable. Indeed, Sue Donaldson's conceptualization of animal citizenship fits well with Saward's theory of representation. If all interests are anyway 'constructed', shaped, and articulated in representative claim-making, this can also be done with animal interests. Human representatives construct them and can feed them into the (human) political processes. There is some extra work needed for construing the relevant interests across the species line, but this is just a matter of degree.[63] The normative drawback of the 'constructivist' view of representation is that it is not democratic, because it ultimately makes the representative the judge of what those represented may want: when the representative shapes or actually makes the latter's interests, he becomes a guardian.[64] And this indeed resembles the relationship between the human intermediaries and the animals.[65]

60 For the purposes of this chapter, I use the terms trustee, guardian, and fiduciary interchangeably. In other discourses, these three concepts are distinguished.

61 See critically Lisa Disch, 'The "Constructivist Turn" in Democratic Representation: A Normative Dead-End?' (2015) 22(4) *Constellations* 487–499.

62 Saward, fn. 56, p. 115.

63 McKay, fn. 56, p. 314. Saward, fn. 56, p. 115: 'Animals can be engaged with, looked for, traced, understood, and appreciated in new ways by humans opening up themselves to new ways of "reading" and " writing" them (. . .). But to do this is to tap into new ideas of what it means to represent, and to make representations, in the senses of both what it can involve and who can do it.'

64 cf Disch, fn. 61, at 496.

65 See for the term 'intermediaries' below Section 9.5.2.4.

I submit that while undemocratic practices of 'representation' persist, democratic representation is normatively preferable. Democratic representation requires that persons whose interests are affected by (or subjected to) the decision-making have an equal opportunity to influence the decisions by selecting (through elections or otherwise) and recalling (disempowering) their representatives. Mechanisms of selection and recall prevent the neglect of interest of those who are absent; they secure 'responsiveness' (Hanna Pitkin's term), an element of what we now call accountability.[66]

The act of voting, thereby replacing one representative with a new one, is the typical democratic sanction that forms part of accountability. Feeble accountability can be realized by means that are softer than elections, such as reporting from the representatives to the represented, through other transparency measures, and through hearings. The possibility of critique can amount to a reputational 'sanction'. The non-availability of strong sanctions makes the accountability weaker. If it is too weak, a scheme of representation (and of accountability) should best not be called 'democratic'. This is a matter of degree and of a minimum threshold.

#### 9.5.2.3 Claimed Versus Authorizing Constituencies

Laura Montanaro has examined (transnational) CSOs as 'self-appointed representatives'.[67] According to her, CSOs such as the WWF can under certain conditions, despite not being elected, nevertheless count as sufficiently 'democratic' representatives. Montanaro argues that the representatives need not inevitably render the accounts to the interest-holders themselves (the represented, i.e. the actual or 'claimed' constituency). Rather, the account-receivers could be someone else (a second constituency that Montanaro calls the 'authorizing constituency'). Thus, the WWF or PETA could make representative claims for and on behalf of the animals by rendering accounts to proxies such as the members and the financial sponsors of the organizations.

Applied to our issue, the 'claimed constituency' are the animals, and the 'authorizing constituency' are members of the animal CSOs, their sponsors and donors. At this point, it should be recalled that when it comes to decision-making

66 Accountability, applied to the framework of 'representation', is the fact that those represented (the constituency) have the right to hold the representatives to a set of standards, to judge whether they have fulfilled their responsibilities in light of these standards, and to impose sanctions if they determine that these responsibilities have not been met (cf Ruth Grant and Robert O. Keohane, 'Accountability and Abuses of Power in World Politics' (2005) 99(1) *American Political Science Review* 29–43).

67 Montanaro, fn. 10.

in IOs, CSOs only have a voice in these processes, not a vote. This means that the 'authorizing' constituencies (the CSOs) are relatively weak anyway.

The next question is whether IOs themselves can be seen as having two constituencies, as in Montanaro's conceptualization. The triangular scheme of self-appointed representative – claimed constituency – authorizing constituency could (with some modification) be applied to IOs. The IOs are not (unlike the CSOs) 'self-appointed' but they are set up by States to fulfil certain functions. Thus, the WOAH could be seen as making representative claims for animals as its claimed constituency, and still have the Member States as its 'authorizing constituency'. Note that this model accepts that the accountability of the representatives to the authorizing constituency is not secured through elections, but for example by withdrawal of financing to the organization, or exit (such as Japan's denunciation of the ICRW and its concomitant withdrawal from the IWC in 2019). Such an exit is not a *democratic* accountability mechanism but a different way of expressing disapproval which at best generates some weak accountability.

One possible tool to hold the representatives accountable to the relevant constituencies are certifications or audits by third parties, notably by CSOs. Some practice in this direction exists both in global governance and for animal issues.[68] This parallel evolution of practices in IOs generally and with regard to animals in domestic governance shows that the problem is (to some extent) analogous: it is the lack of control by those who are absent. CSOs could accredit or certify that the animal intermediaries ('representatives' in a loose sense) fulfil certain criteria of quality and reliability.[69] Such a scheme could be introduced in WOAH and would help to bring animal interests more to bear in its decision-making.

### 9.5.2.4 'Surrogate Representation'?

At this point we need to accept the reality that the animals cannot select nor recall any human 'representatives' themselves. The selection and recall of

68 See for example the certification of animal welfare administrators in the US by the Association for Animal Welfare Advancement. https://learning.theaawa.org/cawa, last accessed 1 February 2026. See in global governance e.g. the civil society network IFOA (standing for 'International Federation of Organic Agriculture Movements') that inter alia certifies agricultural operations for their adherence to a 'family' of organic production and processing standards. www.ifoam.bio/our-work/how/standards-certification/organic-guarantee-system, last accessed 1 February 2026.

69 The follow-up question is how to select and control the certifiers, to prevent misleading certifications. Once we allow *others* to receive the accounts and to sanction (i.e. once we leave the democratic realm of self-rule among equals), the chain of 'controllers' is in theory endless.

these humans must be done by other *humans* who act in the interest of animals. The terminology used for such schemes varies. Those humans who chose (by election or otherwise) and receive the accounts are 'proxies' (to use the term coined by Andrew Dobson with a view to 'representing' future generations of humans)[70] or the 'second constituency' (to use Laura Montanaro's term).[71] The entire scheme has been called a 'surrogate representation',[72] with a 'surrogate accountability'.[73]

However, the challenge for all variants is to secure that the proxies indeed 'stand for' the first, the 'claimed', constituency. All schemes cannot overcome the fundamental fact that the animals – although they can articulate their interests – are not able to select and recall representatives in the human-dominated society. Those who receive the accounts and can draw consequences would never be the animals themselves, but some other institution staffed with humans acting for the animals.

I conclude that all forms of speaking 'for' absent actors who cannot *themselves* select and recall (through elections or otherwise) are only a quasi-representation or 'representation' in quotation marks. This is in line with the terminology of Hanna Pitkin who considers long-term arrangements for securing a regular, systematic potential responsiveness as a key feature of 'representative government' as we understand this elusive concept today.[74] I therefore prefer to call these humans *intermediaries*, because they stand between the animals and the decision-makers. They are – towards the side of the animals – paternalist speakers for the animals. Towards the side of the actual decision-makers (e.g. the Assembly of the WOAH, or a democratic national parliament) these intermediaries may (in the future) be equipped with a range of diverse powers, depending on the institutional framework.[75]

Importantly, in the absence (and genuine impossibility) of mechanisms of election and recall, this scheme of human intermediation needs to build in other mechanisms to prevent the abuse of power of the human intermediaries. The historic experience of abusive guardianship in public and international

70 Andrew Dobson, 'Representative Democracy and the Environment', in William M. Lafferty and James Meadowcroft (eds.), *Democracy and the Environment. Problems and Prospects* (Cheltenham: Edward Elgar, 1996), pp. 124–139, p. 132.

71 Montanaro, fn. 10.

72 Smith, fn. 45, p. 109. She opines that humans could act 'as though' we needed to secure animals' consent, ibid., p. 108.

73 Svenja Alhaus, 'Political Representation of Animals', in Anne Peters, Kristen Stilt and Saskia Stucki (eds.), *Oxford Handbook of Global Animal Law* (Oxford: Oxford University Press, 2026), in press.

74 Pitkin, fn. 59, pp. 232–235.

75 See in detail below Section 9.6.

law (colonies and mandate territories), and in private law (guardianship over women and children) proves the necessity of such safeguards.[76] These are also important for the procedures of considering animals in human political processes.

To conclude, what matters is not the label but the legitimate request to upgrade or strengthen the role of animals in political processes. Independently of the label given, new schemes to bring animal interests to bear in human politics are warranted in normative terms to mitigate the currently unfair neglect of animal interests. With this objective, Janneke Vink proposes to design human 'institutions so that they are forced to pay heed to animals who cannot defend their interests in a political context. Thereby, the interests of animals are institutionally safeguarded and animals get the political consideration they deserve'.[77] Vink has called this the 'consideration right' of animals.[78] Such a consideration right would not lead to democratic animal representation with accountability to the animals themselves, but to a proper 'animal consideration'. This would alleviate the current legitimacy problems of human political processes to some extent.

### 9.5.3 *The Circumscription of the Animal 'Constituency'*

A key question is how and where to draw the boundaries of the group that needs to be represented (or considered) in a given forum.[79] We call this group the 'constituency'.[80] For decision-making in States, this constituency is formed by the citizens, and therefore the question of animal 'citizenship' is so important (see above, Section 9.5.1). IOs do not have a territory and no acknowledged citizens. Therefore, the group to be represented cannot be defined by 'belonginess' or 'community', as often proxied by residence in a given territory and captured or symbolized by citizenship.

With a view to animals in relation to the decision-making by IOs, the 'boundary question' presents itself as a double question: the groups potentially

76 Unlike Robert Goodin, 'Enfranchising the Earth, and its Alternatives' (1996) 44 *Political Studies* 835-849, I do not think that the 'complete incorporation' of animals' (or nature's) interests within the interests of those who are enfranchised generates normatively appropriate outcomes.

77 Vink in Donaldson, Vink and Gagnon, fn. 40, at 83.

78 Vink, *The Open Society and Its Animals*, fn. 40, pp. 53, 347.

79 This has famously been called the 'boundary problem' of democracy by Robert A. Dahl, *Democracy and Its Critics* (New Haven: Yale University Press, 1989), pp. 146–147.

80 The word constituency is used, in a narrow sense, to denote the body of citizens entitled to elect a representative, and also in a broader sense to refer to people involved in or served by any organization.

affected and even subjected to decisions by organizations are not only spatially dispersed, but potentially also comprise more than humans. In order to bring animal interests to bear in the decision-making of IOs, the boundaries of the constituency must not only be pushed across the State boundaries, but additionally across the species lines (see above Section 9.2.2).

So the question is how to circumscribe the circle of animals whose interests should be brought to bear. A widespread premise in democratic theory is that the collective decision-making processes (especially beyond the Nation-State) should grant each human an equal say in decisions *affecting* him or her. This premise is relevant both for decision-making in IOs, and for the unilateral decision-making of States with transnational repercussions for people at other places of the globe, an issue that is not dealt with in this chapter.

The all-affected approach has been extended to animals. It has been said that there is no theoretical reason why the 'all-affected' principle should not transcend the species barrier.[81] Following Robert Garner, the all-affected principle demands 'the inclusion of animals if and when their interests are affected by decisions made. It is clear that many political decisions that are made do impact, often detrimentally and often profoundly, upon animals. Therefore, it follows that animals (more specifically humans acting for animals) ought to have a say in those decisions.'[82]

It is submitted here, in line with other scholarship, that the so-called 'all-affected' principle is too broad. Basically, all human decisions on infrastructure, on the economy, on food, education, sports, affect different groups of animals. If all who are 'affected' by decisions of a State or – for the purposes of this chapter – of an IO were entitled to be represented (or only considered) in its decision-making, this would require to bring into the picture an amorphous group. This is neither morally not warranted nor practicable. Limitations and qualifications are needed.

The desirable and necessary limitations and qualifications can be reached in different strategies. The 'constituency' could be limited to a certain group of actors, namely sentient animals.[83] This is still an exceedingly broad and vague group. A different approach to demarcate animal 'representation' would be to

[81] Lucy J. Parry, 'Deliberative Democracy and Animals: Not so Strange Bedfellows', in Garner and O'Sullivan, fn. 42, pp. 137–154, p. 140; see also Vink, *The Open Society and Its Animals*, fn. 40, pp. 53–54. Concomitantly, animals have been conceptualized as 'stakeholders' in corporate and political processes: Aude-Solveig Epstein and Alice di Concetto, 'Animals in Economic Law: A Research Agenda', in Aude-Solveig Epstein and Alice di Concetto (eds.), *Animals in Economic Law: A New Approach to Protecting Sentient Beings in the EU* (London: Palgrave Macmillan, 2026), in press.

[82] Garner, fn. 42, p. 115.

[83] Ibid., p. 116.

demand such representation only when fundamental or basic interests of animals are probably and deeply affected ('no slaughter without representation').

Alternatively, or cumulatively, the idea of 'subjection' – as propagated for the human say in political decision-making – could be applied to animals. 'Subjection' can be understood in different ways, ranging from being under the formal purview of the law, to being under coercive authority, to being under the sheer exercise of physical power.[84] Animals are in a special way subjected to human laws. Although animals are not expected to abide with the law, they still form the object of regulation, and the human laws apply to them. Also, animals are in factual terms fully dominated through physical violence by humans. Where this is authorized by law, the coercive apparatus of the human State condones this domination. Due to the animals' lack of understanding, the formal aspect of subjection is less relevant, but the physical aspect all the more. In that sense, animals *are* subjected by human decision-making, also when such decisions are taken by IOs.

The aspect of coercion is modified by the fact that most organizations do not possess any enforcement authority, also not over the animals. This does not prevent the animals' constant and intense reduction of life chances and options for flourishment due to the acts of States that implement the relevant organizational acts. Many animals are in this sense 'subjected' to a number of decisions by IOs, most surely to the relevant standards set by WOAH for their species.

The problem remains that the criterion of 'subjection' does not lead to any clear boundary of the 'constituency' either. But such blurriness is not fatal if the animal 'citizens' do not have a vote. Taking their interests into account needs no firm boundaries. The circle of who must be taken into account can be blurry, and it can also be graded. My tentative view is that there should be no hard distinctions along species lines because this would be skewed in favour of rare animals. It also seems that not only domesticated animals but also wild animals need to be considered, because they, too, are harmed by human activity.[85] Further explorations must be left for another paper.

### 9.5.4 *Animal Deliberative Democracy*

With a view to a democratization of decision-making in IOs, many theorists favour deliberative democracy as an alternative or complement

84 Robert Goodin, 'Enfranchising all Subjected, Worldwide' (2016) 8(3) *International Theory* 365–389, at 370–373.

85 Cochrane, fn. 2, pp. 50–55.

to the 'vote-centric' models of democracy. At the same time, this approach has been pursued for environmental and animal-related issues.

Deliberative elements are first of all debates with the goal of reaching an acceptable decision based on good grounds ('deliberations'), the participation of all affected ('stakeholders'), and transparency. In IOs (as in other transnational and international forums), deliberations seem to be easier to realize and are indeed practiced widely (as opposed to transnational or global elections that are fraught with practical and conceptual problems).[86] Along this line, Sabino Cassese has called deliberations a 'surrogate' for the lack of democratic decision-making by IOs.[87]

Environmentalists have espoused deliberative democracy, because deliberative elements are thought to yield better outcomes for nature.[88] The environmentalist ideas have been applied to animal governance.[89] Some authors count communicative exchanges between humans and animals as 'animal deliberation'.[90] Indeed, it is intuitively plausible that the ostensibly beneficial features of deliberations might serve to bring animal interests to bear more in the political process. Generally speaking, deliberations probably enhance rationality, intensify the consideration of the interests of differently situated others, and facilitate mutually acceptable outcomes. They presumably generate more truthfulness, more reason-giving, more social learning, and most of all more reflexivity. All this means that democracy without deliberations would be deficient.

'Animal deliberation' might therefore be a beneficial procedure in IOs such as WOAH. However, the concept of democracy is overstretched when it is applied to mere deliberations without the possibility of electing and recalling representatives. In the absence of voting, deliberations by themselves do not amount to democracy (which needs deliberation and voting), and deliberations do not necessarily involve representation at all, because also those who are absent from a concrete decision-making forum can still participate in deliberations around the decision-making. 'Animal deliberation' might enhance the consideration of animal interests in IOs such as WOAH but would not transform them into more democratic institutions.

86 Even the EU Parliament is not composed of members elected on the basis of an EU-wide procedure in which each citizen has an equal vote.

87 Sabino Cassese, *A World Government?* (Seville: Global Law Press-Editorial Derecho Global, 2018), p. 16.

88 Robyn Eckersley, *The Green State: Rethinking Democracy and Sovereignty* (Cambridge, MA: MIT Press, 2004), pp. 115–119.

89 Parry, fn. 81; Garner, fn. 42, pp. 106–111.

90 Driessen, fn. 49.

## 9.6 CONCRETE PROPOSALS

Political theorists have suggested various novel ways for bringing animals into political (legislative or decision-making) processes.[91] These mainly refer to political processes in democratic States where the principal lawmaker is a democratically elected parliament. Alasdair Cochrane, for example, demanded: 'Animal representatives should act as trustees of the interests of all non-human members of our communities – individuals whose fates are very much entangled with our own. And they should seek to understand those various interests and feed them into impartial deliberations with other policy-makers in their formulations of the public good.'[92] Cochrane also sought to 'explore how certain existing global political institutions, such as the UN General Assembly, might be radically and democratically transformed for the protection of the worth and rights of all sentient creatures'.[93]

The proposals often use the word 'representation' (for example a 'fiduciary representation' of animals)[94] that I will place in quotations marks here, in order to highlight that it is not representation in a strict sense (with accountability to the animals themselves).[95] Still, these schemes seek to bring animal interests to bear in the political process by allowing humans to 'speak for and on behalf' of animals (rather than to 'stand for' or to 'embody' animals). For the reasons explained above (Section 9.5.2.4), this activity is called *animal consideration* (or animal advocacy and animal defence) here.

In the literature, the names given to the humans who are performing the job of bringing animals' interests to bear in human political processes inter alia depend on the type of political forum (parliament or international conference), on the surrounding governance scheme (a democratic Nation-State or an IO), and on the competences given to those humans. They are called animal advocates, defenders, speakers, commissioners, guardians, or

[91] See for an excellent discussion Vink, *The Open Society and Its Animals*, fn. 40, pp. 123–204. See also Marianna Dänner, 'Die Repräsentation von Tierinteressen im politischen Prozess' (2023) 83 *Heidelberg Journal of International Law* 489–516; Ahlhaus, fn. 73; Joe Gray and Patrick Curry, 'Ecodemocracy and Political Representation for Non-Human Nature', in Helena Kopnina and Haydn Washington (eds.), *Conservation: Integrating Social and Ecological Justice* (Cham, Switzerland: Springer, 2020), pp.155-166; for the representation of past and future generations: Hélène Ruiz Fabri, Valérie Rosoux and Alessandra Donati (eds.), *Representing the Absent* (Baden-Baden: Nomos, 2023).

[92] Cochrane, fn. 2, p. 61.

[93] Ibid., p. 132.

[94] Donaldson, 'Animal Citizens and the Democratic Challenge', fn. 47, at 714, 715. She uses the term 'indirect representation', interchangeably.

[95] See above Section 9.5.2.4.

trustees. For the reasons explained above, I prefer the name 'intermediary' (see above Section 9.5.2.4).

The novel ideas differ with regard to *who* is eligible or appointable, *how* (and by whom) the human intermediaries are selected and controlled, *where* these humans act, and *what* their tasks are. As for the tasks, the humans could be allowed to vote on legislative proposals (direct participation as decision-makers); they could be given a right to elect members of a parliament; they could be granted a right to be informed and heard; and they could give advice.

On the domestic plane, in democratic States, these humans' mediating and promotional activity (in the interest of animals) feeds into democratic law-making processes. On the international plane, and especially in IOs, the modes of selecting and controlling those human intermediaries and also their task in the decision-making process would be different ones.

With regard to their selection, the animal intermediaries could be directly appointed, like experts, by the government or by a governmental body. These intermediaries would then enjoy little democratic legitimacy. If the animal intermediary shall be an *elected* office the question is who shall be eligible, by whom, and in which procedures. On this plane, Pablo Magaña distinguishes 'unrestricted' models from 'restricted' models.[96] In the main 'unrestricted' model, all human voters would be allowed to elect, with a second vote, specific animal 'representatives'.[97] However, these 'representatives' would be accountable to the human voters and therefore have little or no incentive to focus on animals' interests.

The 'restricted' variants mean that only *some* humans elect or appoint animal 'representatives'. Building on a proposal that Andrew Dobson made with regard to the 'representation of future generations', Alasdair Cochrane suggested that some humans who have demonstrated a concern for and expertise on animal questions should form a 'proxy electorate'. They would stand for the animals (or for some animals) and thus would be allowed to elect (other) humans, the 'animal representatives', whose task would be to defend (only) animal interests.[98] But this model violates political equality because some humans (the 'proxy electorate') get two votes, one for the 'all-purpose'

96 See for a systematization of institutional proposals Pablo Magaña, 'The Political Representation of Nonhuman Animals' (2022) 48(4) *Social Theory and Practice* 665–690.

97 This proposal has been made by Ekeli for what he calls 'representatives' of future generations, Kristian Skagen Ekeli, 'Giving a Voice to Posterity: Deliberative Democracy and Representation of Future People' (2005) 18 *Journal of Agricultural and Environmental Ethics* 429–450.

98 Cochrane, fn. 2, pp. 47–49; see also Ahlhaus, fn. 73. Seminally Andrew Dobson, 'Representative Democracy and the Environment', in Lafferty and Meadowcroft, fn. 70, pp. 124–139.

representatives and an additional one for the animal 'representatives'.[99] That problem could be solved by forcing the proxy electorate to choose in which elections they want to use a vote; they could give up their general vote in exchange for a vote for the animal 'representative'.[100] However, this scheme would not guarantee that any animal 'representatives' are elected at all.

Another problem is the circumscription of the proxy electorate: how to decide which humans form the 'animal lobby' (the proxy electorate) and should therefore be allowed to elect animal 'representatives'? Alasdair Cochrane has suggested to form the proxy electorate – which he calls 'deliberative citizen assemblies' of voters – by simple lottery.[101] The lottery would resemble the random selection of lay judges or jury members in the criminal courts of many legal systems. These randomly selected citizens might be offered the choice to vote for animal 'representatives' (in addition to, or instead of voting for ordinary representatives in the general elections to parliament).[102]

However, and importantly, all these suggestions suffer from the fatal flaw that they falsely presuppose that animal affairs can be neatly separated from other societal affairs. In reality, these affairs are entangled. More life, liberty, and space for animals inevitably requires to restrict human liberties (to build houses, to eat animal food, to use natural resources, and so on). It is impossible to separate the political competences of the old-fashioned human representatives from those of the novel 'animal representatives'.[103] Therefore, if 'animal representatives' are not elected by everyone in a given jurisdiction and nevertheless are granted a power to participate in political decision-making, their participation (which impinges on human affairs) creates a certain democratic deficit. Human interests will be affected by decisions that are not taken under full popular control. The animal 'representation' would be a counter-majoritarian institution. This is not inconceivable in a democracy, as

[99] Magaña, fn. 96, at 17.

[100] This would be comparable to the Māori electorates in New Zealand. The voters in the Māori electorates vote for reserved positions for representatives of Māori in the New Zealand Parliament. Every area in New Zealand is covered by both a general and a Māori electorate. All registered Māori electors have the opportunity to choose whether they are included on the Māori *or* general electorate rolls, and thus vote for either the general representative or for the Māori representative. The Māori electoral districts are larger than the general electoral districts, their boundaries are superimposed over the boundaries of the general electoral districts. Legal bases are the following: Act to provide for the better Representation of the Native Aboriginal Inhabitants of the Colony of New Zealand of 10 October 1867; Section 45 of the Electoral Act 1993; Electoral (Māori Electoral Option) Legislation Act 2022.

[101] Cochrane, fn. 2, p. 49; Alasdair Cochrane, *Should Animals Have Political Rights?* (Cambridge: Polity Press, 2020), p. 103.

[102] Cochrane, fn. 2, chapter 3.

[103] cf Vink, *The Open Society and Its Animals*, fn. 40, p. 191.

a complement to the majoritarian institutions, but the democratic cost must be factored into any normative assessment of the proposed scheme.

Moreover, all proposed models confront the unyielding fact that any type of 'representative' cannot be politically accountable directly to the animals themselves, due to the animals' lack of political understanding.

The transposal of the schemes to decision-making in IOs faces additional obstacles and requires additional modifications. One aspect is that relevant organizations such as WOAH and WTO, and bodies such as the CITES COPs, the UN Framework Convention on Climate Change (UNFCCC) COPs or the IWC fail to represent humans in a democratic fashion, to begin with.

Further obstacles to a 'representation' of animals on the side of potential human representatives or intermediaries are not unsurmountable. Ignorance, bias, and the value/action gap exist but can be reduced by constant reflexivity.[104] Institutional problems such as the preponderance of organized vested interests, as embodied in the meat lobby and the agricultural lobby, are not uniquely a problem for the representation of animal interests but generally distort political processes. They can be addressed with stricter transparency and conflict of interest rules.

Besides building new institutions, new and additional procedures such as animal mainstreaming[105] or animal impact assessments[106] could be weaved in lawmaking procedures in order to bring animal interests to bear here. All these institutions and procedures could be combined. It is an empirical question whether such a cumulation of, for example, elected intermediaries, non-elected civil society activists, ombudspersons, and mainstreaming would altogether lead to more animal friendly legal outputs, both in domestic legislative (democratic) processes and in the decision-making of IOs.

## 9.7 CONCLUSIONS

It is desirable (normatively appropriate) to bring animal interests to bear in the decision-making of Nation-States and IOs. But such integration faces

104 cf Magaña, fn. 96.

105 Markus Wild, 'Animal Mainstreaming: Motivation und Bedeutung eines neuen Konzepts in der Tierethik', in Elke Diehl and Jens Tuider (eds.), *Haben Tiere Rechte? Aspekte und Dimensionen der Mensch-Tier-Beziehung* (Bonn: Bundeszentrale für politische Bildung, 2019), pp. 323–335.

106 Steven P. McCulloch and Michael J. Reiss, 'Bovine Tuberculosis and Badger Control in Britain: Science, Policy and Politics' (2017) 30 *Journal of Agricultural and Environmental Ethics* 469–484, at 480.

structural and permanent obstacles that root in the animals' lack of understanding and judging of human political processes. It is often said that animal interests are 'mute' or that animal individuals are 'voiceless'.[107] This is an exaggeration, because animals can and do express their preferences. However, they cannot hold humans who disregard their interests to account. These physical limits of human-animal communication not only foreclose representation through elections but also prevent other, looser forms of responsiveness and accountability to the animals themselves. I therefore prefer the term animal consideration rather than animal representation in (democratic) political processes.

Along this line, the institutions and procedures for decision-making in IOs can and should be much improved. To return to the example of WOAH, the office of an animal ombudsperson with a robust mandate should be created; the voice of pro-animal CSOs should be strengthened through compulsory notice-and-comment procedures and extended speaking rights in the WOAH Assembly; all standards should go through mandatory animal welfare impact assessment; and the 'scientific' basis of the standards should be broadened to comprise also ethical arguments.

All attempts for upstepping the existing rudimentary schemes in the direction of a better and stronger consideration of animal interests in human politics will require deep cultural and social change. They depend on the cultivation of a 'sentient solidarity'[108] or 'interspecies solidarity'[109] which is to a large extent beyond the purview of the law.

[107] Magaña, fn. 96.
[108] Cochrane, fn. 2, p. 123.
[109] von Essen and Allen, fn. 48.

# 10

# Democratic Representation in International Institutions: From Great Power Hegemony to Rebellions by the Most Affected

Jochen von Bernstorff

## 10.1 INTRODUCTION

In the history of international institutional law questions of legitimate or 'democratic' representation, participation and decision-making have somewhat regularly re-appeared in both theory and practice over the last 150 years.[1] Concrete controversies usually referred to voting procedures, composition of organs, rules of participation, and the formal status of decisions taken by organs of international institutions. A handful of related dichotomies have structured the associated international legal debates in this field, such as unanimity- versus majority-rule, 'one State one vote' versus weighted voting, binding versus non-binding decisions, diplomatic versus civil society-representation, as well as legislative versus individualized or administrative decision-making. Structurally, these dichotomies revolve around the foundational and enigmatic principle of sovereign equality of States, consent-based lawmaking and the concept of international institutions as creations and subjects of international (treaty-) law. Inevitably, these debates have also been framed against the background of contemporary world-historical developments, such as the creation of the League of Nations and the United Nations (UN) after the two world wars or the decolonization era.

[1] See out of a vast literature for instance the approaches by Anne Peter, 'Dual Democracy', in Jan Klabbers, Anne Peters and Geir Ulfstein (eds.), *The Constitutionalization of International Law* (Oxford: Oxford University Press, 2009), pp. 263–341; Jan Klabbers, 'Law-Making and Constitutionalism', in ibid., pp. 81–125; Gráinne de Búrca, Robert O. Keohane and Charles Sabel, 'Global Experimentalist Governance' (2014) 44(3) *British Journal of Political Science* 477–486; and more recently with a new approach Samantha Besson and José Luis Martí, 'Legitimate Actors of International Law-Making: Towards a Theory of International Democratic Representation' (2018) 9(3) *Jurisprudence* 504–540.

Arguably this holds also true for current scholarly reflections on the democratic legitimacy of international institutions. While being conscious of the ubiquity of the crisis semantics in scholarly discourse, I will nonetheless use the concept of 'planetary crisis' in order to depict the current political context, in which issues of democratic, majoritarian or representative law- and decision-making in international institutions are gaining a renewed prominence: a world-historical situation after a global pandemic, in times of an unfolding climate catastrophe and ongoing nuclear arms race, as well as during a major war of annexation involving a permanent member of the UN Security Council and nuclear power attacking a sovereign neighbouring State. Within and through international institutions, however, public and private, international, transnational, and national actors have reacted to these in many respects catastrophic developments and events by launching new political and legal initiatives. Broad coalitions of small and middle-sized States, including civil society organizations are currently pushing for major institutional reforms in various international institutions reacting rather creatively to a perceived institutional standstill often caused by great powers defending the legal and political status quo.[2]

In the field of disarmament, scholars have observed new coalitions of the 'have-nots' breaking in many ways with the old legal status quo of the Non-Proliferation Treaty (NPT) and confronting the nuclear States with a new complimentary treaty regime (the Treaty on the Prohibition of Nuclear Weapons (TPNW)), which is also informally called the Ban Treaty. Regarding the climate crisis, broad coalitions of smaller States spearheaded by small island States have over the last years put pressure on great powers to introduce major institutional reforms, such as a permanent and compulsory loss and damage fund, as well as new legal avenues for a right to compensation of 'specially affected' countries for climate induced damages through a Vanuatu-spearheaded request by the UN General Assembly (UNGA) for an advisory opinion of the International Court of Justice (ICJ).[3] A growing

[2] Pointing to the possibilities of coalitions of States to compensate for a perceived lack of democratic legitimacy in a particular hegemonic constellation, see Besson and Martí, fn. 1. The authors argue in favour of combining legitimacy resources of (democratic) public and private actors in a 'refined' case by case approach to fora of international lawmaking.

[3] On the struggle for compensation for 'loss and damage' by coalitions of the most affected, see Patrick Toussaint, 'Voices Unheard – Affected Communities and the Climate Negotiations on Loss and Damage' (2018) 3(5–6) *Third World Thematics: A TWQ Journal* 765–784; UNFCCC, 'Report of the Conference of the Parties on its twenty-seventh session, held in Sharm el-Sheikh from 6 to 20 November 2022 (20 November 2022)' (17 March 2023), FCCC/CP/2022/10/Add.1, pp. 5–11; see the UNGA, 'Request for an advisory opinion of the International Court of Justice on the obligations of States in respect of climate change' (1 March 2023), A/77/L.58.

coalition around the most affected small island States is currently in the process of negotiating a 'Fossil Fuel Non-Proliferation Treaty' aiming to put pressure on the Member States of the Paris Agreement to stop the exploration and exploitation of new oil-, gas- and coal fields. Unlike in the decolonization era, these broad coalitions of small and middle-sized States are not necessarily composed of former colonized countries only but include States from all regions and continents.

What holds these coalitions together is a common (public/private) reaction against a perceived standstill or even retrogression regarding the realization of the objectives of the respective international legal regime.[4] While the degree of co-ordination and conflict within these different coalitions certainly differs, they arguably can be seen as joint attempts of the less powerful to breathe life into regimes, which judged by their substantive goals are of existential significance for these States. Small non-nuclear States for instance are more affected by a nuclear arms race than the nuclear powers themselves because of a lack of deterrence capabilities. The likelihood to be attacked, blackmailed, or pushed around by a nuclear power potentially increases with rising stockpiles abroad. Ukraine being a case in point. Or take global health issues as a second example. Countries from the Global South usually have less public and private research capabilities to develop and buy vaccines in times of a pandemic and often this fact coincides with a dysfunctional domestic health system. They are thus more (negatively) affected by a weak and Western-dominated WHO regime, not to mention the effects of an international patent rights regime (the Agreement on Trade Related Intellectual Property Rights (TRIPS)) potentially blocking access to affordable vaccines and other drugs.

All of this goes hand in hand with another recent trend in international institutions, namely the shift from classic non-governmental organization (NGO) representation to privileged participation rights of 'most affected persons' organizations'.[5] Without going too much into detail at this introductory stage, in various international organizations (IOs) Northern-based NGOs over the last decade have been replaced by grass root organizations mainly consisting of individuals personally affected by the decisions of a particular regime, such as

[4] For Becker Lorca the '*solidarité de combat*' (M. Bedjaoui) usually aims at introducing redistributive policies into a certain regime analysing continuities between the New International Economic Order and current developments in the WHO regime, see Arnulf Becker Lorca, 'Contesting Global Justice from the South: Redistribution in the International Order' (2023) 99(1) *International Affairs* 41–60.

[5] Jochen von Bernstorff, 'New Responses to the Legitimacy Crisis of International Institutions: The Role of "Civil Society" and the Rise of the Principle of Participation of the "Most Affected" in International Law' (2021) 32(1) *European Journal of International Law* 125–157.

smallholder farmers from the Global South in the Food and Agriculture Organization (FAO). Taking these trends together arguably justifies speaking of 'coalitions of the most affected', involving both public and private actors, currently resisting and transforming international institutions through various rebellious projects. But what are the institutional or procedural means through which these coalitions aim or have historically attempted to transform fundamental norms or regimes of the international legal order? Historically, the main twentieth-century strategy of broader coalitions of small and middle powers was to use plenary organs of international institutions in order to prepare and promote rebellious projects supported also by civil society actors. Decisive preconditions for such projects were new forms of (majority-based) decision-making in international institutions introduced in the UN era and novel forms of civil society participation. Rebellions, such as the one against the alleged legality of colonialism or for a New International Economic Order, were staged through majority-voting on progressive non-binding UNGA resolutions. An associated rebellious strategy always has been to campaign for progressive treaty projects launched by broad coalitions of States against the declared will of great powers, often prepared by majority decisions of UNGA.[6] As mentioned above, in more recent times, such rebellions included new treaty projects complementing or in fact correcting existing multilateral treaty regimes spearheaded by States and non-State actors particularly affected by the lack of progress and implementation under the existing treaty regimes in times of planetary crisis.

In what follows, I will revisit older debates about majority-rule and large State-coalitions challenging the great powers, as well as foundational approaches to "democratic" legitimacy within and by international institutions (Section 10.2). As a second step, I will analyse in more detail the new concept of the representation of 'the most affected' and a current example of rebellious lawmaking by public/private coalitions of the most affected, notably the TPNW (Section 10.3). By way of conclusion, I will reflect on the broader and more general implications of this trend also for other areas and regimes of international law (Section 10.4).

## 10.2 DECISION-MAKING IN INTERNATIONAL INSTITUTIONS

The first IOs were created in the nineteenth century and dominated by Europe's great powers and their respective national bureaucracies. Decisions

6 See for these decolonization struggles Jochen von Bernstorff and Philipp Dann (eds.), *The Battle for International Law: South-North Perspectives on the Decolonization Era* (Oxford: Oxford University Press, 2019).

were legitimated by sovereign consent (unanimity) and technical expertise. Only in the twentieth century through the UN majority-voting became more common, giving broad coalitions of small and middle powers more influence in decision-making within the UN and other IOs.

### 10.2.1 *The Initial Set-Up: Sovereign Consent and Technical Expertise As Historical Legitimation Narratives in the Nineteenth Century*

The original blueprint for IOs, including the first scholarly reflections on the legitimacy of their lawmaking activities stems from the nineteenth century. Industrialization, scientific, and technical inventions, European imperialism and the associated first wave of economic globalization in the nineteenth century created the perceived need of European national administrations to co-ordinate technical and humanitarian standards. Under the leadership of specific European powers and industrial or philanthropic elites, public international unions and commissions were created by international treaty law, such as the World Telegraph Union, the World Postal Union, or the river commissions for the navigation on the Danube and the Rhine; but also the late nineteenth century international debt commissions which regulated the Egyptian, Turkish, and Chinese debt restructuring programmes or the International Sugar Commission are cases in point. In the field of institutionalized humanitarian and social regulation the Office for the Prevention of Maritime African Slave Trade and Liquor Traffic based in Zanzibar, the Institute for Agriculture in Rome, the International Labor Office in Basel could be added as examples.[7]

The original blueprint of these forms of cooperation is the harmonization of administrative action between European countries on certain issues which in the eyes of Europe's great powers seemed to require international regulation. Particularly obvious was this need for coordinated administrative action in the field of new (communication-) technologies, which had only been invented during that period. The International Telegraphic Union, which later became the International Telecommunications Union (ITU), served as a precedent for the subsequent creation of other permanent forms of administrative cooperation of States.[8] When major European powers, which were particularly advanced in the development of telegraphic technology, realized that the

[7] For an overview, see Inis L. Claude, *Swords into Plowshares. The Problems and Progress of International Organization* (New York: Random House, 1956).

[8] Paul S. Reinsch, 'International Unions and Their Administration' (1907) 1(3) *American Journal of International Law* 579–623.

envisaged global expansion of this technology needed international cooperation, they invited twenty States in 1865 to Paris for a first international conference. States were represented diplomatically by their ambassadors in Paris and by expert delegates from the respective national administrations. The aim of the conference was a continuous harmonization of telegraph administration in the respective countries. Negotiators in Paris differentiated between the convention as a basis for further cooperation and specific harmonized regulations. Even though the convention had to be signed by the ambassadors, the concrete regulations were negotiated by the experts from the national administrations.[9]

In the eyes of great power political elites, legitimacy was formally provided by sovereign consent and substantially by technical expertise. The initial convention foresaw regular conferences of the parties to formally amend its rules and regulations. Conferences would be organized by national administrations on a rotating basis. Only later was a permanent secretariat added to the organizational structure of the ITU with the task to facilitate the application of the convention by national administrations.[10] At an even later stage the organization decided to establish an executive council, consisting of a limited number of Member State-representatives with the task to represent the plenary organ between the regular plenary conferences.

With this organizational set-up, consisting of a plenary of diplomatic representatives, a smaller executive body of diplomatic representatives elected by the plenary, and a secretariat with international civil servants, a model for further IOs had been created: the convention usually established a main diplomatic plenary organ, in which legitimate rule-making in form of resolutions and standard-setting could take place. The plenary organs usually decided on the basis of the 'one State one vote' principle, hereby basing the authority and legitimation of new rules on the principle of sovereign equality. Voting under the unanimity-rule was therefore the standard procedure. The unions also often established a permanent secretariat as a facilitator of future

[9] Anne Peters and Simone Peter, 'International Organizations: Between Technocracy and Democracy', in Bardo Fassbender and Anne Peters (eds.), *The Oxford Handbook of the History of International Law* (Oxford: Oxford University Press, 2012), pp. 170–197, pp. 183–184.

[10] Art. 61 of the Convention télégraphique internationale de Paris: 'Une Administration télégraphique, désignée par la Conférence, prendra les mesures propres à faciliter, dans un intérêt commun, l'exécution et application de la Convention. A cet effet elle organisera, sous le titre de 'Bureau international des Administrations télégraphiques', un service spécial qui fonctionnera sous sa direction, dont les frais seront supportés par toutes les Administrations des Etats'; see Convention télégraphique international de Paris, révisée à Vienne (1868), (adopted 1868, entered into force 1 January 1869). https://search.itu.int/history/HistoryDigitalCollectionDocLibrary/5.2.61.fr.200.pdf, last accessed 30 September 2023.

conferences and for enhancing the application of standards. In the more mature organizations we can then observe the creation of an executive board or council as an executive supervisory organ usually consisting of a limited number of national representatives, elected by the plenary organ and representing the membership.[11]

In all international unions and commissions, the permanent secretariats not only started to employ international civil servants, but they also involved private expertise in their knowledge-creation and dissemination activities.[12] The latter of which was not only the case for unions dealing with technical innovations but was also very common in the financial, humanitarian, and cultural field. Often private technical innovation or philanthropic projects driven by elite-networks led to privately organized international conferences, which preceded the initiation of international diplomatic conferences on the respective matters.[13] Those private associations, scientific institutions, and industry representatives, which had spearheaded technical or humanitarian cooperation, later usually remained an integral part of the knowledge and policy network, at the very heart of the respective international organization. The Egyptian Debt Commission of 1880 for instance consisted of national representatives from the major European creditors, which were in constant contact with the involved banks and their national financial stakeholders. Without the consent of the representatives of the creditor nations in the Commission, the Egyptian government could not incur any expenditures not authorized under the Convention.[14]

Formal legitimation for lawmaking and standard-setting was taken to be provided by sovereign consent, substantively by technical expertise, and culturally by a strong ideology of universal cooperation in a perceived 'common interest'. Decisions by executive bodies would be confined to less fundamental, that is administrative decisions, deriving their legitimacy indirectly from the plenary as an elected body. It goes without saying that colonized societies had no representation in the deliberations of these institutions being excluded from the legal privileges of European sovereignty as so-called 'non-civilized' entities. Colonies of the metropoles, such as the British crown-colony India,

[11] Henry G. Schermers and Niels Blokker, *International Institutional Law: Unity within Diversity*, 3rd ed. (Leiden: Brill/Nijoff, 1995), para. 409.

[12] Claude, fn. 7, pp. 39–40.

[13] Miloš Vec, *Recht und Normierung in der industriellen Revolution: Neue Strukturen der Normsetzung in Völkerrecht, staatlicher Gesetzgebung und gesellsschaftlicher Selbstnormierung* (Frankfurt: Klostermann, 2006), pp. 31 ff; Fassbender and Peters, fn. 12, pp. 186–188.

[14] Reinsch, fn. 8, at 620.

were usually represented by colonial administrations adding hereby to the numerical weight of European empires in these institutions, thus introducing the very first weighted voting procedures. European nineteenth-century observers of this early phase of international organization often waxed lyrical about these new organs, which are seen as an expression of the solidarity between 'civilized' nations in tackling practical questions raised by a rapidly advancing 'European civilization'. Many of these co-operative endeavors in the eyes of European elites had become necessary in order to better administrate and enforce European economic and military imperialism in what contemporaries called 'non-civilized' areas of the world. In that sense European imperialism was not only facilitated by these first international institutions, but Europe's 'civilizing mission' also provided a legitimation for enhanced cooperation between the metropoles. Contemporary literature abounded with the rhetoric of an 'international community' based on common interests. In 1907 the influential American commentator of the move to institutionalized cooperation Paul Reinsch, looking back to this first phase of institutionalization, expressed this optimistic liberal sentiment in the *American Journal of International Law* in the following words:

> During the Middle Ages the unity of civilization rested largely upon a cultural and religious basis. In our own age, such bonds of union have been powerfully supplemented by the growing solidarity of the economic world, as well as by the need of experimental and applied science to utilize the experience and knowledge of all countries. The existence of such an underlying unity of the civilized world has been borne in upon the nations with greater force every succeeding year.[15]

### 10.2.2 *Weighted Versus Majority Voting in the UN System and the First Rebellion of the Third World*

While the League of Nations had preserved the basic nineteenth-century structures of legitimation and decision-making in international institutions, including the 'one State one vote' principle and the unanimity-rule, the UN era introduced both majority voting and weighted voting in various international institutions and organs. The unanimity-rule had been identified by practitioners and scholars as one of the main obstacles to 'getting things done' in international institutions already before and during the Interbellum. Nicolas Politis in 1928 held that 'to lay down the principle that in international

[15] Ibid., at 580.

organizations every important decision must be taken unanimously … is to admit that among nations no real organization is possible, for the rule of unanimity may lead to paralysis and anarchy'.[16] Considering that functionalist aspirations, understood as the common aim of elite-representatives to solve international co-ordination problems, had always been a driving force of the move to institutionalization, the frustration created by small minorities blocking institutional action was felt in various institutional settings since the late nineteenth century.

It may nonetheless seem surprising that in 1945 the US, the USSR, and the still existing European empires could agree on majority voting becoming the default rule in the UN and its specialized agencies; a development described by Wilfred Jenks as 'a revolution of decisive importance' for the future of international organization.[17] For majority voting always comes with the risk of being outvoted by coalitions of smaller States. One explanation for this great power acceptance of majority voting was the new combination with weighted voting procedures understood in a broad sense of the term. A pertinent if not infamous example are the veto rights of the five permanent members of the UN Security Council, entrenching a hegemonic position within a particularly powerful organ of the UN. But not only in the field of international security weighted voting procedures reflected a particular post–Second World War hegemonic status quo. In the Bretton Woods institutions, weighted voting rights equally translated the dominant position of the US and the European empires in the post-War world economy into institutional procedures and the composition of executive bodies. Democratic ideals as well as the principle of sovereign equality in many organs of international institutions gave way to forms of weighted representation according to material contributions, capabilities, and power resources.[18] Formally, unequal representation could of course always be legitimized by small States 'consenting' to accede to the respective regimes, reminding us of Karl Marx criticizing the notion of 'free consent' in the context of a starving worker signing an exploitative labour contract.

16 Nicolas Politis, *The New Aspects of International Law: A Series of Lectures Delivered at Columbia University in July 1926* (Washington, DC: Carnegie Endowment for International Peace, 1928), p. 10.

17 Clarence W. Jenks, 'Some Constitutional Problems of International Organizations' (1945) 22 *British Yearbook of International Law* 11–72, 34–36.

18 Discussing voting rights in the EU from a theoretical perspective, see Samantha Besson and José Luis Martí, 'From Equal State Consent to Equal Public Participation in International Organizations: Institutionalizing Multiple International Representation', in Samantha Besson (ed.), *Consenting to International Law* (Cambridge: Cambridge University Press, 2023), pp. 314–346.

Be that as it may, post-war plenary organs of universal organizations by and large had moved from unanimity to majority voting on a 'one State one vote' basis. That plenary organs with majority voting rules could be used against executive bodies with privileged veto rights had been famously demonstrated in the 1950s by the Uniting for Peace Mechanism, which the US had invented to counter Soviet vetoes in the UN Security Council by UNGA resolutions on matters of war and peace. Unexpectedly, however, during the post-Bandung decolonization era, the US and the other Western great powers increasingly lost control of these plenary organs. The first Third World 'rebellion' started in the UNGA and developed into a broader 'Battle for International Law' in the decolonization era.[19] Legally, the crucial issue for the Third World represented by the Non-Alignment Movement was how to give non-binding majority resolutions of the UNGA, often adopted against the will of great powers, more weight in international legal discourse. It is the time of the debates on 'instant custom', the latter being allegedly created by non-binding resolutions over a short period of time.[20]

Reactions by Western scholars to this rebellion are revealing. Resolutions sponsored by a Third World majority in the context of decolonization and international economic cooperation were criticized by Western politicians, diplomats and scholars as 'reckless', 'irresponsible', and 'undemocratic'.[21] New proposals for weighted voting in plenary organs countering the now deplored 'automatic' majority of Third World States suddenly abounded.[22] Particularly harsh were the reactions in US foreign policy circles given that up until the mid-1950s, the US had dominated the UNGA and practically all other organs of the UN, except for the Security Council where it had to cope from day one with the veto right of the Soviet Union. A US senator in a publication on the future of the UN pointed to the problem of unequal democratic representation because of diverging population-sizes behind the veil of the 'one State one vote' principle. He did so in racialized terms: 'In this grotesque United Nations calculus one African bushman becomes the equivalent of 100 Frenchmen or 400 Americans'.[23] In his very influential monograph on the emergence and

19 Jochen von Bernstorff and Philipp Dann, 'The Battle for International Law: An Introduction', in von Bernstorff and Dann, fn. 6, pp. 1–32.

20 Bin Cheng, *Studies in International Space Law* (Oxford: Oxford University Press, 1997), chapter 7.

21 See collected reactions in Ram P. Anand, 'Sovereign Equality of States in International Law' (1966) 8 *International Studies* 213–241, at 286.

22 Ibid.

23 Thomas J. Dodd, 'Is the United Nations Worth Saving?', in Raymond A. Moore Jr (ed.), *The United Nations Reconsidered* (Columbia, SC: University of South Carolina Press, 1963), pp. 90–109, p. 93.

structures of international institutions published in the 1950s, US scholar Inis L. Claude also warned his readers to be 'on the guard' against those who praise the turn to 'equalitarian' majority voting in international institutions:

> Majority decisions in the equalitarian General Assembly are likely to be undemocratic in the sense that they do not represent a majority of the world's population, unrealistic in the sense that they do not reflect the greater portion of the world's real power, morally unimpressive in the sense that they cannot be identified as expressions of the dominant will be a genuine community, and for all these reasons ineffectual and perhaps even dangerous.[24]

The main problem for the Third World, however, was that the (non-binding) majority resolutions passed in the UNGA against the declared will of the great powers could not lead to new legal obligations under the prevailing doctrine of voluntarist positivism and the mainstream doctrine of sources. Joint Third World efforts during contemporary codification projects, such as the UN Conference on the Law of the Sea, were also only partially successful because of entrenched resistance by great powers in the respective negotiations.[25] As to the claimed new customary rules emerging from UNGA resolutions, the ICJ would confirm new customary rules only in the case of norms from important and unanimous UNGA resolutions, hereby confirming the doctrinal requirement of sovereign (tacit) consent for new international law to emerge.[26] Apart from the gradual incrimination of colonialism, the aspired international legal, political, and economic revolution was eventually thwarted by Western States and their scholars.[27]

One of the main reactions of Western powers during and after decolonization was to sideline those institutions or organs which were now perceived as 'unruly' and difficult to control because of majority voting on a 'one State one vote' basis. Instead, Western great powers enhanced cooperation through institutions, which remained under their political control, such as the G7, the North Atlantic Treaty Organization (NATO), the Security Council, and the Bretton Woods Institutions, often using also informal standard-setting and cooperation mechanisms such as the Basel Committee on banking-regulation. As to formal multilateral treaty-making, treaty projects were usually welcomed

[24] Claude, fn. 7, p. 139.

[25] Surabhi Ranganathan, 'The Common Heritage of Mankind: Annotations on a Battle', in von Bernstorff and Dann, fn. 6, pp. 35–51.

[26] Well known examples are the UNGA Res. 2625(XXV), 'Declaration on Principles of International Law concerning Friendly Relations and Cooperation among States in accordance with the Charter of the United Nations' (24 October 1970) and Res. 3314(XXIX), 'Definition of Aggression' (14 December 1974).

[27] von Bernstorff and Dann, fn. 6.

by great powers once they could help to cement their dominant or advanced position in certain sectors of global politics, be it global trade, investment, armaments, security, health, or communication technologies. Typical examples are the NPT for nuclear weapons, safeguarding an exclusive right of some States to possess nuclear weapons, or the TRIPS Agreement adopted under the WTO roof in the 1990s protecting technical innovations and thus the central position of the largest and most competitive domestic economies in global markets.

## 10.3 'REBELLIOUS' LAWMAKING BY BROAD COALITIONS OF THE MOST AFFECTED

Coalitions of 'the most affected', including public and civil society actors, have recently started to engage in exercises of rebellious treaty-making confronting small groups of great powers and their industrial- or business elites in various institutional settings.

### 10.3.1 *Participation of 'the Most Affected'*

Let me start by explaining the argued recent shift towards enhanced participation of the 'most affected' in international institutional law. On an empirical level this trend is rather obvious for civil society participation in international institutions. If we look back to the 1990s, 'civil society'-participation in 'Global Governance' through involving NGOs was seen as a panacea-like concept to 'democratize' international institutions and to facilitate the realization of 'common interests' in international law. This idea of NGO-representation of abstract common interests, such as environmental protection or fighting impunity from human rights violations, however, has arguably given way to the more recent principle of participation of the 'most affected' in international institutions – the rise of 'affected persons organizations'.[28] Classic

[28] On this trend von Bernstorff, 'New Responses to the Legitimacy Crisis of International Institutions', fn. 5, and Jan Sändig, Jochen von Bernstorff and Andreas Hasenclever, 'Affectedness in International Institutions: Promises and Pitfalls of Involving the Most Affected' (2018) 3(5–6) *Third World Thematics: A TWQ Journal* 587–604. As a non-exhaustive list of institutions currently using the affectedness concept: Intergovernmental Working Group on a UN Declaration on the Rights of Peasants, Working Group on Indigenous Populations (WGIP)/Expert Mechanism on the Rights of Indigenous Peoples (EMRIP), Committee on World Food Security (CFS), The Joint United Nations Programme on HIV/AIDS (UNAIDS), Committee on the Rights of Persons with Disabilities (CRPD), United Nations Permanent Forum on Indigenous Issues (UNPFII), United Nations Environment Programme, Global Fund, Committee on the Rights of the Child (CRC),

NGOs in various fields of law- and policy-making are increasingly replaced by local and transnational social movements, so called 'affected persons' organizations' (APOs) as a reaction to a perceived crisis of legitimacy and a backlash against both international institutions and international NGOs.

This trend has, over the last ten years, already transformed rules of civil society participation in more than twenty prominent IOs. For example, members of indigenous groups and peasant organizations have successfully lobbied for new rights instruments and institutional reforms to ensure protection, participation, and influence in international institutions.[29] Persons affected by HIV/AIDS, tuberculosis, and malaria have been accorded designated seats on decision-making bodies in the Global Fund, UNITAID, and other institutions of global health governance.[30] Organizations of persons with disabilities took on a strong role in the negotiations of the UN Convention on the Rights of Persons with Disabilities. Working children movements from the Global South challenged the Western understandings of child labour in various intergovernmental organizations.[31] Among the first institutions which modified their rules of procedure accordingly were the FAO of the UN in Rome, the Monitoring Mechanism of the Convention on the Rights of Persons with Disabilities, and the WHO. In the FAO, Via Campesina, a global

Climate Investment Fund, Subcommittee of the Strategic Climate Fund for the Pilot Program for Climate Resilience (CIF-PPCR), International Drug Purchase Facility-UNITAID (UNITAID), Committee on Enforced Disappearances (CED), United Nations Collaborative Programme on Reducing Emissions from Deforestation and Forest Degradation in Developing Countries (UNREDD Programme), Forest Carbon Partnership Facility (FCPF), Ad Hoc Open-ended Working Group on Article 8(j) and Related Provisions of the Convention on Biological Diversity (WG8j), World Bank's consultation process for reformed Environmental and Social Framework (WB, ESF consultation), the Arctic Council (1996), United Nations Forum on Forest (UNFF), Global Environment Facility (GEF), Global Agriculture and Food Security Program (GAFSP), WB Inspection Panel. This is one of the empirical findings of an interdisciplinary research project on civil society participation at the University of Tübingen funded by the German Research Foundation, see for the concrete arrangements in the various rules of procedure from a comparative perspective; Markus Hasl, 'Shifting the Paradigm: A Typology of Affected Persons' Participation in International Institutions' (2018) 3(5–6) *Third World Thematics: A TWQ Journal* 626–644.

[29] Jens Dahl, *The Indigenous Space and Marginalized Peoples in the United Nations* (Basingstoke: Palgrave Macmillan, 2012); Nora McKeon, *Food Security Governance. Empowering Communities, Regulating Corporations* (London: Routledge, 2015).

[30] Markus Fraundorfer, 'Experiments in Global Democracy: The Cases of UNITAID and the FAO Committee on World Food Security' (2015) 4(3) *Global Constitutionalism* 328–364; comparing the concrete structure of different civil society mechanisms including 'affected' groups, see Hasl, fn. 28.

[31] Anna Holzscheiter, 'Representation as Power and Performative Practice: Global Civil Society Advocacy for Working Children' (2016) 42(2) *Review of International Studies* 205–226.

peasant movement, has for instance replaced Oxfam and 'Friends of the Earth' in the civil society mechanism.

Classic international NGOs and also States increasingly see political benefits in co-operating with social movements representing the 'most affected'. In the fight against climate change, international institutions are also experimenting with new forms of participation of the most affected from small island States in the form of affected persons organizations and States.[32] In the same field young climate activists claim intergenerational justice as an age group that will be more affected by global warming than the rest of the population. Activists involved in these movements do not want to exercise formalized decision-making powers in these institutions. Rather, the general idea is to participate in institutionalized deliberations in order to influence the content of adopted decisions. For social movements participation in international institutions is one strategy among others aimed at fostering the transnational mobilization of political resistance against perceived hegemonic networks of powerful national administrations, scientific expertise, and influential corporate actors.

The status of speaking for those who are being negatively affected on the ground by certain norms and policies, if credible and well-coordinated, gives these voices moral and sometimes also empirical persuasiveness in these institutional settings. Usually, their positions are more radical and uncompromising than those of classic NGO representatives. Even without formal voting rights, APOs can have a considerable impact on the content of new international norms, standards and decisions; one example being the negotiations on the UN Convention on the Rights of Persons with Disabilities, during which many persons with disabilities representing disability-organizations participated and exerted considerable influence on the content of the convention adopted in 2006.[33]

The general concept of affectedness of course, is neither new, nor has it remained unobserved by researchers in social sciences. It is a basic and long-standing democratic ideal that those who are affected should have a say on issues that concern them.[34] In traditional Western democratic theory, from Emmanuel

[32] On the institutional arrangements aiming at involving the most affected in international environmental law with a focus on UNFCC and REDD+ related negotiations, see Toussaint, fn. 3 and Linda Wallbott and Eugenia Recio, 'Practicing Human Rights Across Scale: Indigenous Peoples' Affectedness and Recognition in REDD+ Governance' (2018) 3(5–6) *Third World Thematics: A TWQ Journal* 785–806.

[33] Convention on the Rights of Persons with Disabilities, 2515 UNTS 44910 (adopted 13 December 2006, entered into force 3 May 2008).

[34] As a general normative ideal also for international institutions, see Klabbers, fn. 1, p. 81 and Richard B. Stewart, 'Remedying Disregard in Global Regulatory Governance: Accountability,

Kant to John Rawls, being affected by rules enforced in a certain delineated territory has been conceptualized as requiring elections of representative bodies on a 'one citizen, one vote' basis, in order to ensure equal influence of affected individuals on the composition of parliaments and executive bodies. More recently, global justice scholars have sought to conceptualize an 'all-affected principle' as a normative expectation for law- and policy-making with *transnational* effects, and discussed its potential implications from the perspective of political philosophy.[35] Even more relevant for the phenomenon under scrutiny here, Nancy Fraser proposed to replace the 'all-affected principle' by a more specific principle of involving all those groups 'subjected' to a given transnational governance structure ('all-subjected principle').[36]

Participation of 'the most affected' also has a constructivist and self-mobilizing dimension, which in this context should not be overlooked. By rallying and articulating their demands on the streets and in conference halls, affected individuals also constitute themselves as a specific collective entity. This self-constitutive mechanism is well known in democratic theory[37] – but now it is no longer 'we the people' but rather 'we the 1.2 billion smallholders' or 'we the 600 million persons with a disability'. Reflected here on a global level is what Pierre Rosanvallon ascertained for the Nation-State: the people (*peuple*) nowadays is only a 'litany of minorities and situations'.[38] Given that organizations representing the 'most affected' do not primarily claim to advance universal or common interests, the question of how they actually managed to be regarded as an actor that can render the work of international institutions more legitimate is not easy to answer. One reason certainly is that under postmodern conditions 'speaking for others' generally has fallen under the suspicion of being another form of hegemonic paternalism. We are also witnessing a widely perceived crisis of representation in Western societies, which arguably comes with the perception that the articulation of one's own interests as a general rule has to be as direct as possible. According to this concept, affected individuals should speak for themselves.

Participation, and Responsiveness' (2014) 108(2) *American Journal of International Law* 211–270.

35 Robert E. Goodin, *Innovating Democracy: Democratic Theory and Practice After the Deliberative Turn* (Oxford: Oxford University Press, 2008); Eva Erman and Sofia Näsström (eds.), *Political Equality in Transnational Democracy* (New York: Palgrave Macmillan, 2013).

36 Nancy Fraser, 'Abnormal Justice' (2008) 34(3) *Critical Inquiry* 393–422, at 411.

37 On this constitutive dimension of the 'we', see Judith Butler, '"Wir sind das Volk': Überlegungen zur Versammlungsfreiheit', in Alain Badiou, Pierre Bourdieu and Judith Butler (eds.), *Was ist ein Volk?* (Hamburg: Laika Theorie, 2017), pp. 17–25.

38 Introduction of Pierre Rosanvallon, *Democratic Legitimacy: Impartiality, Reflexivity, Proximity* (Princeton: Princeton University Press, 2011), p. 4.

And yet 'representation' in the sense of 'making present' something that is literally absent is unavoidable even when the most affected take the floor in international institutions. The small holder-farmer from India is precisely being heard and included because she also claims to speak on behalf of similarly affected persons out there. Employing the categories of representation developed in Hanna Pitkin's seminal monograph, participation of the most affected would fall under forms of 'descriptive' representation resting essentially on the resemblance between the group and its representative.[39] The move to affectedness also has a related performative dimension that is connected to opportunities offered by new media. The authentic testimony of the speaker's own experiences of discrimination, rising sea-levels, violence, or impoverishment is now crucial to have an impact on deliberations in and around international institutions.

Current media-driven campaign concepts, even those of classic NGOs, seem to require the authentic and tangible testimony of affected individuals in order to deliver their own message effectively. Affectedness in that sense has become an element of the political economy of civil society activities, which are always dependent on external donors. The existence of multifaceted relationships between large NGOs and most affected peoples' organizations is therefore not surprising.[40] Allow me one further remark on the political context, in which the rise of the 'most affected principle' takes place: the system of global governance structures, which was erected over the last thirty years, has proven to be quite efficient in creating globalized market structures, but it is increasingly seen as being more or less dysfunctional with regard to the protection of central social, humanitarian, and environmental values of human beings and all other living species inhabiting our planet.

Interestingly, in the nuclear non-proliferation field analysed as an example in more detail in the remainder of my contribution (Ban Treaty), a broad coalition of small and middle powers cooperating with most affected person's organizations and classic NGOs successfully launched a new treaty project in order to correct the old NPT. Interestingly this initiative used majority decisions in the UNGA to create a new dynamic previously blocked by the great powers within the consensus-oriented NPT treaty organs. Creating more progressive treaties alongside existing multilateral regimes is perhaps the most formal approach to launching a rebellion against status quo-oriented great powers.

39 Hanna F. Pitkin, *The Concept of Representation* (Berkeley: University of California Press, 1967), p. 144.

40 See Hasl, fn. 28.

### 10.3.2 *Rebel Treaties*

Surabhi Ranganathan in her pathbreaking work on 'strategically created treaty conflicts' has shown how hegemonic powers (the US in particular) managed to exercise and indeed change multilateral treaty-regimes by a strategic move into bilateral treaty making. These moves served to counter the objectives of lawmaking conventions, such as the UN Convention on the Law of the Sea (UNCLOS) or the Rome Statute.[41] In a similar albeit reversed way broad coalitions of small and medium sized States together with Civil Society groups are currently trying to create new multilateral treaty law in order to put pressure on a small number of hegemonic powers to reform existing treaty regimes, if necessary by creating new complementary treaties. Arguably such rebel treaties are processes of lawmaking, which often aim at turning vaguely termed goals of existing regimes into specific (cross-sectorial) and thus now effective obligations of States in the form of new binding law. The resulting legal rules amount to substantial reforms and as such tend to be in tension with the existing (old) regimes even though they attempt to conceal potential collisions by somewhat euphemistically calling themselves 'complementary' or merely 'concretizing' instruments. One of the first examples of these forms of counter-hegemonic treaty making in the 2000s arguably was the International Treaty on Plant Genetic Resources for Food and Agriculture called 'the seeds treaty'. This treaty set out to correct a hegemonic Western dominated intellectual property protection regime for agricultural seeds established in the 1990s by the Union for the Protection of New Varieties of Plants (UPOV) and the TRIPS regime. Its provisions aim at regulating biodiversity and intellectual property rights' issues through a cross sectorial approach.[42]

From a legal perspective, such rebel treaties complementing the old treaty regime are not able to formally modify another existing treaty with a different set of States parties.[43] Nonetheless rebel treaties can add a number of new obligations and institutional structures to the existing ones and change the

41 Surabhi Ranganathan, *Strategically Created Treaty Conflicts and the Politics of International Law* (Cambridge: Cambridge University Press, 2014). See United Nations Convention on the Law of the Sea, 1833–1835 UNTS 31363 (adopted 10 December 1982, entered into force 16 November 1994); Rome Statute of the International Criminal Court, 2187 UNTS 38544 (adopted 17 July 1998, entered into force 1 July 2002).

42 From a civil society perspective on that struggle between IP-protection and food-sovereignty, see FIAN International, *Farmers' Rights or Corporate Control Over Seeds? Background Paper to the Ninth Session of the ITPGRFA Governing Body* (Heidelberg: FIAN International, 2022). www.fian.org/files/files/EN_FIAN_ITPGRFA-GB9_background-paper_final.pdf, last accessed 30 September 2023.

43 Art. 40(4) and 30(4)(b) of the Vienna Convention on the Law of Treaties, 1155 UNTS 18232 (adopted 23 May 1969, entered into force 27 January 1980).

overall legal landscape, in which the regime operates.[44] Six characteristics of such forms of 'rebellious treaty-making' can be discerned:

- Rebel treaties are conceptualized and put forth as a reaction to 'a failure of the international community in showing solidarity and equity'[45] through existing legal regimes in face of planetary threats and catastrophes;
- These initiatives foresee a special (also performative) role and respect for both States and private groups who are particularly vulnerable or affected ('the most affected') by the failure of the international community to take action on the respective regulatory issue;[46]
- Rather than using only informal policy mechanisms to challenge the status quo through UNGA or other fora, these initiatives aim at formal and 'complementary' treaty-making hereby nonetheless substantially reforming existing international legal regimes without formally replacing or amending treaties already in force. They can be seen as a new counter-hegemonic version of 'strategically created treaty conflicts';[47]
- They also usually go beyond the *Framework-Protocol* approach known from international environmental law by *challenging* fundamental norms of the existing regime rather than concretizing regime-goals through new protocols, decisions, and regulations (framework-protocol approach);
- In their cross-sectorial approach, which reacts to the nature of the crisis phenomena addressed, these treaty projects disregard prior legal boundaries drawn by a deliberately fragmented institutional landscape;
- The new treaty instruments can create new organs but also use existing institutional infrastructures for oversight and monitoring as well as administrative capacities of the pre-existing treaty regime, while delegating new tasks to these bodies.

It is the TPNW which fulfils all of these rebel treaty-characteristics in an exemplary fashion. More than forty years after the adoption of the NPT, a broad coalition of non-nuclear weapons States created a new UN treaty on

44 And Art. 30(4) of the Vienna Convention on the Law of Treaties would only apply if the treaties are indeed regulating the same subject matter, which in case of a 'complementary' treaty is not the case formally; with a detailed historical analysis of the travaux, see Ranganathan, *Strategically Created Treaty Conflicts and the Politics of International Law*, fn. 44.

45 WHO, 'Zero Draft of the WHO CA+ for the consideration of the Intergovernmental Negotiating Body at its fourth meeting' (1 February 2023), A/INB/4/3.

46 Philosophically this claim for participation of the most affected can be based on Nancy Fraser's 'all-subjected' principle, see with further references von Bernstorff, 'New Responses to the Legitimacy Crisis of International Institutions', fn. 5.

47 Ranganathan, *Strategically Created Treaty Conflicts and the Politics of International Law*, fn. 41.

a general prohibition of nuclear weapons (TPNW) alongside the NPT.[48] This initiative had been launched by a broad coalition of civil society organizations and small and middle-sized States.[49] Within the coalition Japanese civil society organizations and representatives of small island States from the Pacific, which had suffered from nuclear testing activities by the US and France in the second half of the twentieth century, played a prominent role. At the first Meeting of States Parties to the TPNW in June 2022 Member States declared that the comprehensive legal prohibition of nuclear weapons had been established by the treaty as a necessary measure to implementing the disarmament pillar of the NPT. The aim of the treaty project was to 'further stigmatizing and delegitimizing nuclear weapons and steadily building a robust global peremptory norm against them'.[50]

What was the prior status quo legalized by the NPT and in which way can the new TPNW with its sixty-eight Member States be seen as a fundamental challenge or correction of the previous legal regime? In 1968 with the adoption of the NPT a compromise had been struck between the then five nuclear powers and the rest of the world. All Member States not belonging to the exclusive group of nuclear powers at that point in time were obliged not to acquire nuclear weapons in the future. In return for taking on this obligation, Member States were allowed to develop civilian usages of nuclear energy facilitated by the nuclear powers. Moreover, Article VI of the NPT requires:

> Each of the Parties to the Treaty . . . to pursue negotiations in good faith on effective measures relating to cessation of the nuclear arms race at an early date and to nuclear disarmament, and on a treaty on general and complete disarmament under strict and effective international control.

48 Treaty on the Prohibition of Nuclear Weapons, 3379 UNTS 56487 (adopted on 7 July 2017, entered into force on 22 January 2021).

49 See on the process, which led to the new treaty: Sascha Hach, *Rule & Resistance in the Nuclear Order. The Subversive Struggle for a Nuclear Weapons Ban* (Bielefeld: Transcript Verlag, 2025); Matthew B. Bolton, Sarah Njeri and Taylor Benjamin-Britton (eds.), *Global Activism and Humanitarian Disarmament* (Cham: Palgrave Macmillan, 2019); Ekaterina Mikhaylenko, *Treaty on the Prohibition of Nuclear Weapons: A New Regime in Formation?* (Ekaterinburg: Ural University Publishing House, 2020); Alexander Kmentt, *The Treaty Prohibiting Nuclear Weapons: How it Was Achieved and Why It Matters* (London and New York: Routledge, 2021); Jean Krasno and Elisabeth Szeli, *Banning the Bomb: The Treaty on the Prohibition of Nuclear Weapons* (Boulder, Colorado: Lynne Rienner Publishers, 2021); Nicholas E. Ritchie, 'An Hegemonic Nuclear Order: Understanding the Ban Treaty and the Power Politics of Nuclear Weapons' (2019) 40(4) *Contemporary and Security Policy* 409–434.

50 Meeting of State Parties to the Treaty on the Prohibition of Nuclear Weapons, 'Draft Vienna Declaration of the 1st Meeting of States Parties to the Treaty on the Prohibition of Nuclear Weapons' (23 June 2022), TPNW/MSP/2022/CRP.8, para. 8.

Additionally, the NPT came with a complex verification system based on differentiated monitoring activities carried out by the International Atomic Agency (IAEA). At the heart of the political mobilization for the new treaty was a sense of frustration among non-nuclear powers that the stockpiles of the five nuclear States had steadily expanded and diversified and that disarmament activities despite certain bilateral disarmament initiatives in the 1980s and 1990s had largely failed. Article 1 of the TPNW fundamentally challenges the NPT-distinction between privileged nuclear States and the 'rest' by generally prohibiting the development, deployment, possession, use, and the threat of use of nuclear weapons. As to its cross-sectorial implications, the TPNW takes a clear stance in the fifty-years-old struggle to ban nuclear weapons as a legitimate means of warfare in international humanitarian law[51] holding in its preambular part that 'any use of nuclear weapons would be contrary to the rules of international law applicable in armed conflict, in particular the principles and rules of international humanitarian law'. No wonder that the five nuclear States privileged by the NPT did not become parties to the TPNW claiming time and again that the new treaty was a dangerous development weakening the existing NPT regime.

But how does the new treaty itself deal with the NPT regime and with potential collisions between the two treaties? It is noteworthy in this context that the coalition driving the drafting process took care to avoid a confrontational stance regarding the NPT regime. Quite the contrary was the case as is reflected in numerous statements by delegations over time and more importantly in various norms of the TPNW. The preamble of the TPNW reaffirms that 'the full and effective implementation of the [NPT], which serves as the cornerstone of the nuclear disarmament and non-proliferation regime, has a vital role to play in promoting international peace and security'. Rather than challenging the NPT explicitly, the Ban Treaty is thus portrayed as being a complementary regime enhancing the implementation of the above cited Article VI of the NPT, which indeed already in 1974 foresaw the conclusion of a disarmament treaty in the future. Not everybody agrees of course. France for example argued that the Ban Treaty created an 'alternative, incompatible and incomplete norm'[52]

[51] On this struggle, see Jochen von Bernstorff, *L'essor et la chute du droit international humanitaire: Une brève histoire de la codification de la protection des civils en temps de guerre* (1899–1977) (Paris: Pedone, 2023).

[52] 10ème Conférence d'examen du Traité sur la non-prolifération des armes nucléaires (New York, 1–26 août 2022). Intervention de l'ambassadeur Yann Hwang, chef de délégation de la France' (4 August 2022). https://reachingcriticalwill.org/images/documents/Disarmament-fora/npt/revcon2022/statements/4Aug_MCI_France.pdf, last accessed 10 May 2023.

undermining the existing non-proliferation regime. Interestingly, Article 18 of the Ban Treaty also holds that '[t]he implementation of this Treaty shall not prejudice obligations undertaken by States Parties with regard to existing international agreements, to which they are party, where those obligations are consistent with the Treaty'. While the first half-sentence of the provision strikes a conciliatory tone ('not prejudice obligations ... '), the second half-sentence establishes a general collision-rule in favour of the provisions of the Ban Treaty hereby implicitly claiming that the Ban Treaty is *lex specialis* vis-à-vis other regimes on nuclear weapons.

As mentioned above, another characteristic feature of these exercises of rebellious treaty-making is the use of organs and institutional features created by the pre-existing regime. The new treaty inserts itself into the existing institutional set-up and monitoring mechanisms extending as a result the old regime without formally amending it. For example, Article 3 not only requires States parties to maintain their existing IAEA safeguards 'without prejudice to any additional relevant instruments' but the treaty also sets the IAEA Comprehensive Safeguards Agreement[53] as a minimum non-proliferation verification requirement, herewith drawing heavily on the existing institutional infrastructure.[54] At the same time this minimum-requirement for all Member States goes beyond the obligations set out in the NPT and from that angle the Ban Treaty strengthens the overall regime.

## 10.4 REBELLIONS IN TIMES OF PLANETARY CRISIS

Historically, each international institution is based on a specific policy network consisting of public and private actors with the aim to foster certain forms of cooperation considered beneficial by this network. It goes without saying that these networks can and do change over time. Nonetheless, great powers and their industrial elites due to their superior diplomatic, administrative, and political resources often managed to preserve a dominant institutional position over time. This may also include a formally privileged position of some of those actors through (weighted) voting procedures or explicit or implicit veto rights. Even in more egalitarian (one State one vote) fora and institutions, strong actors had and still have ways and means to exert more influence on the

[53] IAEA, 'The Structure and Content of Agreements between the Agency and States Required in Connection with the Treaty on the Non-Proliferation of Nuclear Weapons' (June 1972), INFCIRC/153 (Corrected).

[54] IAEA, 'The Structure and Content of Agreements between the Agency and States Required in Connection with the Treaty on the Non-Proliferation of Nuclear Weapons' (June 1972), INFCIRC/153.

institution by withholding or earmarking financial contributions, by impacting on the staff-composition in secretariats and the like. An instructive case in point is the various carrot and stick strategies of one US administration after the other since the 1980s to block and control UN institutions, such as UNESCO, WHO, FAO, and others.

It was the introduction of majority voting in the plenary organs of international institutions after World War II, which provided a platform for a number of rebellions launched by broad coalitions of small and middle powers, often from the Global South, in the decolonization era. These coalitions represented not only a majority of Member States but also usually a majority of the inhabitants of this planet. Especially the UNGA became the facilitator of numerous lawmaking projects during and after decolonization. More recently, broad coalitions of public and private actors arguably adopted a new strategy of lawmaking alongside existing twentieth century treaty regimes, and most importantly perhaps, without the initial support of status quo-oriented great powers (rebel treaties). In the case of the TPNW, great powers protested and pleaded to preserve the status quo ante during the whole process. Interestingly, the initiative to draft and adopt a more progressive new treaty alongside the NPT was again launched by a majority decision of the UNGA.

The late twentieth century turn to informality in global governance structures had been widely identified and perceived of as an instrument for strong actors sidelining egalitarian fora and institutions.[55] The same holds true for what can be called strategic fragmentation of certain issue areas in international law, which have resulted in a highly compartmentalized landscape of different international institutions cementing a hegemonic military or economic role of great powers.[56] Using new cross-sectorial treaty law (rebel treaties) can thus also be interpreted as a counter-reaction of the weak to de-fragment or 'decolonize' international legal regimes.[57] They form broader coalitions under new multilateral treaties aiming at the effective implementation of the objectives of existing but ineffective legal regimes, such as in the field of disarmament or environmental protection. Behind these new coalitions leading public and private actors are thriving on a claim to represent those 'most affected' by the particular regime. If necessary, these treaty projects became realised without the

55 Jan Klabbers, 'The Undesirability of Soft Law' (1998) 67(4) *Nordic Journal of International Law* 381–391.

56 Eyal Benvenisti and George W. Downs, 'The Empire's New Clothes: Political Economy and the Fragmentation of International Law' (2007) 60(2) *Stanford Law Review* 595–631.

57 Cf. Xiaoxiao Kwete et al., 'Decolonizing Global Health: What Should be the Target of this Movement and Where Does It Lead Us?' (2022) 7(1) *Global Health Res Policy* 1–6.

support of great powers, which of course *prima facie* weakens their impact. At the same time, they potentially create a progressive dynamic regarding the underlying norms of a particular treaty regime, hereby increasing the pressure on great powers to join or to move beyond the status quo also within the old treaty regime. After all, the observed public/private coalitions tend to represent the interests of significant segments of the world's population by reacting to a planetary crisis characterized by high-risk scenarios, growing inequity, and potentially or manifestly catastrophic consequences of a prolonged attachment to the status quo.

# PART III

# DEMOCRATIC REPRESENTATION BY INTERNATIONAL ORGANIZATIONS

# 11

# International Organizations as Orchestrators of Represented Constituencies: The Case of the Global Compact on Refugees

Terry Macdonald

## 11.1 INTRODUCTION

International organizations (IOs) now perform many crucial political functions within the interconnected governance systems of the twenty-first century global political order. In recognition of their powerful roles, IOs have been subject to increasing politicization over recent decades,[1] accompanied by widespread challenges to their legitimacy,[2] and calls for democratizing reform.[3] This political concern about IOs' democratic deficits is deeply implicated in wider legitimacy crises facing democratic institutions worldwide – emanating in part from unsettling transformations to democratic States and national societies wrought by global economic, social, and political integration.[4] The institutions of the United Nations (UN) system, in particular, loom large in the conspiracist imaginaries of many populist political movements – cast as emblems of aloof and rapacious global elites, and envisioned as threats to longer-standing democratic practices of legitimate

[1] Michael Zürn, Martin Binder and Matthias Ecker-Ehrhardt, 'International Authority and Its Politicization' (2012) 4(1) *International Theory* 69–106.

[2] Dominik Zaum, 'International Organizations, Legitimacy, and Legitimation', in Dominik Zaum (ed.), *Legitimating International Organizations* (Oxford: Oxford University Press, 2013), pp. 3–25; Jonas Tallberg and Michael Zürn, 'The Legitimacy and Legitimation of International Organizations: Introduction and Framework' (2019) 14 *Review of International Organizations* 581–606.

[3] Klaus Dingwerth, Henning Schmidtke and Tobias Weise, 'The Rise of Democratic Legitimation: Why International Organizations Speak the Language of Democracy' (2020) 26(3) *European Journal of International Relations* 714–741.

[4] Carolien van Ham, Jacques Thomassen, Kees Aarts and Rudy Andeweg (eds.), *Myth and Reality of the Legitimacy Crisis: Explaining Trends and Cross-National Differences in Established Democracies* (Oxford: Oxford University Press, 2017); Nancy Fraser, *The Old Is Dying and the New Cannot Be Born: From Progressive Neoliberalism to Trump and Beyond* (London: Verso Books, 2019).

national self-determination.[5] Against this political background, the question of how best to assess and strengthen the democratic legitimacy of IOs – and of the roles they play within wider governance systems – sits at the centre of broader debates about the prospects and pathways for reviving democratic legitimacy across the global political order.[6]

Some established theoretical work on the democratic legitimacy of IOs has argued that a promising route towards remedying legitimacy problems may be found in strengthening practices of democratic *representation*, since representative democratic instruments can be more successfully adapted to the vast scale and complexity of global governance processes than alternative participatory models.[7] Others, however, have advanced more sceptical assessments of representative practices as vehicles for legitimacy in global institutions. Sociological legitimacy scholars have presented empirical evidence that (at least some) established representative instruments fail to improve attitudinal indicators of IO legitimacy.[8] In parallel, some normative theorists have argued that strong legitimacy can only be achieved through public participation in democratic deliberation,[9] or other forms of active political engagement absent from established representative models.[10] Underlying these sceptical challenges is a recognition that many transnational groups with democratic claims to representative inclusion, in virtue of their experiences of 'affectedness' or

5 Kilian Spandler and Fredrik Söderbaum, 'Populist (De)Legitimation of International Organizations' (2023) 99(3) *International Affairs* 1023–1041.

6 Terry Macdonald, 'Reviving Democracy: Creating Pathways out of Legitimacy Crises' (2023) 22(1) *European Journal of Political Theory* 181–191.

7 Terry Macdonald, *Global Stakeholder Democracy: Power and Representation beyond Liberal States* (Oxford: Oxford University Press, 2008); Andrew Kuper, *Democracy Beyond Borders: Justice and Representation in Global Institutions* (Oxford: Oxford University Press, 2004); Jonathan W. Kuyper, 'Systemic Representation: Democracy, Deliberation, and Nonelectoral Representatives' (2016) 110(2) *American Political Science Review* 308–324; Laura Montanaro, 'The Democratic Legitimacy of Self-Appointed Representatives' (2012) 74(4) *The Journal of Politics* 1094–1107; Jennifer C. Rubenstein, 'The Misuse of Power, Not Bad Representation: Why It Is Beside the Point That No One Elected Oxfam' (2014) 22(2) *Journal of Political Philosophy* 204–230.

8 Lisa Maria Dellmuth and Jonas Tallberg, 'The Social Legitimacy of International Organisations: Interest Representation, Institutional Performance, and Confidence Extrapolation in the United Nations' (2015) 41(3) *Review of International Studies* 451–475.

9 Jens Steffek, 'The Legitimation of International Governance: A Discourse Approach' (2003) 9(2) *European Journal of International Relations* 249–275; Eva Erman, 'In Search of Democratic Agency in Deliberative Governance' (2013) 19(4) *European Journal of International Relations* 847–868.

10 Jens Steffek, Claudia Kissling and Patrizia Nanz (eds.), *Civil Society Participation in European and Global Governance: A Cure for the Democratic Deficit?* (London: Palgrave Macmillan, 2008); Anne Norton, *Wild Democracy: Anarchy, Courage, and Ruling the Law* (Oxford: Oxford University Press, 2023).

'subjection' by international institutions,[11] currently lack those background social and institutional ties that have historically sustained legitimacy within the representative institutions of consolidated democratic States.[12] Whereas contemporary representative theories and practices have mostly been developed to operate with the social relationships that comprise sovereign or self-determining national 'peoples', many represented groups in global institutions are fluid and contested transnational assemblages of diverse political actors, lacking such established social and institutional ties. In their absence, the worry is that practices of democratic *representation* and *legitimation* become politically uncoupled.

My aim in this chapter is to offer a theoretical account of how these challenges to representative democratic legitimation in global institutions may be (at least partially) overcome, and how IOs can contribute to the development of the kinds of representative practices best equipped to strengthen global institutional legitimacy. More specifically, I argue that global representative practice can contribute to democratic legitimacy not only through the representation of groups whose shared claims to representative inclusion are accompanied by established social and institutional ties, which enable their collective judgement and decision as active democratic 'constituencies'.[13] It can contribute further through a distinct set of *constitutive* representative activities, which function to cultivate – within socially and institutionally emergent groups holding democratic representative claims – those ties of political recognition, integration, and commitment required to

[11] Jochen von Bernstorff, 'New Responses to the Legitimacy Crisis of International Institutions: The Role of "Civil Society" and the Rise of the Principle of Participation of the "Most Affected" in International Law' (2021) 32(1) *European Journal of International Law* 125–157; Archon Fung and Sean Gray (eds.), *Empowering Affected Interests: Democratic Inclusion in a Globalized World* (Cambridge: Cambridge University Press, 2024).

[12] David Miller, 'Against Global Democracy', in Keith Breen and Shane O'Neill (eds.), *After the Nation? Critical Reflections on Nationalism and Postnationalism* (London: Palgrave Macmillan, 2010), pp. 141–160.

[13] Here I reserve the term 'constituencies' for groups that are represented not only in the sense of being spoken for by others within international governance processes, but further in the more demanding democratic sense of participating as collectives in the processes of common judgement and action that sustain what can be called the democratic *agency* of the represented within representative practices. By democratic 'agency' here, I mean the exercise of political judgement combined with some substantive power to influence political outcomes in light of that judgement – albeit often indirectly, through complex collective processes such as democratic representation. For further discussion of these concepts see: Nadia Urbinati, *Representative Democracy: Principles and Genealogy* (Chicago: University of Chicago Press, 2006); Terry Macdonald, 'Democratizing Global "Bodies Politic": Collective Agency, Political Legitimacy, and the Democratic Boundary Problem' (2017) 10(2) *Global Justice: Theory Practice Rhetoric* 22–42.

constitute them as active and legitimizing democratic *constituencies*. IOs, more specifically, can engage in this constitutive representation through political practices I describe as the *orchestration of represented constituencies*: intervening in relationships among representatives and their emergent constituents in ways that cultivate their collective legitimating qualities of political recognition, integration, and commitment.

In what follows, I develop these arguments in three steps. First, I examine in greater depth the relationships and tensions between concepts and practices of *democratic legitimation*, on the one hand, and *representation*, on the other; and based on this analysis, I consider how distinctive practices of *constitutive representation* may foster in represented constituencies the qualities of active democratic agency required for sustaining legitimacy (Section 11.2). Second, I examine how IOs can contribute to these practices of constitutive representation – extending established understandings of IOs as *orchestrators* of collective political action to the democratic practices of constituting represented constituencies (Section 11.3). Third, I illustrate and assess these theoretical ideas through an examination of the case of the *Global Compact on Refugees* (GCR): here I examine the roles of the UN High Commission for Refugees (UNHCR) and the UN General Assembly (UNGA) as orchestrators of a transnational represented constituency of refugees,[14] via their work in supporting a range of democratic commitments within the GCR (Section 11.4).

Taken together, these arguments have significance for both theoretical and practical debates about pathways towards global democratic legitimacy. Theoretically, they show how concepts of *representation* can be brought into closer alignment with the functional demands of democratic *legitimation* in the complex and dynamic political circumstances of contemporary global politics. And practically, they highlight a new way in which democratically legitimating forms of representation can be instituted *by IOs* – extending their representative reach not only through participation in external lawmaking processes, but further through supporting the constitution of represented groups as active democratic *constituencies* – whose agency alone confers democratic legitimacy on the governance institutions of the global order.

[14] As discussed at fn. 13 above, a refugee 'constituency' is constituted through the development of those social and institutional ties required for refugee populations to exercise the collective judgement and influence we can call democratic *agency* within representative processes. I take it that whether such agency requires (or is best achieved through) recognition in public law is an empirical rather than a normative or conceptual question – since my account of political *legitimacy* presented in this chapter understands law as just one among many instruments of social and institutional integration that can support democratic legitimation processes. As such, the optimal democratic role for public legal recognition of refugee constituencies may vary across different political contexts within the global order.

## 11.2 REPRESENTATION AS AN INSTRUMENT OF DEMOCRATIC LEGITIMACY

Over the course of its modern history, democratic theory has developed a rich conceptual vocabulary for describing both the justificatory normative grounds, and the operational institutional instruments, required to realize democratic ideals within the vast and complex political orders of modern world society. The concept of *legitimacy* has risen to prominence as a frame for understanding modern democracy's normative grounds; while the concept of *representation* has come to occupy a parallel position in understanding its operational institutional instruments. Despite their proximity as central organizing concepts in modern democratic projects, the ideas of legitimacy and representation have been developed in recent theoretical work with increasing detachment from one another; and their estrangement has nowhere been starker than in theories of democracy within international institutions. In order to develop a model of international representation capable of strengthening global democratic legitimacy, we must therefore begin by considering in more detail: how our concepts of democratic legitimacy and representation have come apart in contemporary theory and governance practice; and how to bring them back into closer political accord.

### 11.2.1 *Legitimacy, Democracy, and Democratic Legitimacy*

The concept of *legitimacy*, first, is commonly invoked as a frame for capturing the underlying normative value that democratic institutions should be designed to deliver. The etymological roots of the legitimacy concept can be traced back to the Latin root *lex*, meaning 'law', and derivatives such as *legitimus*, meaning 'according to law'.[15] But in the early modern period the legitimacy idea evolved to take on more specialized political meanings: first capturing lawfully delegated political powers,[16] and hereditary rights of ruling monarchs;[17] and subsequently expanding to allow scope for subjecting even lawful power to critique in the name of some autonomous set of political agents or reasons.[18] While the precise sources of legitimacy's distinctive

15 Walter W. Skeat, *A Concise Etymological Dictionary of the English Language* (Oxford: Oxford University Press, 1927), p. 290.

16 Jean-Marc Coicaud, *Legitimacy and Politics: A Contribution to the Study of Political Right and Political Responsibility* (Cambridge: Cambridge University Press, 2002), p. 19.

17 Shane P. Mulligan, 'The Uses of Legitimacy in International Relations' (2006) 34(2) *Millennium* 349–375, at 358–359; Arthur Isak Applbaum, *Legitimacy Without Illusions: The Right to Govern in a Wanton World* (Cambridge, MA: Harvard University Press, 2019), p. 82.

18 Mulligan, fn. 17, at 359–360; Applbaum, fn. 17, pp. 81–82.

political normativity remains a matter of ongoing dispute,[19] most theorists understand legitimacy standards as functioning in some sense to remedy *political problems of normative dispute* over the rightful institutional terms of political rule.[20] Remedying such legitimacy problems is commonly valued for helping reconcile political rule with the normative judgements and commitments of free individuals,[21] and further for helping sustain beneficial political cooperation at low enforcement costs.[22]

This modern idea of legitimacy thus captures not any ideal institutional model of political rule, but rather a distinctive normative standard against which institutional models can be judged and designed. It is through this application that the idea of legitimacy has come to be commonly aligned with a reinvigorated modern interpretation of the old Greek idea of *democracy* – defined as a form of political rule or empowerment (*arche*) through which a political community or 'people' (*demos*) engages in collective self-governance. The compound idea of *democratic legitimacy* captures what results when *democratic institutional instruments* successfully function as political remedies to *underlying legitimacy problems* – resolving normative disputes over the institutional terms of political rule through the collectivization of power in democratic decision-making processes.

Not all contemporary justifications of democratic institutions appeal in this way to their value as instruments of legitimation: sometimes democracy is justified instead as a vehicle for some thicker moral conception of justice,[23] or another instrumental moral purpose.[24] Similarly, the concept of 'legitimacy' is sometimes appended to democracy in a more descriptive sense – denoting not its conformity to any substantive normative standard, but rather a generic

[19] Ben Cross, 'Normativity in Realist Legitimacy' (2021) 19(3) *Political Studies Review* 450–463; Eva Erman and Niklas Möller, 'Distinctively Political Normativity in Political Realism: Unattractive or Redundant' (2022) 25 *Ethical Theory and Moral Practice* 433–447; Matt Sleat, 'Realism and Political Normativity' (2022) 25 *Ethical Theory and Moral Practice* 465–478.

[20] Allen Buchanan and Robert O. Keohane, 'The Legitimacy of Global Governance Institutions' (2006) 20(4) *Ethics & International Affairs* 405–437; Terry Macdonald, *Global Political Legitimacy: A Normative Theory of Pluralist World Order*, unpublished manuscript.

[21] Alexander Kaufman, 'Reason, Self-Legislation and Legitimacy: Conceptions of Freedom in the Political Thought of Rousseau and Kant' (1997) 59(1) *The Review of Politics* 25–52; Philip Pettit, 'Legitimacy and Justice in Republican Perspective' (2012) 65 *Current Legal Problems* 59–82.

[22] Christian Reus-Smit, 'International Crises of Legitimacy' (2007) 44 *International Politics* 157–174.

[23] Danielle Allen, *Justice by Means of Democracy* (Chicago: University of Chicago Press, 2023).

[24] Thomas Christiano, 'An Instrumental Argument for a Human Right to Democracy' (2011) 39(2) *Philosophy & Public Affairs* 142–176.

attribution of political justifiability or acceptability, on whatever terms these may be understood.[25] But it was as an instrument of legitimacy in its substantive normative sense that institutional ideals of democracy first gained widespread uptake in modern political thought and practice, under the influence of Jean-Jacques Rousseau's proposed collectivist solution to the legitimacy problems of consolidating European States.[26] And in this same Rousseauvian tradition, deliberative democratic models have attained contemporary theoretical support as instruments of normative legitimacy – entrenching the pairing of *democracy* with *legitimacy* as political *solution* and *problem*, as these function within the State-based institutional orders of modern political life.[27]

### 11.2.2 *Democracy, Representation, and Transnational Legitimacy Problems*

Alongside this normative idea of legitimacy, the concept of *representation* has had enormous theoretical influence in reshaping models of democracy for operation in the modern political world. Like the idea of democracy itself, the concept of representation marks out a model of *the relationships and structures of political rule*, without entailing any particular account of their (justifying or legitimizing) normative grounds. Most broadly, the concept of *representation* means 'making present' in a new sense something which is, in another sense, absent;[28] as such, it has many meanings and applications outside the domain of political life. But when applied to the political context of democratic governance, the concept captures those political relationships and practices through which members of democratic constituencies can be made present in the activities of political rule – even when (due to constraints such as

[25] Rainer Forst, *Normativity and Power: Analyzing Social Orders of Justification* (Oxford: Oxford University Press, 2017), p. 133.

[26] Jean-Jacques Rousseau, *Rousseau: The Social Contract and Other Later Political Writings*, 2nd ed., translated and edited by Victor Gourevitch (Cambridge: Cambridge University Press, 2018); Macdonald, *Global Political Legitimacy*, fn. 20, Chapter 1.

[27] Jürgen Habermas, *Communication and the Evolution of Society*, translated by Thomas McCarthy (Boston: Beacon Press, 1979); Jürgen Habermas, *Between Facts and Norms: Contributions to a Discourse Theory of Law and Democracy*, translated by William Rehg (Cambridge: Polity Press, 2015); Jack Knight and James Johnson, 'Aggregation and Deliberation: On the Possibility of Democratic Legitimacy' (1994) 22(2) *Political Theory* 277–296.

[28] Hanna F. Pitkin, *The Concept of Representation* (Berkeley: University of California Press, 1967), p. 3.

time, distance, resources, competence, or motivation) they do not participate in these directly.[29]

At the heart of all models of democratic representation is some kind of relationship between: the democratic *constituencies* who are (at least in some direct participatory sense) absent from activities of political rule, yet democratically entitled to be present; and their democratic *representatives*, whose characteristics and activities within sites and processes of political rule can make their represented constituencies in some sense present again. Competing theoretical models of democratic representation then vary in how they characterize these political agents and relationships, across several dimensions: the elements of *constituencies' attributes or activities* that representative processes seek to make present; the elements of *representatives' attributes or activities* through which this presence is fostered in sites and processes of political rule; and the features of the *political relationships between representatives and constituents* through which these representative practices are sustained.[30]

In designing and justifying models of political representation along these several dimensions, theorists have not typically undertaken systematic analysis of their implications for political problems of *legitimacy*, in the substantive normative sense of interest here. Rather, a standard analytical strategy has been to assess representative models against the intermediary concept of 'democracy' – assuming that whatever can be upheld as *democratic* warrants an accompanying attribution of normative legitimacy. For some representative theorists an assumption of such equivalence is merely implicit. Others, however, have argued explicitly that the normative assessment of representative institutional designs requires no appeal to any standards exogenous to the concept of democracy itself, but can rather be assessed simply for its 'democraticity' – meaning conformity with the conceptual constraints of the democratic idea.[31] More concretely, this has meant that the assessment of representative designs has mostly focused on the democratic function of representative *inclusion* – aimed at ensuring participants in political rule

[29] It is a contested matter whether direct participation in political rule produces stronger democratic legitimacy than participation as a constituent in representative democratic practice, and some theorists of democratic representation have argued that it does not – for instance Urbinati, fn. 13. My view on this is that both participatory and representative practices are merely *instruments* (as distinct from conceptual or normative constituents) of democratic legitimation, and as such their relative utility for legitimation is an empirical question – the answer to which may vary across political contexts.

[30] Nadia Urbinati and Mark E. Warren, 'The Concept of Representation in Contemporary Democratic Theory' (2008) 11 *Annual Review of Political Science* 387–412.

[31] Hélène Landemore, *Open Democracy: Reinventing Popular Rule for the Twenty-First Century* (Princeton: Princeton University Press, 2020).

(*arche*) include all other members of their political community (*demos*) in their decision-making processes.[32] In this democratic interpretation of the representative challenge, normative evaluation and prescription focuses primarily on the attributes and activities of political *representatives*, whose responsibility it is to include, through their activities of rule, all 'affected' or 'subjected' populations with democratic claims to representation as members of the '*demos*'.[33] The capacity of represented populations to exercise collective judgement and influence as democratic *agents* within representative processes has received much less attention: although the question of constituency agency has received some attention in broader debates on the constitution of the '*demos*' in global democratic practice,[34] its implications for the theory of global democratic *representation* have not been systematically examined.

An important question left open by much of this work concerns *the capacity of representative practice to sustain democratic legitimacy* in contemporary political governance institutions. Some recent work on international and transnational representation invokes the language of legitimacy – suggesting that some prescribed representative innovations, addressed to the remedy of democratic deficits, will also have the advantage of strengthening legitimacy.[35] Such claims have merit insofar as representative practices can fulfil not only the inclusive political function of democraticity, but also the distinct political function of legitimization: resolving normative disputes over the institutional terms of political rule, through the subsumption of divergent individual judgements within a unified institutional framework for collective political agency.[36] One key prerequisite for legitimizing functionality is that the parties to normative disputes over the terms of institutional rule – in democratic terms, those who claim a political 'stake' in its powers as affected parties,[37] or those subjected to demands for institutional compliance or support[38] – are included in the collective democratic decision-making processes that offer

[32] Iris Marion Young, *Inclusion and Democracy* (Oxford: Oxford University Press, 2002).

[33] Macdonald, *Global Stakeholder Democracy*, fn. 7; Kuper, fn. 7; Benjamin Boudou, 'Representing Non-Citizens: A Proposal for the Inclusion of All Affected Interests' (2023) 26(5) *Critical Review of International Social and Political Philosophy* 747–768.

[34] Christian List and Mathias Koenig-Archibugi, 'Can There Be a Global Demos? An Agency-Based Approach' (2010) 38 *Philosophy & Public Affairs* 76.

[35] Montanaro, fn. 7; Sveinung Arnesen and Yvette Peters, 'The Legitimacy of Representation: How Descriptive, Formal, and Responsiveness Representation Affect the Acceptability of Political Decisions' (2018) 51(7) *Comparative Political Studies* 868–899.

[36] Macdonald, *Global Political Legitimacy*, fn. 20.

[37] Macdonald, *Global Stakeholder Democracy*, fn. 7.

[38] Arash Abizadeh, 'The Scope of the All-Subjected Principle: On the Logical Structure of Coercive Laws' (2021) 81(4) *Analysis* 603–610.

some political remedy for these disputes. Insofar as representative innovations are successful in fostering such inclusion – through better aligning the boundaries of governance processes with the boundaries of collective democratic agency – their claim to be contributing to strengthened legitimacy in international institutions can be upheld.

The complex political function of legitimation requires more, however, than merely *aligning the boundaries* of represented constituencies with those of legitimacy problems – representing all democratic claimants in normative disputes over the institutional terms of governance power. For representative inclusion to contribute to remedying legitimacy problems, there is an additional requirement for represented populations to be *actively engaged in representative processes*, to the degree required for sustaining the legitimizing conversion of *normative dispute* among democratic claimants into *collective democratic agency* in the shared exercise of governing power (thus converting diffuse populations of democratic claimants into active democratic *constituencies*). With the shift from participatory to representative democratic models, the expectation for active political engagement of democratic constituents does not extend to their direct involvement in all the activities of political decision-making and implementation that constitute political rule itself. But to foster legitimacy through these democratic practices, representatives must still bring their constituents along through sufficient active political engagements to motivate and guide their support for governing institutions in the ways captured by the distinct normative concept of legitimacy.

More specifically, successful legitimation requires that represented groups have capacities to: *recognize themselves* as democratic constituents of ruling institutions, and as represented by participants in these governance processes;[39] *engage (communicatively or collaboratively) with one another*, in creatively defining the common interests or problems that integrate them as members of democratic constituencies;[40] and *commit to political responsibilities* for democratic burden-sharing and compromise, without which the legitimizing shift from normative contestation to democratic collaboration could not be motivationally sustained.[41] Agentic

39 Eva Erman, 'The Boundary Problem and the Ideal of Democracy' (2014) 21(4) *Constellations* 535–546; Erman, fn 9; Michael Saward, 'The Representative Claim' (2006) 5 *Contemporary Political Theory* 297–318.

40 Norton, fn. 10; Macdonald, 'Reviving Democracy', fn. 6.

41 Iris Marion Young, 'Activist Challenges to Deliberative Democracy' (2001) 29(5) *Political Theory* 670–690; Michael Goodhart, 'Interpreting Responsibility Politically' (2017) 25(2) *Journal of Political Philosophy* 173–195; Avia Pasternak, 'The Collective Responsibility of Democratic Publics' (2011) 41(1) *Canadian Journal of Philosophy* 99–123.

political capacities of these minimal kinds are acknowledged functional requirements already of some theoretical models of 'formal' political representation, which require represented constituents to engage collaboratively and responsibly in activities of authorization and accountability within their representative relationships.[42] As such, these formal representative instruments can make especially clear contributions to legitimation processes. But even with 'substantive' and 'descriptive' representative practices, which are more reliant on the agency of representatives to articulate and embody constituency interests and identities, legitimacy will still depend on constituents possessing these forms of active agency: without constituents' active recognition, integration, and commitment operating in the background, representative rule would not convert to legitimizing support from institutions' democratic claimants.

There is a longstanding and live democratic debate about whether representative legitimation of these kinds can realistically be achieved in political practice. An influential tradition of thought on democratic legitimacy – originating in Rousseau's well-known claim that the democratic general will cannot be represented – contends that representative practices are incapable of empowering and sustaining adequate capabilities of these kinds for the exercise of legitimizing democratic agency.[43] The contemporary political circumstances of transnational democratic projects produce some compelling grounds for supporting such sceptical views. Current configurations of global governance institutions – viewed systemically, as subsuming all governance levels and institutional types interacting within the overarching global order – are complex and dynamic, with uneven and shifting impacts on local and transnational populations.[44] As a consequence, many populations of democratic claimants are themselves diffuse and dynamic – with contested and shifting boundaries, dispersed and diverse memberships, and weak political relationships to their purported representatives within governance institutions. This systemic disjuncture between populations of democratic claimants, and those connected socially and institutionally as active democratic constituencies, produces significant

[42] Pitkin, fn. 28; Macdonald, *Global Stakeholder Democracy*, fn. 7.

[43] Nadia Urbinati, 'Rousseau on the Risks of Representing the Sovereign' (2012) 53(4) *Politische Vierteljahresschrift* 646–667; Robin Douglass, 'Rousseau's Critique of Representative Sovereignty: Principled or Pragmatic?' (2013) 57(3) *American Journal of Political Science* 735–747.

[44] Michael Zürn, *A Theory of Global Governance: Authority, Legitimacy, and Contestation* (Oxford: Oxford University Press, 2018); Kenneth W. Abbott, Jessica F. Green and Robert O. Keohane, 'Organizational Ecology and Institutional Change in Global Governance' (2016) 70(2) *International Organization* 247–277.

challenges for the development of legitimate representative instruments of global democracy.[45]

### 11.2.3 *Constitutive Representation As Remedy for Transnational Legitimacy Problems*

Given these challenges, proponents of representation as an instrument of global legitimation must consider further what instruments within representative practices can best foster and sustain the requisite dimensions of active democratic agency within represented constituencies. Here I propose that such practices can be helpfully conceptualized as a variant of what is sometimes called *constitutive* (or in more common terms, 'constructivist') representation.[46] This idea captures the creative potential that arises in any representative process, which re-presents its subject in a new and different form from its original condition:[47] not just describing or displacing a subject already adequately formed, but *re-constituting the represented subject itself* through the representative process. Established theoretical accounts of constitutive representation have been mostly concerned with the *symbolic* dimensions of representative practice – that is, the ways in which cultural categories of political interest and identity can be creatively constructed by representational activities of depiction, narration, and interpretation, prior to the wider ideational uptake of these categories by institutionally affected or subjected democratic claimants.[48] Some theorists have deployed these representative concepts to capture the way self-appointed representatives can call forth or mobilize new constituencies in dynamic and contested governance contexts, such as those emerging in response to new transnational or global political problems.[49]

45 Gerald Gaus, *The Open Society and Its Complexities* (Oxford: Oxford University Press, 2021); Kate Macdonald and Terry Macdonald, 'Liquid Authority and Political Legitimacy in Transnational Governance' (2017) 9(2) *International Theory* 329–351.

46 Lisa Disch, *Making Constituencies: Representation as Mobilization in Mass Democracy* (Chicago: University of Chicago Press, 2021); Lisa Disch, Mathijs van de Sande and Nadia Urbinati (eds.), *The Constructivist Turn in Political Representation* (Edinburgh: Edinburgh University Press, 2019); Urbinati, fn. 13.

47 Stuart Hall (ed.), *Representation: Cultural Representations and Signifying Practices* (London: Sage Publications, 1997); Saward, fn. 39.

48 Judith Squires, 'The Constitutive Representation of Gender: Extra-Parliamentary Re-Presentations of Gender Relations' (2008) 44(2) *Representation* 187–204; Michael Saward, 'Authorisation and Authenticity: Representation and the Unelected' (2009) 17(1) *Journal of Political Philosophy* 1–22; Disch, fn. 46.

49 Kuyper, fn. 7; Saward, 'Authorisation and Authenticity: Representation and the Unelected', fn. 48; Eline Severs, 'Representation as Claims-Making: Quid Responsiveness?' (2010) 46(4) *Representation* 411–423; Montanaro, fn. 7.

Here, I propose that this established concept of constitutive representation can be expanded to capture the practices through which representatives operate to constitute not only *cultural categories* of political membership, but further *political capabilities* for the exercise of legitimizing democratic agency. More specifically, we may consider how constitutive representation can function to cultivate, among members of fluid and emergent transnational constituencies, those capabilities for constituency *self-recognition*, communicative or collaborative *engagement*, and responsible political *commitment*, which we have established are required to support the active political agency that is the source of democratic legitimacy in representative practice. First, representatives may support the constitution of represented constituencies in the dimension of *self-recognition* by creatively interpreting and projecting latent or contested group identities – metaphorically, painting a portrait rather than holding up a mirror; in doing so, they may help constituents gain stronger recognition of their political status as a collective, and their democratic claims against international governance institutions. Second, representatives may support the constitution of represented constituencies in the dimension of communicative or collaborative *engagement* by supplying the interactive infrastructures and attentional salience required to bring disparate constituents together into creative political engagements of their own – building new and dynamic understandings of the content of shared interests in their governance institutions. And third, representatives may support the constitution of represented constituencies in the dimension of responsible political *commitment* by brokering engagements between their own represented constituents and other groups with competing represented interests – thus helping to contain partisanship among their represented subjects within the bounds and burdens of political responsibility to the wider democratic order.

More work needs to be done, however, to consider how such constitutive representation may function in practice in international institutions, to help remedy problems of legitimacy arising across the transnational constituencies of the global democratic order. It is accordingly to these more concrete political issues that we must turn our attention next; and in doing so, we will take up more directly the question of the role played by IOs in fostering these distinctive representative practices.

## 11.3 THE REPRESENTATIVE FUNCTION OF IOS AS ORCHESTRATORS OF DEMOCRATIC CONSTITUENCIES

So far, we have been discussing issues about the functions of democratic and representative instruments, as remedies to political legitimacy problems, at a very general level of theoretical analysis. With this broad conceptual framework now in place, we are ready to turn to the more specific questions that focus inquiry in this volume – concerning the role of IO representation in fostering democratic legitimacy within international lawmaking processes. As set out in this volume's framing introductory discussion,[50] IOs contribute to international lawmaking processes in a variety of important ways, and correspondingly serve as institutional hubs for diverse representative practices. As others in the volume are discussing, practices of political representation with legitimizing democratic qualities can be supported: *inside* IOs, when representative inclusion is cultivated within their internal decision-making processes; *through* IOs, where IO processes serve as sites for collaborative decision-making involving outside representative parties; and *by* IOs, where IOs themselves serve as agents of representative practice within wider processes of international lawmaking.

Here I am considering the third of these modes of IO representation; though the instrument for this role that I will describe is less direct than some other instances of representation by IOs, such as when IOs take on representative roles as members of other IOs, or as participants in external lawmaking processes. More specifically, I will examine in what follows how IOs can represent transnational constituencies through the indirect process of *orchestrating the constitution of represented constituencies* within international lawmaking processes, in circumstances where constituencies may otherwise lack the political capacities for participation in representative legitimation of international law. Before moving on to illustrate this kind of representative practice, with the case of IO orchestration of refugee constituencies through the GCR, it is helpful to begin by explaining in more detail the proposed political instruments of these constitutive practices of IO representation. This requires saying more: first about the idea of *orchestration*, as an instrument of IO agency in representative political practice; and second about the concrete activities through which IOs can orchestrate *the constitution of represented constituencies* as democratic agents in international lawmaking processes.

### 11.3.1 *Orchestration as an Instrument of IO Representation*

The traditional conceptual categories of modern political analysis are notoriously challenged by the theoretical task of capturing the distinctive forms of political agency embodied in IOs, as they now function within the complex governance systems of our contemporary global order. Modern theories of

[50] See also Besson, Chapter 1 in this volume.

political power, legitimacy, and democracy have built conceptual apparatuses around the governance systems of sovereign States – drawing a clear conceptual line between the *governing* agency of political rule (centred on the lawmaking and enforcement powers of the State), and the *democratic* agency of the ruled (exercised collectively through representative or other practices of democratic legitimation). IOs do not fit neatly on either side of this conceptual divide, as they are both instruments and subjects of the sovereign powers of States, which invest them with their varied organizational powers. Moreover, any delegated ruling powers invested in IOs by States are subject further to the structural dynamics of a complex global governance system, in which a multiplicity of political agents must navigate and negotiate competing aims and powers to advance their governing or legitimizing aims.[51] Any theoretical account of IOs' political agency within a democratic global order – whether focused on the side of governance or legitimation functions – must grapple with these systemic complexities.

These theoretical challenges have been the focus of significant attention from International Relations scholars seeking to account for the distinctive forms of political agency IOs exercise within processes of global governance – or in other terms, in activities of institutional rule. While many IOs still engage heavily in traditional State-centred forms of governance activity – such as negotiation of treaties, operation of interstate dispute resolution mechanisms, or monitoring of compliance – there is now wide recognition that their governance performance is often improved by utilization of soft and indirect forms of political agency, operating through the mobilization of 'intermediary' actors such as non-governmental organizations (NGOs), businesses, transgovernmental networks, transnational partnerships, and other IOs, in support of their governance goals. The concept of 'orchestration' is often used to describe these indirect modes of IO influence – serving as an umbrella concept for a wide variety of political strategies IOs use to support, facilitate, coordinate, and steer global governance activities via intermediary actors operating across a complex global institutional system.[52]

[51] Karen J. Alter and Sophie Meunier, 'The Politics of International Regime Complexity' (2009) 7(1) *Perspectives on Politics* 13–24; Alexander Betts, 'Regime Complexity and International Organizations: UNHCR as a Challenged Institution' (2013) 19(1) *Global Governance* 69–81; Karen J. Alter and Kal Raustiala, 'The Rise of International Regime Complexity' (2018) 14 *Annual Review of Law and Social Science* 329–349.

[52] Kenneth W. Abbott, Philipp Genschel, Duncan Snidal and Bernhard Zangl, 'Orchestration: Global Governance through Intermediaries', in Kenneth W. Abbott, Philipp Genschel, Duncan Snidal and Bernhard Zangl (eds.), *International Organizations as Orchestrators* (Cambridge: Cambridge University Press, 2015), pp. 3–36.

Some theoretical attention has been given to the question of how IO orchestration in global governance practices can itself be legitimized or democratized, as an instrument of institutional rule.[53] But there has been less consideration of how the indirect forms of IO political agency captured by the orchestration concept may also help model IOs agency exercised on the other side of the democratic leger – in new kinds of representative practices that adapt democratic instruments to the complex social and institutional order of twenty-first century world politics. Here I propose that the concept of orchestration can instructively be applied in this latter way, to capture some important roles IOs can play in supporting, facilitating, coordinating, and steering a range of intermediary actors engaged in activities of *constitutive representation* – which cultivate in emergent constituencies, across the global order, the qualities required to support their roles in representative legitimation. Through so doing, IO orchestration activities can potentially support not only the functional efficacy of global governance practices, but also their democratic legitimacy.

### 11.3.2 *How IOs Can Orchestrate the Constitution of Represented Constituencies*

What, then, are some of the political activities through which IOs can orchestrate the constitution of represented constituencies, as democratic agents in international lawmaking processes? In exploring these activities, we can extrapolate and apply established theoretical work on the varied *techniques of IO orchestration* commonly deployed through intermediaries in support of global governance goals – exploring how these techniques may further be utilized in practices of constitutive representation.[54] While IO orchestration capabilities and techniques are diverse, and vary greatly across contexts, existing orchestration scholarship has identified several with especially wide application: *convening* engagements among intermediaries, to catalyse collaborations; *agenda-setting* for programmes of collaborative work; financial and administrative *assistance*, to expand the material capabilities of intermediary

[53] Kenneth W. Abbott, Philipp Genschel, Duncan Snidal and Bernhard Zangl, 'Two Logics of Indirect Governance: Delegation and Orchestration' (2016) 46(4) *British Journal of Political Science* 719–729; Karin Bäckstrand and Jonathan W. Kuyper, 'The Democratic Legitimacy of Orchestration: The UNFCCC, Non-State Actors, and Transnational Climate Governance' (2017) 26(4) *Environmental Politics* 764–788.

[54] For further discussion see Samantha Besson, 'Democratic Representation within International Organizations: From International Good Governance to International Good Government' (2022) 19(4) *International Organizations Law Review* 489–527.

actors; *endorsement*, to raise profiles or status of intermediary activities; and *coordination*, to increase collaborative synergies and impact.[55] To map out how such orchestration techniques may be applicable within practices of constitutive representation, we can consider how they may operate to support the constitution of each of the legitimizing capabilities within transnational constituencies identified earlier: democratic *self-recognition*, *engagement*, and *commitment*.

First, IO orchestration activities may contribute to the constitution of *democratic self-recognition* within represented transnational constituencies – supporting the interpretation and projection of latent or contested identities among constituents who have been brought together not by longstanding historical trajectories of shared culture, but rather by more recent impositions of institutional affectedness or subjection producing a shared democratic claim. Two important orchestration techniques IOs can deploy to support these constitutive representative practices are *convening* and *endorsement*: here IOs can leverage their access to a range of (contextually varying, public or private) influential actors in their governance domains to identify representative intermediaries with inspirational visions and leadership capabilities; and they can further supply these representatives with the institutional platforms and networks required to project their visions across audiences wider institutional stakeholder constituencies. Administrative and financial *assistance* will typically be a further essential component of orchestration activities of this kind – whether this supports the convening of high profile representative public events or forums, or the brokerage of ongoing relationships between visionary representatives and their wider constituencies at more localized levels, which allow for wide political transmission of representative interpretations of collective democratic identities.

Second, IO orchestration activities may contribute to the constitution of communicative or collaborative *engagement* within represented transnational constituencies – supplying not only platforms for representatives to disseminate inspirational visions of the democratic identities and claims of their represented constituencies, but further opportunities for disparate members of transnational constituencies to contribute themselves to defining the political interests associated with these memberships. As above, orchestration techniques of *convening* and *assistance* can play important roles in supporting these constitutive practices. Here, however, the emphasis will be less on support for high profile platforming of representative visions, and more on support for deliberative network infrastructures and local community

[55] Abbott *et al.*, *International Organizations as Orchestrators*, fn. 52, pp. 14–16.

engagements diffused across the wider memberships of represented constituencies. To provide structure and focus for these diffused political processes of communicative and collaborative engagement, there may often be roles also for orchestration techniques of *agenda-setting* and *coordination*. Here, IOs can support the deliberative articulation of constituency interests by helping to frame questions, establish deliberative forums and processes, and create shared records of dialogues among members of transnational constituencies, in support of these legitimizing forms of collective democratic engagement.

Third, IO orchestration activities may contribute to the constitution of responsible political *commitment* within represented transnational constituencies – by fostering understandings not only of their internal democratic identities and interests, but also their political responsibilities to others across the wider global political order, with whom legitimate settlements must be reached through shared governance institutions. Supporting the constitution of wider political commitments of this kind may require an array of orchestration techniques – with *agenda-setting* playing an especially important role in framing representative engagements around problems and challenges of common global concern, as distinct from narrower partisan issues, and *coordination* helping to define clear norms for responsible political engagement of constituents with the wider governance institutions and communities through which their interests are to be advanced. These responsible political engagements can be aided further through building and disseminating more knowledge about constituencies' mutual vulnerabilities and interdependencies, and through building capacity for secure and strong political leadership structures within represented constituencies. Here, *assistance* may also be a crucial feature of IO orchestration activity in this area – insofar as IOs' financial, administrative, and technical resources can make valuable contributions to these knowledge- and capacity-building practices.

## 11.4 IO ORCHESTRATION OF REPRESENTED REFUGEE CONSTITUENCIES: THE CASE OF THE GLOBAL COMPACT ON REFUGEES

The democratic roles that IO orchestration can play, in supporting legitimizing practices of constitutive representation in global governance, can be illustrated by examining the work of the UNHCR and the UNGA in the development and implementation of the *Global Compact for Refugees* (GCR). The GCR is a framework of principles, formulated to guide international cooperation among IOs, governments, NGOs, and other refugee and host community stakeholders in the pursuit of more equitable and effective global responsibility-sharing for supporting refugees and their host communities. Its development was motivated by increasing international recognition of the deficiencies of existing global governance instruments for addressing the escalating refugee crises of the early twenty-first century – catalysed in particular by the Syrian refugee crisis of 2015 – and a corresponding shared commitment to strengthening international cooperation in refugee protection and assistance.[56] The GCR was formally adopted by the UNGA on 17 December 2018, following over two years of consultations with UN Member States, IOs, refugee communities and leaders, civil society and private sector stakeholder organizations, and academic experts, led by the UNHCR.[57]

As momentum was built through this process for international commitments to developing stronger institutional instruments for political governance of refugee protection and assistance, increasing attention turned to the question of how these new international principles and processes could achieve *legitimacy* – of the loosely democratic kind associated with commitments to participatory and representative principles of political inclusion.[58] Commitments to legitimizing principles of stakeholder participation, representation, and localization were by this time already well-entrenched within international governance practices in a range of humanitarian and development fields.[59] But their importance in the field of refugee protection and assistance is heightened further by the special political situation of refugee populations – being alienated from the routine avenues for participatory and representative inclusion associated with secure State citizenship. As a result, these principles gained prominence within international discussions on the design and legitimation of this emerging governance architecture – led by the emphasis placed on this issue by refugee communities themselves.[60]

56 Gillian D. Triggs and Patrick C. J. Wall, '"The Makings of a Success": The Global Compact on Refugees and the Inaugural Global Refugee Forum' (2020) 32(2) *International Journal of Refugee Law* 283–339.

57 UN, *Global Compact on Refugees* (New York: United Nations, 2018). www.unhcr.org/media/37797, last accessed 1 June 2023.

58 Dana Schmalz, *Refugees, Democracy and the Law: Political Rights at the Margins of the State* (London: Routledge, 2021).

59 Ghazala Mansuri and Vijayendra Rao, *Localizing Development: Does Participation Work?* (Washington, DC: World Bank, 2013); Hugo Slim, 'Localization Is Self-Determination' (2021) 3 *Frontiers in Political Science* 1.

60 Stefan Rother and Elias Steinhilper, 'Tokens or Stakeholders in Global Migration Governance? The Role of Affected Communities and Civil Society in the Global Compacts on Migration and Refugees' (2019) 57(6) *International Migration* 243–257.

In the decades leading up to the establishment of the GCR, significant work had already been done – by refugees themselves, and by other organizations and analysts – to establish the idea that refugees may have democratic claims to recognition as a distinctive constituency within international society, entitled to some forms of democratic representation operating independently from State-based vehicles for political inclusion.[61] This idea had been advanced in three institutional contexts in particular: first, in work towards strengthened refugees' democratic inclusion in the governance of refugee camps;[62] second, in debates about refugees' rights to vote or otherwise participate within host community democratic processes;[63] and third, in proposals for direct representation of refugee communities within UNHCR decision-making processes.[64] As the scope of the framework for international cooperation on refugee issues expanded through the development of the GCR, refugee leaders advocated strongly for the parallel expansion of international commitments to principles of refugees' democratic inclusion – to include the wider range of local and transnational contexts in which key issues affecting the lives of refugees are politically settled.[65] These broad commitments were ultimately codified within the GCR itself, which prescribes that:

> [R]elevant actors will, wherever possible, continue to develop and support consultative processes that enable *refugees and host community members* to assist in designing appropriate, accessible and inclusive responses. States and relevant stakeholders will explore how best to include refugees and members of host communities, particularly women, youth, and persons with disabilities, in key forums and processes, as well as diaspora, where relevant.[66]

61 Schmalz, fn. 58.

62 Felix Bender, 'Should Refugees Govern Refugee Camps?' (2021) 27(4) *Critical Review of International Social and Political Philosophy* 441–464; Jennifer Hyndman, 'A Refugee Camp Conundrum: Geopolitics, Liberal Democracy, and Protracted Refugee Situations' (2013) 28(2) *Refuge: Canada's Journal on Refugees* 7–15; Schmalz, fn. 58; Jennifer Hyndman, 'Refugee Self-Management and the Question of Governance' (1997) 16(2) *Refuge: Canada's Journal on Refugees* 16–22.

63 Ruvi Ziegler, *Voting Rights of Refugees* (Cambridge: Cambridge University Press, 2017); Felix Bender, 'Enfranchising the Disenfranchised: Should Refugees Receive Political Rights in Liberal Democracies?' (2021) 25(1) *Citizenship Studies* 56–71.

64 Carolina Moulin and Peter Nyers, '"We Live in a Country of UNHCR": Refugee Protests and Global Political Society' (2007) 1(4) *International Political Sociology* 356–372; Haqqi Bahram, 'Between Tokenism and Self-Representation: Refugee-Led Advocacy and Inclusion in International Refugee Policy' (2020) 58 *RESPOND Working Paper Series Global Migration: Consequences and Responses* 1–18; Bahati Kanyamanza and Emily Arnold-Fernandez, 'Meaningful Representation Starts at the Top: Refugees on UNHCR's ExCom' (2022) 70 *Forced Migration Review* 21–24.

65 Rother and Steinhilper, fn. 60; Triggs and Wall, fn. 56.

66 UN, *Global Compact on Refugees*, fn. 57, para. 34 (emphasis original).

While these very general commitments to refugees' democratic inclusion have gained international endorsement within the GCR framework at the level of principle, there is nonetheless wide recognition that their implementation in practice faces significant political obstacles. Even leaving aside difficulties associated with conflicts of interest between these democratic principles and other political goals that States and non-State actors bring to their cooperative activities on refugee issues, there are some significant barriers to democratic inclusion associated with aspects of refugee constituencies themselves. These arise because many of the same features of refugee situations which generate the imperative for international refugee protection and assistance, in the first place, also undermine some important social prerequisites for the exercise by refugee constituencies of legitimizing democratic agency. Though many individuals live with the precarity of refugee status for extended periods, membership of a transnational refugee constituency is nonetheless fluid and dynamic – lacking the secure integration and commitment of permanent citizenship; refugees as a transnational constituency are geographically dispersed, and culturally and linguistically diverse, posing barriers to political communication; and perhaps most crucially, the physical, economic, social, and cultural vulnerability and estrangement experienced in many situations of refugeehood can deter or preclude taking on the additional risks and burdens that accompany political engagement.

Achieving political legitimacy in the global governance of refugee issues thus requires addressing such barriers through systematic political interventions to support the development and preservation of refugees' capabilities for democratic political agency. As David Owen has put it, this involves at the most basic level supporting the constitution of refugees as agents 'who can make choices and plans about their futures that are not simply driven by the urgent requirements of practical necessity and who have some ability to shape the social environment in which those choices and plans are made'.[67] More specifically, it requires some practices of the kind described earlier as *constitutive representation*: political interventions aimed at cultivating within refugee constituencies the capabilities of democratic self-recognition, engagement, and commitment – established earlier as the minimal forms of collective political agency required to sustain democratic legitimacy through representative practice.

In response to this demand for legitimacy in their governance operations, the UNHCR and the UNGA have engaged in a range of activities, through their work in developing and implementing the GCR framework, which can

67 David Owen, 'Refugees, Legitimacy and Development' (2021) 14 *Ethics & Global Politics* 86–97.

be characterized as *orchestration of constitutive representation* – or to put this differently, *orchestration of refugee constituencies* as represented collectives of active democratic agents. Through these orchestration activities, the role of IOs in representative practices goes beyond opening up IOs' internal decision-making processes and institutional spaces to access by established refugee representatives; it extends further to *external* interventions in the political relationships among members of refugee communities and their political representatives, with the aim of strengthening their legitimizing capacities.

To illustrate these activities, we can first examine how the UNHCR and UNGA have helped to orchestrate the constitution of *democratic self-recognition* within refugee constituencies, through supporting the activities of refugee leaders in interpreting and projecting mutual understandings of refugeehood as a democratic political identity with legitimate claims to international representation. Some of the most important IO contributions here have deployed orchestration techniques of *convening* and *endorsement* – leveraging access to their organizational networks and prestige to bring together visionary and well-connected refugee leaders from across disparate geographical and cultural contexts, and to raise the political profiles of their democratic political advocacy. An important example of such activities is the UNHCR's work in convening and endorsing the 2018 Global Summit of Refugees,[68] and the subsequent Global Refugee Forums, hosted annually from 2019 as platforms for the collective promotion of new 'forms of behaviour and identity'[69] more conducive to representative international decision-making on refugee issues. This prominent support from UNHCR, and the high-status endorsement from the UNGA through its adoption of the GCR framework, has in turn inspired wider commitments to refugee participation and representation among other governmental and NGO actors,[70] thus expanding the scope of refugees' political recognition as a transnational democratic constituency. The provision of administrative and financial *assistance* to refugee leaders, and to the other actors supporting these developing representative practices at more local levels, has been another important element of IO orchestration techniques in this area – with significant

68 Mauricio Vilori, Diana Ortiz, Najeeba Wazefadost and Mohammed Badran, 'The Global Summit of Refugees and the Importance of Refugee Self-Representation' (2018) 59 *Forced Migration Review* 62–63.

69 Triggs and Wall, fn. 56, at 321.

70 Institute of Democracy and Electoral Assistance, *Political Participation of Refugees: Bridging the Gaps* (Stockholm: Institute for Democracy and Electoral Assistance, 2018).

investments of resources by the UNHCR to support the elevation of refugee voices through these new international forums and networked engagements.[71]

Second, the UNHCR and UNGA have helped to orchestrate the constitution of communicative and collaborative *engagement* within refugee constituencies: extending support beyond the platforming and endorsement of selected refugee leaders advocating for refugees' democratic empowerment; and further fostering the involvement of wider members of refugee communities in defining the substantive refugee interests to be represented by leaders in protection and assistance operations. Here orchestration techniques of *convening* and *assistance* can be seen in some material support UNHCR has provided for grassroots refugee networks and local community groups to expand the scope of refugee participation in the design and delivery of refugee assistance programmes, within refugee camps as well as some transit and resettlement situations.[72] In addition to such support for widening the participatory base of political engagement within refugee communities, the UNHCR has also orchestrated the empowerment of refugee agency through *agenda-setting* and *coordination* activities, which help to frame, endorse, and disseminate new principled frameworks and recommendations to guide the work of other governmental, civil society, and business actors in fostering opportunities and supports for refugee participation. These include the broadly democratic principles that are incorporated (with UNGA endorsement) in the GCR itself; and they further include those more detailed recommendations that have been developed within independent refugee-led forums convened with IO support,[73] such as the Representation and Participation Working Group of the International Refugee Congress – a non-profit organization initially established with UNHCR support.[74]

Third, these IOs have helped to orchestrate the constitution of responsible political *commitment* within refugee constituencies, by working to support

[71] UN High Commissioner for Refugees, 'Budget and Expenditure' (2017). https://reporting.unhcr.org/dashboards/budget-and-expenditure?year=2017, last accessed 18 September 2023.

[72] Kate Pincock, Alexander Betts and Evan Easton-Calabria, *The Global Governed?: Refugees as Providers of Protection and Assistance* (Cambridge: Cambridge University Press, 2020); Evan Easton-Calabria and Kate Pincock, 'Refugee-Led Social Protection: Reconceiving Refugee Assistance' (2018) 58 *Forced Migration Review* 56–58; Kate Pincock, Alexander Betts and Evan Easton-Calabria, 'The Rhetoric and Reality of Localisation: Refugee-Led Organisations in Humanitarian Governance' (2021) 57(5) *The Journal of Development Studies* 719–734.

[73] International Refugee Congress, 'International Refugee Congress 2018 Consultation Report' (2018).

[74] Refugee Congress, 'About Refugee Congress'. https://refugeecongress.org/about-refugee-congress, last accessed 2 June 2023.

political engagements not only within refugee communities, but also between refugees and their host communities, and other global stakeholders in refugee protection and assistance. Orchestration techniques of *agenda-setting* and *coordination* have been deployed here via the emphasis placed in GCR principles upon a 'whole-of-society' approach to responsibility-sharing for refugee protection and assistance,[75] and related orchestration instruments such as proposals within the GCR for future 'solidarity conferences' and platforms, intended to bring refugees and other stakeholders together in community-building dialogue around responsibility-sharing commitments.[76] This principled approach to responsibility-sharing identifies the intersecting contributions required from varied social actors – State and non-State, local and international – and further seeks to balance an emphasis on refugee rights with a discourse of mutual and shared political responsibility between refugees and other stakeholders in refugee governance instruments.[77] IO support for constituting these dimensions of refugee agency is advanced further through extensive *assistance* invested in data-collection and scholarly analysis of collective refugee protection and assistance instruments, aimed at building stronger capacities within and beyond refugee communities for upholding these shared responsibilities.[78]

These various activities undertaken by the UNHCR (some with endorsement and other support from the UNGA) have made some meaningful impact: both in building international recognition of the legitimate claims of refugee communities to inclusion in the governance of those refugee protection and assistance issues that affect their lives; and in taking first steps in a larger programme of work towards the empowerment of refugee's political agency as participants in representative decision-making practices. As instruments for establishing the representative democratic legitimacy of political decision-making around refugee protection and assistance, however, they are

[75] Tamara Domicelj and Carolina Gottardo, 'Implementing the Global Compacts: The Importance of a Whole-of-Society Approach' (2019) 60 *Forced Migration Review* 79–82; UN, *Global Compact on Refugees*, fn. 57.

[76] Bhupinder S. Chimni, 'Global Compact on Refugees: One Step Forward, Two Steps Back' (2018) 30(4) *International Journal of Refugee Law* 630–634; Alexander Betts, 'The Global Compact on Refugees: Towards a Theory of Change?' (2018) 30(4) *International Journal of Refugee Law* 623–626.

[77] Matthew Gibney, 'The Duties of Refugees', in David Miller and Christine Straehle (eds.), *The Political Philosophy of Refuge* (Cambridge: Cambridge University Press, 2019), pp. 132–153.

[78] Chimni, fn. 76; Volker Türk, 'The Promise and Potential of the Global Compact on Refugees' (2018) 30(4) *International Journal of Refugee Law* 575–585; Jeff Crisp, 'A Global Academic Network on Refugees: Some Unanswered Questions' (2018) 30(4) *International Journal of Refugee Law* 640–642.

limited in several important dimensions. First, IO efforts to orchestrate refugee constituencies' democratic *self-recognition* raise questions about whether those refugee leaders selected for invitation through IO networks can reflect the wide diversity of refugee experiences – particularly including experiences of those in the most marginalized and vulnerable positions; moreover, there are worries that refugees may be 'tokenized' through IO orchestration activities,[79] without parallel inclusion in the more ongoing and mundane protection and assistance activities that impact refugee lives.[80] At the same time, IO orchestration instruments for fostering refugees' political *engagement* at such localized levels are typically not sufficient to overcome the deeper sources of physical vulnerability, economic precarity, social exclusion, and future uncertainty, that work to undermine secure opportunities for refugees' communicative and collaborative political participation.[81] Work to orchestrate refugee constituencies' responsible political *commitment* faces related constraints, due to the risks that political discourse around shared responsibility may be used, in contexts of persistent power asymmetries, to shift burdens prematurely and inappropriately onto refugee communities without adequate capacity and support to uphold them.[82]

Some aspects of these challenges may be partially overcome through greater investment of political capital and material resources by IOs in the scope of their orchestration efforts. Others, however, have deeper structural drivers that cannot be adequately overcome through IOs acting within siloed fields of governance responsibility – since the social prerequisites for legitimizing democratic agency traverse many functional and territorial governance fields and corresponding political constituencies. The democratic work of constituting legitimizing capability within represented constituencies must accordingly always retain a commitment to some cosmopolitan principle of 'whole-of-society' global responsibility, such that IOs pursue this orchestration work as a coordinated part of much wider global projects of collaborative political change.

79 Sana Mustafa, 'Nothing About Us Without Us: Why Refugee Inclusion Is Long Overdue', *Refugees Deeply*, 20 June 2018. https://deeply.thenewhumanitarian.org/refugees/community/2018/06/20/nothing-about-us-without-us-why-refugee-inclusion-is-long-overdue, last accessed 18 September 2023.

80 Mustafa Alio, Shaza Alrihawi, James Milner, Anila Noor, Najeeba Wazefadost and Pascal Zigashane, 'By Refugees, for Refugees: Refugee Leadership during COVID-19, and Beyond' (2020) 32(2) *International Journal of Refugee Law* 370–373; Rother and Steinhilper, fn. 60.

81 Institute of Democracy and Electoral Assistance, fn. 70.

82 Pincock *et al.*, *The Global Governed?*, fn. 72; Pincock *et al.*, 'The Rhetoric and Reality of Localisation', fn. 72.

## 11.5 CONCLUSIONS

Just as IOs play important roles in international lawmaking, and political governance more broadly, the analysis here has shown one way in which they can also play important roles in *legitimating practices of political representation*. Just as IOs' roles in global governance are often indirect – orchestrating intermediary governmental, civil society, and other social actors instead of imposing direct political control – so too their roles in legitimizing representation can operate indirectly, through practices of *representative orchestration*. The orchestration practices examined here have been addressed to one particular element of representative practice that IOs are particularly well-positioned to support: activities of *constitutive representation*, which cultivate within transnational constituencies those forms of political recognition, integration, and commitment required to support democratic legitimacy. Examining these practices as undertaken by the UNHCR and UNGA, in their work around the development and implementation of the GCR, has illustrated some valuable democratic contributions, alongside significant structural limitations, of IO efforts to foster stronger democratic agency and legitimacy in global governance. Taken together, these remind us that even while the activities of democratic governance and legitimation can take diverse political forms for different actors and in different operational contexts, the political work of establishing the shared democratic identities, relationships, and commitments required for strong legitimacy will always demand persistent attention to the collective problems and responsibilities that connect stakeholders across the global order as a whole.

# 12

# No International Democratic Representation without Institution

## *Lifting the Democratic Veil of Functionalist, Incorporation, and Agency Theories of Representation by International Organizations*

Samantha Besson and José Luis Martí

### 12.1 INTRODUCTION

Many contemporary international organizations (IOs) are empowered to adopt international law that claims to bind their Member States (and, directly or indirectly, their peoples). Certain IOs have also become members of other IOs or, at least, active participants in international lawmaking processes that claim to bind those IOs and their Member States (and their peoples). Generally speaking IOs play a central role in contemporary international lawmaking: they institutionalize most of the processes through which international law is adopted today, be it through international conferences, international courts, or as IO secondary law. From the perspective of the democratic legitimacy of international law, this raises the question of the conditions under which those IOs may be regarded as democratic representatives of their Member States' peoples and, accordingly, under which the international law they have the right or discretion to adopt inside and outside of IO organs and processes may claim to bind those peoples legitimately.

When one knows how powerful and even dominating certain IOs and, within those IOs, certain States and their governments (usually not the most democratic ones) have become,[1] the stakes of those IOs' democratic representativeness are

Many thanks to Louis Hill and Mathilde Vigné for their editorial assistance, and to Charles Girard, Oliver de Frouville, Folke Tersman, Patricia Mindus, Olle Risberg, Max McLoughlin, and Silvana Hultsch for helpful comments.

[1] See Andrew Hurrell and Nicholas Lees, 'International Organizations and the Idea of Equality', in Bob Reinalda (ed.), *Routledge Handbook of International Organization* (London/New York: Routledge, 2013), pp. 106–118; Lora A. Viola, *The Closure of the International System: How*

extremely high. As a matter of fact, the stakes of the democratic representativeness of IOs are not only international.[2] As we know by now, the deficit in democratic representation by and in IOs has also fuelled the so-called 'crisis' of democratic representation domestically, including its populist critique of both governments and parliaments.[3] The future of domestic representation is therefore bound to that of international representation, and vice-versa.

Curiously given the importance of those international and domestic stakes, however, the democratic representativeness of IOs does not seem to be much of a concern of IOs and their Member States, at least if one refers to the international law of IOs and the related international law scholarship.[4]

There are many reasons for the contemporary sidelining of the question of democratic representation by and in IOs.

One of the main reasons for the neglect of democratic representation *by* IOs is that their capacity to represent has mostly been approached as 'non-political' in international law.[5] Representation by IOs is indeed often organized so as to follow a functional approach to legitimacy by output only: it should ensure the implementation of delegated State functions and hence the protection of their Member States' interests. When it is exceptionally framed by reference to input legitimacy, representation by IOs remains functional, moreover. It relies on IOs' integrated or independent organs' expertise, for instance, in implementing States' functions and protecting their interests.

Moreover, to the extent that IO Member States, but also other public and private institutions participate in IO procedures and hence are to be represented *in* IO organs according to IO law, it is usually as such, and not

*Institutions Create Political Equalities and Hierarchies* (Cambridge: Cambridge University Press, 2020); Samantha Besson, 'L'égalité des États membres de l'Union européenne: un nouveau départ en droit international de l'organisation des États?', in Édouard Dubout (ed.), *L'égalité des États membres de l'Union européenne* (Brussels: Bruylant, 2022), pp. 261–298.

2 On the continuity between domestic and international democracy, see Samantha Besson, 'The Authority of International Law: Lifting the State Veil' (2009) 31(3) *Sydney Law Review* 343–380; Samantha Besson, 'Investment Citizenship and Democracy in a Global Age: Towards a Democratic Interpretation of International Nationality Law' (2019) 29(4) *Swiss Review of International and European Law* 525–547.

3 See Nadia Urbinati, *Me the People: How Populism Transforms Democracy* (Cambridge, MA: Harvard University Press, 2019); Joachim Blatter and Johannes Schulz, 'Intergovernmentalism and the Crisis of Representative Democracy: The Case for Creating a System of Horizontally Expanded and Overlapping National Democracies' (2022) 28(3) *European Journal of International Relations* 722–747; Kilian Spandler and Fredrik Söderbaum, 'Populist (De) Legitimation of International Organizations' (2023) 99(3) *International Affairs* 1023–1041.

4 On the reasons for the similarly meagre discussion of representation in international democratic theory, see Besson, Chapter 1 in this volume.

5 See also Marieke Louis and Lucile Maertens, *Why International Organizations Hate Politics: Depoliticizing the World* (London: Routledge, 2021). See Section 12.4.1 below.

necessarily as political representatives.[6] In the increasing number of cases where their representativeness in IOs is actually required, it is mostly functional, however, and measured by reference to certain characteristics of States or civil society organizations (CSO) that may be of instrumental relevance for the IO. One may think here of the economic, financial, military, or technoscientific power of some of its Member States (usually a few of them) in the IO's interstate organs, on the one hand, and of the expertise and financial resources of some CSOs (usually just a few as well), on the other. For the rest, the democratic emphasis in that debate has been placed on ensuring more 'participation', 'deliberation', and 'inclusion' in IOs,[7] for instance of the so-called 'affected persons' and other 'stakeholders'.[8] This assumes that there could be participation or deliberation without representation. Participation is usually organized indeed without reference to the representative credentials of those participants in IO processes except as self-representing or as self-appointed representatives, and without any concern about their impact on the concurrent representation of the very same people(s) by States within those IOs.

It is this gap that the present chapter purports to fill. To do so, it builds upon our previous work on international democratic representation and brings our argument in favour of IOs as 'multiple international representation systems' one step further.[9] Our earlier publications addressed various issues pertaining to the deficit of the democratic representation by States and by other public

[6] There are exceptions, of course, such as the ILO's representative tripartism (see Marieke Louis, *Qu'est-ce qu'une bonne représentation? L'Organisation internationale du travail de 1919 à nos jours* (Paris: Dalloz, 2016); Marieke Louis, 'Who Decides? Representation and Decision-Making at the International Labour Organization' (2019) 11 *International Development Policy* 40–58), but they are rare. See Section 12.4.2 below.

[7] See Anne Peters, 'International Organizations and International Law', in Jacob Katz Cogan, Ian Hurd and Ian Johnstone (eds.), *The Oxford Handbook of International Organizations* (Oxford: Oxford University Press, 2016), pp. 33–59, pp. 51–52; Klaus Dingwerth and Patrizia Nanz, 'Participation', in Cogan *et al.*, ibid, pp. 1126–1145.

[8] See Terry Macdonald, 'Citizens or Stakeholders? Exclusion, Equality and Legitimacy in Global Stakeholder Democracy', in Daniele Archibugi, Mathias Koenig-Archibugi and Raffaele Marchetti (eds.), *Global Democracy: Normative and Empirical Perspectives* (Cambridge: Cambridge University Press, 2011), pp. 47–68; Coline Ruwet, 'Que représentent les *stakeholders*?' (2010) 60(6) *Revue Française de Science Politique* 1115–1135; Jochen von Bernstorff, 'New Responses to the Legitimacy Crisis of International Institutions: The Role of "Civil Society" and the Rise of the Principle of Participation of the "Most Affected" in International Institutional Law' (2021) 32(1) *European Journal of International Law* 125–157, at 141ff.

[9] See Samantha Besson and José Luis Martí, 'The Legitimate Actors of International Law-Making: Towards a Theory of International Democratic Representation' (2018) 9(3) *Jurisprudence* 504–540; Samantha Besson, 'COVID-19 and the WHO's Political Moment' (2020) *EJIL:Talk!* www.ejiltalk.org/covid-19-and-the-whos-political-moment/, last accessed 28 August 2023; Samantha Besson and José Luis Martí, 'Cities as Democratic Representatives in

and private institutions *in* IOs and in their various organs in which those States and other public and private institutions are represented and arguably represent the same States' peoples,[10] on the one hand. There, we also discussed democratic representation *through* IOs and the legal and institutional requirements the latter could and should posit to the democratic representativeness of States and other public and private institutions and of their respective representatives inside IOs' lawmaking organs and processes so as to both correct and complement their respective democratic deficits and organize a multiple international representation system,[11] on the other. What has been left out from the scope of our inquiry so far is the further question of democratic representation *by* IOs, in and of themselves. The time has come to address it directly since the three forms of democratic representation are intimately related.

The issue of democratic representation by IOs is a broad one. What we will focus on here therefore are two questions: the subjects represented (the *who* of democratic representation by IOs) and the representation relation (the *how* of democratic representation by IOs). Scope precludes addressing the related

International Law-Making', in Helmut P. Aust and Janne E. Nijman (eds.), *Research Handbook on International Law and Cities* (London: Edward Elgar, 2021), pp. 341–353; Besson, 'L'égalité des États membres de l'Union européenne', fn. 1; Samantha Besson, 'Democratic Representation within International Organizations: From International Good Governance to International Good Government' (2022) 19(3) *International Organizations Law Review* 489–527; Samantha Besson and José Luis Martí, 'From Equal State Consent to Equal Public Participation in International Organizations: Institutionalizing Multiple International Representation', in Samantha Besson (ed.), *Consenting to International Law* (Cambridge: Cambridge University Press, 2023), pp. 314–346; Samantha Besson, 'Pour une représentation démocratique multiple au sein de l'Organisation mondiale de la Santé', in Olivier de Frouville and Dominique Rousseau (eds.), *Démocratiser l'Espace-Monde* (Le Kremlin Bicêtre: Mare & Martin, 2024), pp. 199–218; Samantha Besson, 'The Politics of Regional International Organizations: A New Dawn for the Political Legitimacy of International Law' (2024) 21(1) *International Organizations Law Review* 87–114; Samantha Besson, 'We the Peoples of the United Nations: From Single Separate Instituent Powers to Multiple Nested Instituted Publics', in Peter Niesen, Marcus Patberg and Lucia Robinelli (eds.), *The Oxford Handbook of Constituent Power* (Oxford: Oxford University Press, 2026), pp. 531–544; Samantha Besson and José Luis Martí, 'Republican Sovereignty', in Mortimer Sellers and Frank Lovett (eds.), *The Oxford Handbook of Republicanism* (Oxford: Oxford University Press, 2026) (online edition, Oxford Academic, 23 January 2024, https://doi.org/10.1093/oxfordhb/9780197754115.013.35, last accessed 16 January 2026).

[10] See Besson, 'Democratic Representation within International Organizations', fn. 9; Besson and Martí, 'From Equal State Consent to Equal Public Participation', fn. 9.

[11] See Besson, 'Democratic Representation within International Organizations', fn. 9; Besson, 'L'égalité des États membres de l'Union européenne', fn. 1; Besson, 'Pour une représentation démocratique multiple au sein de l'Organisation mondiale de la Santé', fn. 9; Besson, 'The Politics of Regional International Organizations', fn. 9.

issue of the democratic representation *of* IOs, that is, the democratic representativeness of the organs representing IOs for the latter to represent their Member States' peoples and other publics democratically. This includes very important questions, however, such as the required content of the minimal public organization law of IOs[12] and the separation of powers within IOs.[13]

Our claim in this chapter is that the protection of self-government and popular sovereignty against domination by IOs requires the public re-institution of IOs in international law so that they can represent the peoples of the world, and not only their Member States, and so that they can do so democratically, and not only instrumentally. More specifically, the chapter calls for a reform of the current international law of representation by IOs, including of its functional-democratic ambivalence for more input legitimacy, on the one hand, and of the private law analogies behind its agency-based and incorporation-based approaches to representation for more public legitimacy, on the other. Thereby, the chapter also contributes to current debates in democratic representation theory.[14] It is our claim indeed that international law and its complex institutional framework provide a unique opportunity to bring the twin instituting and authorizing dimensions of democratic representation back together again and make their necessary complementarity more visible domestically as well. This could help countering what some critiques have referred to as the contemporary reduction and 'flattening' of the tridimensional relation of political representation into a purely bidimensional and mirroring one between the represented people and their representatives.[15]

[12] See Jochen von Bernstorff, 'Procedures of Decision-Making and the Role of Law in International Organizations', in Armin von Bogdandy, Rüdiger Wolfrum, Jochen von Bernstorff, Philipp Dann and Matthias Goldmann (eds.), *The Exercise of Public Authority by International Institutions: Advancing International Institutions Law* (Heidelberg: Springer, 2010), pp. 777–806; Besson, 'Democratic Representation within International Organizations', fn. 9.

[13] See Joana Mendes and Ingo Venzke (eds.), *Allocating Authority: Who Should Do What in European and International Law?* (Oxford: Hart, 2018); Miriam Cullen, 'Separation of Powers in the United Nations System? Institutional Structure and the Rule of Law' (2020) 17(3) *International Organizations Law Review* 492–530.

[14] For those critiques, see Nadia Urbinati, 'Representative Democracy and its Critics', in Sonia Alonso, John Keane and Wolfgang Merkel (eds.), *The Future of Representative Democracy* (Cambridge: Cambridge University Press, 2011), pp. 23–49; Sofia Näsström, 'Where is the Representative Turn Going?' (2011) 10(4) *European Journal of Political Theory* 501–510.

[15] See Pierre Musso, *Le temps de l'État-Entreprise: Berlusconi, Trump, Macron* (Paris: Fayard, 2019), pp. 133–137; Samantha Besson, *Reconstructing the International Institutional Order* (Paris: OpenEdition Books/Collège de France, 2021), para. 53.

The structure of this chapter's argument is three-pronged. The first section sets the *conceptual* framework for the argument by presenting what is meant by international 'democratic legitimacy' and 'representation' in the chapter (Section 12.2). The second section specifies the *subjects* of democratic representation by IOs. It argues against an approach, now common both in international democratic theory and in the international law of IOs, that considers States to be the subjects of international representation as opposed to peoples, and States' peoples only as opposed to the multiple publics those peoples, but also others, are re-instituted into by different public institutions now involved in international lawmaking (Section 12.3). In the third and final section, the chapter turns to the *relation* of democratic representation by IOs. It criticizes three existing accounts of that relation for their lack of democratic legitimacy: functionalism, incorporation, and agency (Section 12.4).

Before we start, it is important to clarify what is meant by 'international organizations' in the chapter. Of course, specifying that notion raises a well-known difficulty to the extent that there are as many legal statuses of IOs[16] in international law as there are IOs. We consider that the corresponding categorical malaise[17] actually reflects the very 'institutional' problem with IOs this chapter purports to address, and especially the issue of their democratic representativeness.[18] Indeed, it is the proposed argument's premise that no complete conceptual clarification of the institutions referred to as IOs may be provided outside of a legal and hence normative argument about what kind of public institutions they should be and, more specifically, about how they should relate to the peoples whose legitimate law they claim to adopt. It is indeed the point of IOs *qua* institutions to be instituted, ordered, or literally 'organized' in a specific way.[19]

To the extent, however, that a preliminary clarification is required as to the identity of the IOs whose democratic legitimacy is at stake here, two delineations may be drawn. First, the chapter uses the term IO to refer to a legal understanding of IO with independent *legal personality*. Accordingly, it does

16 See Laurence Dubin and Marie-Clotilde Runavot, 'Propos introductifs', in Laurence Dubin and Marie-Clotilde Runavot (eds.), *Le phénomène institutionnel international dans tous ses états: Transformation, déformation ou reformation?* (Paris: Pedone, 2014), pp. 5–17.

17 See Angelo Golia and Anne Peters, 'The Concept of International Organizations', in Jan Klabbers (ed.), *Cambridge Companion to International Organizations Law* (Cambridge: Cambridge University Press, 2022), pp. 25–49.

18 See Besson, *Reconstructing the International Institutional Order*, fn. 15, paras. 75–80.

19 See Besson, 'The Politics of Regional International Organizations', fn. 9; Besson, 'We the Peoples of the United Nations', fn. 9.

not examine forms of international institutional cooperation with no organizational independence, such as networks or mere conferences. The latter cannot adopt (binding) international law on their own. Within this first subset of IOs, second, this chapter concentrates on organizations whose members are States, that is, on so-called *public*, 'interstate', or 'intergovernmental' organizations. This excludes purely private organizations or hybrid and public-private ones even when they are active internationally. The chapter draws no further distinctions between the IOs just identified, including by reference to their scope, size, resources, or area of specialization, even when they present themselves as 'technical' and not 'political' as a result. Democratic legitimacy should be expected of all of them when they claim to adopt international law and engage politically therefore. Of course, the institutional design of international representation depends largely on context and there can be no 'one (institutional) design fits all'. The scope of this chapter precludes, however, addressing the institutional reform of each IO in detail.[20]

Methodologically, what this chapter proposes is an argument in normative international legal theory: it puts forward an interpretation of international law and institutions, and in this case IOs and their international law, that best fits and justifies their practice. More specifically, it defends a democratic interpretation of that practice. Although the proposed democratic approach to international law relies at least in part on some ideal understanding of democracy, the argument is primarily an exercise in non-ideal normative political theory: it reacts to deficits in political legitimacy in the international legal and institutional order, and especially in democratic representation, by making non-ideal reform proposals. It is to be expected therefore that some of its proposals may suffer from legitimacy deficits of their own.

## 12.2 THE CONCEPT OF DEMOCRATIC REPRESENTATION BY INTERNATIONAL ORGANIZATIONS

This first section sets the conceptual framework for the chapter's argument by presenting what it means by 'democratic legitimacy' (Section 12.2.1) and 'representation' (Section 12.2.2) in international law and institutions.

[20] Besson and Martí, 'The Legitimate Actors', fn. 9, at 538. On the WHO, see Besson and Martí, 'From Equal State Consent to Equal Public Participation', fn. 9; Besson, 'Pour une représentation démocratique multiple au sein de l'Organisation mondiale de la Santé', fn. 9. For an ILO/WHO comparison, see Besson, 'We the Peoples of the United Nations', fn. 9.

### 12.2.1 *International Democratic Legitimacy*

The representation of peoples[21] by IOs is a question of *political legitimacy*. By political legitimacy, we mean a form of legitimacy that is not descriptive or subjective and cannot be reduced to popular acceptability, but is *normative* or objective.

More specifically, it is a form of normative *procedural* legitimacy we are concerned about. It focuses on the procedural aspects of lawmaking and should therefore be distinguished from more substantive forms of normative political legitimacy, such as justice. This brings us to another well-known distinction in the realm of political legitimacy: the distinction between input and output legitimacy. Theories of input legitimacy claim that the normative legitimacy of law derives from a combination of prior facts considered as 'inputs' into the lawmaking process. By contrast, output legitimacy refers to the substantive merits of international legal norms, be it their substantive justice or efficiency or both and therefore focuses on the 'outputs' of the lawmaking process. With its focus on procedural normative legitimacy,[22] this chapter sides, even if it objects to the terminology and to the distinction itself between output and input, with *input* accounts of political legitimacy.

This chapter understands political legitimacy, in quite a standard way, to refer to the normative questions of who has the right to rule (or the right to adopt legal norms or participate in the adoption of such norms) and how such a right to rule should be exerted in order to generate obligations for those subject to such rule.[23] Under this standard account, these questions have usually been given a democratic response, and it is the case in this chapter as well. Only democratic political systems, in very broad terms and perhaps with a few exceptions, are regarded as legitimate, while authoritarian or mixed regimes are considered illegitimate. This means, still broadly speaking, that

[21] In this chapter (see Besson and Martí, 'From Equal State Consent to Equal Public Participation', fn. 9), we understand a 'people' as a political community or citizenry and, more specifically, as a 'public', i.e. an instituted people, by opposition to a 'nation' or 'society' or any community allegedly pre-existing its institution, on the one hand, but also by opposition to the 'civil society' that may organize itself alongside its public institution, on the other. This covers the peoples or publics of States, as much as those of infranational, international, or supranational public institutions that re-institute the same peoples into multiple different publics. This conception of 'people' explains why there cannot be, as of yet, talk of a single global people or public for lack of a global institution of global law, a global law and institution one may argue would not be normatively desirable in any case.

[22] Both dimensions of normative legitimacy need not be entirely disconnected, however, as exemplified by the requirement of human rights protection in the account of democratic legitimacy proposed later in this section.

[23] See Besson and Martí, 'The Legitimate Actors', fn. 9, at 508–509.

lawmaking should ultimately be able to be attributed to the people subject to the law,[24] with some additional democratic requirements we will revert to below.

Input legitimacy in general, and democratic legitimacy in particular, as they are understood here, are regarded as the standard way of legitimizing domestic law and institutions. On the international plane, however, discussions have taken a somehow different turn. In the last few decades, indeed, many authors have assumed that democratic principles cannot apply to international law-making processes. This has brought them to endorse output legitimacy as an alternative way to provide a normative justification of international law.[25]

This exclusive focus on the output legitimacy of international law and institutions is problematic. There is no doubt that the substantive quality of international law is a matter of utmost importance, including for its normative justification. The main problem with output legitimacy, however, is that it identifies legitimacy entirely with either justice or efficiency. By doing so, it can no longer address the distinctive and important normative question of who should rule and how. When the sole focus of legitimacy is on output, indeed, the only way to address that question becomes instrumental. If the unique goal is to maximize the probability of adopting good (e.g. just or efficient) laws, the answer can only be that such laws should be adopted by those with the most capacity to do so. Important as this consideration might be in deciding who should have representative power to make public decisions in the first place, it does not resolve the problem of whom those representatives should be accountable to and hence of whom they should represent.

As a matter of fact, considerations of output legitimacy do not exhaust our concerns about the legitimacy of law and institutions domestically. Whatever should be the exact balance between expertocracy and democracy in any particular context, indeed, our concerns about normative legitimacy at the domestic level are never exhausted by considerations of output legitimacy. The reason is that our concerns about input legitimacy are considered as self-standing and not only instrumental to output. Given the identity of the ultimate individual subjects to the authority of both domestic and international law, that is, the same peoples albeit re-instituted in different publics,

[24] The scope of the chapter precludes exploring the close ties between democratic legitimacy and representation and especially how representation has nowadays become constitutive of democratic legitimacy, but also how it is constrained by the latter. See on that mutually constitutive relationship, Nadia Urbinati, *Representative Democracy: Principles and Genealogy* (Chicago: Chicago University Press, 2006), pp. 4–6, 17–20.

[25] See Fritz Scharpf, *Governing Europe: Effective and Democratic?* (Oxford: Oxford University Press, 1999).

those considerations about the self-standing importance of input legitimacy should also apply to the political legitimacy of international law.[26]

In this chapter, we propose that the democratic legitimacy of any lawmaking institution should be assessed by reference to four basic, scalar abstract principles common to most accounts of democracy.[27] First of all, the principle of *ultimate, effective popular control*. It derives directly from the ideal of self-government or popular sovereignty: all peoples subjected to law should have a relevant say in the process of making that law. They may, of course, confer that power to representatives. The peoples should, however, retain ultimate, effective control over their representatives (who may otherwise only claim to be such) and, through them, over institutions and decision-making processes in order to make self-government possible. Second, the principle of *political equality*. The people represented should have an equal say, directly or through their representatives, in holding that ultimate power of control. That means that no citizen or group of citizens should be able to impose their views unilaterally or have significantly greater political power to determine the law than others. Third, the principle of *deliberative contestability*. The peoples – or their representatives – should be able to contest, through deliberation, all the laws and decisions made. They should also have the capacity to engage in deliberative interaction with each other, thus promoting public (formal and informal) debate. Fourth, the principle of *human rights' protection*. Individuals' human rights that are constitutive of their basic moral equality and enable them to exercise ultimate control should also be protected in lawmaking processes and institutions in order for the latter to be democratically legitimate.

How do these four democratic principles apply to international institutions in general, and to IOs in particular?

[26] The continuity between domestic and international democracy, including democratic representation, is actually required by international democracy law, and especially by international human rights law. See e.g. UN General Assembly (UNGA), 'Letter dated 17 December 1996 from the Secretary-General addressed to the President of the General Assembly' (20 December 1996), A/51/761, paras. 67–70, 72–73; UN Human Rights Committee (HRC), 'CCPR General Comment No. 25: Article 25 (Participation in Public Affairs and the Right to Vote), The Right to Participate in Public Affairs and the Right of Equal Access to Public Service' (12 July 1996), CCPR/C/21/Rev.1/Add.7, para. 5; UNGA Res. 75/178 (16 December 2020) paras. 6(g), 6(h), 6(i). See also Nahuel Maisley, 'The International Right of Rights? Article 25(a) of the ICCPR as a Human Right to Take Part in International Law-Making' (2017) 28(1) *European Journal of International Law* 89–113; Hilary Charlesworth, 'International Legal Encounters with Democracy' (2017) 8(S6) *Global Policy* 34–43.

[27] See Besson and Martí, 'The Legitimate Actors', fn. 9, at 510–511.

The first democratic principle is quite clear in this respect, and it is the one which we will pay attention to in this chapter.[28] Given that the peoples of the world cannot rule directly at the international level – in fact, they cannot do so at the domestic level either – they should confer their power to rule to representative institutions and to those institutions' organs. This turns the question of the democratic legitimacy of international law into one of democratic representation. Accordingly, the assessment of the democratic legitimacy of institutions of international lawmaking crucially depends on whether those institutions, and IOs in particular, can be said to have been conferred their powers by the peoples subjected to the decisions to be made (the so-called 'authorization') and, even more importantly, on whether the peoples may access effective mechanisms of ultimate control over their representatives and over the decision-making system as a whole (the so-called 'control').

It is important to emphasize that representation would be required even if direct popular participation were feasible internationally: not only does democratic participation require the primary institution of the people as such and hence a form of representation of that people in the first place, but representation is also required to guarantee political equality and to organize equal participation and deliberation all along. Contrary to what one often reads, therefore, the relationship between the concepts of democracy and representation is not instrumental and contingent, but intrinsic and constitutive.[29] This is an important point because various forms of compensatory participation and deliberation are often put forward precisely in lieu of international representation that is held too difficult to organize by many authors[30] – usually, moreover, because it is also wrongly identified with and reduced to electoral representation. What those authors do not understand, however, is that representation and participation are in a mutual and constant relationship to the extent that the represented should also be able to participate in representative lawmaking processes and deliberate continuously with their representatives and vice-versa for the latter to represent them.[31]

[28] On the others and especially political equality, see Besson and Martí, 'From Equal State Consent to Equal Public Participation', fn. 9; Besson, 'L'égalité des États membres de l'Union européenne', fn. 1.

[29] See Urbinati, *Representative Democracy*, fn. 24, pp. 4–6, 7–20; Ernst-Wolfgang Böckenförde, 'Demokratie und Repräsentation: Zur Kritik der heutigen Demokratiediskussion', in Ernst-Wolfgang Böckenförde, *Staat, Gesellschaft und Freiheit. Studien zur Staatslehre, Verfassungstheorie und Verfassungsgeschichte* (Frankfurt: Suhrkamp Verlag, 1991), paras. 10–28.

[30] See e.g. Ian Johnstone, 'Deliberation', in Klabbers, fn. 17, pp. 173–198, p. 176; Dingwerth and Nanz, fn. 7, p. 1127; Peters, fn. 7, pp. 51–52.

[31] See Urbinati, *Representative Democracy*, fn. 24, p. 3.

In our traditional (modern) understanding of representative democracy, at least when applied to domestic lawmaking, these four principles have required the existence of a parliament with fundamental lawmaking powers whose members are elected democratically, a directly or indirectly elected executive and an independent and self-standing judiciary, among other democratic institutions. Nothing like this, of course, exists (yet) at the international level, including in most IOs. This is even the case in the European Union (EU) where the directly elected parliamentary organ of the EU holds neither the lawmaking initiative nor the legislative monopoly and does not elect either of the two executive organs of the EU. To that extent, the proposed conception of the democratic legitimacy of IOs cannot be that of a worldwide or global democratic State with a single global people or instituted public represented by various directly or indirectly elected officials organized in parliamentary, executive, and judicial authorities.[32] As a result, whether or not one considers that such a cosmopolitan and monist account of international democratic representation is justifiable under ideal circumstances, it is clearly far from being possible in present, deeply pluralist, real conditions. Importantly, however, this does not imply that the principles of democratic legitimacy cannot be respected through other institutional configurations. Those principles albeit developed for States are actually general enough to adapt to the international institutional context.

Before turning, in the next sections, to the crucial two questions of whom IOs should 'democratically' represent and how, it is important to briefly specify what democratic 'representation' amounts to more specifically.

### 12.2.2 *International Democratic Representation*

The conceptions of political and especially democratic representation we use today are very recent: they are modern, even if earlier traces may be found, of course.[33] The origin of these modern conceptions, however, is medieval. They arose from numerous theological and legal permutations that took place in Europe from the twelfth century onwards.

32 See e.g. Robert A. Dahl, 'Can International Organizations Be Democratic? A Skeptic's View', in Ian Shapiro and Casiano Hacker-Cordón (eds.), *Democracy's Edges* (Cambridge: Cambridge University Press, 1999), pp. 19–36; Mathias Koenig-Archibugi, 'International Organizations and Democracy: An Assessment', in Luis Cabrera (ed.), *Institutional Cosmopolitanism* (Oxford: Oxford University Press, 2018), pp. 154–186.

33 See Samuel Hayat, Corinne Péneau and Yves Sintomer, 'Introduction', in Samuel Hayat, Corinne Péneau and Yves Sintomer (eds.), *La représentation avant le gouvernement représentatif* (Rennes: Presses Universitaires de Rennes, 2020), pp. 7–28, pp. 7–8.

These so-called 'political-legal' conceptions of representation originated in the reception of Roman private law and constitute the core of the medieval *jus commune* of representation.[34] In short, they developed on the basis of two conceptions of representation elaborated by lawyers, first in canon law and then in civil law, especially in the Germanic and Italian traditions thereof.

The first conception of representation relies on the notion of corporation or legal person such as a city or the Church (and the *pars pro toto* representation *by* this incorporated or legal person and, by extension, the representation *of* this legal person by a particular physical person therein, that is, its 'head' – *caput* – or 'organ'). The most famous discussion thereof was that of Marsilius of Padua in the thirteenth century.[35] We speak here of 'personal representation' or 'incorporation-based representation' because the representative acts 'as' or 'like' the represented: it stands as them (*stand as* representation). The second medieval conception of representation is that of the mandate or legal delegation (and the principal-agent relation) developed in particular by Bartolus of Saxoferrato in the fourteenth century.[36] We speak here of 'conventional representation' or 'agency-based representation' because the representative acts 'for' the represented: it acts in their place (*act for* representation).

With the advent of modernity, this medieval private law of representation gave rise, in domestic law, to the public law of political representation. The latter still bears the traces of the former's two conceptions of representation, however.[37] The first conception of incorporation-based representation gave rise, in the seventeenth century, to the political notion of the person of the State and its sovereign, and then of the sovereign State itself and its organs. The second conception, that of agency-based or delegation-based representation, gave rise to the democratic notion of the electoral and, more generally, to the political 'mandate' of the representative from the nineteenth century onwards. As we will explain in Section 12.4, the international law of representation actually bears the traces of the medieval private law of representation even more directly than domestic law.

A common feature of the various contemporary conceptions of democratic representation that ensued from this modern understanding is the idea that representatives should take into account and promote the interests of the

[34] See Yves Sintomer, 'Le sens de la représentation politique: Usages et mésusages du débat contemporain' (2013) 50 *Raisons politiques* 13–34; Hasso Hofmann, *Repräsentation: Studien zur Wort- und Begriffsgeschichte von der Antike bis ins 19. Jahrhundert*, 4th ed. (Berlin: Duncker & Humblot, 2003).

[35] See Alessandro Mulieri, 'La représentation-incarnation chez Marsile de Padoue' (2018) 72 *Raisons Politiques* 71–88.

[36] See Sintomer, fn. 34, at 20.

[37] Ibid.

represented. This is clearly the case of contemporary agency-based conceptions in which the agent should act not only in the name of the represented ('as' them), but also to their benefit ('for' them).[38] However, it is also true of the so-called 'symbolic' and 'descriptive' conceptions of representation according to which the representative relationship depends on other, constitutive features that are related to the protection of their interests.[39] It even applies to the so-called 'constructive' or 'claim' conceptions of representation, according to which the only definitional requirement of representation is that an agent claims to represent another one in terms that might prove acceptable through a constructive process of the represented's interests and this, whether the latter have authorized and controlled those terms or not.[40]

To revert to our earlier discussion of input and output legitimacy, the fact that representatives should take into account and promote the interests of the represented in most contemporary accounts of democratic representation[41] does not, however, imply that the corresponding notion of political legitimacy is necessarily a substantive one and based on output only. Nor does it imply that input legitimacy should only be understood in instrumental terms. Many modern views of political representation, starting with Thomas Hobbes',[42] have indeed made the latter dependent on formal acts of authorization, whether ex ante or ex post. This is the case, for instance, of the so-called 'trustee' and 'delegate' models of representation.[43] In both cases, representatives act for the represented on the basis of some kind of authorization. They differ, however, in the degree of autonomy that representatives should enjoy in

[38] See e.g. Bernard Manin, *The Principles of Representative Government* (Cambridge: Cambridge University Press, 1997).

[39] See e.g. Jane Mansbridge, 'A Deliberative Theory of Interest Representation', in Mark P. Petracca (ed.), *The Politics of Interests*, 2nd ed. (New York: Routledge, 2018), pp. 32–57; Sintomer, fn. 34.

[40] See e.g. Michael Saward, *The Representative Claim* (Oxford: Oxford University Press, 2010); Jonathan W. Kuyper, 'Systemic Representation: Democracy, Deliberation, and Nonelectoral Representatives' (2016) 110(2) *American Political Science Review* 308–324.

[41] In any case, democratic representation does not, strictly speaking, have 'objects' to represent, but 'subjects'. The fact is, of course, that not all dimensions of the represented subject can always be represented, hence the common reference to an object to represent. In the history of democratic representation, these objects have been very varied: they have ranged from will, interests, and preferences to judgement. It is the latter, however, that seems the most relevant to the authorized and then controlled activity of representation. Representation is indeed a matter of authorizing and controlling political decision-making on what is the right thing to do and, in the case of lawmaking, of justifying the authority of law, and this implies an exercise of judgement.

[42] See Quentin Skinner, 'Hobbes on Representation' (2005) 13(2) *European Journal of Philosophy* 155–184, at 167.

[43] For a discussion, see Urbinati, *Representative Democracy*, fn. 24, pp. 30–35.

order to effectively represent the represented. While the delegate model claims that representatives should operate under the tight terms of an explicit act of delegation or mandate, the trustee model relies on the representative's relative independence in order to best protect the interests of the represented.

Accordingly, and regardless of how those debates have evolved domestically and without entering into those details here, there are two conditions which political representation should comply with in order to be regarded as democratically legitimate, and which are of utmost importance to the institutional organization of international representation as well.

The first one derives from the principle of ultimate, effective popular control. Representatives should be *authorized* by the people they are meant to represent, and should also be ultimately and effectively *controlled* by those people.[44] Independently of the degree of autonomy representatives might be granted, the represented should always possess effective mechanisms to hold the representatives accountable and retain ultimate control over their actions. Periodic elections with electoral mandate have proven to be a relatively successful institutional mechanism to do so. However, they are neither a necessary nor a sufficient condition of democratic legitimacy. Indeed, elections do not necessarily guarantee ultimate, effective control by the people in domestic democratic systems. Moreover, there might be other mechanisms that could complement or even replace elections as instruments of ultimate, effective popular control. Many modern conceptions of representation have been excessively dependent on electoral accountability by making it a conceptual requirement of democratic legitimacy.[45] As a result, in contexts where such electoral control does not yet or simply cannot exist or is difficult to organize, as it is on the international plane, this has brought many to give up on democratic representation or, by extension, on democratic legitimacy altogether, as mentioned before.

The second condition is a consequence of the first one and is even more crucial to international representation than it is domestically. Democratic representation inherently possesses an *instituting* dimension. This has often been overlooked at the domestic level because the institutional framework of the State is long-lasting and usually taken for granted when organizing democratic representation. Political representation can only occur through law and institutions. It follows that democratic representatives should operate in institutional and legal frameworks and should be instituted themselves as such by

[44] See Jane Mansbridge, 'Clarifying the Concept of Representation' (2011) 105(3) *American Political Science Review* 621–630, at 624.

[45] For this critique, see Urbinati, *Representative Democracy*, fn. 24, pp. 1–3.

those legal frameworks. To revert to a point made before, the way in which representatives are instituted and hence constructed is actually a mutual constructive process that also includes the institutional construction of the represented themselves as a people or a public in return.[46] Importantly, therefore, and even though there is something that has long been identified as paradoxical about it,[47] that process should also fall under the principle of ultimate, effective control and be adequately institutionalized. This is actually why the instituting dimension of democratic representation should not be separated from the authorizing one, and vice-versa.[48] This is another reason why participation and representation should always go hand in hand, as argued before.

To recapitulate, then, this chapter approaches democratic representation as a relation that institutes, authorizes, and holds power accountable under the ultimate control of the people and thereby contributes to the justification of political authority, including of lawmaking authority. It gives the representative a claim to act as and for the represented, leading to the attribution of those acts to the represented if the conditions of authorization and control are fulfilled.

## 12.3 THE SUBJECTS OF DEMOCRATIC REPRESENTATION BY INTERNATIONAL ORGANIZATIONS: FROM STATES TO MULTIPLE PUBLICS

As mentioned in the introduction, a prevalent understanding in international law is that IOs should represent the States that have organized them.[49] IOs are construed as inter-institutional systems that include other institutions as 'members', that is, States, and whose organs are mostly interstate, at least their plenary interstate organs in charge of lawmaking and their non-plenary interstate organs in charge of implementation and operations. This is sometimes under the assumption or, more rarely, under the condition that those States themselves adequately represent their peoples.

[46] Ibid., pp. 2–4.

[47] See Manuela Albertone and Michel Troper, 'Penser la représentation: Une introduction', in Manuela Albertone and Michel Troper (eds.), *La représentation politique. Anthologie* (Paris: Classiques Garnier, 2021), pp. 7–32, pp. 18, 23.

[48] See also Urbinati, *Representative Democracy*, fn. 24, pp. 23–25.

[49] See e.g. Laurence Dubin and Marie-Clotilde Runavot, 'Représentativité, efficacité, légitimité: Des organisations internationales en crise?', in Évelyne Lagrange and Jean-Marc Sorel (eds.), *Droit des organisations internationales* (Paris: LGDJ, 2013), pp. 77–103, pp. 89–93; Stephen Mathias and Stadler Trengove, 'Membership and Representation', in Cogan *et al.*, fn. 7, pp. 962–984, pp. 974–976.

In previous publications, we have identified some weaknesses in this view and several deficits in the international democratic representation of peoples by their States. Given these democratic deficits of State-based representation of peoples *in* IOs, we have explored various ways to enhance the representation of those peoples *through* IOs and especially through IO law, in order to improve the democratic representation by States themselves inside IO organs, but also the compensatory democratic representation by other public institutions such as cities or regions or even by private organizations such as non-governmental organizations involved in IO lawmaking processes.[50] In this section, we summarize those arguments before bringing them one step further and explaining how that representation should also be ensured directly *by* IOs themselves.

This may be done, we would like to argue, by changing the current understanding of the subjects of international democratic representation in at least two ways: first, by focusing on *peoples* instead of their States in the representation by IOs and, second, by recognizing the importance of representing *multiple other publics* besides States' peoples. Not only is such multiple representation already partly at work de facto in the non-ideal world of IOs, with all the inegalitarian shortcomings that flow from those various forms of participation growing outside of any international legal status of those different publics. We also submit that it should be articulated further as a system of 'multi-public' representation and ordered de jure as such in future reforms of those IOs.

Our argument is two-pronged and based, first, on the insufficiency of States as democratic international representatives of their peoples and, second, on the democratic virtues of the multiple representation of the same peoples albeit as multiple publics instituted and represented by many different public institutions besides States.

First of all, it is important to start by explaining why State-based representation of *States' peoples* in IOs cannot be regarded as sufficient and why those peoples should be represented directly *by* IOs as well.

At first sight, of course, one may consider that the subjects democratically represented by States *in* IOs and those who should be represented *by* IOs are in fact the same: States' peoples. The representation of States by IOs therefore seemingly equates that of those States' peoples. In practice, however, States are far from being perfect democratic representatives of the peoples they institute as publics. More specifically, the interests of representative organs within those States, such as governments or parliaments, and especially those of the

[50] See the references in fn. 10.

elected or non-elected officials holding those representative positions might differ from the interests of the people they claim to represent.[51]

Of course, as we argued elsewhere,[52] in the non-ideal circumstances that currently prevail, States should still be considered as the most effective institutions to ensure the democratic representation of the peoples of the world, and especially the ultimate, effective popular control of those peoples over international lawmaking processes and institutions and their political equality. As such, they should play a primary role in the democratic representation of their peoples in their IOs' organs, be it in internal or external international lawmaking procedures. And, doing so, they can significantly contribute to those IOs' democratic representativeness.

Because of their many democratic deficits, however, we also argued that States should not be considered as the exclusive international representatives of their peoples *in* IOs.[53] The most obvious of those deficits is that many States are not democratic. As a result, the officials representing those States in IOs cannot be said to legitimately represent their peoples. In addition, even in democratic States, existing domestic mechanisms of ultimate, effective popular control over the external policy of States might prove to be insufficient for their peoples to control their international decisions. Indeed, international issues are usually less salient in domestic electoral politics, and other non-electoral mechanisms of popular authorization and control of State officials active internationally, especially over governments and diplomats, are usually absent. Finally, even when State officials are effectively accountable domestically for their international decisions, there might still be important democratic concerns with respect to the representation of stateless peoples (e.g. refugees) or even of certain peoples within States (e.g. indigenous peoples or regional minorities).

Importantly, as we also argued,[54] there are other institutions that might help both correct those deficits in the State-based democratic representation of peoples in IOs and complement their representation in those IOs. This is the case of other public institutions, such as regions or cities, but also of private

51 See Besson, 'The Authority of International Law', fn. 2, at 361–362; Jeremy Waldron, 'Are Sovereigns Entitled to the Benefit of the International Rule of Law?' (2011) 22(2) *European Journal of International Law* 315–343, at 329–330.

52 See Besson and Martí, 'The Legitimate Actors', fn. 9; Besson and Martí, 'From Equal State Consent to Equal Public Participation', fn. 9.

53 See Besson and Martí, 'The Legitimate Actors', fn. 9; Besson, 'Democratic Representation within International Organizations', fn. 9; Besson and Martí, 'From Equal State Consent to Equal Public Participation', fn. 9.

54 See Besson and Martí, 'The Legitimate Actors', fn. 9; Besson and Martí, 'Cities as Democratic Representatives in International Law', fn. 9; Besson, 'Democratic Representation within International Organizations', fn. 9.

organizations, such as non-governmental organizations, transnational corporations, religious organizations or trade unions that are increasingly involved, in various participatory or deliberative capacities, in IOs' lawmaking processes. This is what we have referred to as democratic representation *through* IOs. As orchestrators of 'multiple international systems of representation' and of what one of us has coined 'multipartism' in IOs,[55] IOs can indeed contribute to enhance the democratic representation of the otherwise underrepresented peoples of their Member States. This can occur through reinforced requirements, in IO law, of democratic representativeness not only on the part of Member States' representatives, but also of those of all the other public institutions and private organizations involved.

The fact is, however, that none of these other public institutions or private organizations is free from deficits as democratic representatives. Not the least because most of them still lack a complete institutionalization under current public international law.[56] In addition, many of them, especially the private ones, also lack mechanisms of ultimate, effective popular control. This is why the creation of further mechanisms of ultimate, effective popular control *over* IOs themselves as democratic representatives and over their systems of multiple international representation should be a priority. For IOs to be able to claim to legitimately represent their Member States' peoples, they should themselves be organized so as to comply with the four principles of democratic legitimacy presented in Section 12.2.

Apart from this first argument for the direct democratic representation of States' peoples by IOs, however, there is also a second argument in favour of the representation of the same peoples *qua other publics* by IOs alongside States' publics.

As we argued elsewhere,[57] indeed, the same peoples may be instituted and re-instituted in different publics in a multiplicity of ways, and thus may be represented by multiple public institutions including infranational ones such as cities, regions, or indigenous peoples, but also by international ones like IOs. One of the advantages of approaching the issue through the proposed idea of multiple representation is that it breaks with the assumption that the only

[55] See Besson 'Pour une représentation démocratique multiple au sein de l'Organisation mondiale de la Santé', fn. 9; Besson, 'We the Peoples of the United Nations', fn. 9.

[56] See Besson, *Reconstructing the International Institutional Order*, fn. 15, paras. 81–82.

[57] See Besson and Martí, 'The Legitimate Actors', fn. 9; Besson, 'Democratic Representation within International Organizations', fn. 9; Besson and Martí, 'From Equal State Consent to Equal Public Participation', fn. 9; Besson, 'The Politics of Regional International Organizations', fn. 9. On the multi-public instituent powers of IOs, see also Besson, 'We the Peoples of the United Nations', fn. 9.

instituted peoples or public to be represented in, through, and by IOs are States' peoples or publics.

Of course, approaching democratic representation in IOs as multiple might have a cost in terms of political equality, and hence of democratic legitimacy.[58] This could be the case, for instance, when some peoples are re-instituted many times by different public institutions and represented by them in IOs, such as by States and cities, while others, such as those living in rural regions, are not or at least without the corresponding inclusion of their second tier of institutions internationally. The representation of the same peoples as many publics by both States and cities in IOs in this case may lead to over-represent part of those peoples and underrepresent another.[59]

This is why we argued against a radically pluralistic approach to multiple international representation and for a systemic or ordered approach instead.[60] What we have advocated is that IOs should re-organize their internal processes and bodies in order to allow multiple public and private representatives to participate in their lawmaking processes, but should do so in a systemic way so as to take into account their respective shortcomings as legitimate representatives.[61] They should also aim at minimizing potential conflicts among representatives and at maximizing the overall representativeness of each of them, calling for constant adjustments and contextualization. This systemic balance, among other considerations, should generally give priority to public institutions over private organizations. However, no representative public institution, including States, may legitimately claim to democratically represent a people at the exclusion of others.

Even if such a system or ordering of multiple international representation in and through IOs were to be organized, the fact remains that all peoples and the re-instituted publics in the world also have a claim to be adequately represented by the different IOs' multiple international systems themselves. To that extent, IOs' democratic representativeness matters in itself. For this to be the

58 The same objection has been raised with respect to popular sovereign equality for the latter has been wrongly reduced to States' (peoples') sovereign equality. For a full egalitarian and hence democratic argument in favour of multiple sovereignty, see Besson and Martí, 'Republican Sovereignty', fn. 9; Besson, 'The Politics of Regional International Organizations', fn. 9.

59 See Besson and Martí, 'Cities as Democratic Representatives in International Law-Making', fn. 9, p. 351. On multiple representation in the WHO and the ILO, see also Besson, 'We the Peoples of the United Nations', fn. 9.

60 On representative systems in general, see Felipe Rey, 'The Representative System' (2023) 26(6) *Critical Review of International Social and Political Philosophy* 831–854.

61 See Besson, 'Democratic Representation within International Organizations', fn. 9; Besson and Martí, 'From Equal State Consent to Equal Public Participation', fn. 9.

case, the ultimate, effective popular control by those peoples and their multiple publics over IOs should be secured.

## 12.4 THE RELATION OF DEMOCRATIC REPRESENTATION BY INTERNATIONAL ORGANIZATIONS: BEYOND FUNCTIONALISM, INCORPORATION, AND AGENCY

Besides its exclusive focus on States as the sole subjects of representation instead of States' peoples and multiple other publics, the international law of IOs may also be criticized for the way it contributes to the organization of the relation of representation by IOs. Indeed, it does so in functionalist as opposed to political terms (Section 12.4.1) and relies on private law models of representation by incorporation and/or by agency instead of public law ones (Section 12.4.2).

In this section, those two approaches to the relation of representation are assessed by reference to the democratic principles identified earlier: the functionalist approach to the legitimacy of IOs is criticized because it does not allow for input legitimacy, and the incorporation-based and agency-based approaches are qualified because they do not address IOs, nor their Member States as a matter of fact, as public institutions. Generally, what those approaches to the representation by IOs elude is the primary institutional role of representation by IOs in re-instituting their various Member States' peoples before those IOs' representative organs can even be authorized to represent them. Hence this chapter's title "No International Democratic Representation without Institution".

### 12.4.1 *Against Functional Representation by International Organizations: Input Matters*

To date, representation in the international law of IOs has been approached mostly as a form of instrumental representation of States' functions and framed as providing IOs with output legitimacy. To that extent, the legitimacy of IOs and the representation by IOs may be described as 'functional'.

Things are more complicated than that, however, and there is a certain ambivalence nowadays between functional and democratic legitimacy in IO law and hence between output and input legitimacy. One may distinguish two periods in this respect: a first one that goes from the foundation of the early IOs in the nineteenth century, and a second one that opens with the end of the Cold War.[62] While the second period has brought in a new emphasis on

[62] See von Bernstorff, 'New Responses to the Legitimacy Crisis of International Institutions', fn. 8, at 130–140; Besson, 'Democratic Representation within International Organizations', fn. 9.

democratic input legitimacy, it has not succeeded in trumping functional output legitimacy entirely. As a result, both concerns coexist today in the international law of representation by IOs.

First period: the carelessness of *functional good governance*. When the first IOs were established in the late nineteenth century, they were to remain under the sovereign control of their Member States. Conceived from a functionalist perspective, IOs were simply to perform the 'functions' that their Member States had 'delegated' to them, as opposed to exercising the 'sovereign powers' those States could have 'conferred' to them.

In this context, expecting IOs to conform to the principles of democratic good government and represent their Member States' peoples would have been contradictory. Indeed, to the extent that States were to remain in charge of the sovereign 'government' of their peoples, IOs were not designed to 'govern' those peoples. According to that conception, if IOs were to be described as 'public', it was only so in a functional or instrumental way.[63] They could be considered public only insofar as they had been established to serve the 'public functions' of their Member States. As for their alleged 'public authority', it amounted at most to the exercise of a de facto authority. There was no claim that that authority was exercised on behalf of an instituted public that would have authorized its exercise, nor was it to be controlled by that public in return, a public that could not therefore be considered as the 'author' of IO law.

Clearly, then, and despite many rhetorical preambles (such as the United Nations (UN) Charter's reference to 'We the peoples of the United Nations'), IOs have not yet been organized or ordered by their Member States' peoples as political institutions representing them. Worse, many IOs have actually been organized by their States to remain 'apolitical'.[64] This explains why IO Member States did not initially consider it necessary to insert rules and principles of public law into the internal law of their IOs in order to organize the latter's good government, including their democratic representativeness.[65] For example, there was and still is no trace of a principle of separation of powers and even less of a democratic principle in most IOs but the EU.

63 See Samantha Besson, 'The International Public: A Farewell to Functions in International Law' (2021) 115 *American Journal of International Law Unbound* 307–311. For an alternative argument, see Samantha Besson, 'In What Sense are International Organizations "Public"? A Plea for a Public International Law of Organisation' (2026) *Leiden Journal of International Law* in press; Samantha Besson, 'What can Public international Law do against Privatization?' (2024) 15:3 *Transnational Legal Theory* 341–369.

64 See Louis and Maertens, fn. 5.

65 See von Bernstorff, 'Procedures of Decision-Making and the Role of Law', fn. 12, pp. 781–783.

No wonder then that the representation by IOs has mostly been organized so as to follow a functional approach to legitimacy by output: it should ensure the implementation of State functions and hence the protection of their Member States' interests. When it is exceptionally framed as input legitimacy, which is also sometimes the case, representation by IOs remains functional, however. It relies on the IO's organs' expertise, for instance, in implementing its Member States' functions and protecting their interests. The same applies to the representation of States or even of CSOs in IOs. The latter does not necessarily seek to represent the peoples of those States or the civil society organized through those CSOs. Their representativeness is measured by reference to certain characteristics of States or CSOs that may be of an instrumental purpose for the IO, such as the economic, military, or financial power of some of its Member States (usually a few of them)[66] and the expertise and financial resources of certain CSOs.[67]

This is problematic from a democratic legitimacy perspective that places emphasis on the distinct relevance of input legitimacy, as argued in Section 12.2.1. Even more so as the protection of the represented's interests through representation does not exclude the relevance of input legitimacy through authorization and control, as argued in Section 12.2.2. Important as it is to take into account the quality of output under such instrumental approaches to representation by IOs and to rely on experts within those IOs' organs when making law, securing ultimate, effective popular control over our representatives should also matter from a non-instrumental perspective of democratic legitimacy. Following Ernst-Wolfgang Böckenförde, one should consider democratic representation as a form of 'material' rather than merely 'formal' representation of pre-existing interests.[68] Representation enables the people(s) to specify, through their institutions' deliberation, what actually amounts to their public interest. One may argue therefore that the international 'public' and, by extension, its 'public interest' does not actually pre-exist international political representation.

Importantly, there was a turning point in the 1990s and a second period opened in the international law of IOs: the call for *democratic good*

66 See Besson, 'Democratic Representation within International Organizations', fn. 9, at 495–498, 522. See also Cogan, Chapter 4 in this volume.

67 See Besson, 'Democratic Representation within International Organizations', fn. 9, at 498–501. On the essentially functional representation by private organizations under the WHO's Framework of Engagement of Non-State Actors and especially its para. 4, see Besson, 'Pour une représentation démocratique multiple au sein de l'Organisation mondiale de la Santé', fn. 9.

68 See Böckenförde, fn. 29, paras. 30–32.

*government*. It was during that period indeed that many IOs became more autonomous in their international lawmaking procedures, subjecting States and, directly or indirectly, their peoples to their legal authority. Hence the growing need to justify that authority and hence to control their power in order to make it legitimate, including through democratic representation.

The end of the Cold War also corresponded to the rekindling of international democracy law, including in its application to the international institutional order.[69] The specific obligation of IO Member States to organize their IOs in a democratic manner may be grounded in the human right to democratic participation under Article 25(a) of the International Covenant on Civil and Political Rights.[70] Unfortunately, States are still deeply divided over the scope of application of those international democracy law obligations: Southern and Eastern States oppose its domestic application inside States and require more international democracy including in IOs, while Northern and Western States oppose its international application including inside IOs.[71]

Unsurprisingly, therefore, it is the new avatar of good government in domestic public law, that is, the public-private approach to 'good governance', that has been transposed to IOs.[72] This explains how the so-called process of 'constitutionalization' of IOs[73] has in fact largely turned into an exercise of technocratic 'rationalization'.[74]

What makes this current system of 'techno-democratic'[75] governance of IOs difficult to criticize, however, is that the appearances of democratic legitimacy have been saved. Terms are regularly borrowed from the lexicon of input

69 See UNGA Res. 75/178, fn. 26, paras. 6(g), 6(h), 6(i).

70 See Maisley, fn. 26, at 107–113.

71 See Hilary Charlesworth, 'Democracy and International Law' (Volume 371) *Collected Courses of the Hague Academy of International Law*, 2015, pp. 43–152; Charlesworth, fn. 26.

72 See e.g. Ayelet Berman, Tim Büthe, Martino Maggetti and Joost Pauwelyn, 'Introduction: Rethinking Stakeholder Participation in Global Governance', in Joost Pauwelyn, Martino Maggetti, Tim Büthe and Ayelet Berman (eds.), *Rethinking Participation in Global Governance: Voice and Influence after Stakeholder Reforms in Global Finance and Health* (Oxford: Oxford University Press, 2022), pp. 3–30.

73 See Anne Peters, 'Dual Democracy', in Jan Klabbers, Anne Peters and Geir Ulfstein (eds.), *The Constitutionalization of International Law* (Oxford: Oxford University Press, 2009), pp. 263–341; Anne Peters, 'Constitutional Theories of International Organisations: Beyond the West' (2021) 20(4) *Chinese Journal of International Law* 649–698.

74 See von Bernstorff, 'Procedures of Decision-Making and the Role of Law', fn. 12, p. 797. For a similar concern, see Peter Niesen, 'Constituent Power in Global Constitutionalism', in Anthony F. Lang Jr. and Antje Wiener (eds.), *Handbook on Global Constitutionalism*, 2nd ed. (Cheltenham: Edward Elgar, 2023), pp. 318–330.

75 For this term, see René-Jean Dupuy, 'L'organisation internationale et l'expression de la volonté générale' (1957) 59 *Revue générale de droit international public* 527–579, at 563.

legitimacy, even if they are deprived of their original meaning. This is what Ayelet Berman has referred to as the 'false sense of legitimacy' of IOs.[76]

To be sure, 'participation' or 'inclusion' in IOs together with their 'accountability' are often emphasized in those proposals. However, and to start with the term 'participation', it is mostly used to refer to various types of partnerships with 'non-State actors' including those from the private sector, and not to the participation of citizens themselves.[77] It does not, moreover, and curiously, concern itself with the representativeness of those so-called 'participants'. Those non-State actors such as CSOs cannot indeed claim to participate in and of themselves and should somehow be related to the segment of the civil society they are contributing to organize and hence to represent. More generally, as mentioned earlier in the chapter, there can be no democratic participation without some form of representation in order to guarantee political equality and organize self-government.

As to the term 'inclusion', second, it usually refers to 'stakeholders' in that context, that is, pre-established interest groups.[78] Unlike the latter social groups, however, peoples institute themselves through their representatives in order to participate in their self-government and thereby to emancipate themselves as publics from their prior collectives.[79] And the same may be said of CSOs (e.g. trade unions) whose representative self-organization contributes to transform prior social groups (e.g. workers). Finally, 'accountability' is a curious in-between.[80] Its procedures are not usually approached as political unlike authorization or election, on the one hand, and its consequences are not political or even legal unlike responsibility, on the other.[81] It is achieved through various 'audits' and other self-referential effectiveness assessment mechanisms stemming from business management that allow IOs to provide evidence of their 'compliance' with 'good governance' standards.[82]

76 See Ayelet Berman, 'Between Participation and Capture in International Rule-Making: The WHO Framework of Engagement with Non-State Actors' (2021) 32(1) *European Journal of International Law* 227–254, at 229.

77 See e.g. Pauwelyn *et al.*, fn. 72.

78 Ibid.

79 For this critique, see Urbinati, *Representative Democracy*, fn. 24, p. 4.

80 See Koenig-Archibugi, fn. 32; Dominik Zaum, 'Legitimacy', in Cogan *et al.*, fn. 7, pp. 1107–1125.

81 See Megan Donaldson and Surabhi Ranganathan, 'Accountability', in Klabbers, fn. 17, pp. 50–75.

82 See Laurence Dubin and Pierre Bodeau-Livinec, 'La responsabilité des institutions internationales dans tous ses états', in Dubin and Runavot, *Le phénomène institutionnel international dans tous ses états*, fn. 16, pp. 231–261.

Ironically for our purpose in this chapter, 'representation' is not usually mentioned expressly in this 'window dressing' exercise in the legitimation of IOs. This may be because of the ambivalence between functional output legitimacy and democratic input legitimacy: democratic representation requires popular input and hence ultimate, effective popular control of the represented over the representatives.

Clarifying this is particularly pressing as alternative forms of international democratic representation are currently discussed in democratic theory that are more output oriented and instrumental to the representation of interests. It is the case, for instance, of 'mimetic' or, at least, 'statistic' representation,[83] 'altruistic' representation[84] and/or 'epistemic' representation.[85] All three purport to represent pre-identified traits or interests to be promoted (functional output) or, at least, knowledge or expertise in how to do so (functional input). Those forms of representation are gaining traction in discussions of international democracy as well.[86] Not only, indeed, do they fit the prevalent functionalist approach to representation by IOs and its output legitimacy framework just described. They also claim to vest it with a democratic justification without, however, reverting to the proposed conception of democratic representation that requires authorization and control. This may be because the proponents of those alternative forms of democratic representation wrongly conflate the latter conception with electoral representation. In light of the many hurdles in the organization of international elections, they then disparage ultimate, effective popular control from the realm of realistic possibilities in international representation and hence revert to alternatives.

Whatever the virtues of those alternative forms of representation as complements to international democratic representation, they cannot be regarded as democratically legitimate in themselves, and actually amount to illegitimate 'shortcuts', to cite Cristina Lafont.[87] Those alternative forms of representation should never be regarded as substitutes for wider democratic deliberation and

[83] See e.g. Sintomer, fn. 34 (who refers to 'mimetic' representation). See also Yves Sintomer, *The Government of Chance: Sortition and Democracy from Athens to the Present* (Cambridge: Cambridge University Press, 2023); John Gastil and Erik Olin Wright, *Legislature by Lot: Transformative Designs for Deliberative Governance* (London: Verso Books, 2019).

[84] See e.g. Mansbridge, 'Clarifying the Concept of Representation', fn. 44 (who refers to 'gyroscopic' representation).

[85] See e.g. Philip Pettit, 'Representation, Responsive and Indicative' (2010) 17(3) *Constellations* 426–434 (who refers to 'indicative' representation).

[86] See e.g. Inigo Gonzalez-Ricoy and Felipe Rey, 'Enfranchising the Future: Climate Justice and the Representation of Future Generations' (2019) 10(5) *WIREs Climate Change* e598.

[87] Cristina Lafont, *Democracy Without Shortcuts: A Participatory Conception of Deliberative Democracy* (Oxford: Oxford University Press, 2019).

hence representation in the strong democratic sense. They cannot be regarded as legitimate in the absence of explicit and effective forms of authorization and control. Indeed, what authorization rules out, first, is the self-appointment of the representative, including in the form of self-representation by mimetism or statistical reproduction. The requirement of authorization also excludes the random selection of representatives by a third party (or by lot) unless there has been some form of ex ante authorization to that random selection. Second, control implies that the represented disposes of ultimate, effective means of supervision over the activity of the representative. The mere 'claim' to represent is not enough to respect the equal autonomy of the represented citizens, therefore.[88]

### 12.4.2 *Against Incorporation and Agency Representation by International Organizations: Publicness Matters*

If the international law of representation has generally made very little room for the political dimension of international representation, it is also because the private law analogies that have prevailed in the moulding of the modern law of public representation domestically have remained even more prevalent in international law. As a matter of fact, the public turn has not yet taken place in the international law of representation.

The reason for this is very simple: from the twelfth century onwards, and since the first diplomatic exchanges between Italian cities, the international law of representation has developed as a private law of representation in the mould of the nascent medieval *jus commune* of representation.[89] This was confirmed by the consolidation of classical international law in the seventeenth century, an international law conceived, yet again and more generally, on a private law model and which approached the rights and obligations of States by analogy with those of private individuals.

This actually echoes a more general feature of the international legal order. Because of what one of us has referred to as international law's

[88] Contra e.g. Saward, fn. 40; Kuyper, fn. 40. For the same critique, see Nadia Urbinati, 'Representative Constructivism's Conundrum', in Lisa Disch, Mathijs van de Sande and Nadia Urbinati (eds.), *The Constructivist Turn in Political Representation* (Edinburgh: Edinburgh University Press, 2019), pp. 182–202.

[89] On those origins, see Dante Fedele, 'Between Private and Public Law: The Contribution of Late Medieval *Ius Commune* to the Conceptualisation of Diplomatic Representation' (2020) 18 *Clio@Themis* 1–16; Niels F. May, 'Le cérémonial diplomatique et les transformations du concept de représentation au XVII$^{e}$ siècle', in Daniel Aznar, Guillaume Hanotin and Niels F. May (eds.), *À la place du roi: Vice-rois, gouverneurs et ambassadeurs dans les monarchies française et espagnole (XVI$^{e}$-XVIII$^{e}$ siècles)* (Madrid: Casa de Velázquez, 2015), pp. 35–49.

'methodological statism', the international law of statehood has eluded the political origin of the State and its publicity is simply built upon domestic public law.[90] As a result, until this day and most of the time, the public and, by extension, the political dimension of States has been ignored in the legal organization of their international representation. It has been relegated to the realm of domestic public law and hardly any corresponding international public law has developed on the issue. Sometimes, the question of the representativeness of States' international representatives is even relegated to the side, as a matter of 'fact' rather than law.[91] States being the 'original persons' of international law, it is their own representation that is at stake *qua* persons as opposed to public institutions, by analogy with legal persons of private law.

In turn, this explains why the international law of representation has been more concerned with the representatives *of* States than by States themselves as representatives – or only as representatives of other States. By analogy, this is also what applies to the representation *of* IOs rather than *by* IOs in the international law of representation. IOs are represented as 'persons' under international law as opposed to public institutions. Their representatives are not considered to represent peoples, as a result, hence actually the equivocation between IO 'organs' and their 'agents'.

To be sure, the question of representation *by* IOs also arises in international law. It does so only to address the representation *of States* by IOs, however, and not that of those States' peoples by those IOs. Even when IOs represent their Member States, indeed, and with exceptions such as the EU, IO law does not also position those IOs as representatives of the peoples of these States. Sometimes, of course, the representation of these States in their IOs' interstate organs requires that State representatives should also represent their peoples democratically. It is then organized by the internal law of some IOs so as to be democratic. One may think here of certain IO's parliamentary interstate bodies or of the democratic credentials required of State representatives of certain IOs at the time of accreditation or even for purposes of State accession/suspension/exclusion of the IOs.[92]

[90] See Besson, *Reconstructing the International Institutional Order*, fn. 15, para. 71.

[91] See Maurice Kamto, 'La volonté de l'État en droit international' (Volume 310) *Collected Courses of the Hague Academy of International Law*, 2004, pp. 9–428, p. 86; Jean Salmon, 'Representatives of States in International Relations', in Rüdiger Wolfrum (ed.), *Max Planck Encyclopedia of Public International Law* (Oxford: Oxford University Press, 2007).

[92] See Jean d'Aspremont, 'Legitimacy of Governments in the Age of Democracy' (2006) 38(4) *New York University Journal of International Law and Politics* 877–918, at 899–909; Alison Duxbury, *The Participation of States in International Organisations: The Role of Human Rights and Democracy* (Cambridge: Cambridge University Press, 2011), pp. 288–292.

In all these cases, however, it is the representation *by States* in those IOs that should be democratic, that is, what we have referred earlier to as democratic representation *in* and *through* IOs, and not the representation *by* the IOs themselves – even if the former contributes to the latter, of course.

Again, the reason for this is straightforward under international law. An IO is considered a legal person distinct from its Member States and established precisely to represent its Member States. IOs are not usually ordered so as to institute the peoples of their Member States as new public institutions and, as such, are not considered to represent those peoples. This is considered to be the price of safeguarding their Member States' sovereignty and, by extension, sometimes those States' peoples' popular sovereignty, albeit wrongly so as we argued earlier.[93]

Just as the international law of representation of States by States, the international law of representation of States by IOs has been articulated around two models originating from the medieval *jus commune* of representation: *conventional* and *personal* representation. In what follows, we will assess them in turn, before criticizing their lack of combination in a third step.

First, *conventional* or agency-based representation. This type of international representation is inspired by the private law of agency and articulates the relation of delegation between a principal and an agent.

Conventional representation applies to representation between any persons or subjects of international law and, by extension, between IOs.[94] Conventional representation sometimes also applies to the representation of States by IOs. This is only the case, however, insofar as it does not concern relations of 'membership' of those States in the IO. Those relations, indeed, are in principle covered by the internal law of the IO, to the extent that the activity of the IO falls within the scope of the powers that its Member States have conferred to it. In such cases, it is the second type of personal or incorporation-based representation of States by the IO that applies. We will revert to this alleged incompatibility and tension between the two approaches to representation at the end of this section.

93 For a full argument, see Besson and Martí, 'Republican Sovereignty', fn. 9. See also Besson, 'The Politics of Regional International Organizations', fn. 9.

94 See Angelo Piero Sereni, 'La représentation en droit international' (Volume 73) *Collected Courses of The Hague Academy of International Law*, 1948, pp. 69–166; Riad Daoudi, *La représentation en droit international public* (Paris: LGDJ, 1980); Salmon, fn. 91. See also in International Relations theory, Zaum, fn. 80; Johnstone, fn. 30. For a critique, see Pieter Jan Kuijper, 'Delegation and International Organizations' (Volume 426) *Collected Courses of the Hague Academy of International Law*, 2022, pp. 9–240, pp. 23–25.

Because conventional representation works along the lines of a delegation or mandate between two private persons, it does not take into consideration the representative dimension of these 'persons' themselves and hence their institutional dimension. And this, even if the represented person is also a public institution under domestic law and a democratic State as it is or should be the case of IO Member States. This is highly regrettable from a democratic point of view.

As a matter of fact, resorting to principal-agent delegation as a model for democratic representation has been criticized in a domestic context as well.[95] Indeed, despite its historical origins, many authors consider that the relationship of political representation should now be distinguished from a relationship of mandate, delegation, or agency in private law. Among the difficulties raised by the agency analogy, one should mention, first of all, its reliance on the pre-existing legal personalities of both the representatives and the represented and, further, on their independence, as opposed to their mutual construction as political institutions, that is, both as representative institutions and as their peoples. A second difficulty pertains to the agency analogy's reliance on a one-way relationship of delegation from the principal to the agent and its absence of mutuality, as opposed to the constant participation and to-ing and fro-ing between political representatives and represented. Finally, a third difficulty lies in the agency model's voluntarist approach to authorization by simple consent or veto, as opposed to other modes of political authorization and control, for instance through participation.[96]

Once applied to IOs, those three difficulties are magnified. First of all, by treating IOs and States as distinct and independent persons of international law as opposed to composite institutions, the conventional model of representation neglects not only the institutional continuity between IOs and their Member States, but also their institutional ties to the publics they institute and re-institute. In fact, applying a private law analogy to the international representation by IOs is even more problematic than it is in the case of the international representation by States. There is indeed no internal IO public law to organize the representation by those IOs and hence no background legal and institutional framework. Merely resorting to analogies with Member States' domestic public law as a complement only makes things worse in this respect.[97] Indeed, those public law analogies suffer from the same neglect of

95 See especially Urbinati, *Representative Democracy*, fn. 24, pp. 57–59.

96 See Besson and Martí, 'From Equal State Consent to Equal Public Participation', fn. 9.

97 For such analogies, see Dan Sarooshi, *International Organizations and their Exercise of Sovereign Powers* (Oxford: Oxford University Press, 2005), pp. 14–17; Fernando Lusa Bordin,

the composite institutional nature of IOs for they treat the latter as public institutions separate from their Member States and place them on an equal plane as comparable institutions.[98] Second, and it is related, the agency-based approach to representation by IOs, by conflating public and private powers, cannot prevent the confusion between the conferral of powers by States to IOs and their transfer by IOs to private persons. As a matter of fact, the confusion has been enhanced by the generalized recourse to the private law term 'delegation' to cover both cases,[99] and the public-private interchangeability of 'functions' the term seems to condone. The privatization of IO powers today may therefore be attributed in great part to the conventional understanding of representation by IOs.

The second type of international representation of States by IOs one encounters in the international law of representation is *personal* or incorporation-based representation. It relies on the second private law dimension of the medieval *jus commune* of representation, that is, the law of legal persons or corporations.

It is the most common of the two models of representation by IOs. Indeed, the IO and its distinct personality are not organized separately from its Member States for their own sake, but in order to personify the ensemble of its Member States and hence to represent them so as to bind them together through the internal and external actions of its organs. Still, one should not go as far as to resort here to the term 'institutional' representation used by Évelyne Lagrange[100] when referring to this understanding of the representation by IOs. And this, in order precisely to avoid any confusion with the representation that institutes or rather re-institutes a given IO's Member States' peoples as new publics. With some exceptions, such as the EU, indeed, the international law of IOs does not yet consider States' peoples as publics to re-institute and then represent in international law in the manner of new publics and sovereign international institutions. It does not treat IO Member States as re-instituted public institutions,[101] but only by analogy to private persons who become members of a private corporation and are re-personified as such.

*The Analogy between States and International Organizations* (Cambridge: Cambridge University Press, 2018), pp. 13–86.

98 See Samantha Besson, 'Review of Fernando Lusa Bordin's *The Analogy between States and International Organizations*' (2020) 31(2) *European Journal of International Law* 771–776; Besson, 'What makes International Organizations "Public"?', fn. 63.

99 See also Kuijper, fn. 94, pp. 74–76.

100 Évelyne Lagrange, *La représentation institutionnelle dans l'ordre international: Une contribution à la théorie de la personnalité morale des organisations internationales* (The Hague: Kluwer Law International, 2002), pp. 1–3, 8, 48.

101 On IO Member States as re-instituted States, see Samantha Besson, 'International Courts and the Jurisprudence of Statehood' (2019) 10(1) *Transnational Legal Theory* 30–64, at 49–50,

This missing public institutional dimension of representation by IOs is the key objection to the personal model. It undermines their democratic legitimacy, especially with respect to ultimate, effective popular control. The incorporation-based representation of States by their IOs throws a 'democratic veil' over States at the same time as it knits a corporate or personal veil around IOs.[102] That veil interrupts the relationship of democratic representation that should link an IO's Member States to their peoples by interposing the screen of the IO's legal personality.

Besides those two critiques against the conventional and personal approaches to the representation by IOs separately, the most important and third set of critiques actually pertains to their lack of combination.

As mentioned in Section 12.2.2, democratic representation when it institutes and then authorizes and controls political power is a relation of mediation: it does not only bring together the represented and the representatives, but it also separates them at the same time.[103] When it institutes this power, democratic representation therefore constructs, by separating them, the subjects of representation which do not pre-exist their representation. It is through the institution of the State, indeed, that the State's people is instituted into a public. When, in a second step, democratic representation enables the represented to authorize and control the exercise of instituted power, it makes it possible to separate, once again, the representatives (this time, the parliamentarians or the government) from the represented (this time, the citizens or the governed) while tying them to each other.

Democratic representation thereby brings together two subjects in two successive and intertwined relations: first, it links the State, or any other institution of public law, to the people which the State institutes as a public, contributes to create as such and consequently represents (this is what one may refer to as 'institution-representation', whose ancestor is incorporation-based representation or 'stand as' representation); and, then, in a second stage, democratic representation connects the representatives of that State, that is to say its organs, to the represented people, that is to say the citizens (this is what one may refer to as 'authorization-representation', whose ancestor is the agency-based representation-mandate or 'act for' representation). Both

drawing on Christopher Bickerton, 'Nation State to Member State. Trajectories of State Reconfiguration and Recomposition in Europe', in Patrick Le Galès and Desmond King (eds.), *Reconfiguring European States in Crisis* (Oxford: Oxford University Press, 2017), pp. 45–61.

102 On the latter, see Catherine Brölmann, *The Institutional Veil in Public International Law: International Organisations and the Law of Treaties* (Oxford: Hart Publishing, 2007).

103 See Böckenförde, fn. 29, para. 32.

dimensions are essential to democratic representation. Too often, indeed, contemporary discussions of domestic democratic representation are torn between two extremes: either they reduce representation, following a constructivist and almost neo-Hobbesian tendency, to the moment of the institution of the people without regard to the need for constant re-authorization and control thereafter between representatives and represented as guarantors of self-government and political equality;[104] or they reduce representation to the electoral mandate, following an ontological and neo-Schmittian move that ignores all too quickly that the people and the citizens do not pre-exist the figuration of representation and must first be instituted as such.[105]

In fact, it is the characteristic of the State's internal constitutional framework, a framework that is destined to last, that explains how easily it has become today to forget the first instituting dimension of representation in favour of the second, that is, the representation-authorization, which takes place much more regularly. Providentially, international law and its complex institutional framework gives us the opportunity to capture them together again. The multiplicity of representative institutions in the international legal order helps us re-connect the two dimensions of democratic representation and make them both visible again. Thereby, international representation by IOs may contribute to counter what some critiques have referred to as the 'flattening' of the tridimensional relation of political representation and its reduction to a bidimensional and horizontal authorizing dimension.[106]

For this to be the case, however, the instituting dimension of the personal model of representation by IOs and the authorizing dimension of the conventional model need not only to be fixed in themselves, as we proposed earlier in this section, but also brought together in future interpretations of the international law of representation by IOs. At the moment, indeed, they coexist as juxtaposed approaches to representation by IOs in the international law of representation without being articulated with one another.[107] The instituted IO is exempted from the need for further authorization and control, thereby giving rise to a risk of domination; and the authorized IO is taken to exist without a prior institution, thereby giving rise to a risk of political inequality.

104 For a similar critique, see Urbinati, *Representative Democracy*, fn. 24, pp. 3–5; Näsström, fn. 14, at 507.

105 For a similar critique, see Urbinati, *Representative Democracy*, fn. 24, pp. 4–6.

106 See Musso, fn. 15, pp. 133–137; Besson, *Reconstructing the International Institutional Order*, fn. 15, para. 82.

107 See e.g. Sarooshi, fn. 97.

Worse, both dimensions of democratic representation are also opposed at times, and treated as incompatible as mentioned earlier in this section.

## 12.5 CONCLUSION

To date, there has been relatively little treatment of the notion of international representation from a democratic, non-formalist perspective. Moreover, the existing literature has mostly focused on the circumstances in which States and other public and private institutions may be regarded as legitimate representatives. Only a small portion thereof has focused on representation of those States' and other public institutions' peoples *in* IOs, for instance in some of their organs, and *through* IOs when the latter contribute to enhancing their Member States and other participating public or private institutions' representativeness. However, even fewer authors have provided an account of the conditions under which IOs themselves might be regarded as legitimate representatives of their publics, that is, the peoples that integrate their constituencies and which they contribute to re-instituting as publics.

Democratic representation *by* IOs is the gap in international democracy law and democratic theory the present chapter has purported to fill. The gist of the proposed conception of democratic representation by IOs has been institutional. The argument has spelled out the primarily re-instituting dimension of representation by IOs and hence its contribution not only to the authorization and control of IO representatives, but also to the multiple public re-institution of sovereign power internationally.

The proposed 'international turn' in democratic representation may actually also prove beneficial to the future of democratic representation in general. Instead of rushing to conclusions in terms of post-representation or towards alternative constructive or symbolic forms of representation, we should indeed consider the deficits in international democratic representation and the related crisis of domestic democratic representation as an opportunity for the future of democratic representation in general. They could and should trigger an in-depth and across the board revision of the electoral-only model of democratic representation and of the many private law analogies that have shaped our conceptions of democratic representation for too long and from which originate much of today's pushback against democratic representation, both domestically and internationally.

# 13

# Democratic Representation in the European Union: Democratizing Democracy?

Édouard Dubout and Dominique Ritleng

## 13.1 INTRODUCTION: EXPANDING THE FRAMEWORK

Since 2009, the founding treaty of the European Union (EU) has provided that '[t]he functioning of the Union shall be founded on representative democracy'.[1] This statement offers much to consider.

It is well-known how complicated the relationship between the EU and democracy is. The EU's confrontation with democratic standards very often leads to the lazy denunciation of a democratic deficit. Assuming such a denunciation is justified, it would still be necessary to agree on its meaning. Democracy refers to a principle of power legitimacy that makes the people the foundation of political power, and to a form of government requiring that political power be exercised by the people, or by organs elected by the people. The creation of the Union is undoubtedly not the result of the manifestation of the will of an original constituent power, that is, an act of political self-institution by a European people. The foundation of European political power rather resides in the acceptance of the treaties by the peoples of the Member States or by their representatives, an acceptance which is often expressed in a national constitutional clause. Once democratically ratified, the founding treaties established an organization to which decision-making power was transferred 'in ever wider fields',[2] which enables it to adopt common rules directly applicable not only to Member States, but also to their nationals. It is easy to perceive to what extent the legitimacy of the EU depends on the form of government in which

This chapter was translated from French by Sévrine Knuchel, thanks to the financial support of the College of France's Foundation.

[1] Art. 10(1) of the Consolidated Version of the Treaty on European Union, OJ 2012 No. C326, 26 October 2012, p. 13, introduced by the Treaty of Lisbon amending the Treaty on European Union and the Treaty establishing the European Community, OJ 2007 No. C306, 17 December 2007, p. 1, which entered into force in 2009.

[2] Opinion 1/09, EU:C:2011:123, 8 March 2011, para. 65.

the exercise of such a normative power – unprecedented for an international organization – takes place. But how, in the absence of a people to represent, could the EU claim to be a 'representative' form of democracy? The endeavor seems all the more risky that the representative model is experiencing a deep crisis[3] just when the EU is trying to fit into it to counter the lack of legitimacy that would affect its form of government.[4] How could a *transnational* form of democratic representation be established, when it is called into question in the national State framework that has seen it flourish?

Nonetheless, the European experience may lead us to reconsider our way of thinking about democratic representation. This chapter aims at showing that, by expanding the framework of democratic representation to a transnational dimension, the EU is exacerbating a founding aporia and outlining a way of overcoming it. Our research reveals that, paradoxically, the development of a European democratic representation requires an association with non-representative forms of citizen participation, even though such forms were originally considered as competing with the representative government.[5] The idea of democratic representation takes on a different meaning which presupposes, rather than opposes, the development and diversification of more 'direct' forms of citizen involvement in European political decision-making.[6] In other words, democratizing democracy in the EU implies expanding its framework, not only *vertically* by adding a level of political representation, but also *horizontally*.

The unprecedented context of the EU invites us to consider democracy in a pragmatic way, or – as John Dewey expresses it – as a constant effort to 'adapt old institutions and ideas to situations created by new material conditions'.[7] The challenge is to create a *more complex democratic feeling*, one that goes beyond the existence of, or the belonging to, a national State. Yet, much of this challenge remains to be met, as the process of expanding the framework for

3 As illustrated by populism's expansion into the very heart of democracies; see Nadia Urbinati, *Me the People: How Populism Transforms Democracy* (Cambridge, MA: Harvard University Press, 2019).

4 The management of the 'Greek crisis' only exacerbated this lack of democratic legitimacy. See Jürgen Habermas,*La Constitution de l'Europe* (Paris: Gallimard, 2012), pp. 76ff.

5 On this tension, see Bernard Manin, *Principes du gouvernement représentatif* (Paris: Flammarion, 1996).

6 For a demonstration of the 'representative' character of so-called 'direct' forms of democracy, see Olivier Jouanjan, 'Échapper au concept hobbesien de "représentation" en démocratie?' (2023) 29 *Jus politicum* 65–76, at 74ff.

7 John Dewey, 'La démocratie créatrice. La tâche qui nous attend' (1995) 5(2) *Horizons philosophiques* 41–48 (translation of the conference published in 1940). See also, John Dewey, *The Public and its Problems* (New York: Holt Publishers, 1927).

democratic representation in the EU continues to face major difficulties.[8] This contribution seeks to trace the genealogy of the obstacles, both conceptual and institutional, that have stood and continue to stand in the way of going beyond the State framework of democratic representation in the EU. These consecutive difficulties are of three kinds: the issue of the unity of representation (Section 13.2), the issue of the representation of a distinctly European citizenship (Section 13.3), and, finally, the transition from representation to the representativeness of the European society (Section 13.4).

## 13.2 REPRESENTING THE EUROPEAN UNITY

### 13.2.1 *The Unity of the Represented*

The first difficulty when thinking about democratic representation in the EU is to identify the entity represented. Most political theories of representation view it as an operation whereby a more or less complex authority expresses a position on behalf of another entity, generally considered both unique and ultimate. For instance, Michel Troper and Manuela Albertone try to identify a 'meta-concept' of political representation with the following two elements: 'on the one hand, the capacity of an authority to want or act on behalf of another entity to which that will and those acts are imputed. On the other hand, the supremacy of that authority and the function it exercises.'[9] The characteristics of the entity represented – its unity and superiority – are conceived around the idea that the operation of representation would precisely aim at making an *identifiable* totality express itself, or even exist. According to these authors, the legitimizing function of representation in political theory consists 'in justifying power by claiming that it is exercised in another's name',[10] so that rulers would not act in their own name, but on behalf of another higher entity, namely – in democratic theory – the *demos*. The unitary character of the represented is particularly problematic because it is based on a fiction, or, at the very least, a stripped-down reality. Whereas, in the monarchical era, the unity of the representative made it possible to embody the multitude and conceive it as a whole, the advent of the

8 For an effort to (re)think democracy in order to conceive it at the EU level, see Daniel Innerarity, *Democracy in Europe. A Political Philosophy of the EU* (Cham: Palgrave Macmillan, 2018).

9 Manuela Albertone and Michel Troper, 'Penser la représentation: Une introduction', in Manuela Albertone and Michel Troper (eds.), *La représentation politique. Anthologie* (Paris: Classiques Garnier, 2021), pp. 7–32, p. 15.

10 Ibid., p. 29.

democratic ideal now postulates the unity of the represented.[11] It is the case of the invention of the 'nation', which is generally conceived as a purely abstract entity, or even of a 'people', whose representation cannot account for the complexity of the society that composes it. Henceforth, the unity of the represented has become a logical requirement of political representation. Representation requires assuming the unity of the entity represented, and, therefore, ignoring the diversity and complexity of its composition and the conflictual relationships that run through it. If the represented was fragmented into several independent entities, it would be impossible to make it express itself or even exist *as such*. Representation presupposes the autonomy of the represented, whether it is a people, a nation, a society, regardless of its components.

### 13.2.2 *The Issue of Federative Duality*

This conceptual approach to representation that presupposes the unity of the represented raises an important issue in federative type groups which, like the EU, are defined by the duality and equality of the federal and federated levels. The combination of federated and federal wills can hardly be appended to that of an encompassing totality that would subsume them, without risking at the same time to dilute them in the new entity. This is why the thinkers of federative theory believe that 'in a federal structure, there are, legally speaking, two peoples: the federated people and the federal people'.[12] The notion of 'people', like that of sovereignty, becomes problematic when thinking about the duality inherent in federalism.

It is from this perspective that one must understand the ambiguity of Article 10 of the Treaty on European Union (TEU) on the democratic principles of the EU. Article 10(1) TEU states that 'the functioning of the Union shall be founded on representative democracy' and yet, no *demos* is identified in whose name the *cratos* would be exercised. In order to circumvent the difficulty of having to choose between a single people or multiple peoples as represented entities, Article 10(2) TEU designates two collective entities: first, the 'citizens', who are 'directly represented at Union level in the European Parliament'; and second, the 'Member States', that are represented in the

[11] Pierre Rosanvallon, *Le peuple introuvable* (Paris: Gallimard, 1998), p. 20. There is a permanent tension between the need for a unified fiction and the need to take into account the diversity of the interests to be represented, or the people 'appears continually separated from themselves', see Rosanvallon, ibid., p. 53.

[12] Olivier Beaud, 'La représentation dans l'État fédéral', in Albertone and Troper, fn. 9, pp. 439–457, p. 455.

European Council and in the Council by representatives who are said to be 'themselves democratically accountable either to their national Parliaments, or to their citizens'. The latter results from the Treaty of Lisbon, which, by taking the Councils out of the orbit of pure interstate representation and into the democratic field, breaks with the conception that tended to present the European Parliament as holding the monopoly of democratic representation within the institutional system of the Union.[13] Article 10(2) TEU recognizes the democratic nature of the representation of Member States in intergovernmental institutions by highlighting that it is the representation of the national political communities of the Member States that is ensured by that representation. This convoluted construction tries to restore the idea of the complex nature of the EU, which is sometimes referred to as a 'democratic federation of States and citizens' to express the duality it embodies.[14] The distinction between 'direct' (parliamentary) and 'indirect' (intergovernmental) forms of representation may seem surprising at first, since, by hypothesis, representation presupposes intermediation and is generally opposed to so-called 'direct' democracy (which itself is never really such). Only the need to emphasize the unsurpassable duality of the federative structure explains the need to resort to this distinction between 'direct' and 'indirect' democratic representation.

The dual approach to democratic representation, however, often gives rise to the impression that its direct and indirect forms are in competition. Democratic representation in the EU would operate according to a 'connected vessels' system,[15] in which the strengthening of direct democratic representation in Parliament would necessarily detract from indirect democratic representation in the Councils. For example, according to Dieter

[13] That approach led the Court of Justice to favour the provision most closely associating the Parliament with an act's adoption when the act in question equally pursued the objectives set forth in two different legal bases (see CJEU, *Commission v. Council* (Case C-300/89) EU:C:1991:244 [1991] ECR I-02867, 11 June 1991), and to impose respect for the legislative procedure which gives the parliamentary institution the most power in the event of a combination of legal bases providing for a different decision-making process (see CJEU, *Parliament v. Council* (Case C-155/07) EU:C:2008:605 [2008] ECR I-08103, 6 November 2008; *Parliament v. Council* (Case C-166/07) EU:C:2009:499 [2009] ECR I-07135, 3 September 2009). For a critique based on the balance between the national and European dimensions of the Union's democracy (embodied respectively by the Council and the Parliament), see CJEU, *Commission v. Parliament and Council* (C-411/06) EU:C:2009:189 [2009] ECR I-07585, 26 March 2009, Opinion of Advocate General Poiares Maduro, para. 6.

[14] Louis Dubouis, 'La nature de l'Union européenne', in Gérard Cohen-Jonathan and Jacqueline Dutheil de la Rochère (eds.), *Constitution européenne, démocratie, et droits de l'homme* (Brussels: Bruylant/Nemesis, 2003), pp. 81–196, p. 93.

[15] The expression 'connected vessels' is borrowed from Étienne Balibar, *Europe, crise et fin?* (Lormont: Le Bord de l'eau, 2016), p. 207.

Grimm, 'the transformation of the Union into a parliamentary system would weaken rather than strengthen democracy in Europe', because it increases the risk 'that a Member State will be subject to a law that has not been approved by its democratically elected and controlled organs'.[16] For this author, in the absence of a genuine European *demos* whose members imagine themselves as such, for want in particular of a European public space linking European citizens and their representative organs, any increase in the powers of the European Parliament, which can only lead to a corresponding decrease in the powers of the Councils, would weaken the democratic legitimacy of the Union, which essentially emanates from the national *demoi* and their control over the positions of their national representatives within the Councils. In other words, the strengthening of 'direct' democratic representation would necessarily be at the expense of 'indirect' democratic representation. Yet, in the event of a conflict, 'indirect' democratic representation, which is rooted in Member States, would be the true source of democratic legitimacy.[17]

This is why the hybrid form of dual democratic representation of the federated and federal levels is perceived as conflictual, unstable, and unsatisfactory. The concept of democratic representation seems to be captive of the State and unitary context in which it was mainly deployed. How do we escape this aporia of the unity of the represented? One solution is to duplicate, rather than oppose, the two components of democratic representation in the European federative context, that is, the States and the citizens.

### 13.2.3 *A Solution? Dual Political Citizenship*

The temptation to oppose the two levels of democratic representation, or to play the federated people against the federal people, underestimates the *ubiquity* of the represented components. Each of them includes two sides: one federated, and the other federal. Because they each are twofold, they

[16] Dieter Grimm, 'Quand le juge dissout l'électeur', *Le Monde diplomatique*, July 2017, p 19. The author's position is constant. It is expressed many times in Dieter Grimm, *The Constitution of European Democracy* (Oxford: Oxford University Press, 2017).

[17] This would even justify that Member States' representatives in the Councils retain a right of veto in the event of a decision taken by qualified majority (Luxembourg compromise), because, in this way, a Member State could not be subject to a European norm not approved by its democratic organs. The French Constitutional Council considers that substituting a qualified majority for a unanimous decision of the Council or conferring decision-taking power on the European Parliament would infringe upon the essential conditions of the exercise of national sovereignty. See French Constitutional Council, *Traité de Lisbonne*, 31 December 2007, Decision 2007-560 DC, para. 20.

cannot fully oppose each other without contradicting themselves. Yet, the question of the duplication of each of the components of democratic representation does not arise in the same terms.

The duplication of the State component of representation is classic. EU States may act as 'members' of the Union, thus participating in its representation, but also as 'monadic' States, representing themselves. It therefore seems simplistic, even erroneous, to oppose the European and national levels of democratic representation in the EU, since the former already comes in part from the latter. State duplication means that, on the one hand, the Union can only be democratic if its Member States are democratic, and, on the other hand, the latter can only remain democratic if the Union is democratic too. Admittedly, the boundary between the two 'hats' of 'member' or 'monadic' State is not always easy to draw, particularly when government representatives collectively exercise their competence outside the EU institutions.[18] But the idea of a functional duplication of representative State organs is not fundamentally problematic. It can be solved by a duplication of legal orders depending on whether States act as monads in the international legal order, or as members in the European legal order.[19]

The idea of duplicating the citizen component of representation seems at first sight more problematic. It is implicitly conveyed by Article 10(2) TEU when it states that citizens are represented in the European Parliament 'at Union level'. While it might seem like a pleonasm, since the European Parliament is obviously situated 'at Union level', it is meant to emphasize that citizens are also represented at another level, that of their Member State, which forms the other 'indirect' component of representation in the Union (see above, Section 13.2.2). This is also the meaning that can be given to Article 9 TEU *in fine*, reproduced by Article 20 of the Treaty on the Functioning of the European Union (TFEU) and according to which '[c]itizenship of the Union shall be additional to and not replace national citizenship'.[20] Yet, while it may seem

[18] See, for example, the agreement with Turkey on the outsourcing of the control of asylum seekers, CJEU, *NF v. European Council* (Joined Cases C-208/17 P to C-210/17 P) EU:C:2018:705, 12 September 2018.

[19] Édouard Dubout, 'La relativité de la distinction des normes internationales et européennes', in Laurence Burgorgue-Larsen, Édouard Dubout, Alexandre Maitrot de la Motte and Sébastien Touzé (eds.), *Droit de l'Union européenne et droit international: les interactions normatives* (Paris: Pedone, 2012), pp. 17–52.

[20] Art. 20 of the Consolidated Version of the Treaty on the Functioning of the European Union, OJ 2012 C326, 26 October 2012, p. 47. On the idea that democratic representation in the Union must be conceived by starting from citizenship, see also Armin von Bogdandy, 'The European Lesson for International Democracy: The Significance of Articles 9 to 12 EU Treaty for International Organizations' (2012) 23(2) *European Journal of International Law* 315–334, at 322.

conceivable that a complex and abstract entity such as a State be duplicated in some cases, the duplication of the citizen as an individual endowed by definition with a single will faces an obvious objection: how could one and the same citizen be represented at two levels, without risking self-contradiction in the event of a conflict between these levels of representation?

This situation is fairly common. It is the case, for instance, when in the State context, a local representative institution collides with a national representative institution, but the issue is then decided based on a hierarchy of levels of representation articulated around the idea of a single and indivisible people. In the absence of such a single people, multiple citizenship is again problematic, even schizophrenic. An example of such a situation was when British nationals tried to pit their status as European citizens against that of national citizens in order to challenge the Brexit effects and continue to benefit from their rights deriving from their previous European citizenship. Presented with such a claim, the Court of Justice merely established a chronological relationship between the two forms of citizenship, national and European, and held that, *after* the entry into force of the withdrawal, the applicants could no longer claim their European citizenship since they 'no longer hold the nationality of a Member State, but that of a third State'.[21] Such a chronological approach is questionable: not only does it obscure the fact that, unlike with third-country nationals, European citizenship had been acquired before being revoked,[22] but it also introduces a form of hierarchy between citizenships. It is difficult to understand how the exercise of national citizenship can call into question the existence of European citizenship, without assuming a form of superiority of one over the other. In fact, what this case law highlights is the derivative character of EU citizenship in relation to the citizenship of a Member State. This example shows the difficulty of articulating a dual and *equal* citizenship.

One way to overcome the difficulty of the egalitarian duplication of citizenship is to take into account the *political* nature of representation. As Jürgen Habermas highlights, the construction of citizens' political opinions takes place within a *public space* of deliberation that 'constitutes the necessary connecting element between the political autonomy of the individual and the formation of the common political will of all citizens of the State'.[23] It is

[21] CJEU, *EP v. Préfet du Gers and Institut National de la Statistique et des Études Économiques (INSEE)* (Case C-673/20) EU:C:2022:449, 9 June 2022, GC, para. 56 (emphasis added).

[22] Niamh Nic Shuibhne, 'Protecting the Legal Heritage of Former Union Citizens: EP v. Préfet du Gers' (2023) 60(2) *Common Market Law Review* 475–516.

[23] Jürgen Habermas, *Espace public et démocratie délibérative: un tournant* (Paris: Gallimard, 2023), p. 10. [Translator's note: The use of the expression 'public space' follows the initial French translation of Habermas' *Strukturwandel der Öffentlichkeit Untersuchungen zu einer*

therefore necessary to distinguish the 'raw' interest of the individual as a member of society (*Gesellschaftsbürger*) from the final interest of the citizen as a member of the political collectivity (*Staatsbürger*), which is formed only through a space of collective deliberation. The political preferences expressed by citizens are embedded in communication structures that guide their choices, depending on the preferences of the other participants in the deliberation and the available strategies. However, nothing prevents this public space from being dual (national and European), including with a level of porousness between the two, so that the same citizen will be able to formulate different political demands depending on the space of deliberation in which they participate. Thus, under the condition of a two-level public space sufficiently developed to establish a close connection between the citizens and their representatives, the citizens could very well be, or feel, involved in the definition of the national interest that will be defended by their representatives in the Council, and of the transnational interest defended by the European Parliament. Admittedly, conflicts between the results expressed in these two spaces may arise, but this does not necessarily require reducing the citizen to a single or ultimate deliberative community. On this condition, a dual political citizenship in the same space need not be perceived as completely confrontational.

At this stage, one may formulate a first intermediate conclusion to resolve the aporia of the unity of the represented in the European context. The represented is the citizen, himself conceived as a member of two political communities, which justifies that he is represented at European level both 'directly' (via the Parliament) as a member of the European political community, and 'indirectly' (via the Council) as a member of the national political community. With such a reading, the democratic failure of one level of representation necessarily impacts on the democratic quality of the other. Far from opposing each other, the two levels of representation are bound to strengthen each other.[24] The question then arises as to whether the conditions

*Kategorie der bürgerlichen Gesellschaft* (1962) as *L'espace public, archéologie de la publicité comme dimension constitutive de la société bourgeoise* (Paris: Payot, 1978)].

24 See also, defending the same idea that the different channels of representation in the Union, including participatory arrangements, should be seen as complementary and, therefore, strengthen their interconnectedness, Richard Bellamy and Sandra Kröger (eds.), *Representation and Democracy in the EU: Does One Come at the Expense of the Other?* (London: Routledge, 2015). On the idea that federalism can increase the 'agency and political power' of citizens by offering them more opportunities to rally a majority, see also Francis Cheneval, 'Une petite philosophie de l'égalité des États', in Édouard Dubout (ed.), *L'égalité des États membres de l'Union européenne* (Brussels: Bruylant, 2022), pp. 299–308, p. 307.

for a duplication of political citizenship in the EU are really met. Which leads to the second difficulty: European political citizenship still seems to be largely correlated to the national public space. In those circumstances, it is difficult to consider its holders to be represented as such.

## 13.3 REPRESENTING THE EUROPEAN CITIZEN

### 13.3.1 *From Peoples to Citizens*

Pursuant to Article 10(2) TEU, citizens are 'directly' represented at the Union level by the European Parliament. But what citizenship does the European Parliament represent? A truly autonomous European citizenship, or a derivative, or even 'indirect', form of national citizenship? The question is whether, from an institutional and procedural point of view, the parliamentary system of European representation is giving itself the means to achieve the ambition it displays. If an evolution is occurring, it is still in progress.

The establishment of a form of democratic representation of a parliamentary type within the institutional system of the Community was necessary from the outset. It mirrored the creation of international assemblies by numerous treaties after the war (Western European Union, Council of Europe, North Atlantic Treaty Organization (NATO), etc.), but also stemmed from the desire to establish a democratic control over the activities of this independent supranational authority, the High Authority, precursor to the current European Commission. The European Coal and Steel Community (ECSC) already included a Common Assembly. The European Economic Community (EEC) retained the same institutional structure, including an assembly that was intended to reflect the association between the citizens of the Member States and the construction of Europe. This assembly, which took the name 'European Parliament' in 1962,[25] is today the parliamentary institution of the EU.

Article 137 of the Treaty of Rome of 25 March 1957 establishing the EEC provided that the Assembly 'shall be composed of representatives of the peoples of the States united within the Community'.[26] This formula set aside the idea of representing *a* European people in favour of representing national political communities. The *demoi*cratic nature of representation in

[25] In 1986, the Single European Act incorporated this designation into primary law. See Single European Act, OJ 1987 No. L169, 29 June 1987, p. 1.

[26] See also, with regard to the Common Assembly of the ECSC, Art. 20 of the Treaty instituting the European Coal and Steel Community, 261 UNTS 3729 (adopted 18 April 1951, entered into force 23 July 1952).

the European Parliament was further reinforced by the method of appointment initially chosen. This method established an organic link between national and European parliamentarians because Members of the European Parliament (MEPs) were chosen by the national parliaments from among their members in accordance with the procedure laid down by each Member State.[27] Admittedly, the principle of election by direct universal suffrage had been provided from the outset.[28] Article 21 of the ECSC Treaty left it to the discretion of each Member State to have members of the national parliament chosen from among its members or to provide for the election of MEPs by direct universal suffrage. Article 138(3) of the EEC Treaty instructed the European Parliament to prepare a draft to that effect, on which the Council had to decide unanimously and which had to be ratified by all the Member States in accordance with their respective constitutional requirements. It was not until 1976 that the principle of the election of MEPs by direct universal suffrage was put into practice.[29] But direct election did not change the nature or scope of representation. As the French Constitutional Council emphasized, the Act concerning the election of the Assembly of the Communities by direct universal suffrage does not intend to 'modify the nature of this Assembly, which remains composed of representatives of each of the peoples of these States' or 'to create sovereignty'.[30] The election was organized within the Member States, which were free to determine the holders of the right to vote and stand as a candidate. In principle, they reserved it for their nationals.[31]

One might have thought that the introduction by the Maastricht Treaty of EU citizenship (to which is attached the right to vote and stand as a candidate in European elections in the Member State of residence under the same conditions as nationals) was an innovation.[32] This seemed to be confirmed by the Treaty of Lisbon which finally established a link between European

[27] See Art. 138(1) of the Treaty establishing the European Economic Community (hereafter TEC), 294–298 UNTS 4300 (adopted 25 March 1957, entered into force 1 January 1958).

[28] On the evolution of the rules governing the designation of MEPs see, Frédéric Allemand, 'L'évolution de la désignation des membres du Parlement européen: le principe électif dans tous ses états', in Laurence Potvin-Solis (ed.), *Le principe électif dans l'Union européenne* (Brussels: Bruylant, 2021), pp. 91–122.

[29] See the Act concerning the election of the representatives of the Assembly by direct universal suffrage, OJ 1976 No. L278, 8 October 1976, p. 5.

[30] See Conseil Constitutionnel, *Décision du Conseil des communautés européennes relative à l'élection de l'Assemblée des Communautés au suffrage universel direct*, 30 December 1976, decision 76–71 DC, paras. 3–4.

[31] However, some Member States, such as Ireland and the Netherlands, recognized the right to vote also to nationals of other Member States residing on their territory. See Jean Boulouis, *Droit institutionnel des Communautés européennes* (Paris: Montchrestien, 1983), p. 49.

[32] See Treaty on European Union, OJ 1992 No. C191, 29 July 1992, p. 1.

citizenship and representation in the European Parliament. The hitherto immutable formula describing the European Parliament as an assembly consisting of 'representatives of the peoples of the States brought together in the Community'[33] no longer appears. From then on, the Treaty provides that 'citizens are directly represented, at Union level, in the European Parliament'[34] and describes MEPs as 'representatives of the Union's citizens'.[35]

According to the French constitutional judge, there had been a change. In 2003, the French Constitutional Council found that the creation of eight electoral constituencies instead of a single jurisdiction did not infringe the principles of the indivisibility of the French Republic and of the unity of the French people. According to the French Constitutional Council (*Conseil constitutionnel*), since the Treaty confers on EU citizens the right to vote and to stand as a candidate in elections to the European Parliament in the State of residence under the same conditions as nationals of that State, 'Members of the European Parliament elected in France shall be elected as representatives of the citizens of the European Union residing in France'.[36] This highlights a change, or a potential change, in the nature of the democratic representation assured by the European Parliament. The Parliament would no longer be the representative organ of the national political communities of Member States, but that of a new body politic transcending national political bodies and made up of European citizens. In other words, the European Parliament would have become the organ of expression of a European people which is, if not already there, at least in the making, if we are willing to believe in the performative function of law and legal language and admit that political representation constitutes the represented subject. An additional sign of this change in the nature of representation in the European Parliament would be the severance of the link between the European Parliament and the national parliaments in 2002 by the decision amending the Act concerning the election of the representatives of the European Parliament by direct universal suffrage, which made the national and European parliamentary mandates incompatible (as was already the case in France).[37] But the text of the treaty is not unequivocal and several elements might question this reading.

33 See Art. 137 of the Treaty instituting the European Coal and Steel Community, which became Art. 189 TEC.

34 See Art. 10(2) TEU.

35 See Art. 14(2) TEU.

36 French Constitutional Council, *Loi relative à l'élection des conseillers régionaux et des représentants au Parlement européen ainsi qu'à l'aide publique aux partis politiques*, 3 April 2003, Decision 2003–468 DC, para. 37.

37 Council Decision 2002/772/EC of 25 June 2002 and 23 September 2002 amending the Act concerning the election of the representatives of the European Parliament by direct universal suffrage, OJ 2002 No. L283, 21 October 2002, p. 1.

### 13.3.2 A 'Second-Order' European Political Citizenship?[38]

First, the national fragmentation of the electorate and the ballot's territorialization into States persist. The State remains the electoral basis for the European elections, which are organized in each Member State for the representatives elected in that State.[39]

Second, the distribution of seats in the European Parliament is subject to quotas per Member State and does not apply strict demographic proportionality. Indeed, according to Article 14(2) TEU, '[r]epresentation of citizens shall be degressively proportional, with a minimum threshold of six members per Member State', with the specification that '[n]o Member State shall be allocated more than ninety-six seats'. This means that 'the ratio between the population and the number of seats of each Member State … shall vary in relation to their respective populations', but 'each Member of the European Parliament from a more populous Member State represents more citizens than each Member from a less populous Member State and, conversely, that the larger the population of a Member State, the greater its entitlement to a large number of seats'.[40] The application of that principle of degressive proportionality results in an imbalance in demographic representation, such that the vote of the citizen of the least populous Member State weighs approximately twelve times more than the vote of the citizen of the most populous State. However, as the German Constitutional Court (*Bundesverfassungsgericht*) observed,[41] if the European Parliament were the representative body of European citizens taken as a political unit, such an imbalance would not be acceptable because it would disregard the democratic principle and its corollary, the equality of citizens in the representation of the vote. It can only be explained and justified because, despite the assertions of the Treaty, the European Parliament remains an institution partly representative of the peoples of the Member States. Therefore, equality between Member

[38] By analogy with the idea that European elections would, in reality, be 'second-order' national elections; see Karlheinz Reif and Hermann Schmitt, 'Nine Second-order National Elections: A Conceptual Framework for the Analysis of European Election Results' (1980) 8(1) *European Journal of Political Research* 3–44.

[39] As provided by primary law, namely, Council Decision 2002/772/EC, fn. 37. See, in particular, Art. 1: 'In each Member State, members of the European Parliament shall be elected on the basis of proportional representation, using the list system or the single transferable vote.'

[40] Art. 1 of the Council Decision 2013/312/EU of 28 June 2013 establishing the composition of the European Parliament, OJ 2013 No. L181, 29 June 2013, p. 57.

[41] See German Constitutional Court, *Lisbonne*, 30 June 2009, BVerfG, 2/08, paras. 277–287.

States legitimately tempers demographic proportionality[42] because the allocation of national contingents of MEPs responds not so much, or not only to, the concern to guarantee equal suffrage for citizens, but also to the need to ensure adequate representation of national democracies. This system is capable of reflecting at the level of the European Parliament the balance of political forces in even the smallest Member States.[43] For a while, the amendment to Article 190(2) Treaty establishing the EEC introduced by the Treaty of Amsterdam emphasized this point: by stating that 'the number of representatives elected in each Member State must ensure appropriate representation of the peoples of the States brought together in the Community', it tended, in the minds of its initiators, to ensure that 'the representation of the smaller Member States should be sufficient to enable the main political currents of a State to have a seat'.[44] In other words, the principle of degressive proportionality which governs the State allocation of MEP mandates is justified by maintaining the division of the European electorate into national electorates whose political pluralism must be represented in the European Parliament.[45]

Third, the delimitation of national electorate bodies for the European elections remains within the competence of Member States to determine. EU law does not determine who is entitled to vote and stand as a candidate at elections to the European Parliament. All it obliges Member States to do is enlarging the national electorate to include the European citizens who reside on their territories.[46] As for the conditions for integration, they are freely determined by the State, provided that they are the same for citizens of the Union and for nationals. The Netherlands is thus theoretically entitled to decide that the Overseas Countries and Territories (OCTs) (Netherlands

[42] Ibid., para. 284; Claude Blumann and Louis Dubouis, *Droit institutionnel de l'Union européenne*, 7th ed. (Paris: LexisNexis, 2019), p. 282.

[43] See European Parliament, 'Rapport relatif à l'adoption d'un projet de convention instituant l'élection des membres du Parlement européen au suffrage universel direct – Rapporteur: S. Patijn' (13 January 1975), Doc. PE 368/74, which underlined that the proposed allocation of seats pursued the maximum proportionality between the population of a State and the number of its representatives in the European Parliament, and ensured that all the essential political forces of a State were represented in the European Parliament.

[44] Jean-Paul Jacqué, *Droit institutionnel de l'Union européenne*, 7th ed. (Paris: Dalloz, 2012), p. 257.

[45] See Jelena von Achenbach, 'The European Parliament as a Forum of National Interest? A Transnationalist Critique of Jürgen Habermas' Reconstruction of Degressive Proportionality: The European Parliament as a Forum of National Interest?' (2017) 55(2) *JCMS: Journal of Common Market Studies* 193–202.

[46] See Arts. 20(2)(b) and 22(2) TFEU; Art. 39 of the Charter of Fundamental Rights of the European Union, OJ 2000 No. C364, 18 December 2000, p. 1.

Antilles) are not part of the electoral territory and, therefore, to exclude from the right to vote and to stand as a candidate the European citizens residing in the OCTs. It is only to the extent that Netherlands law recognizes the right to vote and to stand as a candidate to Netherlands nationals residing in a third country that the European principle of equal treatment prohibits them from doing so.[47] Even more so, the United Kingdom has been able to grant the right to vote and to stand as a candidate in European elections to Commonwealth citizens (Gibraltar residents)[48] even though they are not British nationals and, therefore, citizens of the Union, on the ground that, under a national constitutional tradition, they have a 'close connection' with the United Kingdom.[49] This does not imply that Commonwealth citizens who are residents of Gibraltar become citizens of the Union and entitled to vote in European elections in another Member State to which they have transferred their residence. The competence of the State to determine the holders of the right to vote and to stand as a candidate in elections to the European Parliament implies an imperfect overlap between the subject which, according to the Treaties, is represented in the European Parliament and the European electorate defined by the States.[50] In principle, the right to vote should be recognized to each of the citizens of the Union.[51] This does not mean, however, that this right must be exercised by each of them, since the State is free to set the conditions (age, residence, ineligibilities,[52] incompatibilities, etc.), or even that this right must be reserved exclusively to them. Political unity remains defined nationally. The right of political representation at the Union level 'is in no way the attribute of belonging to a new political

[47] See CJEU, *Eman and Sevinger v. College van burgemeester en wethouders van Den Haag* (Case C-300/04) EU:C:2006:545 [2006] ECR I-08055, 12 September 2006, GC.

[48] The United Kingdom's decision was prompted by the need to comply with the *Matthews* judgment by which the European Court of Human Rights had condemned it for violation of the right to free elections for having consented to the Act concerning the election of the European Parliament by direct universal suffrage of 1976 which excluded Gibraltar from the electoral territory of the United Kingdom. See European Court of Human Rights, *Matthews v. United Kingdom* (No. 24833/94) (1999) 28 EHRR 361.

[49] See CJEU, *Spain v. United Kingdom* (Case C-145/04) EU:C:2006:543 [2006] ECR I-07917, 12 September 2006, GC; Laurence Burgorgue-Larsen 'L'identité de l'Union européenne au cœur d'une controverse territoriale centenaire' (2007) (1) *Revue trimestrielle de droit européen* 25–46.

[50] See Case C-145/04, fn. 49 and *Eman and Sevinger* (C-300/04) [2006] ECR I-07917, 6 April 2006, Opinion of Advocate General Tizzano, paras. 81–88.

[51] See Case C-145/04, fn. 49, para. 76; CJEU, *Thierry Delvigne v. Commune de Lesparre-Médoc, Préfet de la Gironde*, (Case C-650/13) EU:C:2015:648, 6 October 2015, GC, para. 44.

[52] See Case C-650/13, fn. 51. French legislation that attaches the deprivation of the right to vote and to stand as a candidate in elections to the European Parliament to a criminal penalty does not violate EU law.

or European community … but rather the mark of integration into a given national community'.[53] Together with civil, economic, and social rights, the political rights attached to EU citizenship contribute to endowing their holders with the status of 'quasi-nationals'.[54]

If one adds that European elections are still not organized according to a uniform electoral procedure,[55] and, on a political level, the transnational dimension of the public space is not yet sufficiently developed to allow European elections to generate a fully European political agenda,[56] one must admit that, even under the Treaty of Lisbon, representation in the European Parliament continues to be 'nationally mediated',[57] and a member of the European Parliament largely remains an emanation of a national community. In sum, the democratic legitimacy of the European Parliament remains more plural than unitary. Symptomatic of this is the fact that the entry into force of the Treaty of Lisbon did not lead the Court of Justice to change its qualification inaugurated in 1980[58] according to which the involvement of the European Parliament in the Union's decision-making process reflects 'the fundamental democratic principle that *the people* should

53 Loïc Azoulai, 'La citoyenneté européenne, un statut d'intégration sociale', in Gérard Cohen-Jonathan (ed.), *Chemins d'Europe. Mélanges en l'honneur de Jean-Paul Jacqué* (Paris: Dalloz, 2010), pp. 1–28, p. 14.

54 Ibid., p. 15.

55 Only 'principles common to all Member States', in accordance with the alternative opened up by Art. 223(1) TFEU, could be adopted: proportional representation voting, which can be organized in constituencies provided that the proportional nature of the vote is not undermined; voting may be preferential; a minimum threshold of votes may be provided for the allocation of seats, which may not exceed five per cent of the votes cast. See Council Decision 2002/772/EC, fn. 37, amended by Council Decision (EU, Euratom) of 13 July 2018 amending the Act concerning the election of the members of the European Parliament by direct universal suffrage, annexed to Council Decision 76/787/ESC, EEC, Euratom of 20 September 1976, OJ 2018 No. 178, 16 July 2018, p. 1. On the expected benefits of a European electoral reform, see Fabio Pascua Mateo, 'European Parliament and Representation of the Union's Citizens: What Can Be Expected from Electoral Law from a Democratic Standpoint?' (2022) 28 *European Law Journal* 63–88.

56 To put it more bluntly, 'elections to the European Parliament are largely organized in accordance with national rules, … and votes are cast for national parties with national candidates on the basis of national programmes'. 'Proposal for a Council Regulation on the election of the Members of the European Parliament by direct universal suffrage, repealing Council Decision 76/787/ECSC, EEC, Euratom and the Act concerning the election of the members of the European Parliament by direct universal suffrage annexed to that Decision' (20 May 2022), 2022/0902(APP), para. 5.

57 Boulouis, *Droit institutionnel des Communautés européennes*, fn. 31, p. 49. For a similar view, see André Moine, 'La représentation parlementaire des citoyens européens', in Potvin-Solis, fn. 28, pp. 199–217, p. 199.

58 CJEU, *Roquette Frères SA v. Council* (Case C-138/79) EU:C:1980:249 [1980] ECR 03333, 29 October 1980, para 33.

take part in the exercise of power through the intermediary of a representative'.[59]

How might it be possible remedy this indexation of European political citizenship on the national public space, this national compartmentalization of the parliamentary representation of European citizens?

### 13.3.3 *Transnationalizing the Public Space and Democratic Representation*

Despite the persistent national origin of MEPs, elements of a transnationalization of democratic representation in the European Parliament already exist.

First, the presentation of candidates for MEP under the aegis of European political parties is encouraged. Although the first European political parties were formed in the 1970s with the specific goal of coordinating electoral campaigns in the context of European elections, the Maastricht Treaty enshrined their role in primary law, which is, according to Article 10(4) TEU, to 'contribute to forming European political awareness and to expressing the will of citizens of the Union'. After the Treaty of Nice included a legal basis to that end,[60] the EU created a European legal status and established a public financing mechanism to promote their emergence and development.[61] To benefit from it, the political party must be transnational in scope, that is, represented in at least a quarter of the Member States by MEPs, in national or regional parliaments or in regional assemblies; or have obtained, in at least one quarter of the Member States, at least three per cent of the votes cast in each of those Member States in the last elections to the European Parliament. Moreover, it also must have taken part in the elections to the European Parliament or have publicly expressed its intention to

59 Ibid. (emphasis added). While the English version renders 'the people' as singular, the French version, renders people as plural ('*les peuples*'): '*l'expression d'un principe démocratique fondamental selon lequel les peuples participent à l'exercice du pouvoir par l'intermédiaire d'une assemblée représentative*'. See CJEU, *Slovakia v. Council and Hungary v. Council* (Joined Cases C-643/15 and C-645/15) EU:C:2017:631, 6 September 2017, GC, para. 160; *RPO* (Case C-390/15) EU:C:2017:174, 7 March 2017, GC, para. 25; *Parliament v. Council* (Case C-263/14) EU:C:2016:435, 14 June 2016, GC, para. 70; *Parliament v. Council* (Case C-658/11) EU:C:2014:2025, 24 June 2014, GC, para. 81; *Parliament v. Council* (Case C-130/10) EU:C:2012:472, 12 July 2012, GC, para. 81; *Syrian Lebanese Commercial Bank v. Council* (Joined Cases T-174/12 and T-80/13) EU:T:2014:52, 4 February 2014, para. 16.

60 See Art. 224 TFEU, previously Art. 191(2) TEC.

61 See Regulation (EU, Euratom) No 1141/2014/EU of the European Parliament and of the Council of 22 October 2014 on the statute and funding of European political parties and European political foundations, OJ 2014 No. L317, 4 November 2014, p. 1, modified by Regulation (EU, Euratom) 2018/673/EU of the European Parliament and of the Council of 3 May 2018, OJ 2018 No. L114I, 4 May 2018, p. 1.

participate in the next elections to the European Parliament. This clearly shows the desire to make European political parties vehicles for the Europeanization of democratic representation. Today, there are nearly fifteen European political parties, formed by grouping together national parties. To give just one example, the European People's Party, which was created in 1976, today brings together more than eighty political parties, some thirty of which do not come from EU Member States. Yet, the development and constitutional role of these parties remain limited.[62] Deprived of members and partisans (other than through the membership of affiliated national parties) and hampered in the elaboration of global societal projects by the heterogeneity of the conceptions of their member parties and the limitation of the competences of the Union, they hardly are instruments of mobilization and political socialization of European citizens. The electoral manifestos they issue in preparation for the European elections have little echo on the different national stages during the European elections, and MEPs remain preselected by the national parties. At most, they are able to coordinate the positions of the MEPs within the transnational political groups.

As early as 1953, the MEPs decided to sit by political groups and not by national delegations. The transnational dimension of these groups was gradually reinforced by legal texts. In 1997, while the Rules of Procedure of the European Parliament still allowed for the formation of political groups comprising only Members from a single Member State, in an effort to promote the transnational dimension of the political groups, the minimum number of Members required for a group was lowered in proportion to its increase in multinational character.[63] Today, the Rules of Procedure of the European Parliament of April 2023 only allow the formation of transnational political groups. Article 33 provides that a political group must have at least twenty-three members elected in at least one quarter of the Member States. This structuring according to a transnational political logic is unanimously seen as a sign of 'fusion' of European representation, and therefore of the 'generality' of the mandate.[64] Far from being the representatives of the national political bodies from which they come, MEPs collectively represent the indivisibility of

62 See Paul Magnette, *Le régime politique de l'Union européenne*, 4th ed. (Paris: Presses de Sciences Po, 2017), pp. 214–218.

63 See Art. 29 of the Rules of Procedure of the European Parliament, OJ 1997 No. L49, 19 February 1997, p. 1.

64 See Catherine Castor, *Le principe démocratique dans le droit de l'Union européenne* (Brussels: Bruylant, 2012), p. 248; Olivier Costa, *Le parlement européen assemblée délibérante* (Brussels: Éditions de l'ULB, 2001), p. 279.

the European peoples whose collective interest is distinct from the sum of their particular interests. Even the European judge emphasized that the grouping of MEPs by political affinities 'enables local political particularities to be transcended and promotes the European integration', and aids in realizing the constitutional objective assigned to European political parties of forming a European consciousness and expressing the political will of European citizens.[65] Representation would thus constitute the represented as an indivisible body politic. Let us beware, however, of giving too much credence to this sign of the mandate's generality. As evidenced by the fate of the Member of Parliament (MPs) elected in the United Kingdom who, following Brexit, had to leave the European Parliament, the mandate of MEPs cannot be compared to that of a Member of the French National Assembly who, although elected in a constituency, does not represent that constituency, but the nation as a whole.[66] Moreover, the partisan structure of the assembly does not prevent members of the same nationality of a political group from forming national delegations to which, depending on the group, a greater or lesser degree of autonomy is recognized, which allows them, in certain cases, to free themselves from the group voting discipline.[67]

The prohibition of binding mandates may also contribute to a transnationalization of representation in the European Parliament despite the national fragmentation of the electorate. Article 4(1) of the Act concerning the election of the representatives of the Assembly by direct universal suffrage provides that '[r]epresentatives shall vote on an individual and personal basis. They shall not be bound by any instructions and shall not receive a binding mandate'.[68] The mandate's representative nature thus frees MEPs from the duty to look after the interests of their national electorate. MEPs are therefore legally in a position to determine the collective interest of European citizens in a complete independence. By way of a parallel, it is worth recalling that the abolition of binding mandates by the deputies of the Third Estate in 1789 in

65 CJEU, *Martinez and Others v. Parliament* (Joined Cases T-222/99, T-327/99 and T-329/99) EU:T:2001:242 [2001] ECR II-02823, 2 October 2001, para. 148.

66 The French mandate's generality allowed Alsatian and Lorraine deputies to keep their seats, even as their constituencies were hit by the annexation of Alsace-Lorraine by Germany in 1871. In 1962, it was only because of political imperatives that the generality of the mandate was obscured: an ordinance put an end to the mandate of Algeria's elected representatives in the French National Assembly.

67 See Costa, *Le parlement européen assemblée délibérante*, fn. 64, pp. 331–338.

68 For a reminder in the same terms, see Art. 3 of the Decision 2005/684/EC of the European Parliament of 28 September 2005 adopting the Statute for Members of the European Parliament, OJ 2005 No. L262, 7 October 2005, p. 1.

France was intended to allow them to speak on behalf of a collective person rather than merely reflect a will that predated their action.

In the future, the establishment of transnational lists of candidates for the European elections would certainly go a long way towards remedying the national partition of democratic representation in the European Parliament. This proposal is old. Already in 1998, the European Parliament adopted a report which suggested electing 10 per cent of MEPs on transnational lists within the framework of a single electoral constituency.[69] President Macron took up this idea in his speech at the Sorbonne University on 26 September 2017 when he suggested using the quota of departing British MPs for this purpose in view of the 2019 European elections.[70] Since the Treaty of Lisbon, this proposal no longer necessarily requires a revision of the Treaties because Article 14 TEU provides that the European Parliament represents the citizens of the Union. Yet, it nonetheless requires amending the Act concerning the election of the representatives of the European Parliament by direct universal suffrage, which lays down the principle of the distribution of seats by State, and, as such, makes the Member State the electoral territorial basis of European representation. Such an amendment would have to follow a particularly burdensome procedure.[71] That is why the proposal did not advance.[72] But it has since been renewed in the European Parliament with the aim of applying it to the 2024 European elections.[73] It is also one of the forty-nine proposals that emerged from the Conference on the

[69] Report on a proposal for an electoral procedure incorporating common principles for the election of Members of the European Parliament of 2 June 1998 (2 June 1998), A4-0212/98. It was adopted on 15 July 1998, see European Parliament, Resolution on a draft electoral procedure incorporating common principles for the election of Members of the European Parliament, OJEC 1998 No. C292, 21 September 1998, p. 66.

[70] Élysée, 'President Macron gives speech on new initiative for Europe' (26 September 2017). www.elysee.fr/en/emmanuel-macron/2017/09/26/president-macron-gives-speech-on-new-initiative-for-europe, last accessed 18 October 2023.

[71] Requiring, inter alia, the unanimous agreement of the Council, approval by Parliament by a majority of its members and ratification by all Member States, in accordance with their respective constitutional requirements, see Art. 223(1) TFUE.

[72] The proposal was abandoned and twenty-seven of the seventy-three seats were eventually redistributed, mainly in favour of the larger States to somewhat remedy the imbalance in demographic representation. The remaining forty-six seats were put in reserve for future EU enlargement. See European Council Decision (EU) 2018/937 of 28 June 2018 establishing the composition of the European Parliament, OJ 2018 No. L165I, 2 July 2018, p. 1.

[73] See the Domènec Ruiz Devesa, 'Report on the proposal for a Council Regulation on the election of the members of the European Parliament by direct universal suffrage, repealing Council Decision (76/787/ECSC, EEC, Euratom) and the Act concerning the election of the members of the European Parliament by direct universal suffrage annexed to that decision' (4 April 2022), Report A9-0083/2022, as well as the European Parliament legislative resolution of 3 May 2022 on the proposal for a Council Regulation on the election of the members of the

Future of Europe.[74] The system devised by the European Parliament provides for the election of twenty-eight candidates from lists drawn up at the Union level, with voters being called upon to vote twice in the elections: once for a list drawn up within the national framework, and another time for a transnational list. This structure strives to respect the principle (imposed by primary law) of degressive proportionality even for the composition of transnational lists. For this purpose, Member States are classified into three categories, comprising, respectively, the most populous, the medium-sized, and the least populous States. Each list will have to include a succession of groups of three candidates, and each candidate from a group will have to belong to a different category of States. Since the twenty-eight seats are distributed according to the D'Hondt method, each category of States can hope to be represented.

Such a reform would clearly represent a substantial step forward towards the emergence of a European civic community and for the development of a European public sphere. It would strengthen the European dimension of the electoral campaign at a time when it is still too often fragmented by State and focused on national issues. It would also encourage the emergence of European political parties, or European confederations of national political parties. The draft reform further provides that equal treatment and opportunities must be reserved in each Member State for transnational lists as compared to national lists. If, in fulfilment of the European Parliament's wishes,[75] the establishment of transnational lists were, moreover, coupled with the institutionalization of the currently informal mechanism of the lead candidate (*Spitzenkandidat*) – which would stand on a transnational list for the votes of all European citizens to defend a political programme – the power of collective self-determination of European citizens and the politicization of the European democratic system, including the democratic dimension of the election of representatives to the European Parliament, would increase significantly.[76]

Finally, the development of mechanisms for democratic participation also contributes to the transnationalization of European representation. Activated

European Parliament by direct universal suffrage, repealing Council Decision (76/787/ECSC, EEC, Euratom) and the Act concerning the election of the members of the European Parliament by direct universal suffrage annexed to that Decision (2020/2220(INL) – 2022/0902(APP)).

74 See EU, *Report on the Final Outcome of the Conference on the Future of Europe* (Luxembourg: Publications Office of the European Union, 2022).

75 See the European Parliament legislative resolution of 3 May 2022, fn. 73.

76 See Olivier Costa, 'Des listes transnationales au Parlement européen?' (2021) (3) *Revue des Affaires Européennes* 479–490; Christine Verger, 'Vers des listes transnationales en 2024' (2022) (279) *Policy paper Institut Jacques Delors* 1–11; Jean-Paul Jacqué, 'Chron. Droit institutionnel de l'Union européenne' (2022) (4) *Revue trimestrielle de droit européen* 795–816.

upstream of decision-making, these participatory mechanisms have the common characteristic of involving individuals in the European decision-making process regardless of nationality. They therefore invite the European representative institutions (the Council and the Parliament) to be more attentive to the expectations of an emerging European society. The expected result is twofold: transnationalizing and democratizing the Union's representative system.[77] The transnationalization effect of the European legislative process stems in particular from the European citizens' initiative, which, in order to be admissible, must be signed by at least one million Union citizens from at least a quarter of the Member States.[78] It also derives from the contribution of European social democracy to European representative democracy. Whether European social democracy takes the form of professional representation such as the European Social Committee (whose consultation is binding on the European legislator in the cases provided for by the Treaty), or that of the European social dialogue (which involves the social partners in the development of social standards), it brings not the citizen, but the 'situated man' to the political scene, that is to say, the 'man conditioned by his environment'[79] to give voice to the demands called for by his concrete economic situation.

Promoted by the Treaty of Lisbon,[80] participatory democracy is conceived as a means of correcting 'the persistent State-national bias of representative democracy in the Union'.[81] By striving to bring out and give voice to the European society, it also pushes European democracy to be more representative of that society.

## 13.4 REPRESENTING THE EUROPEAN SOCIETY

### 13.4.1 *Representation and Representativeness*

In recent decades, the demand for democratic representation has become more sensitive to taking into account society's diversity.[82] It is no longer

[77] For advocacy for the development of European participatory democracy, see Joshua Cohen and Charles Sabel, 'Directly-Deliberative Polyarchy' (1997) 3(4) *European Law Journal* 313–342.

[78] See Art. 11(4) TEU, as specified in Regulation (EU) 2019/788 of the European Parliament and of the Council of 17 April 2019 on the European citizens' initiative, OJ 2019 No. L130, 17 May 2019, p. 55.

[79] Georges Burdeau, *Traité de science politique*, tome VII (Paris: LGDJ, 1973), p. 40. English translation of 'l'homme situé' and of 'l'homme conditionné par son milieu'.

[80] See Art. 11 TEU.

[81] Édouard Dubout, *Droit constitutionnel de l'Union européenne*, 2nd ed. (Brussels: Bruylant, 2023), p. 313.

[82] Bernard Manin, 'La démocratie menacée? Résilience des institutions représentatives' (2015) 1 *Argomenti* 5–17, at 7.

satisfied with representing the people conceived as a body of citizens equal in rights, but aspires to make representation more faithful to the reality of the *body politic*, more 'descriptive', in particular by improving its inclusive character, or – at least – by remedying its tendency to exclude certain vulnerable groups. The evolution in the vision and perception of society as being composed of multiple identity groups, sometimes antagonistic, often subject to relations of domination and in constant search of emancipation explains this shift to a representation that is more representative. A better representation of these vulnerable groups at the political level would guarantee democratic improvement, by ensuring that political decision-making no longer perpetuates exclusionary phenomena in a systemic way. Yet, by being assigned an objective of inclusion and emancipation of vulnerable groups, representation also changes its *nature*: it ceases to be seen as mainly procedural or formal and takes on a substantial and more 'distributive' dimension of social justice, one of access to positions that determines, by the adoption of laws, the allocation of other valued social goods (education, employment, health, and so on). Such a transformation of the representative ideal raises a challenge that is not unique to European democracy, but also (and primarily) concerns democracy at the national level. Nevertheless, the clash between the change of scale (Europeanization) and the change in nature (substantialization) of democratic representation raises in the EU a particular difficulty which is mainly due to the lack of both institutional and mental structures to signify and politically represent the diversity of a European society *under construction*. The current modern ideal of representativeness usually develops as a higher and later stage of representation of an already existing national society. In contrast, aiming for a more faithful representation of social diversity on a European scale requires breaking down the elements of a social whole even before it is fully formed and imagines itself as such. As it stands, it is difficult to affirm the existence of a European society sufficiently organized to be *re*-presented in its diversity. Admittedly, Article 11 TEU includes, among the democratic principles of the EU, the open and transparent dialogue with 'civil society'.[83] In practice, however, the dialogue with civil society takes place through the best organized and most powerful actors at the European level, including lobbies, to the point that it is difficult to see it as a true emanation of the European society.[84] This is why, at the European level, representation is

83 See Arts. 11(1) to 11(3).

84 See Paul Magnette, 'European Governance and Civic Participation: Beyond Elitist Citizenship?' (2003) 51(1) *Political Studies* 144–160; Piotr Staszcyk, A *Legal Analysis of NGO's and European Civil Society* (Alphen aan den Rijn: Kluwer Law International, 2019).

torn between two poles: to strive to create a homogeneous whole that does not yet exist, and to reproduce the heterogeneous reality of this inchoate whole.

A move towards a more substantialist approach to European representation should however not be ruled out. Its first translation can be seen in the proposal of Council Regulation to replace the Act concerning the election of the MEPs by direct universal suffrage that was approved by the European Parliament.[85] In addition to allowing for the establishment of transnational lists, the proposal requires respect for gender equality in the determination of candidate lists 'without infringing the rights of non-binary people', and provides for the possibility of exemptions from nationally provided thresholds for the allocation of seats for political parties representing recognized national and linguistic minorities.[86] Yet, until the adoption of this reform, the efforts for representativeness continue to come from, and depend on, applicable national electoral laws. Moreover, the issue of gender and minorities obviously does not exhaust the ideal of representativeness of different social groups. This is why the shift towards a greater representativeness of the European society seems to require the introduction of new forms of participation and direct involvement of citizens in European political decision-making.

### 13.4.2 *The Representation and Participation of Society*

The desire to represent and involve categorical or sectoral social interests is reflected in the introduction of specific organs and procedures at the Union level, such as the European Social Dialogue or the European citizens' initiative. Apart from the fact that their transnational dimension contributes to a decompartmentalization of the public space (see above, Section 13.3.3), these participatory mechanisms tend to compensate, to some extent, for one of the weaknesses of the Union's representative system with regard to at least one of the principles governing 'representative government', which is to be accountable during elections and, therefore, responsive to the citizens' preferences.[87] Despite institutional arrangements and the strengthening of the political link between the Commission and the Parliament, the system is still unable to establish a link between the outcome of European Parliament elections and the choice of those who govern and the adopted policies. It

[85] See the European Parliament legislative resolution of 3 May 2022, fn. 73.

[86] See Arts. 10 and 13 of the proposal for a Council Regulation on the election of the members of the European Parliament, fn. 73.

[87] Manin, *Principes du gouvernement représentatif*, fn. 5, pp. 223–224.

therefore offers voters little opportunity to 'punish representatives in the polls'.[88] However, these participatory mechanisms giving voice to sectional interests remain confined to a complementary or even secondary role in relation to parliamentary political representation at the European level. The clear mistrust of these participatory mechanisms probably stems from the fact that parliamentary representation at the European level remains recent and fragile, so that the addition of these mechanisms – which potentially challenge majority choice – is perceived as posing a risk of further weakening representation.

As for social partners, negotiation may lead to the adoption of European legislation on social matters. The Single European Act opened the possibility that European social dialogue[89] could lead to the adoption of social rules by means of an agreement,[90] a possibility that was consolidated by subsequent revisions of the founding Treaties and is now regulated by Articles 154 and 155 TFEU. Several directives, relating for instance to working hours or safety at work, have been adopted following trade union negotiations at the European level, giving rise to a form of European social democracy.[91] At first, such a procedure was widely promoted, and the jurisprudence even considered it to be an element of 'the principle of democracy, on which the Union is founded' because it ensured that, in the absence of participation by the European Parliament in the process of adopting a legislative act, 'the participation of the people in that process be otherwise assured'.[92] Social democracy was at that time considered an *equivalent* to parliamentary democracy. Later, however, the social dialogue mechanism not only ran out of steam and

88 See, among others, Joseph H. H. Weiler, 'European Democracy and its Critics: Polity and System', in Joseph H. H. Weiler, *The Constitution of Europe* (Cambridge: Cambridge University Press, 1999), pp. 264–284, p. 264; Andreas Føllesdal and Simon Hix, 'Why There is a Democratic Deficit in the EU: A Response to Majone and Moravscik' (2006) 44(3) *JCMS: Journal of Common Market Studies* 533–562; Dominique Ritleng, 'L'Union européenne, un système démocratique, un vide politique' (2019) 2 *Titre VII – Les Nouveaux Cahiers du Conseil constitutionnel* 2–10.

89 Which encompasses the consultation, information, and negotiation procedures between the European social partners. See Emmanuelle Mazuyer, 'Retour sur l'âge d'or du dialogue social européen', in *Liber Amicorum en hommage à Pierre Rodière, Droit social international et européen en mouvement* (Paris: LGDJ, 2019), pp. 287–296, p. 269.

90 See Art. 118 B TEC introduced by the Single European Act, fn. 25: '[t]he Commission shall endeavour to develop the dialogue between management and labour at European level which could, if the two sides consider it desirable, lead to relations based on agreement'.

91 Dominique Ritleng, 'La démocratie européenne par la démocratie sociale (De l'actualité de la pensée de Marx)', in Éric Carpano and Gaëlle Marti (eds.), *Démocratie et marché dans l'Union européenne* (Brussels: Bruylant, 2021), pp. 445–465.

92 CJEU, *UEAPME v. Council* (Case T-135/96) EU:T:1998:128 [1998] ECR II-02335, 17 June 1998, para. 89.

struggled to produce new texts, but it was not viewed as triggering any obligation for the Commission to legislatively implement an agreement negotiated by the European social partners.[93] This institution, whose democratic legitimacy is only indirect, has a right of veto for the sake of protecting its initiative power, which allows it to define the general European interest independently. Admittedly, if the European social agreement had a greater scope, the social partners would have been granted a right to undertake a European legislative initiative, which, for the moment, is not granted to the European Parliament itself.[94] The restriction of the weight of social democracy thus seems justified by the weakness of European parliamentary democracy, which it was supposed to complement, or even compensate for.

The same dilemma applies to the new European citizens' initiative procedure provided in Article 11(4) TEU. On the one hand, this form of participatory democracy at the European level is supposed to bring the Union's institutions closer to its citizens, by giving them the opportunity to directly orient European political action. It contributes to the creation of a transnational public space (see above, Section 13.3.3), by stimulating the formation of sectoral demands within European society. This is why the Court of Justice has chosen to develop its potential, by relaxing the material conditions for the admissibility of an initiative,[95] and by obliging the Commission to cooperate more with the initiators.[96] On the other hand, the Court's case law has upheld the procedure's main obstacle, which is to leave the Commission free to decide on the follow-up to be given to a citizens' initiative. The justification for this blocking power lies in the fear of a competition between 'representative' democracy and 'participatory' democracy,[97] as the latter can only '*complement*', and not supplant, the former.[98] As the Court of Justice specifies, the interest of the citizens' initiative procedure remains limited: it is not to impose

[93] CJEU, *European Federation of Public Service Unions (EPSU) v. Commission* (Case C-928/19 P) EU:C:2021:656, 2 September 2021, GC.

[94] 'If management and labour had the power to require the Commission to submit a proposal with a view to having their agreements implemented at EU level, they would be able to exercise much greater influence over the content of legal acts adopted in the social policy field than the Parliament, which is merely informed of the implementation of agreements on the basis of Art. 155(2) TFEU'. See CJEU, *EPSU v. Commission* (Case C-928/19 P) EU:C:2021:38, 20 January 2021, Opinion of Advocate General Pikamäe, para. 76.

[95] CJEU, *Efler and Others v. Commission* (Case T-754/14) EU:T:2017:323, 10 May 2017, para. 42.

[96] CJEU, *Izsák and Dabis v. Commission* (Case C-420/16 P) EU:C:2019:177, 7 March 2019.

[97] Dominique Ritleng, 'L'initiative citoyenne européenne entre démocratie représentative et démocratie participative', in Édouard Dubout, Francesco Martucci and Fabrice Picod (eds.), *L'initiative citoyenne européenne* (Brussels: Bruylant, 2019), pp. 87–103.

[98] CJEU, *Puppinck and Others v. Commission* (Case C-418/18 P) EU:C:2019:1113, 19 December 2019, GC, para. 65 (emphasis added).

a political agenda on the representative institutions, but only 'to initiate debate on policy'.[99] This explains why the European Commission retains its veto. Again, as long as the EU Parliament does not have a right of legislative initiative, there can be no question of recognizing such a right for citizens' associations.[100] This would extend participatory democracy beyond its role of 'complement[ing]'[101] the democratic legitimation of European public authority.

It is difficult to assess the sincerity of the argument of a risk of rivalry between the classic form of political representation and the newer form of citizen participation at the European level.[102] The real fear may be that of creating a way to challenge the actions of the EU institutions. In practice, many European citizens' initiatives call into question the political choices of the majority made by the representative institutions.[103] Yet, a living democracy, one that is truly representative of the diverse aspirations of its society, would probably benefit from taking a better account of dissent and giving it a voice so that it can exert a real influence on its representatives, or else it might reinforce the idea that citizen mobilization only bears fruit at the national level.[104] To integrate protest, it is necessary to be able to respond to it, by organizing the deliberation of society with itself on a European scale.

### 13.4.3 *Representation and Deliberation in Society*

For the first time, a 'Citizens' Conference' was held at the European level in 2021–2022 to outline the prospects for the EU's institutional and political evolution. The participatory mechanism established by the Conference on the Future of Europe was special in that it emphasized its deliberative dimension. This deliberative turn extends to the European level a paradigm that is spreading within national democracies with the ambition of taking better account of what citizens want, but also, and above all, of focusing on the way in which citizens *form* their political will, which must be egalitarian and inclusive. The deliberative process matters as much as its outcome, given that

99 Ibid., para. 70.

100 Ibid., para. 61.

101 In the words of the German Constitutional Court in its judgment on the Treaty of Lisbon, fn. 41, para. 272.

102 On the alleged opposition between democratic representation and democratic participation, see Nadia Urbinati, *Representative Democracy: Principles and Genealogy* (Chicago: University of Chicago Press, 2006).

103 Édouard Dubout and Francesco Martucci, 'L'initiative citoyenne et le sens de la participation dans l'Union européenne', in Dubout *et al.*, fn. 97, pp. 13–39.

104 Balibar, fn. 15, p. 201.

deliberative exchanges are supposed to influence the outcomes, by transforming the initial aspirations of the participants who are guided by both individual and collective reason.[105] This democratic form, which somehow reconnects with the roots of the democratic model, aims to generate 'a new type of representatives'.[106] It is no longer a question of appointing a governing elite, nor of representing sectoral interests, but of deliberating individuals 'randomly chosen, for a short period, as ordinary citizens and for specific and limited tasks'.[107] The figure of the 'citizen-representative' reappears.[108] But since these are 'representatives' without a mandate or popular responsibility, their democratic legitimacy depends above all on the transparency and quality of the deliberative process in which they participate.[109]

Yet, this new paradigm generally presupposes the prior existence of a single or ultimate democratic perimeter, within which the deliberative mechanism is instituted.[110] In addition to the difficulty of organizing deliberations on a 'large scale',[111] in the EU there is also the difficulty of organizing them on a 'double scale'. The initial obstacle of the duality of democratic levels in the EU strikes again. This is why the composition of the Citizens' Conference on the Future of Europe sought to combine the two dimensions of citizenship, national and European. On the one hand, citizens' conferences were organized in parallel at both levels: national and European. In the latter case, four panels of 200 citizens from across the Union were formed by taking into account the geographical origin (nationality and urban/rural environment), gender, age, as well as socio-economic background and education level. This guaranteed a certain form of representativeness, especially for young people (one third of participants were young people aged sixteen to twenty-five). On

105 Bernard Manin, 'Volonté générale ou délibération? Esquisse d'une théorie de la délibération démocratique' (1985) 33 *Le Débat* 72–94; Bernard Manin, 'Un paradigme et ses problèmes', in Bernard Manin and Loïc Blondiaux (eds.), *Le tournant délibératif de la démocratie* (Paris: Presses de Sciences Po, 2021), pp. 9–23; Charlotte Girard, *Délibérer entre égaux. Enquête sur l' idéal démocratique* (Paris: Vrin, 2019).

106 Gordon Gibson, 'Deliberative Democracy and the B.C. Citizens' Assembly', Speech delivered on 23 February 2007, quoted by Yves Sintomer, 'De la démocratie délibérative à la démocratie radicale? Tirage au sort et politique au XXIème siècle' (2019) 23 *Participations* 33–59, at 52.

107 Ibid.

108 Denis Baranger, 'Citoyen-représentant: Une lecture de l'article 6 de la Déclaration des Droits de l'Homme et du Citoyen de 1789' (2023) 29 *Jus politicum* 77–107.

109 See Hélène Landemore, *Open Democracy: Reinventing Popular Rule for the Twenty-First Century* (Princeton: Princeton University Press, 2020).

110 Justine Lacroix, 'Pensons tous ensemble' (2020) *La Vie des idées*. https://laviedesidees.fr/Charles-Girard-Deliberer-entre-egaux-ideal-democratique, last accessed 11 October 2023.

111 Charlotte Girard, 'La démocratie délibérative à grande échelle: des arènes locales à la délibération de tous', in Manin and Blondiaux, fn. 105, pp. 67–96.

the other hand, the final Citizens' Conference, which was responsible for summarizing national and European deliberations and adopting the final recommendations, was composed of eighty citizens from the *European* panels, but also of one citizen from each *national* panel. That is, 107 citizens initially designated by a random drawing, plus the President of the European Youth Forum. A whole series of other representatives still completed this citizens' assembly of 108 people, which gave it a plethoric and hybrid composition, half-deliberative and half-representative.[112] A total of 449 participants adopted forty-nine proposals, which were further divided into more than 300 concrete measures. A digital platform also collected nearly 50,000 contributions to the debate.

It is not easy to measure the real contribution of this type of complex deliberative structure at the European level.[113] Although it lasted for more than two years, it remained largely unknown to public opinion and the national media. From this point of view, it does not seem to have contributed much to the transnationalization of public space.[114] The experience of the Citizens' Conference could, however, pave the way for other forms of transnational deliberation, such as the convening of thematic Citizens' Conferences prior to European legislative work. Moreover, unlike the European citizens' initiative, which was perceived as contesting and competing with parliamentary representation, the experience of the Citizens' Conference seems to be more congruent. It is interesting to note that the Conference came out in favour of strengthening European parliamentarism, notably by proposing to confer a right of legislative initiative on MEPs or to set up transnational European elections (proposal n°38). Supporters of a strengthening of the 'direct' form of democratic representation could thus draw from transnational citizen deliberation a democratic justification for a real overcoming of the national State framework of democracy.[115] On the other hand, if

112 It also included one hundred eight MEPs, one hundred eight national parliamentarians, fifty-four representatives of the Council, three representatives of the European Commission, eighteen representatives of the Committee of the Regions, eighteen representatives of the Economic and Social Committee, six elected representatives from regional authorities, six elected representatives from local authorities, twelve representatives of the social partners, and, finally, eight representatives of civil society.

113 Compare Céline Spector, 'La Conférence sur l'Avenir de l'Europe: un exercice démocratique?' (2021) 3 *Revue des Affaires européennes* 463–471, with Alberto Alemano and Kalypso Nicolaïdis, 'L'Europe puissance citoyenne' (2021) 3 *Revue européenne du droit* 7–17; Sandro Gozi, 'La conférence sur l'avenir de l'Europe. Analyse juridique de la plus grande expérience démocratique du continent' (2022) 1 *Revue du droit de l'Union Européenne* 171–189.

114 Ben Crum, 'EU democracy Beyond Participation: Building an EU Political Space', in Göran von Sydow and Valentin Kreilinger (eds.), *Making EU Representative Democracy Fit for the Future* (Stockholm: SIEPS, 2022), pp. 18–32, p. 22.

115 Costa, 'Des listes transnationales au Parlement européen?', fn. 76.

most of the proposals of the Citizens' Conference were to go unheeded, which is not to be ruled out in the light of national experiences, a new democratic disappointment will then likely arise.

## 13.5 CONCLUSION

Could the new challenge of democratic representativeness, which is to establish within European society more inclusive and deliberative forms of political decision-making, make it possible to overcome the initial obstacle of the constitutive duality of the EU and of the representation of an autonomous European citizenship? As discussed above, the vertical superimposition of democratic representation at the European level requires the horizontal development of other processes of transnational citizen involvement. While the representative form of democracy was conceived in opposition to the more direct forms of democracy, transnational experience rather suggests their complementarity, or even their co-institutive character of a complex citizenship. In other words, the EU is revisiting the concept of political representation in the sense of a confluence of the representative and non-representative forms of democracy.

Does this extension of the framework present a danger for national democracy? It seems unlikely to us that, in the historical and political context of Europe, the empowerment and diversification of the European dimension of citizenship will weaken national political citizenship to the point of tipping over into a form of European Nation-State that would dissolve it. On the contrary, the transnationalization of a new common public space could promote the democratization of European political regimes. By opening new procedures for election, participation, or deliberation, the construction of a European democratic area promotes a broader and deeper discussion of common political issues within society, in order to respond to common problems.

But are the social and cultural conditions met for such a transnational discussion of European political issues to take place serenely? The new challenge facing political citizenship in the Union is rather that of the axiological background in which it unfolds. Is democracy only procedural, or also substantive? In other words, does European democratic representation presuppose a minimum prior agreement on common values, or is it, on the contrary, the condition for overcoming the inevitable conflicts when time comes to give them a tangible content? Another debate emerges on what the democratic ideal *represents* in the minds of European citizens.

# 14

# Extending the Sphere of Deliberation in Universal International Organizations: An Alternative to the Elusive Democratic Representation in/by International Organizations

Évelyne Lagrange

'Extend the sphere . . .'

James Madison,
The Federalist no. 10, 1787

## 14.1 INTRODUCTION

International organizations (IOs), in the sense here of interstate organizations, stand out amid the madding crowd of international institutions.[1] They are formed at the will of States, possibly in competition with existing IOs, and personify the collectivity of the Member States.[2] Their autonomy is recognized and protected de jure, although de facto it is only relative insofar as they remain dependent on their Member States institutionally (decision-making power rests with Member States in their principal organs), functionally (their powers do not usually extend to the enforcement of their acts and policies), and financially (their own resources being limited). In other words, IOs have a separate existence from their Member States, but Member States have rights collectively over them and individually within them (rights of representation, voting rights, participation in the procedure for amending the constituent instrument, etc.) as well as obligations towards them.

Translation established with the help of Christopher Sutcliff.

[1] See Évelyne Lagrange, 'La catégorie "organisations internationales"', in Évelyne Lagrange and Jean-Marc Sorel (eds.), *Droit des organisations internationales* (Paris: LGDJ, 2013), pp. 35–70, pp. 54–59.

[2] Évelyne Lagrange, *La représentation institutionnelle dans l'ordre international: Une contribution à la théorie de la personnalité morale des organisations internationales* (The Hague: Kluwer Law International, 2002), p. 258.

As public bodies of a special kind, IOs remain essential components of internationalized governance despite the surge in informal modes of cooperation that compete with or subordinate them. Neither their 'antiquity' nor the degree of formalization of their activities spare IOs from criticism. On the contrary, they are reputed to suffer from a deficit of legitimacy or democratic legitimacy, which supposedly reflects poorly on their Member States – and on internationalized governance as a whole. Delegitimization 'by ricochet' results from the fact that the exercise of State power and the conduct of public policy are 'embedded'[3] in internationalized governance and depend, in varying extents, on ex ante or ex post prescriptions from IOs, which are channelled through a wide range of instruments; with the transfer of power to IOs that lack mechanisms of representation or participation of peoples equivalent to those found in democratic States,[4] democratic legitimacy is supposedly diluted in the internationalization of the exercise of power. This widely shared diagnosis needs to be addressed before proposals for institutional reform are considered.

### 14.1.1 *A Look Back at the Crisis of IO Legitimacy*

The recurring theme, in legal doctrine, of the deficit or crisis of legitimacy of IOs[5] calls for certain clarifications and nuances to unveil possible biases.

While normative legitimacy cannot readily be disentangled from the sociological legitimacy of institutions,[6] a first bias – of approximation (or exaggeration) – is detectable in the perception by scholars of a widespread crisis of legitimacy of IOs. When subjected to closer scrutiny, sociological surveys

[3] Tine Handieder and Bernhard Zangl, 'The Embedded State. The New Division of Labor in the Provision of Governance Function', in Stephan Leibfried, Evelyne Huber, Matthew Lange, Jonah D. Levy and John D. Stephens (eds.), *The Oxford Handbook of Transformations of the State* (Oxford: Oxford University Press, 2015), pp. 253–268.

[4] States whose form of government guarantees that power is exercised for, by and under the control of the people, through their direct participation or through their freely appointed representatives, while respecting pluralism (making alternation possible), fundamental human rights and the rights of minorities, under the supervision of independent authorities.

[5] See e.g. Laurence Dubin and Marie-Clotilde Runavot, 'Représentation, efficacité, légitimité: des organisations internationales en crise?', in Lagrange and Sorel, fn. 1, pp. 77–103; Emanuel Castellarin, Évelyne Lagrange and Paolo Palchetti (coord.), *White Paper on Global Governance / Multilateralism* (Paris: ILA, 2022); Samantha Besson, 'Democratic Representation within International Organizations: From International Good Governance to International Good Government' (2022) 19(4) *International Organizations Law Review* 489–527; Besson and Martí, Chapter 12 in this volume.

[6] Dominik Zaum, 'Legitimacy', in Jacob Katz Cogan, Ian Hurd and Ian Johnstone (eds.), *The Oxford Handbook of International Organizations* (Oxford: Oxford University Press, 2016), pp. 1107–1125. The normative standard varies with periods and communities, and beliefs evolve with the normative standard to which institutions refer.

show that the crisis of confidence in or legitimacy of IOs is not as deep-rooted as is suggested;[7] it could have its roots far from the institutional structures of IOs, in the degree of intersubjective trust that prevails in a society,[8] or in IOs' incapacity to tackle the concrete problems facing populations; and, finally, it does not generate a particularly strong demand for the democratization of IOs,[9] at least in the sense of the institution or 're-institution of IOs'[10] by the people or peoples they supposedly represent or of making IOs more representative of Member States and infra-State constituencies.

Dramatization can also result from the evaluation of IOs' legitimacy deficit in terms of normative standards that are not firmly enshrined in positive law, even though they may be there in outline. This is particularly true of the lack of democratic legitimacy attributed to IOs. This grievance is all the more serious given that the real power of IOs, understood here in the Foucauldian sense of their capacity to exert an action on the actions of others, far exceeds their formal power (IOs' power to prescribe and condition public policies exceeds, for example, the decision-making power attributed to them by their constituent treaty). While a principle subjecting IOs to a requirement of direct or even indirect democratic legitimization would contain an obvious promise of emancipation for peoples and individuals in relation to the inter-statism still prevalent in international society, its existence in positive law remains dubious. Even if the principle of democratic legitimacy could be invoked against their members, which is far from certain, most IOs have been deliberately instituted and have persevered in being on the basis of an exclusively

7 See especially Edelman Trust, 'Edelman Trust Barometer 2022' (2022), pp. 47–48. www.edelman.com/trust/2022-trust-barometer, last accessed 15 September 2023; James Bell, Jacob Poushter, Moira Fagan, Nicholas Kent and J. J. Moncus, 'International Cooperation Welcomed Across 14 Advances Economies' (2020) *Pew Research Center*. www.pewresearch.org/global/2020/09/21/international-cooperation-welcomed-across-14-advanced-economies/, last accessed 15 September 2023.

8 Lisa Maria Dellmuth and Jonas Tallberg, 'Why National and International Legitimacy Are Linked: Social Trust as an Antecedent Factor' (2020) 15 *The Review of International Organizations* 311–337.

9 Jan Aart Scholte, Soetkin Verhaegen and Jonas Tallberg, 'Elite Attitudes and the Future of Global Governance' (2021) 97(3) *International Affairs* 861–886. This study measures the expectations of elites (governmental and non-governmental) in a panel of six countries (including three BRICS), which are rather high with regard to 'democracy', in IOs, albeit reduced to transparency, and rather low with regard to their contribution to the democratization of states compared to their capacity to develop solutions to problems. This finding is to be treated with caution, given the variations in the concept of 'democracy'.

10 Samantha Besson, 'We the Peoples of the United Nations: From Single Separate Instituent Powers to Multiple Nested Instituted Publics', in Peter Niesen, Marcus Patberg and Lucia Robinelli (eds.), *The Oxford Handbook of Constituent Power* (Oxford: Oxford University Press, 2026), pp. 531–544.

governmental representation of States – and, through them only, of peoples – without regard to the democratic form of State government. This could correspond to a *lex specialis*.

Focusing on the legitimacy of IOs considered in isolation is another possible bias. Since IOs rarely have the full power to adopt, impose, and implement norms (or policies), the legitimacy of this whole process can only vary with two factors: the balance achieved between international and national bodies and the interplay of the principles of legitimacy operating within the IO and in the Member States. A growing 'democratic discontinuity'[11] can undoubtedly be observed between the real seat of decision-making, shifted outside the State, increasingly distant from its original consent and less and less controlled by the people or their elected representatives, and the space of democratic legitimization of power, enclosed within States. This is not to say that the State should be idealized as the ultimate instance of true democratic legitimization. On the one hand, national decision-making procedures, unless specially prescribed (e.g. in the form of an obligation to carry out an impact assessment), are not designed to take into consideration the voices of other States and populations affected by instruments or public policy subject to validation by the people or their representatives. Conversely, the detour via IOs and submission to majority rule in IOs have the advantage of forcing, *to a certain extent*, national bodies to take into consideration points of view other than strictly national interests or the interests of the most powerful groups at national level.[12] On the other hand, while certain questions of general interest can be decided within the framework of the Nation-State, and while certain interdependencies are reversible, others are irreducible, notably in environmental and economic matters (barring a sudden disruption in globalization). The leeway that the people or their representatives give themselves is sometimes illusory, and reactions to unreasonable displays of unilateralism (perhaps legitimized by the command of a majority) are often entirely for form. For these reasons, the relevant scale for constructing and assessing processes of political legitimization is probably neither that of the State alone, nor that of IOs alone, but either that, on a meso-scale, of the whole formed by an (or several) IOs and its (their) members, or that, on a micro-scale, of 'transverse institutional arrangements' which associate organs of one or more IOs and organs of Member States in the processes of drawing up and enforcing norms (or policies).[13]

[11] See Besson and Martí, Chapter 12 in this volume.

[12] See Robert O. Keohane, Stephen Macedo and Andrew Moravcsik, 'Democracy-Enhancing Multilateralism' (2009) 63(1) *International Organization* 1–31.

[13] Évelyne Lagrange, 'Introduction générale. Le pouvoir en mouvement' (Seminar at Aix-Marseille-Université, delivered 14 March 2022); '(Re)-légitimer le pouvoir dans les

Finally, beyond the original and therefore distant legitimization of the IO by the consent of the Member States and debatable legitimization by the output (i.e. legitimization that ignores the political principles of the founding and framing of power), the legitimacy deficit may arise from the discrepancy between the purpose for which the IO is set up and its results, or between its stated goals and the interpretation of its mandate by intergovernmental bodies (set up according to principles that do not, or no longer, provide sufficient legitimacy). Leaving aside the risk of projecting onto IOs values, expectations, or ends that are those of the observer rather than of the members or constituencies underpinning the IO, political reform of IOs for the purpose of re-legitimizing these bodies should indeed envisage the revision of their goals, functions, competences, and powers, the determination of the normative constraints weighing on them in view of their nature (notably in terms of the protection of human rights), as well as the redefinition of the conditions under which public affairs (or questions of international public interest) are brought up for discussion, the related instruments deliberated upon, adopted, and monitored, and their authors held to account. Disregarding a critical discussion of IOs' future purposes and obligations is nothing more than a convenient fiction in this academic exercise.

Under the benefit of this delineation, it appears that legal doctrine, whether or not it tends towards a radical critique of the current IO model, relates their legitimacy deficit to several of their institutional features:

(1) *unequal representation* of Member States: the strictly egalitarian representation of States does not, in itself, ensure that less powerful States make their voices effectively heard in IOs; the differentiation of representation rights in IOs (in the form of privileges such as a permanent seat with a veto, or a weighting of votes, or eligibility criteria in restricted bodies) feeds the suspicion that IOs are designed to prolong relations of domination: ultimately, the distortion between, on the one hand, the relatively fixed distribution of seats and votes and, on the other, the current redistribution of power or competences in the international system reproduces and amplifies inequalities rooted in the experience of colonization;

(2) the '*disordered plurality*'[14] that has governed participation in standard-setting processes in IOs since the 1990s: the attempt to make IOs more

instances de gouvernance internationalisées' (Conference at Aix-Marseille Université, delivered 17 October 2022).

14 Besson, 'Democratic Representation Within International Organizations', fn. 5; Besson and Martí, Chapter 12 in this volume.

'democratic' or 'inclusive' promotes a degree of blurring between the formal prerogatives of IO bodies (intergovernmental or otherwise) and the power conquered by non-State actors[15] (NSAs) over certain decision-making processes; conversely, although NSAs are most often confined to the margins of bodies and selected on the basis of ill-defined or dysfunctional procedures or principles, their presence, according to certain institutional and doctrinal discourses, (re-)legitimizes IOs' action;

(3) the monopolization of power within the institution by government representatives or by experts lacking representative status;

(4) the preference for a *logic of depoliticization* of the issues brought before the IO, to the detriment of a logic of confrontation pitting States and, possibly, social groups against each other.[16]

Ultimately, the cumulative effect of these discrepancies would be to widen the gap between the degree of power that certain IOs can exercise over their members and over the living conditions of populations or private individuals, and the legitimacy of that power.

### 14.1.2 *A Look Back at Some Responses to the Legitimacy Deficit Through the Democratization of IOs*

In response, a number of internationalists have come up with ambitious ideas on the updating of constitutionalist approaches to IOs,[17] the advent of a 'cosmopolitical transition law'[18] or the transformation of IOs into democratic institutions.[19] Whether idealistic or explanatory or 'non-ideal' theories, these proposals are centred on the principle of equality among States, peoples, or individuals (depending on the perspective) and on the right to equal participation and consideration of all those who are or could be affected by the

15 Here, by convention, we mean players other than State, interstate or infra-State public authorities.

16 See Marieke Louis and Lucile Maertens, *Why International Organizations Hate Politics: Depoliticizing the World* (London: Routledge, 2021).

17 See Anne Peters, 'Constitutional Theories of International Organisations: Beyond the West' (2021) 20(4) *Chinese Journal of International Law* 649–698.

18 Olivier de Frouville, 'Vers une théorie démocratique du droit international', in Marie-Clotilde Runavot (ed.), *La démocratie appliquée au droit international: de quoi parle-t-on?* (Paris: Pedone, 2018), pp. 143–152.

19 See Anne Peters, 'Dual Democracy', in Jan Klabbers, Anne Peters and Geir Ulfstein, *The Constitutionalization of International Law* (Oxford: Oxford University Press, 2009), pp. 263–341, pp. 268–271; Hilary Charlesworth, 'Democracy and International Law' (Volume 371) *Collected Courses of the Hague Academy of International Law*, 2015, pp. 43–152, pp. 54–64.

exercise of power by these institutions. In a 'non-ideal' theory of 'international democratic representation', Samantha Besson argues that IOs must be 're-instituted' as representatives of peoples, without, however, ousting either States or their representatives. Without waiting for this constitutive moment, the potential of a 'multiple representation system' dominated by the principle of democratic legitimacy should be explored in and through IOs.[20]

While lacking the space here to enter into the detailed discussion that these proposals deserve, it is worth pausing to consider the idea that IOs are subject, or subjectable, to the principle of democratic legitimacy. However alive democracy may be as a practice or an experience,[21] however flexible the concept, in the current state of international law, this principle can only be found, unadulterated, in IOs that follow the model of the club of States or pursue an integration project, provided that their Member States all share the same conception of democracy and make it a condition of (initial or ongoing) participation in the IO.[22] It remains alien to the institutions with a universal vocation (hereafter: universal IOs) on which our attention will focus.[23]

Three considerations drawn from the current state of law and institutions underpin this objection. First, the principle of democratic legitimacy is, at best, emerging in international law at the universal level, and suffers from profound divergences as to what constitutes democracy.[24] Second, its

20 See Samantha Besson and José Luis Martí, 'Legitimate Actors in International Law-Making: Towards a Theory of International Democratic Representation' (2018) 9(3) *Jurisprudence* 504–540; Besson, 'Democratic Representation Within International Organizations', fn. 5; Besson, 'We the Peoples of the United Nations', fn. 10; Besson and Martí, Chapter 12 in this volume.

21 Rosanvallon, Chapter 2 in this volume; Pablo de Greiff, Papia Sengupta and Arthur Giannattasio (coord.), *White Paper on Democracy and International Law in Support of Democracy and the Rule of Law* (Paris: ILA, 2023), part 1.

22 For a definition of integration, see Lagrange and Sorel, fn. 1, pp. 68ff.

23 Or IOs whose functions are deemed to be of interest to all States, in all regions, and whose membership or admission procedures are designed or implemented to limit the exclusionary effect of the conditions imposed on participation in the IO. Organizations of the UN system are a case in point. See Guillaume Devin, *Les organisations internationales. Entre intégration et différenciation* (Malakoff: Armand Colin, 2022), pp. 91ff. This category is used here as an ideal-type. Given the diversity of purposes and institutional structures, a detailed diagnosis and proposals for institutional reform should be tailored to each corresponding IO as a second step. See also, while dismissing a functionalist approach, Besson 'Democratic Representation Within International Organizations', fn. 5.

24 See Sigrid Boysen, 'Remnants of a Constitutional Moment: The Right to Democracy in International Law', in Andreas von Arnauld, Kerstin von der Decken and Mart Susi (eds.), *The Cambridge Handbook on New Human Rights – Recognition, Novelty, Rhetoric* (Cambridge: Cambridge University Press, 2020), pp. 465–480. *Opinio juris* is weakened by the equivocality of concepts and practice, which is inconstant (including on the part of defenders of democracy in the liberal tradition) and not fully representative.

transposition into the sphere of universal IOs can accommodate neither the omnipresence of the State, interposed before peoples, communities, and individuals, nor the presence, in numbers, of non-democratic States.[25] Third, the regime of universal IOs is the product of a 'mix of egalitarian and hierarchical arrangements':[26] equality among States is a founding fiction that makes it possible to institutionalize inequalities among members (and therefore among peoples or individuals); thus, this regime is a hybrid of unequal representation by States and participation by NSAs, that may be viewed as 'drowned' in a multitude of processes and statuses. Unequal representation or participation is thus embedded, to varying degrees, in the very structure of IOs.[27] But after all, it may be said, no political form is set in stone, and it is conceivable that IOs could mutate: from interstate bodies instituted with a view to fulfilling a mandate conferred by States, they could become democratic or cosmopolitical bodies forging decisions in the general interest at the universal level; in a less radical variant of the mutation, they could serve as vectors for a *more* democratic representation of peoples and individuals.[28]

But a 'non-ideal' theory of international democratic representation would then come up against another set of objections, this time drawn from the contemporary political context. Unless we project ourselves towards the utopia of a new kind of IO constituted without or against States, the balance of power and the political mindsets of States are decisive, since institutional reforms and, a fortiori, a redesign or refoundation of IOs presuppose, in one way or another, an agreement among States. However, the current political climate does not seem conducive to the deployment of democratization of IOs or democratic representation in and by IOs.[29] On the one hand, the beneficiaries of the current institutional arrangements, including some of the most

[25] Subject to the practical possibility of organizing it on a universal level (for an attempt, see the Global Assembly (2021) https://globalassembly.org/, last accessed 15 September 2023), direct representation of peoples and individuals in IOs could only be democratic if electors and representatives enjoyed civil and political rights in their own States. If their representation remained assured by the States, the acts of IOs would have no more democratic legitimacy for the whole of their addressees if they were approved by less democratic States 'representing' a majority of the world's population than by more democratic States representing only a minority.

[26] Lora A. Viola, *The Closure of the International System. How Institutions Create Political Equalities and Hierarchies* (Cambridge: Cambridge University Press, 2020), p. 167.

[27] In the sense that IOs cannot simultaneously ensure the egalitarian representation of States, peoples, and individuals.

[28] Thomas M. Franck, *Fairness in International Law and Institutions* (Oxford: Oxford University Press, 1998), pp. 481–484.

[29] But see Besson, 'Democratic Representation Within International Organizations', fn. 5, at 493.

democratic States[30] (sometimes exposed to a phenomenon of democratic backsliding), are a priori more interested in fine-tuning than in the complete dismantling of these arrangements.[31] On the other hand, the challenge to the established institutional order is not led only by States in a position of institutional inferiority or of dependence on IOs, all supposedly eager to continue 'opening up' the IOs until they are fully democratized. It is also vigorously opposed by openly 'illiberal' States (to use an all-encompassing category), whose project is to confine IOs to the representation and protection of States alone, as sovereigns over their territory. The lack of consensus and the paradoxical distribution of votes on a series of United Nations General Assembly (UNGA) resolutions on a Democratic and Equitable International Order (DEIO) reveal the depth of divisions in international society over the very notion of democracy and the desirability of transposing it into the international institutional system.[32] While the DEIO is pledged to '[t]he right to equitable participation of all, without any discrimination, in domestic and global decision-making',[33] some fifty Western and allied States are opposed to it, while the sponsors of the latest resolution (2022) are drawn from among the most illiberal and authoritarian States, including Russia and China, which are engaged in a coordinated effort to subvert concepts borrowed from Western liberal-inspired political rhetoric and redefine the modalities of multilateralism, in a more oligarchic than democratic sense.[34] To attempt to rush this *momentum* by formulating reform proposals based entirely

[30] It is important to think in relative terms, first because the concept of democracy or democratic regime evolves over time, and second because domestic political regimes can change significantly. Existing international rankings are based on (necessarily debatable) complex indicators and tend to reflect these evolutions. See Economist Intelligence Unit, 'Democracy Index 2022. Frontline Democracy and the Battle for Ukraine' (2023); IDEA International, The Global State of Democracy 2022: Forging Social Contracts in a Time of Discontent (Stockholm: International IDEA, 2022).

[31] Viola, fn. 26, p. 172.

[32] These many long-standing divisions are a subject of study in themselves. See Charlesworth, fn. 19, pp. 96ff, 108ff and, with the benefit of a comparative analysis of votes on successive DEIO resolutions and on other resolutions dealing with the various topics (from democracy to disarmament) interwoven in this concept: Daniel Ventura, 'Ordre international démocratique et équitable. Vingt ans d'une aspiration démocratique équitable' (Seminar at the Institute for Peace and Development, delivered 12 April 2023). www.youtube.com/watch?v=1pZonZapRfY, last accessed 15 September 2023.

[33] UNGA Res. 77/215, 'Promotion of a democratic and equitable international order' (15 December 2022) para. 6h. This resolution has been renewed and enriched from year to year since UNGA Res. 55/107, 'Promotion of a democratic and equitable international order' (4 December 2000) in a geopolitical context that has evolved since then.

[34] Achilles Skordas, 'Authoritarian Global Governance? The Russian-Chinese Joint Statement of March 2021' (2021) 81 *Zeitschrift für ausländisches öffentliches Recht und Völkerrecht* 293–302.

on democracy is to run the risk of devitalizing or subverting the concept in the international political arena, or even of creating a formidable 'paradox of consequences' (M. Weber).[35] Indeed, IOs have once again become an arena for ideological confrontations over the foundations and limits of power: States taking political control of them, either as a result of a shift in power, or as a result of a redistribution of seats and votes dictated by the imperative of true equality between States, peoples, or individuals, will be able to impose their conception of 'international democracy' on fragile or hesitant States, and protect themselves against the assertion of a universal and robust principle of democratic legitimacy.

For all these reasons, 'democratic representation' seems to have no explanatory power for the current structure and operation of IOs (which bring together States and NSAs) and a weak justificatory value for upcoming political reforms of universal IOs. Nothing in this observation precludes reflection on the hypothetical conditions for potential or ideal political models that would transcend national frameworks to guarantee public participation whenever issues of international or transnational interest are at stake. There may even be an urgent need to do so,[36] given the widening gap between existing political models – including representative democracy – and the challenges we face, particularly environmental ones. But if, in the current context, reflection tends towards the prescription of remedies to the legitimacy deficit of existing universal IOs,[37] it cannot follow the path of 'democratization' of IOs that remain interstate, largely open to non-democratic States, and permeable to manipulations of the idea of democracy.

### 14.1.3 *Searching for an Alternative Route*

The alternative approach proposed here takes as its starting point today's universal IOs and the under-exploited potential of positive international law, while remaining guided by the necessity to preserve the basic conditions and virtues of democracy in the State.[38] This requires some degree of methodological and political cautiousness. As a preliminary, no-harm rules can be formulated. The first principle is that IO reform should be designed in such

35 Max Weber, *Wirtschaft und Gesellschaft* (Tübingen: Mohr, 1972). See also the warnings by Peters, fn. 17, at 679ff.
36 Évelyne Lagrange, 'Conclusions', in Daniel Erasmus Khan, Évelyne Lagrange, Stefan Oeter and Christian Walter (eds.), *Democracy and Sovereignty. Rethinking the Legitimacy of Public International Law* (Leiden: Brill/Nijhoff, 2023), pp. 430–440, pp. 438–439.
37 Keeping in mind that the loss of legitimacy varies with the specific characteristics of each IO.
38 See fn. 4.

a way that IOs do not become, on the pretext of equal representation (of States, peoples, individuals), the crucible of a political project to annihilate the democratic legitimization of power or of organized resistance either to the crystallization of a general principle of democratic legitimacy in a national or international framework or to a more inclusive deliberation within IOs. The second principle, which is also negative, is that the political reform of IOs should not prejudice the regime of political entities that have a democratic regime or are converting to one, since the democratic dynamic can only be expressed, for the time being, within a national or integrative framework (with the limits pointed out in this chapter). In addition, since we must start from what already exists, one fact stands out: universal IOs do not make their Member States' participation conditional on the existence of an unequivocally defined democratic regime. This absence of democratic conditionality is obviously the sine qua non for maintaining a framework conducive to the indispensable cooperation among, potentially, all States, from the least to the most democratic, that we hold to be indispensable.

Building thereon, we propose to define, positively, principles of political reform of IOs that do not relate their legitimacy either solely to the consent initially given by the State, or to a hypothetical democratic representation in and by IOs. This reflection is rooted in the matrix of IOs: multilateralism. Whatever the degree of concordance between States' political values, multilateralism on a universal scale is defined and justified as a principle articulated to values, a method of cooperation, and a space for apprehending objects from a multitude of sides. In this way, these objects become truly common and can, if need be, give rise to common questions and answers.[39]

However, and this is what this contribution will focus on, as States and their representatives are not in a position on their own to identify objects that transcend their interests and go beyond their borders, the space of international deliberation needs to be restructured to accommodate, in bodies that have yet to be created for the most part, voices other than those of States, in a way that makes it possible to clearly identify the share of each voice in an *enlarged, pluralist multilateral deliberation*. In concrete terms, the challenge is to identify why, and under what conditions, new subsidiary bodies should and could contribute to:

(1) improving the quality of deliberation *within* IOs, by ensuring that voices other than those of States or a few 'stakeholders' are heard;

[39] See Guillaume Devin, 'L'avenir du multilatéralisme', unpublished manuscript, 2021. www.sciencespo.fr/ceri/fr/content/lavenir-du-multilateralisme.html, last accessed 15 September 2023.

(2) creating fora for coordinated discussion of projects (instruments and actions) or of the track record of IOs with related, complementary or overlapping skills (better deliberation *among* IOs);
(3) or promoting accountability (better deliberation *about* IOs).

'Reinvigorating multilateralism', 'constructing international public space' within the IOs themselves,[40] this is the contribution that can be expected, on a theoretical level, from a 'reconceptualization' of the IO's functions (Section 14.2) and, on a more practical level, from the creation of new subsidiary bodies with consultative functions alongside intergovernmental bodies, welcoming participants from civil society and others (referred to here as NSAs) (Section 14.3).

## 14.2 ARGUMENTS FOR A PLURALIST APPROACH TO DELIBERATION WITHIN IOS

The review of the functions of IOs allows us to identify both a metafunction (deliberation) and an organizing principle (pluralism) that can serve as guidelines for a political reform of universal IOs. When the question of representation and representativeness resurfaces, it does so in a secondary role and without the ballast of a democratic requirement that cannot be transposed to this type of IO as it stands.

### 14.2.1 *Rethinking the Functions of IOs and Their Reform*

Much has been written in international law on the limits of a functionalist approach to IOs, weakened by 'blind spots' (the rights of third parties and human rights) and tainted by biases inherent in the principle-agent theory, the fictitious nature of their political neutrality, or the fragmentation of competences.[41] Our intent here is not to fuel a plethoric doctrinal debate that has helped to renew our understanding of IOs, and to reevaluate 'functional necessity'. However, the relevance of these criticisms does not render the notion of function useless in understanding IOs, since they remain institutions established for *certain purposes* or with a view to the fulfilment

[40] These two expressions are borrowed respectively from Marie-Clotilde Runavot, 'Rapport introductif', in Runavot, fn. 18, pp. 7–42, p. 40 and Patrick Jacob, 'Démocratie et participation aux institutions internationales', in Runavot, fn. 18, pp. 127–141, p. 140.

[41] Jan Klabbers, 'The Transformation of International Organizations Law' (2015) 26(1) *European Journal of International Law* 9–82 and subsequent debates in (2015) 26 *European Journal of International Law*.

of *certain functions* which the Member States agree to exercise in common or through them, or to consider as falling solely within the remit of an IO.[42] Goals, functions, competences, and attributed powers can be said to form together the mandate of the IO.[43] If we are willing to accept this constitutive feature of existing IOs, legitimization through functions remains inherent in them. This is not to say, of course, that it is or should be exclusive of any other principle of legitimacy, nor that it is never misused. On the contrary, it can only be maintained under certain conditions.

However diverse universal IOs may be, unless they have strictly operational or jurisdictional functions, they are invested with 'metafunctions' that override their respective mandates. The historical metafunction of this type of IO is undoubtedly to provide a framework for the coexistence of States that are always likely to compete for power, influence, and control over space and resources, a framework that relatively pacifies their relations, at the cost of inequalities in member representation (notably to keep the most powerful States in the institutional system). But there are other metafunctions which today constitute the ultimate *raison d'être* of universal IOs:

(1) opening up spaces for confrontation and *deliberation*;[44]
(2) defending *universalizable values* translated into universal legal principles *and common interests*;
(3) understanding complex *interdependencies* that transcend national borders;
(4) contemplating the *long-term*, since they are disconnected from national political fluctuations which are not themselves synchronous;
(5) and, perhaps, taking into account *planetary boundaries*.[45]

[42] Michel Virally, 'La notion de fonction dans la théorie de l'organisation internationale', in *Mélanges offerts à Charles Rousseau: La Communauté internationale* (Paris: Pedone, 1974), pp. 277–300, p. 277.

[43] Far from being set in stone, it is subject to a process (permanent or intermittent depending on the case) of interpretation, contestation and redefinition, involving the IO's bodies, its Member States and also third parties, particularly the NSAs with an interest in this mandate.

[44] This function of IOs, commonly accepted in law and political science applied to IOs, is sometimes termed 'forum'. See Gérard Cahin, 'La variété des fonctions imparties aux organisations internationales', in Lagrange and Sorel, fn. 1, pp. 679–683; Guillaume Devin, Franck Petiteville and Simon Tordjman (eds.), *L'Assemblée générale des Nations Unies. Là où le monde se parle depuis 75 ans* (Paris: Presses de Sciences Po, 2020); Ian Johnstone, 'Deliberation', in Jan Klabbers (ed.), *The Cambridge Companion to International Organizations Law* (Cambridge: Cambridge University Press, 2022), pp. 173–198.

[45] See Sandrine Maljean-Dubois (ed.), *La définition des limites planétaires. Quelles implications pour le droit et la gouvernance internationale?* (Paris: Pedone, 2023).

The 'forum' function is the 'only utility that is not contested (at least in the plenary bodies)'.[46]

To put it more succinctly, the ultimate function of universal IOs is to constitute the perennial framework for inter- and transnational deliberation on common objects defined by a space, a temporality, and constraints that do not coincide with the coordinates of deliberation in any other public institution at State or sub-State level.

### 14.2.2 *Rethinking the Functional Legitimacy of IOs Based on Their 'Deliberation' Metafunction*

'Deliberation' might seem at odds with the mundane understanding of States' interplay in/through IOs, supposedly based on bargaining (under threat sometimes) and negotiating. Negotiation is defined, negatively, as 'neither the result of an aggregate of individual choices (like voting), nor that of a single decision taken by a hierarchical authority'[47] and, positively, as a mode of 'joint decision-making' among parties who, having divergent interests, seek a mutually acceptable solution.[48] By contrast, deliberation is '[e]xamining, weighing up all the elements of a question with other people, or possibly oneself, before making a decision, in order to reach a conclusion'.[49] Deliberation, then, may or may not lead to the unilateral adoption of an act, which may or may not be legally binding, depending on the features of the law-making, evaluation, or control procedure considered. On closer scrutiny, IOs are indeed the seat of deliberation and voting, both of them permeated by transactions.

It remains to be explained how the concept of deliberation can be transposed to IO theory without contradicting the assertion that democracy is not a relevant concept for universal IOs. It is true that, in political theory, deliberation has often been closely associated with democracy, right up to the construction of a model of 'deliberative democracy' according to which 'the norm is legitimate only if it is based on public reasons resulting from an inclusive and equitable deliberative process in which all citizens can

46 Devin, fn. 23, p. 91.

47 Translated from Delphine Placidi-Frot, 'Les négociations internationales à travers le prisme des sciences sociales', in Franck Petiteville and Delphine Placidi-Frot (eds.), *Négociations internationales* (Paris: Presses de Sciences Po, 2013), pp. 27–76, p. 39.

48 Ibid.

49 Translated from Trésor informatisé de la langue française, 'Délibération'. http://atilf.atilf.fr/, last accessed 15 September 2023.

participate and in which they are led to cooperate freely'.[50] Yet, deliberation is not a concept captive to that of democracy, and the conditions for good or better deliberation do not necessarily exclude all forms of transaction – not even in a deliberative theory of democracy. Deliberation can also be articulated with 'non-deliberative procedures', such as voting. A more comprehensive approach envisions that participants might have both the common good and their 'self-interests' in sight, that they might resort to 'non-coercive forms of negotiation' and, ultimately, that lingering divergences might usher in the 'clarification' and 'structuring' of conflict instead of consensus.[51] Conceived of as an alternative to ideal 'deliberative democracy', this expanded conception of democratic deliberation can in fact be transposed to non-democratic universal IOs. After all, general principles binding members of IOs are not so remote from the prerequisites for 'mutual justification' as to be the 'central task' of deliberation between citizens: 'mutual respect, equality, reciprocity, mutual justification, the search for fairness, and the absence of coercive power'.[52] What is more, IO members have no less interest in arguing than in bargaining.[53]

Finally, decisions by IOs (even if not unanimous) can be considered legitimate through the combination of the legitimacy derived from the State's initial consent, from the IO's metafunction (deliberation) and specific functions, from the respect for its particular mandate (subject to evolving interpretation), and ultimately from the fairness of the deliberative process.

### 14.2.3 *Rethinking Pluralism in IOs Beyond the Requirement for Democratic Representation*

When one focuses on democratic representation in IOs, a series of a priori requirements, in particular equality of participation in decision-making bodies and procedures, or representativeness, are to be imposed on the constitution of IO bodies. But when the purpose is to define the conditions for good or better deliberation in IOs, the yardstick to determine which voices should

[50] Translated from Loïc Blondiaux and Yves Sintomer, 'L'impératif délibératif' (2002) 57 *Politix* 17–35. See also, Bernard Manin, 'Volonté générale ou délibération? Esquisse d'une théorie de la délibération politique' (1985) 33 *Le Débat* 72–94.

[51] Jane Mansbridge, James Bohman, Simon Chambers, David Estlund, Andreas Føllesdal, Archon Fung, Cristina Lafont, Bernard Manin and José Luis Martí, 'The Place of Self-Interest and the Role of Power in Deliberative Democracy' (2010) 18(1) *The Journal of Political Philosophy* 64–100.

[52] Ibid., at 94.

[53] Jon Elster, 'Arguing and Bargaining in Two Constituent Assemblies' (2000) 2 *Journal of Constitutional Law* 345–421, at 405–421.

have which share – given that different perspectives should be confronted but that each is imbued with a potential bias towards unilateralism – is to be found in their metafunctions and specific functions. These conditions prefigure and configure the exercise of each IO's own mandate.

Several avenues can be explored, simultaneously or not, to (re)create or maintain a space for interstate and transnational deliberation that is as open as possible, and therefore pluralist, enabling the settlement of public affairs and the assumption of functions of international public interest (within the mandate of each IO).

Hence, the rebalancing of *State representation* within IOs. While this is impossible to justify in terms of democratic requirements,[54] it can be done, classically, by updating the representation of the collectivity of Member States, per se (egalitarian or specular representation) or with regard to the functions of the IO (a potentially differentiated representation) or, in the perspective defended here, with regard to the need for pluralization of the voices heard in IOs. Institutional arrangements are available, such as the enlargement of restricted bodies to currently under-represented States, the rotation of seats on restricted bodies, or the maintenance of the 'one State one vote' rule in combination with complex decision-making rules that protect all members against automatic majorities or institutionalized unilateralism, and force Member States, to either compromise or display outright opposition. The IO's capacity to take decisions may suffer as a result, but this is the price to pay if the greatest number of States are to retain a genuine interest in international cooperation. In order to re-establish a certain continuity in the legitimization of the power shared between States and IOs, the participation of people's representatives, designated within a national framework, in the definition of positions taken by the Member States in the IO and in the adoption of IO instruments may involve the systematic inclusion of parliamentarians in national delegations, or the creation of (inter)parliamentary bodies.[55] This will not result in democratizing decision-making in IOs since not all representatives of the people will be freely appointed. Nonetheless, deliberation in IOs could thus be more pluralistic.

[54] See Joseph H. H. Weiler, 'The Geology of International Law: Governance, Democracy and Legitimacy' (2004) 64 *Zeitschrift für ausländisches öffentliches Recht und Völkerrecht* 547–562.

[55] See, *mutatis mutandis*, Florian Couveinhes' proposals along these lines, with regard to conventional normative activity, 'Les parlements et les traités internationaux', in Frédérique Coulée (ed.), *Le droit des traités entre États – Pratique et mutations 1969-2019*, unpublished manuscript, Les parlements et les traités internationaux. See also Runavot, Chapter 6 in this volume.

The expansion of multilateral deliberation should not, however, benefit only Member States and their parliaments. Indeed, universal IOs are already marked by the strong presence of NSAs. It was enough for Member States to support or tolerate the opening up of universal IOs to entities other than themselves for multiparty 'representation' or participation to take root. It is not 'democratic' (despite the institutional rhetoric) but could gain in legitimacy and legitimizing force if justified and adjusted to the requirements of better deliberation. This presence should be amplified, but rationalized, for reasons of principle: the object of deliberation in IOs cannot be apprehended solely through the confrontation or a sum of statist points of view because States are themselves subject to limitations arising from their difficulty in projecting themselves into the long-term,[56] in apprehending the negative cross-border externalities of public policies,[57] and, even in the most democratic States, in hearing the plurality of all relevant voices on a subject.

Deliberation institutionalized in the IO can and must therefore *in abstracto* accommodate persons with a representative mandate associated with IO membership, but also experts (subject to robust and controlled rules of independence) without a representative mandate,[58] as well as persons giving voice either to natural entities (with or without legal personality) or making their point of view heard or to groups that find no satisfactory political expression in any State (e.g. refugees or migrants), to peoples without a (universally recognized) State, to marginalized groups, and so on.[59] Deliberation can also be enriched by the ad hoc direct participation of

[56] See Yukio Adachi, 'How is it Possible for Democracies to Effectively Tackle Long-Term Problems?' (2019) 21(1) *Journal of Comparative Policy Analysis: Research and Practice* 116–129.

[57] See Mattias Kumm, 'Sovereignty and the Right to be Left Alone: Subsidiarity, Justice-Sensitive Externalities, and the Proper Domain of the Consent Requirement in International Law' (2016) 79(2) *Law and Contemporary Problems* 239–258.

[58] One of the functions of universal IOs is to produce information, to reduce asymmetries in access to information, or to make expertise available to States with the fewest resources. Epistocratic legitimacy is part of the functional legitimacy for some universal IOs. In times of a resurgence of populism and deliberate dissemination of misinformation, the participation of experts in IO deliberations should be strengthened by (1) promoting the pluralism of expertise, debates among experts, and the contestability of experts and expertise, and (2) dialogue among experts, State representatives, and NSAs. On lessons learned from the IPCC, see Kari De Pryck, 'La voix du climat' (Conference at the Collège de France, delivered 29 March 2023). www.youtube.com/watch?v=NNmpPnBLHOo, last accessed 15 September 2023.

[59] The requirement of 'democratic representation' needlessly complicates the search for an adequate justification (by reference to a people) for mechanisms giving voice to transnational human collectivities with a community of interests but not necessarily of destiny, to collectives that do not operate on the model of democratic representation (like colleges of experts) or to natural (or non-human) entities.

particularly interested categories of people, in the form of petitions or 'pure' or hybrid[60] transnational citizens' conventions. In fact, deliberation can be adapted, according to the functional specificities of each IO in terms of designating the categories of subjects, interests, or perspectives that are granted an institutional role and/or status, and defining the procedural rights of each. The proposal to transform universal IOs from fora in which a 'polylateral diplomacy' with multiple channels or voices already unfolds[61] into restructured and structuring spaces for inter- and transnational deliberation is clearly liberal in inspiration: a quest for greater inclusivity and greater rationality in the product of deliberation is at stake.[62]

Focusing on IOs, a good or better deliberation will be one that:

(1) may lead to varying degrees of *change in positions* initially defined from a necessarily one-sided perspective or on the basis of partial information;
(2) will lead, at best, to a *reasoned outcome*, taking the form of a majority decision or no decision at all, or at least to a '*reasonable dissensus*';[63]
(3) affords *comparison* between the final outcome and the particular positions of each party at each stage, on the one hand, and between the arguments exchanged, on the other.

The concrete determination of the parameters of this space for deliberation takes place by descending from the level of the metafunction to the functions and powers of the IO and the bodies designated to carry them out.

## 14.3 ARGUMENTS FOR A RENEWED INSTITUTIONAL MODEL

Historically, pluralism in deliberation within IOs has been fostered by two main models: the inclusion in State delegations of representatives of non-State interests, as with tripartism at the International Labour Organization (ILO), the extension of which would presuppose a revision of the constituent instruments of IOs; the proliferation of official participation by NSAs in the work or activities but not as members of IO bodies. This participation itself follows two

60 With the participation of experts.

61 Expression taken from Auriane Guilbaud, 'La diplomatie des acteurs non étatiques', in Thierry Balzacq, Frédéric Charillon and Frédéric Ramel (eds.), *Manuel de diplomatie* (Paris: Presses de Sciences Po, 2018), pp. 213–226, who borrows it from Geoffrey Wiseman.

62 See Jean d'Aspremont, 'Do Non-State Actors Strengthen or Weaken International Law. The Story of Liberal Symbiosis', in Heike Krieger, Georg Nolte and Andreas Zimmermann (eds.), *The International Rule of Law: Rise or Decline? Foundational Challenges* (Oxford: Oxford University Press, 2019), pp. 130–143, p. 130.

63 Drawn from Yves Sintomer, 'Délibération et participation: affinité élective ou concepts en tension?' (2011) 1 *Participations* 239–276, at 262.

main patterns: the 'social participation model', which enables them to be involved without voting power in the work and debates of an IO body (sometimes at the cost of their own identity or their power to contest); the 'partnership model', which associates NSAs with the implementation of IO policies, making them IO's auxiliaries.[64] The permanent movement maintained by NSAs masks the limits of these models: the efficiency of NSAs involvement in the work of intergovernmental bodies can be low;[65] the legibility, then contestability, of the game played by these actors and their contributions are cumbersome; the non- or under-representation of the most vulnerable populations, future generations, and natural entities persists.[66] Various biases (capture by profit-seeking actors, instrumentalization by States, over-representation of Western perspectives, categorization of actors, etc.) are likely to distort both the deliberation itself, and the public's perception of it. A third model, sometimes referred to as the 'stakeholder model', is currently being tested with the Committee on World Food Security (CFS) which, in 2009, became a de facto multi-stakeholder body[67] bringing together voting members (States), participants (including NSAs that take part in deliberations but not in voting), and observers. Two mechanisms, one for the civil society sector and the other for the private sector, coordinate the preparation of these groups' contributions to the CFS, with the support of the Food and Agriculture Organization (FAO). A disagreement of a sector with the CFS can occasionally be formalized either on the substance or on the procedure followed.[68] The model is innovative but not yet taken up elsewhere.

[64] For further details, see Olivier Nay, 'Introduction: Le tournant social des organisations internationales: dynamiques d'ouverture et jeux de frontière', in Delphine Lagrange, Marieke Louis and Olivier Nay (eds.), *Le tournant social de l'international: Les organisations internationales face aux sociétés civiles* (Rennes: Presses Universitaires de Rennes, 2021), pp. 11–33.

[65] For an attempt to measure the impact of civil society groups on the texts finally adopted, see Leah Rachel Kimber, 'The Architecture of Exclusion at the United Nations: Analyzing the Inclusion of the Women's Group in the Negotiations of the Sendaï Framework for Disaster Risk Reduction', PhD thesis, University of Geneva, 2020.

[66] The decision to give priority within the CFS to those most affected by food insecurity is a significant development.

[67] Even if its intergovernmental nature is reaffirmed on the occasion of the reform, see FAO, 'Reform of the Committee on World Food Security' (14, 15, and 17 October 2009), CFS:2009/2 Rev.2.

[68] See the studies by Auriane Guilbaud, 'La réforme des organisations internationales de développement par le modèle des parties prenantes. Les effets d'un double mouvement contradictoire sur la contestation internationale' (2022) 126 *Cultures et conflits* 19–40; Jessica Duncan, Nadia Lambek and Priscilla Claeys, 'Le Comité de la sécurité alimentaire mondiale après la réforme', in Antoine Bernard de Raymond and Delphine Thivet (eds.), *Un*

It may sound more promising to limit NSAs participation in IO deliberations to outside bodies or on the basis of informal arrangements, in order to avoid State blockages or promote bottom-up IO reform. On the contrary, there are a number of reasons for renewing the institutional model and structure of universal IOs. First, consideration for the many facets of the issues addressed by IOs should be permanently regulated by institutional law rather than decided on a case-by-case basis by intergovernmental bodies, according to the interests of the moment. Moreover, the involvement of NSAs must be controllable, notably by the public. Finally, the integration of NSAs into the IO's own institutional structure could make it possible to limit the effects of exclusion (or over-representation) and reduce the control exercised either by intergovernmental bodies or by the IO's administrative bodies over 'authorized' NSAs. This proposal may seem paradoxical, given that any further institutionalization of NSAs' roles in the deliberation process would ultimately depend on the consent of the Member States. This does not mean, however, that the definition of new spheres of deliberation within the IO, and the designation of eligible actors, should be left to them in detail. Indeed, if we accept that IOs are 'spaces of struggle' more or less 'detached from the mandates given by States'[69] and that NSAs are already active protagonists, the operation cannot be envisaged without the active participation of the latter.

### 14.3.1 *Reshaping the Institutional Architecture*

Institutional architecture follows basic patterns that spread by isomorphism. The dominant, strictly intergovernmental models are still so powerful that the International Renewable Energy Agency (IRENA) was set up in 2009 without a body designed to accommodate NSAs, despite the sensitivity of its field of competence to actors engaged in the ecological transition.[70] However, the functioning of IOs already depends on the possibility granted to actors other than members to participate in the deliberation process (with the rights that are those of an observer, for example) and on the creation of additional, so-called subsidiary bodies. These bodies may themselves be intergovernmental, but they can also accommodate people with no representative mandate, as is

*monde sans faim. Gouverner la sécurité alimentaire* (Paris: Presses de Sciences Po, 2021), pp. 97–128.

69 Delphine Lagrange, 'Espaces ouverts, pouvoir clos. Une approche sociologique des organisations internationales', in Lagrange *et al.*, fn. 64, pp. 173–182, para. 4.

70 Victor Grandaubert, 'L'agence internationale pour les énergies renouvelables à l'heure de la "guerre des métaux rares"' (2022) 68 *Annuaire Français de Droit International* 496–508.

the case with expert bodies. In this way, they offer a particularly interesting institutional format for remedying, in part, the growing dissociation between the purpose of IOs, which is no longer strictly interstate, and their structure, dominated by intergovernmental bodies with a contested balance.

Designed for one, two, or more of the IO's intergovernmental bodies, and open to actors other than States or IOs (grouped here under the generic name of NSAs) to enhance their deliberation, consultative bodies would be distinct from multi-stakeholder fora, networks, or platforms set up by an IO with the explicit aim of helping it fulfil one of its prime objectives, under the control of the integrated administrative body.[71] Functionally, they would be closer to certain recurring multi-stakeholder fora which, like the Youth Forum of the Economic and Social Council (ECOSOC), can lead to NSAs adopting their own positions.[72] Their institutional status, however, would be that of IO bodies with attributions formally articulated to those of the main bodies.[73] This is an essential point. The UN Permanent Forum on Indigenous Issues created by the ECOSOC in 2000 as a subsidiary organ with representatives of indigenous peoples sitting in their personal capacity as 'independent experts' could inspire further practice.[74]

71 See WHO, 'Terms of Reference of WHO Youth Council' (2021). https://cdn.who.int/media/docs/default-source/youth-engagement/tor_whoyouthcouncil.pdf?sfvrsn=fc962b80_4, last accessed 15 September 2023.

72 The UN presentation of the 2023 edition of this forum refers to the adoption of various types of acts, including an 'informal summary of the proceedings by the President of ECOSOC, a document capturing key messages and findings of the different sessions' and a preparatory document drawn up by organizations representing young people. See ECOSOC, 'ECOSOC Youth Forum 2023'. https://ecosoc.un.org/en/what-we-do/ecosoc-youth-forum/about-youth-forum/ecosoc-youth-forum-2023, last accessed 15 September 2023.

73 Following on from his report *Our Common Agenda* published in 2021, the UN Secretary-General has proposed the transformation of this forum into a subsidiary body with a strengthened, but as yet undefined, mandate under the name United Nations Youth Townhall or Permanent Youth Assembly. See UNGA, 'Guidance Note No. 3: Meaningful participation of young people in policy and decision-making' (23 March 2023), A/77/CRP.1/Add.2, paras. 37, 16.

74 ECOSOC Res. 2000/22, 'Establishment of a Permanent Forum on Indigenous Issues' (28 July 2000); Benedict Kingsbury, 'Indigenous Peoples', in Rüdiger Wolfrum (ed.), *Max Planck Encyclopedia of Public International Law* (Oxford: Oxford University Press, 2006), para. 16. The UNGA also created in June 2023 an Independent Institution on Missing Persons in the Syrian Arab Republic which 'shall have a structural element that ensures the full and meaningful participation and representation of victims, survivors and the families of missing persons in the Syrian Arab Republic in its operationalization and work'. UNGA, 'Independent Institution on Missing Persons in the Syrian Arab Republic' (26 June 2023), A/77/L.79, para. 3. The modalities remain to be determined.

#### 14.3.1.1 Creation of New Subsidiary versus External Bodies

A first method – the creation of new subsidiary bodies – makes it possible to include the expression of non-strictly State interests or perspectives in the IO's institutional structure. A second method – the creation of a body external to the IO – facilitates contributions from NSAs and makes them more visible, without formally integrating them into the IO. The risk is that this may encourage the creation of an autonomous sphere of deliberation with no knock-on effect on deliberation within intergovernmental bodies. In practice, however, as the experience of the Council of Europe shows, the links can be quasi-organic between the interstate structure and the 'external' body.[75]

The most complete scheme is probably to combine the institution of a new subsidiary consultative body open to NSAs and IO support for fora that enable NSAs to structure themselves, in order to determine common positions and designate participants for deliberation within the subsidiary body.

#### 14.3.1.2 Creation of New Consultative Bodies: Closer Scrutiny

The institutional architecture of IOs can easily be expanded to include, alongside the main bodies (or only the intergovernmental, main or subsidiary bodies),[76] new subsidiary bodies resulting from secondary legislation adopted by one, two, or even more bodies of the IO. Created, reformed, or abolished by a simple act of secondary legislation, they are part of the necessary but equivocal 'transformism' of the IO.[77] These bodies may even be common to two IOs (as in the case of the Codex Alimentarius, common to the FAO and World Health Organization (WHO)). This process is commonplace in IO law[78] but the main intergovernmental bodies' creativity is limited by certain rules. Needless to say, subsidiary bodies are subject to various forms of pressure from the main organ if the balance of power allows.[79]

The power to create subsidiary bodies is often provided for in the constitution, either generally or for the benefit of certain IO bodies. Otherwise, the

75 Birte Wassenberg, 'La place des ONG au Conseil de l'Europe de 1952 à nos jours' (2012) 152 *Relations internationales* 77–92.

76 Only this hypothesis will be considered here.

77 Laurence Burgorgue-Larsen, 'La structure institutionnelle de l'organisation internationale', in Lagrange and Sorel, fn. 1, pp. 375–401.

78 See Laurence Boisson de Chazournes and Vassilis Pergantis, 'A Legal Framework on Internal Matters. Please Mind the Gap', in Klabbers, fn. 44, pp. 113–118.

79 On subsidiary bodies of the UNGA and the UNSC, see Pieter Jan Kuijper, 'Delegation and International Organizations' (Volume 426) *Collected Courses of the Hague Academy of International Law*, 2022, pp. 9–240, pp. 109ff, 152ff.

theory of implied powers can justify their creation on the fundamental proviso that they are necessary for the fulfilment of the functions of the IO and the principal organ, as interpreted in the light of generally accepted IO practice.

The second condition for a main organ to be able to appoint one or more subsidiary bodies without dispute is that the former does not delegate to the latter the exercise of powers that the constituent instrument would require it to exercise itself. This does not prevent the main body from creating, for the performance of its own functions, a body with a composition quite different from its own and appropriate to the exercise of the powers assigned to it. This may include, if necessary, a body of experts, or even a jurisdictional body whose acts the intergovernmental body cannot reverse, and which it could not have adopted itself. Apart from this very special case, 'not a complete delegation by which the principal organs would be definitively divested, but rather a kind of provisional and precarious delegation, the exercise of the delegated powers being subject to a permanent right of revision by the principal organ'.[80] The main bodies would probably not be able to share with or delegate to subsidiary bodies the power to *decide* on matters falling within their own prerogatives and subject to the voting rules defined by the constituent instrument (unless the composition and operating rules of the body reproduces those of the main body, or allows a reversion to them). In other words, the power to adopt binding secondary legislation could not be delegated to a subsidiary body made up of non-State delegates. At a minimum, if such an instrument were adopted by a majority of the main organ, its own regularity could be challenged. If not, it is possible that, in time, such an innovation should become accepted practice, but it is more likely that, fairly quickly, there will be Member States of the main intergovernmental body to propose reversing the acts of the subsidiary body, notwithstanding the terms of the institutive resolution, and a (qualified) majority to follow them.[81] As the law and practice stand, the main intergovernmental bodies can associate themselves with subsidiary bodies intended to exercise, *under their control*, a power of recommendation or decision, *or* with bodies whose *opinion* they would *merely consult*, it being up to the main organs to draw the consequences from this in the exercise of their own normative power. In this way, the IO and its members would retain political responsibility for their actions and decisions. Still, implied powers may develop overtime.

[80] Translated from Paul Reuter, 'Les organes subsidiaires des organisations internationales', in *Hommage d'une génération de juristes au Président Basdevant* (Paris: Pedone, 1960), pp. 415–440, p. 433.

[81] Kuijper, fn. 79, pp. 80ff.

### 14.3.1.3 Expected Functional Benefits

In theory, institutionalizing the participation of NSAs in the deliberations of the IO offers a series of advantages compared to contemporary practice, from the increased legibility of debates to the production of either common positions or statements of disagreement, not to mention the (at least partial) control of the agenda by the members of the subsidiary body, or the possibility of hearing whistle-blowers or independent experts, or receiving petitions.

For NSAs, the creation of such bodies would represent a substantial enhancement of their institutional status. They are currently confined to a variable consultative status with intergovernmental bodies that may have no decision-making powers[82] or to sitting in a council attached to the integrated administrative body with sometimes very vague remits.[83] Instead of or in addition to these positions, they could join subsidiary bodies set up under the main bodies (possibly the ones endowed with extensive normative powers) and intended to enlarge the sphere of deliberation within the IO. The public at large would be able to follow these deliberations, within the limits of the body's attributions, and enjoy ready access to the minutes and the output of their work.

From the point of view of the operation of IOs, where decision-making power remains with intergovernmental bodies, a fourfold contribution could be expected.

First, they could contribute *to improving deliberation in intergovernmental bodies*, provided that a series of procedural rules, under IO secondary legislation, rigorously articulate the different circles of deliberation. These rules could provide for the possibility or obligation for the main organ (or another organ) to refer a request for an opinion to the subsidiary organ, which would then be incorporated into the material for its own deliberation, or for the subsidiary organ to request the inclusion of a recommendation on the principal organ's agenda and the right to obtain a response, or even an obligation for the principal organ to decide on an opinion or recommendation presented by the subsidiary organ (while retaining its freedom of decision). A modification of the main body's rules of procedure would be necessary for these purposes, which raises no legal difficulty as long as they are compatible with *the*

[82] See Saïda El Boudouhi, 'Les qualités autres que celle(s) de membre', in Lagrange and Sorel, fn. 1, pp. 350–371, p. 360.

[83] See Julian A. Hettihewa, 'Looking Behind the UN Youth Office: Considering Structural Limitations of Youth Participation after the Party' (2022) *EJIL:Talk!* www.ejiltalk.org/looking-behind-the-un-youth-office-considering-structural-limitations-of-youth-participation-after-the-party/, last accessed 15 September 2023.

*provisions of the constituent treaty and do not undermine its normative power* (see above, Section 14.1.1). The public could thus understand more clearly which proposals or opinions emanating from NSAs sitting on the subsidiary body have been opposed, successfully or unsuccessfully, by (certain) States within the main body, or which divisions have prevented the adoption of an opinion or recommendation within the subsidiary body.

Second, these subsidiary consultative bodies could contribute *to enriching the deliberations of national legal systems*, taking into account the interests of other populations or expertise without equivalent in the State, provided that these consultative bodies include delegations of national parliamentarians (in necessarily limited numbers) or are duly articulated with (inter)parliamentary bodies, or see their opinions transmitted to national parliaments for discussion.

Third, *these bodies could deliberate on the operation or achievements of the international organization* or, as the case may be, of one of its bodies. There is nothing, other than political reluctance, to prevent endowing a subsidiary consultative body with the power to open a debate and, possibly, formulate an opinion on the achievements or future orientations of the IO or one of its bodies – in conjunction, where appropriate, with an interparliamentary body and after having heard from the heads of integrated bodies, presidents, or members of the office of the presidency of intergovernmental bodies. Going a step further, the consultative body could be empowered to organize annual Q&A sessions with the presidency of the principal body. More or less formalized practices already involve NSAs in exchanges with candidates for the position of head of the secretariat in certain IOs, or with the secretariat on the IO's achievements and prospects. They could be institutionalized. The value of this power of control obviously depends in part on the composition of the advisory body.

Fourth, these bodies could contribute to *better coordination between IOs through deliberation*. It is widely acknowledged that there is a division of competences between universal IOs, with no formal hierarchy and no satisfactory coordination, thus opening up the possibility for those IOs with the greatest real power, because of their dispute settlement system or the financing capacities made available to their Member States, to ignore, thwart, or ruin the mandate of other IOs. The consultative subsidiary bodies envisaged here could contribute to confronting the Member States of these IOs with contradictions between IO mandates or in the positions taken by their representatives of the same State in different IOs, a fortiori if the subsidiary bodies were common to two IOs.

No sphere falling within the competence of an IO can be excluded a priori from the benefits expected from an extended deliberation on the pretext that it would be either too political, or too technical: the objects of deliberation in IOs always ultimately concern human communities. It is likely, however, that the creation of subsidiary consultative bodies cannot be generalized to all intergovernmental bodies, or even in every IO. In some cases, the strict delimitation of these bodies' mandates, excluding them from expressing opinions on specific situations (of States or other subjects), will be the condition for their political acceptability. In other cases, it might prove impossible to mobilize people capable of voicing the plurality of non-State perspectives in multiple fora imposing a timetable and a certain formalism. But in any case, the possibility for NSAs to act on the margins of the bodies or from the outside on the IO's work should be preserved. This is a sine qua non if the institutionalization of their contribution to deliberation is not to become a pretext for re-closing interstate organizations in on themselves.

### 14.3.2 *Participation of Non-State Actors in Consultative Subsidiary Bodies*

Defining rules for participation is key for adequately enlarging and improving deliberation within IOs.

#### 14.3.2.1 Homogeneous or Multiparty Bodies

Given that the aim is neither to guarantee the perfect representativeness of the IO (by piercing the screen of the collectivity of Member States), nor to democratize its operation, but to improve the conditions of deliberation, the rules governing the composition of the new subsidiary bodies can be guided, primarily, by a concern to redress the biases in interstate deliberation that would be identified as *the most detrimental to the fulfilment of the IO's mandate*, or, to put it positively, to ensure that voices are distinctly heard, the consideration of which would enable the IO to best fulfil its primary functions.

There are two main options:

(1) to give precedence to one class of interests or non-State perspectives that would otherwise be marginalized or would necessarily have to be heard by the intergovernmental body, or;
(2) to bring together diverse interests and perspectives.

These bodies can therefore be of homogeneous or multiparty composition, with many variations.

In theory at least, and depending on the IO's functions, it is conceivable that the consultative subsidiary body could only accommodate people whose mandate would be either to make the voice of populations from the South heard, if they are the ultimate recipients (with interests or expectations that may vary) of the instruments, projects, or policies under discussion, or to highlight the stakes, for a natural entity or ecosystem, of the discussions underway. In practice, for reasons relating to the need to invigorate the feeling of international solidarity, the desire to organize the confrontation of radically antagonistic points of view, or the positions already acquired with IOs by many NSAs who will become players in the creation of such bodies,[84] multiparty bodies should often be preferred.

This formula could see the coexistence of State representatives who volunteer or are designated for this purpose by an intergovernmental body (and/or State representatives designated for this purpose by national parliaments and/or representatives of local and regional authorities) with NSA delegates. Alternatively, a multiparty body could host solely delegates from civil society or the private for-profit sector and/or persons in charge of the interests of natural entities and/or persons designated for their scientific expertise and/or representatives of non-State or transnational communities (indigenous peoples, refugees, women, etc.).

The choice of a combination will depend both on the functions of the IO and of the subsidiary body, and on a balance being struck between the interest of multiplying perspectives and the constraints inherent in the time available for debate within an IO. The aim could be for instance to bring together different types of expertise (e.g. scientific and citizen), or to make the voice of future generations heard, by bringing together scientists working on planetary boundaries and representatives of younger generations, and so on.

#### 14.3.2.2 NSA Eligibility and Appointment Methods: The Role of Self-organization

The definition of eligibility criteria is a sensitive issue. Functionalist logic, in relation to the deliberative function of IOs, provides arguments for excluding a priori interest classes that are already over-represented or benefit from other channels for making their voices heard. Here, we are of course thinking primarily of multinational corporations, or even non-profit players who already occupy a dominant position, such as certain foundations. Whatever the choice made in this respect, structuring the participation of NSAs in subsidiary consultative bodies could aim for the reproduction of civil society in all its diversity, the due representation of all those affected by or subject to

84 See the CFS precedent described by Guilbaud, fn. 68.

the IO (or the most affected, the most directly subject, etc.),[85] the confrontation between representatives of different pre-identified classes of interests, or the presence of different perspectives, irreducible to homogeneous and pre-identifiable interests. The introduction of thematic or regional quotas,[86] could be envisaged, if necessary to make heard the voices that State representatives fail to convey and that a given IO needs to hear to fulfil its functions.

Formally, it is up to the main body to adopt the by-laws of its subsidiary bodies, and to lay down the rules governing their composition. Once the main principles of eligibility (which are also necessarily principles of exclusion) have been laid down, there is nothing to prevent the body from making room for the self-organization of NSAs called upon to sit on it in one capacity or another.[87] In so doing, it would reduce the well-known risk of accreditation procedures being used to discipline NSAs, either as a group or one by one, or to admit organizations that are no more than a front for States. By opting to grant NSAs relative freedom in the modalities and the choice of those among them who will sit on the consultative body, the IO would give an additional chance to a transnational political space to structure itself – in line with the objectives it pursues. This experiment is already underway with the nine major groups identified since 1992 in the United Nations system for their contribution to the theme of sustainable development.[88] By design, the freedom given to NSAs should be exercised within the limits set by the statutes and under the ultimate control of the main body, according to the modalities it has itself defined in the exercise of its power of self-organization.

#### 14.3.2.3 Institutional Status and Statutory Protection

These subsidiary advisory bodies will need premises, administrative support, interpreters, and so on, but also funds to facilitate the participation of some

85 See Jochen von Bernstorff, 'Authority Monism in International Organisation. A Historical Sketch', in Joana Mendes and Ingo Venzke (eds.), *Allocating of Authority: Who Should Do What in European and International Law?* (Oxford: Bloomsbury, 2018), pp. 99–114; Jochen von Bernstorff, 'New Responses to the Legitimacy Crisis of International Institutions: The Role of "Civil Society" and the Rise of the Principle of Participation of the "Most Affected" in International Institutional Law' (2021) 32(1) *European Journal of International Law* 125–157.

86 Besson, 'Democratic Representation Within International Organizations', fn. 5, at 519.

87 Leaving it up to them to decide whether mandates should be 'mimetic' or 'altruistic', e.g. Besson and Martí, Chapter 12 in this volume.

88 See Sarah Jamal, 'Les 10 ans de l'Assemblée des Nations Unies pour l'environnement: un organe à composition universelle en droit de l'environnement' (2022) 68 *Annuaire Français de Droit International* 453–465.

NSAs. The financing of bodies whose creation falls within the scope of the IO's activities is based on the organization's budget. It is not hard to imagine that some Member States might object to financing via compulsory contributions, and argue for financing at least part of the costs through voluntary contributions. All considerations of IO budgetary law aside, the latter type of funding entails obvious risks of bias and instability, and should be rigorously supervised. The quality of the work produced by these bodies will depend, in part, on the amount of funding they receive from the IO budget. It is a safe bet that the managerial logic at work in IOs, sometimes used as a front for political reluctance or resistance, will impose limits on sessions, speaking time, and so on, here as elsewhere. Preserving them is a matter of balance of power.

The status of members of the consultative subsidiary body is another delicate issue. Unlike observers or beneficiaries of consultative status, who act at their own expense (except in the case of financial support from the IO for certain categories of them), under their own responsibility and with very limited privileges, the members of these consultative bodies would sit on them in the interests of the organization *lato sensu*, to enable it to perform its functions to the best of its ability. As members of an IO body without being members of the organization, contributing to the exercise of its functions without being its agents, they could benefit from a status inspired by that of independent experts mandated by the IO. All their mission expenses could then be covered by the IO which would not be held responsible for their actions, since they would act for the IO without its acting through them. Finally, they would have to be granted privileges (e.g. access to the territory of the host State of the advisory body) and immunities: immunity from arrest for the duration of the mission; immunity from jurisdiction for acts and writings carried out in the context of their participation in the work of this body.[89] This guarantee would be essential to the freedom of expression of the members of these bodies, itself indispensable to improving deliberation in the IO. Taking functionalist logic to its logical conclusion, this immunity would have to be made systematically enforceable against States of nationality and residence. The context of democratic backsliding and resurgent authoritarianism that forms the backdrop to these proposals obviously argues in favour of greater protection for the members of the consultative body, and therefore, of its role.

[89] See, by way of inspiration, Art. VI of the Convention on the Privileges and Immunities of the United Nations, 1 UNTS 4 (adopted 13 February 1946, entered into force 17 September 1946).

## 14.4 CONCLUSION

The proposed approach is modest, as it does not presuppose the search for agreement between States on a concept of democracy, which could ultimately be weakened: it simply involves going back to the primordial function of institutionalized multilateralism, and adding to the intergovernmental bodies holding the bulk of the power in the new IO bodies endowed with consultative power and formally integrated into the deliberation in the IO. The aim is to build up, through the reasoned consideration of varied arguments, an international, transnational, transgenerational, cross-border perspective through deliberation and to articulate shared and individual, local, and global perspectives.

This proposal may be politically feasible if the Western States, which (still) occupy a dominant position in IOs shaped by their own hands – and which are (still) among the most democratic in the sense of international rankings – understand that it is in their interest to open up universal IOs to a certain extent, at the same time as the States that are under-represented in them, particularly those from the South, realize that their best interests lie in a combination of correcting imbalances in State representation and further institutionalizing the involvement of NSAs in all their diversity – *and therefore of NSAs from the South* – in the interpretation and fulfilment of the IO's mandate.[90]

Some diffuse 'democratization' effects might be observed here and there: truly pluralist deliberation in universal IOs would contribute not only to keeping alive the idea of international and transnational solidarity, but also to preserving the chances of progress for the democratic idea within a national framework.[91] This hoped-for democratization effect will result from the opportunities that IOs can offer for learning new political practices or from the protected spaces for free expression, particularly of the 'voiceless' in their own State. However, these are not principled justifications for expanding multilateral deliberation, but simply possible desirable consequences.

[90] Caution is still called for, since the archives of the IOs contain a wealth of reform proposals. See the Cardoso Report on UN-Civil Society Relations (2004), admittedly drafted under the aegis of their 'democratization', which the Member States have preferred to forget: UNGA, 'We the peoples: civil society, the United Nations and global governance. Report of the Panel of Eminent Persons on United Nations–Civil Society Relations' (11 June 2004), A/58/817.

[91] Peters, fn. 17, at 694.

# 15

# Conclusions

Olivier de Frouville

## 15.1 INTRODUCTION

We should warmly thank Samantha Besson for choosing the theme of 'good representation in international law' as the subject of her 2023 annual course at the College of France. And then for having decided that 'Democratic Representation in and by International Organizations' would be the subject of her annual conference. The responses that will be given in the coming years to the questions asked by Samantha Besson may have a major influence on the future of Humanity. This is about the present and future of democracy which might well be an existential issue at the global level. There are many signs in the current state of the world that the idea of democracy is under attack, and that existing democracies are deeply fragilized. Alternative authoritarian models represented by States like Russia and China are gaining ground. This also goes with an alternative model of international law to the one that emerged after the Second World War, based on the prohibition of the use of force in international relations and the respect for human rights. This model is no longer self-evident, it needs to be justified and defended.[1] Even more so as the States that originally promoted it are betraying its promises, caught in the trap of their double standards.

I was asked not to 'summarize or close the debate' but instead to try to enable to revert to the main issues addressed during the conference and maybe identify further issues for research. So, the 'conclusions' are not meant to close the discussion, but rather, to some extent, to re-open the discussion and to leave it open until next time . . . In listening to the participants (and in reading

[1] Olivier de Frouville, 'Justifying International Law, Defending Cosmopolitanism', in Olivier de Frouville, *From Cosmopolitanism to Human Rights* (Oxford: Hart Publishing, 2021), pp. 106–125.

thoroughly their contributions), I identified four questions that could serve as an outline for these conclusions.

The first question is: Why should we be discussing democratic representation in and by international organizations (IOs) in the first place (Section 15.2)? Although objections could be conceived, all participants developed convincing reasons to show that this discussion not only made sense but was important. This, in turn, raised the question of whether we need the concept of 'representation' when discussing the democratization of IOs (Section 15.3)? And assuming the response is 'yes', what is meant by 'representation', considering the various meanings that this word took in political science and in law (Section 15.4)? And the final question was: what are the main models or projects proposed when speaking about democracy in and by IOs (Section 15.5)?

## 15.2 WHY DISCUSSING DEMOCRACY AND REPRESENTATION IN AND BY INTERNATIONAL ORGANIZATIONS?

Democracy on an international or global scale has for long been a subject of reflection for specialists in international relations and philosophy, in the line of perpetual peace projects and in particular Emmanuel Kant's cosmopolitanism. It has not been such a popular topic for international lawyers. Although the discussion was 'invigorated by the "turn to governance"', "democracy" may have never reached the limelight in the first place, perhaps because it is not easy to translate the vocabulary of democracy into the reality of the international legal (governance) system', as very well explained by the organizers of a recent EJIL Symposium issue.[2] Most international lawyers would still hold that democratic theory is limited to the borders of the State and is hardly applicable to the 'international sphere', with the exception maybe of the European Union.[3] The classical view on 'democracy in international organizations' is that one can only speak of 'democracy' is a very loose sense, that is: (1) IOs are a 'democracy of States', because most of those organizations, including the United Nations (UN), rely on the principle 'one State, one vote', even though there are notable exceptions such as the UN Security

[2] Jan Klabbers, Doreen Lustig, André Nollkaemper, Sarah Nouwem, Michal Saliternik, and Joseph H. H. Weiler, 'International Law and Democracy Revisited: Introduction to the Symposium' (2021) 32(1) *European Journal of International Law* 9–15, at 10–11.

[3] See especially Édouard Dubout, *Droit constitutionnel de l'Union européenne* (Brussels: Bruylant, 2021); Stefan Oeter, 'Federalism and Democracy', in Armin von Bogdandy and Jürgen Bast (eds.), *Principles of European Constitutional Law*, 2nd ed. (Oxford: Hart Publishing, 2009), pp. 55–82, p. 55.

Council or the financial institutions; (2) even if one is to adopt a more demanding conception of democratic theory that says that not only States but also peoples should participate to decision-making, such a classical view would respond that this is already the case: based on an *indirect representation* system, if States represent their peoples, and IOs are made of States, then IOs are at least *indirectly* representing peoples. But the two arguments are misleading. Against the first one, Anne Peters for instance recalls that '[t]he reference point of democracy should be natural persons (human beings), not States'.[4] And against the second, Samantha Besson explains that 'States are far from being perfect democratic representatives of the peoples they institute as public',[5] because of mainly two reasons (1) some States are undemocratic; (2) even in democratic States, peoples are generally not associated with decisions on international and global affairs, including through their representatives. Add to this that the Westphalian principle of 'one State one vote' cannot account for the democratic principle of equal participation by all peoples and individuals, since the size of the population varies considerably from one State to another.[6] Under a more specific angle, Marie-Clotilde Runavot shows the very ambiguous status of members of domestic parliaments in IOs and the fact that parliamentarians have no real democratic representation functions in IOs, but can only enjoy, at best, a slightly more privileged status than civil society organizations.[7]

The consequence of that could be that the topic is not worth spending much scientific energy, except in the context of a purely speculative theory, something that the lawyers should leave for the philosophers. However, a minority of international lawyers have argued that a serious discussion on democracy in IOs is not only possible but also of major importance, for mainly two sets of reasons.

4 Anne Peters, 'Constitutional Theories of International Organisations: Beyond the West' (2021) 20(4) *Chinese Journal of International Law* 649–698. In 1963, René-Jean Dupuy already articulated the same type of refutation, René-Jean Dupuy, 'Démocratie et société internationale', in René-Jean Dupuy, *Dialectique du droit international* (Paris: Pedone, 1999), pp. 71–86, p. 71.

5 Besson and Martí, Chapter 12 in this volume. The authors also state: 'More specifically, the interests of representative organs within those States, such as governments or parliaments, and especially those of the elected or non-elected officials holding those representative positions might differ from the interests of the people they claim to represent.'

6 This was very well explained by Michel Virally in 1961, see Michel Virally, *L'ONU d'hier à demain* (Paris: Seuil, 1961), pp. 114–115.

7 Runavot, Chapter 6 in this volume.

The first set relates to *normative reasons*. These lawyers, including the ones participating in the conference, could agree that democratization is necessary because:

(1) In contemporary politics, peoples may think that they are unable to decide anymore on important questions that affect their lives because these questions are decided 'above' in IOs, without their participation. This 'democratic deficit' creates frustration and in turn a rise of populism, which puts in danger national democracy.[8] In other words, not democratizing IOs would be a serious risk upon existing democracies at the domestic level.
(2) There are more and more global issues that affect the daily lives of peoples in the States – like climate change, migration, population ... – and IOs regulate those global issues, so peoples should be able to participate in their decision-making procedures.[9] Moreover, and according to a cosmopolitan perspective, moral obligations of justice as well as legal obligations under international law, especially international human rights law,[10] extend beyond borders, which calls not only to reconceive modern States as 'cosmopolitan States'[11] but also to establish effective global institutions with democratic legitimacy.
(3) Following this cosmopolitan perspective, the human right to participation in public affairs, under Article 25 of the International Covenant on

[8] See among others the analysis by Steven Wheatley, *The Democratic Legitimacy of International Law* (Oxford: Hart Publishing, 2010) chapter 1. It should be noted that Évelyne Lagrange somehow dissents with this view of the majority of contributors. See Lagrange, Chapter 14 in this volume.

[9] David Held speaks of the 'paradox of our times': 'the inconsistency between the global nature of many of our pressing problems (from climate change to nuclear proliferation and global poverty) and contemporary forms of governance rooted in the nation state'. David Held, *Cosmopolitanism. Ideals and Realities* (Cambridge: Polity Press, 2010), p. 23.

[10] Referring here to the literature linking global justice to international human rights extraterritorial obligation as well as extraterritorial criminal jurisdiction, conceived as 'cosmopolitan obligations': among others Malcolm Langford, Wouter Vandenhole and Martin Scheinin (eds.), *Global Justice, State Duties. The Extraterritorial Scope of Economic, Social and Cultural Rights in International Law* (Cambridge: Cambridge University Press, 2013); Danielle Ireland-Piper, 'Extraterritorial Criminal Jurisdiction and the Cosmopolitan: A Double-Edged Sword', in Richard Beardsworth, Garrett Wallace Brown and Richard Shapcott (eds.), *The State and Cosmopolitan Responsibilities* (Oxford: Oxford University Press, 2019), pp. 147–169; H. Patrick Glenn, *The Cosmopolitan State* (Oxford: Oxford University Press, 2013), pp. 147–169.

[11] By that I mean a non-solipsist State, that is a State that is able to think of itself at the same time as a national and a global institution, and that does include that thinking into its legal and constitutional arrangements, allowing itself to exercise domestic as well as global competences. See also for other but approaching concepts of that notion Beardsworth *et al.*, fn. 10.

> Civil and Political Rights,[12] is to be understood to extend not only domestic public affairs but also international public affairs.[13] And this right to participate is a good legal basis for a multi-level or cosmopolitan democracy that includes cosmopolitan States and global institutions, as well as other levels of public authorities (cities, regions ...) and other actors, including private actors.

The second set of reasons relates to what can be scientifically observed. In fact, participation of actors others than States *does* effectively take place on the international plane. And not only does it take place as a fact, but this participation is more and more accepted and more officially and legally recognized not only by IOs secretariats but also by States themselves. This is of course not to say that participation of non-State actors is new: the International Labour Organization (ILO) for instance has been cited several times, and the case of the International Organization of Employers (IOE) was also mentioned, among other examples. But in the last thirty years participation of non-State actors has grown in an unprecedented manner in history. And it's obviously not only a quantitative change, but also a qualitative change: more actors are participating in a more substantive way. IOs themselves have recently shifted their models of relations with non-State actors, from a consultative instrumental model to more participatory models – where civil society organizations (CSOs) are invited to participate as 'stakeholders' or 'partners'.[14] This growing participation can be verified in all functions fulfilled by IOs: standard-setting, litigation, and operations. Évelyne Lagrange has noted more generally:

> [U]niversal IOs are already marked by the strong presence of [non-State actors]. It was enough for Member States to support or tolerate the opening-up of universal IOs to entities other than themselves for multiparty 'representation' or participation to take root.[15]

12 International Covenant on Civil and Political Rights, 999 UNTS 171 (adopted 16 December 1966, entered into force 23 March 1976).

13 Olivier de Frouville, 'Vers une démocratie continue à l'échelle globale? Nouvelles perspectives sur le droit de participer aux affaires publiques', in *Mélanges en l'honneur du professeur Dominique Rousseau. Constitution, justice, démocratie* (Paris: LGDJ, 2020), pp. 395–408; Claire Callejon, 'Les études de l'ONU sur le droit à la participation publique et la participation de la société civile', in Olivier de Frouville and Dominique Rousseau (eds.), *Démocratiser l'espace-monde* (Le Kremlin-Bicêtre: Mare & Martin 2024), pp. 93–106.

14 Olivier de Frouville, 'Civil Society's Role in International Organizations. Theori(es) and Practice(s)', in de Frouville, *From Cosmopolitanism to Human Rights*, fn. 1, pp. 175–189; Jonas Tallberg and Anders Uhlin, 'Civil Society and Global Democracy', in Daniele Archibugi, Mathias Koenig-Archibugi and Raffaele Marchetti (eds.), *Global Democracy. Normative and Empirical Perspectives* (Cambridge: Cambridge University Press, 2011), pp. 210–232.

15 Lagrange, Chapter 14 in this volume.

Although she expresses doubts about whether this has to do with 'democracy' as such, she agrees that at least this raises new questions about the structuring of the exercise of power within IOs, beyond the presupposition of the representation of peoples by States.

Not only a discussion on democracy and representation in and by IOs cannot be said to be purely speculative or theoretical, but it seems necessary today, in a situation where effective participation of non-State actors in IOs is taking place. I think all contributors to this volume agree with that conclusion. It is when delving deeper into the issue that the controversies appear. And first and foremost, when asking the question on whether the concept of representation is necessary to understanding and theorizing participation and democracy in IOs.

## 15.3 DO WE NEED THE CONCEPT OF REPRESENTATION?

Samantha Besson and José Luis Martí's response to that question in their chapter is a clear 'yes'.[16] And the main reason they are putting forward is that 'the relationship between the concepts of democracy and representation is not instrumental and contingent … but intrinsic and constitutive'.[17] And this is because, according to them, only representation can 'guarantee political equality and … organize equal participation all along'.[18] The thesis is therefore that there cannot be democracy without representation. Although for Besson and Martí, representation alone is not democracy, because they submit democratic legitimacy should be assessed by reference to four basic principles, namely:

- The principle of ultimate, effective popular control;
- The principle of political equality;
- The principle of deliberative contestability, and;
- The principle of human rights protection.

In other words, even if representation is not the main ingredient to democratic legitimacy, it is an indispensable ingredient. Besson and Martí oppose the idea that deliberation or participation could come 'in lieu' of representation.

The question of the link between democracy and representation is almost as old as the theory of democracy. There has been and there is still, to some extent, a debate on whether representation is even compatible with

[16] Besson and Martí, Chapter 12 in this volume.
[17] Ibid.
[18] Ibid.

democracy.[19] In the *General Theory of Law and the State*, Hans Kelsen is affirmative that strictly speaking representation without imperative mandate is non-democratic and that representation has never been a democratic principle but is rather drawn from a particular conception of the division of labour in the society based on the idea that some people are to exercise power, while most of the others are not.[20] Although Kelsen accepts that representation became part of the democratic theory in the eighteenth century, with John Stuart Mill or l'Abbé Siéyès, he remains reluctant to put an equal sign between representation and democracy, without further refinement. Bernard Manin, in his landmark study on representation, describes representation as a compromise, a sort of mix between 'democratic elements' and 'oligarchic elements'.[21] Other authors consider not only that representation is not intrinsically linked with democracy, but that democracy can exist without representation. In his contribution to the present volume, Philip Pettit writes:

> Peoples may exercise democratic control over an organization in a variety of ways that do not directly involve representation: for example, by constitutionally or otherwise requiring that it operate under certain constraints, that appointments be made according to strict procedures, that it offers broadly public-interest reasons for its decisions, and that it be subject to monitoring and auditing by an independent body.[22]

And from a completely different standpoint, one of the promoters of the theory of global administrative law, Sabino Cassese, wrote:

> There is no representative democracy and there are no periodic elections at the global level; but deliberative democracy can work as a surrogate, granting participation in the decision-making processes.[23]

This quote gets to the heart of the argument, opposing a cosmopolitan deliberative model of democracy and a model based on representation. A deliberative cosmopolitan theory would argue, as Sabino Cassese does in this quotation, that representative democracy is non-existent and cannot practically be put in place at the international level. However, that does not prevent democratization of international law, which can occur through the putting in place of 'deliberative systems' as conceived by authors like Jane

19 Nadia Urbinati, *Representative Democracy: Principles and Genealogy* (Chicago: University of Chicago Press, 2006).
20 Hans Kelsen, *General Theory of Law and State* (Cambridge, MA: Harvard University Press, 1945), p. 289 about the 'fiction of representation'.
21 Bernard Manin, *Principes du gouvernement représentatif* (Paris: Flammarion, 1996), p. 306.
22 Pettit, Chapter 3 in this volume.
23 Sabino Cassese, *A World Government?* (Sevilla: Global Law Press, 2018), p. 16.

Mansbridge and others[24] and applied by John Dryzek to global law in several contributions.[25]

This discussion leaves however open the question of whether, as a project of reform, we could have both systems at the international plane, side by side, and seconding each other's, so to say, like we have in domestic systems. And, again, Besson and Martí's proposal does not exclude deliberative systems, but say they cannot be dissociated from representative systems.[26] And this leads us to the next question which is: if we consider that representation is needed in IOs, what is the concept of representation we would be using?

## 15.4 WHAT CONCEPT OF REPRESENTATION SHOULD WE USE?

In the context of their mixed concept of democratic legitimacy, Besson and Martí give a very strict definition of what we could be called 'the representation principle', that is 'ultimate, effective popular control':

> [T]he assessment of the democratic legitimacy of institutions of international lawmaking crucially depends on whether those institutions, and IOs in particular, can be said to have been conferred their powers by the peoples subjected to the decisions to be made (the so-called 'authorization') and, even more importantly, on whether the peoples may access effective mechanisms of ultimate control over their representatives and over the decision-making system as a whole (the so-called 'control'). . . . Many modern views of political representation, starting with Thomas Hobbes', have indeed made the latter dependent on formal acts of authorization, whether *ex ante* or *ex post*. . . . [W]hat authorization rules out, first, is the self-appointment of the representative, including in the form of self-representation by mimetism or statistical reproduction. The requirement of authorization also excludes the random

[24] Jane Mansbridge and John Parkinson (eds.), *Deliberative Systems: Deliberative Democracy at the Large Scale* (Cambridge: Cambridge University Press, 2012).

[25] John S. Dryzek, *Foundations and Frontiers of Deliberative Governance* (Oxford: Oxford University Press, 2010), pp. 10–14; Hayley Stevenson and John S. Dryzek, *Democratizing Global Climate Change* (Cambridge: Cambridge University Press, 2014), pp. 12–36.

[26] Besson and Martí, Chapter 12 in this volume. The link between representation and deliberation in fact goes back to the origins of the concept of representation. For instance, Manin shows that Siéyès did not conceive representation separate from discussion – the two were linked and only from discussion between representative could come up an appropriate conception of general interest (which is never pre-given), Manin, fn. 21, pp. 240–241. He concludes: '*Le principe du gouvernement représentatif doit donc être formulé de la façon suivante: une mesure quelconque ne peut acquérir une valeur de décision que si elle a emporté le consentement de la majorité à l'issue d'une discussion. Le consentement de la majorité, et non la discussion elle-même, constitue ainsi la procédure de décision*', ibid., pp. 242–243. See also James Bohman, 'Representation in the Deliberative System', in Mansbridge and Parkinson, fn. 24, pp. 72–94.

selection of representatives by a third party (e.g. by lot) unless there has been some form of *ex ante* authorization to that random selection. Second, control implies that the represented disposes of ultimate, effective means of supervision over the activity of the representative. The mere 'claim' to represent is not enough to respect the equal autonomy of the represented citizens, therefore.[27]

Other authors – including some contributors to this volume – have defended more flexible conceptions of 'representation', which do not necessarily imply authorization nor control, belonging more to the sort of what Pitkin called 'descriptive representation'.[28] Édouard Dubout and Dominique Ritleng in their contribution have focused on the Conference on the Future of Europe Citizens' Assembly and on the participation of citizens that were drawn by lot. In the authors' opinion those participants constitute 'mini-publics' and their members are 'a new type of representatives ... without a mandate or popular responsibility [because] their democratic legitimacy depends above all on the transparency and quality of the deliberative process in which they participate'.[29]

In the same line of thinking, in Jacob Katz Cogan's fourth 'mode of representation', civil society representatives or most affected persons in the boards of the Global Fund to Fight AIDS, Tuberculosis, and Malaria and of the Gavi – the Vaccine alliance, are not 'representative' in the strict sense, that is they have not been elected or nominated by their constituencies but rather because they are active in the field (for CSOs) or because they are part of a larger group of affected peoples.[30]

Near to that conception but more on the side of 'epistemic' representation, Anne Peters speaks about 'self-appointed representatives' for those who are considered to represent a 'cause', like the World Wildlife Fund (WWF) or People for the Ethical Treatment of Animals (PETA) who 'have not been elected'. Neither were they selected, mandated, or nominated by the people they are representing by speaking on their behalf or by reporting on their situations.[31]

27 Besson and Martí, Chapter 12 in this volume.

28 Hanna F. Pitkin, *The Concept of Representation* (Berkeley: University of California Press, 1967), pp. 60ff. For a criticism of the too narrow conception of 'descriptive representation' based on experiences of deliberative democracy: Yves Sintomer, 'Le sens de la représentation politique: Usages et mésusages du débat contemporain' (2013) 50 *Raisons politiques* 13–34.

29 Dubout and Ritleng, Chapter 13 in this volume.

30 Cogan, Chapter 4 in this volume.

31 Peters, Chapter 9 in this volume.

Jochen von Bernstorff also mentioned the case of the 'most affected persons' groups and the striking example of an Indian farmer who, when speaking before IOs about his/her experience is also somehow claiming to 'represent' the common experience of one billion of other farmers in India.[32] I would personally add to this another example: take a mother of a person who was forcibly disappeared in a particular country and who gives her personal testimony to and participates in the legislative work of the UN. She only 'represents' herself, she does not even belong to an association, but still is 'representative' of a group of people who share the same horrendous experience of searching for their loved ones in the very same context, because the enforced disappearance is part of a pattern.[33] In that, she has some legitimacy in participating as a 'representative' in a democratic process – for instance in the drafting of norms related to enforced disappearances.[34]

Another interesting perspective was introduced by Melissa J. Durkee who supported the view that representation should be understood as 'a claim', that is a 'discursive practice' that operates and produces effects when a particular institution values that representation discourse.[35] In other words, democratic participation is granted to whoever 'claims' to be representative and is recognized as such by a given institution.

Finally, Anne Peters introduced the topic of democratic representation of those who cannot speak for themselves, by focusing on the case of animals, but recognizing that the problem extends the representation of other non-present or non-speaking entities such as elements of the biosphere and future generations. She proposes various procedures to appoint animals' representatives with the view to 'bringing animals to bear in the decision-making of IOs'.[36] She admits that this would be speaking of political representation 'only in a loose sense', taking the examples, in liberal democracies, of small children and disabled persons. Although it could be objected that these cases are mostly concerned with legal, but not political representation, and that as far as disabled persons are concerned, the legal argument has evolved and tends to deny or at least reduce to the minimum possible legal representation for the

32 von Bernstorff, Chapter 10 in this volume.

33 Olivier de Frouville, 'La Convention des Nations Unies pour la protection de toutes les personnes contre les disparitions forcées: les enjeux juridiques d'une négociation exemplaire' (2006) 6 *Droits fondamentaux* 1–92.

34 We will come back in Section 15.5 on forms of democratic legitimacy.

35 Durkee, Chapter 8 in this volume.

36 Peters, Chapter 9 in this volume. See also Anne Peters, 'Animals in International Law' (Volume 410) *Collected Courses of the Hague Academy of International Law*, 2020, pp. 95–544, pp. 509ff.

purpose of political agency/participation.[37] As far as animals are concerned, Peters finally comes to the conclusion that the 'physical limits of human-animal communication not only foreclose representation through elections, but also other, looser forms of responsiveness and accountability to the animals themselves', and that is thus preferable to speak of 'animal consideration rather than animal representation in (democratic) political processes'.[38]

It appears clearly that none of these use or concepts or definitions of 'representation' would achieve the functions assigned by Besson and Martí to 'democratic representation', that is guaranteeing political equality and organizing equal participation.[39] But then it seems that the question boils down to what our definition of 'democracy' or 'democratic institutions' means. Should we hold that an institution is 'democratic' only if a set of preconditions is fulfilled? Or that 'democracy' is rather a continuum allowing to find a given institution 'more or less' democratic? In other words, 'democracy' as an ideal-type, rather than a series of strict conditions and thresholds?

Kelsen's concept of democracy is based on the principle of *autonomy*, leading him to reduce the classical typology of political regimes to two ideal-types: autocracy and democracy. Autocracy, according to Kelsen, is a political regime based on the principle of heteronomy (subjects are 'excluded from the creation of the legal order');[40] whereas democracy is defined as a political regime founded on the principle of autonomy (where the 'subject of a legal order … participates in the creation of that order').[41] Every constitution – and thus every institution, including IOs – lies somewhere between these two poles: according to Kelsen, there can never be a 'pure' autocracy (i.e. a constitution based entirely on the principle of heteronomy) or a 'pure' democracy (based entirely on the principle of autonomy). The point, then, is not to establish a kind of dualism, but rather to highlight the complexity of constitutional experiences, which each combine and associate, in various

37 See Marie Baudel, 'Droit international et santé mentale', PhD thesis, Nantes Université, 2021, especially pp. 279ff. More specifically and in relation to Art. 12 of the Convention on the Rights of Persons with Disabilities, 2515 UNTS 44910 (adopted 13 December 2006, entered into force 3 May 2008) and corresponding General Comment no. 1 of the Committee, see Faraaz Mahomed, Michael Ashley Stein, Vikram Patel and Charlene Sunkel, 'A "Paradigm Shift" in Mental Health Care', in Michael Ashley Stein, Faraaz Mahomed, Vikram Patel and Charlene Sunkel (eds.), *Mental Health, Legal Capacity and Human Rights* (Cambridge: Cambridge University Press, 2021), pp. 1–16.

38 Peters, Chapter 9 in this volume.

39 Besson and Martí, Chapter 12 in this volume.

40 Kelsen, fn. 20, p. 333.

41 Ibid.

proportions and configurations, legal procedures that, in some cases, tend towards autonomy and, in others, towards heteronomy.

It may well be that there are in fact two distinct projects: the first consisting of turning IOs into democratic institutions, and the second aiming more modestly to 'democratize' IOs – in other words, to bring these institutions into a (never-ending?) process towards a more *inclusive participation* in their decision-making process, so that the 'subject of a legal order . . . participates in the creation of that order'.[42] It is true though that Besson and Martí's strict representation concept as ultimate and effective popular control is conceived as 'scalar' and thus subject to progressive realization[43] and balanced with other principles and practices such as deliberation between the represented and their representatives, and respect for human rights without discrimination. At the same time, posing an intrinsic link between democracy and such a strict concept of representation is a feature that clearly distinguishes this theory from others, such as a deliberative theory, which may conceive democracy *without* representation based on authorization and control, or going along and in parallel with more flexible concepts of representation.[44]

The question that was then raised by the contributors was: what the best model would be, if any, so as to push forward the agenda of democratic representation and/or democratization of IOs (which all, as said in Section 15.2, accepted as being not only desirable, but also necessary)?

## 15.5 WHAT MODELS TO PUSH FORWARD THE DEMOCRATIZATION OF IOS AGENDA?

All contributions in the volume are converging in trying to shape 'non-ideal' models of democracy in IOs. Accordingly, options are discussed not only through a theoretical lens, but also through a practical lens: what models could be said to be both theoretically consistent and sufficiently in adequation with the existing practice, and able to produce practically feasible proposals? In that spirit, several contributions address the challenges met by a 'democratic representation' in and by IOs based on a strict representation concept. At the same time, alternative sources of legitimacies are also discussed, as well as existing processes of democratization of IOs.

42 Ibid.

43 Samantha Besson and José Luis Martí, 'Legitimate Actors of International Law-making: Towards a Theory of International Democratic Representation' (2018) 9(3) *Jurisprudence* 504–540.

44 For instance, see Iris Marion Young, *Inclusion and Democracy* (Oxford: Oxford University Press, 2002).

### 15.5.1 *Challenges of Democratic Representation in and by IOs*

Contributors are raising a number of questions in relation to democratic representation in and by IOs. Some of them are quite specific, others have a broader scope and mean to go to the core of the argument. Without the ambition of being exhaustive, I am mentioning four of these challenges below.

#### 15.5.1.1 How Does Representation Work If Not Through Elections?

Samantha Besson and José Luis Martí speak of 'consent' from the represented to the representatives but do not make explicit which mechanisms may be used to ensure that consent is given, by other means than elections.[45] This is of particular concern when it comes to reflecting upon how CSOs should be 'organized' or 'authorized',[46] with conditions put upon their formation and structure, so as to ensure their 'representativity' might and in fact will not be used by States to exclude the most efficient and very often the most 'representative' (in the loose sense) non-governmental organizations (NGOs) from participation in the work of IOs. We will come back to this in the final part of these conclusions.

#### 15.5.1.2 Does Representation in IOs Means Giving Automatic Primacy to State Representation in All Cases?

In the 'multiple international representation system' (the 'MIRS') proposed by Samantha Besson and José Luis Martí, 'States should still be considered as the most effective institutions to ensure the democratic representation of the peoples of the world' and should thus 'play a primary role in the democratic representation of their peoples in their IOs' organs'.[47] The authors admit however that there are important deficits of States' representation: (1) 'many States are not democratic'; (2) 'even in democratic States, existing domestic mechanisms of ultimate, effective popular control over the external policy of States might prove to be insufficient for their peoples to control their international decisions'; (3) 'even when State officials are effectively accountable domestically for their international decisions, there might still be important

45 Besson and Martí, Chapter 12 in this volume; see also Samantha Besson and José Luis Martí, 'From Equal State Consent to Equal Public Participation in International Organizations: Institutionalizing Multiple International Representation', in Samantha Besson (ed.), *Consenting to International Law* (Cambridge: Cambridge University Press, 2023), pp. 314–346.

46 For concrete proposals in this regard, see Besson and Martí, 'Legitimate Actors of International Law-Making', fn. 43.

47 Besson and Martí, Chapter 12 in this volume.

democratic concerns with respect to the representation of stateless peoples (e.g. refugees) or even of certain peoples within States (e.g. indigenous peoples or regional minorities)'.

The response to this concern is to have other institutions helping to 'correct those deficits in State-based democratic representation of peoples in IOs', such as other public institutions like 'regions or cities, but also of private organizations, such as non-governmental organizations, transnational corporations, religious organizations or trade unions that are increasingly involved, in various participatory or deliberative capacities, in IOs' lawmaking processes'.[48] Even these complements and corrections are not enough in the opinion of the authors, because 'none of these other public institutions or private organizations is free from deficits as democratic representatives'.[49] This would justify going even further, by creating 'further mechanisms of ultimate, effective popular control *over* IOs themselves'.[50] Still, in the meantime, States should have a sort of precedence, and 'public institutions' (such as cities or regions) should themselves be given a 'priority' over 'private organizations' (such as CSOs).

The idea of the precedence of the State versus other actors and of the public versus the private can also be found in other proposals put forward by some contributors, although from very different points of view. Philip Pettit proposes a model which gives precedence to the State in the sense that non-State actors should generally be allowed to represent their constituencies, *unless* the State objects or puts its veto to their decisions.[51] Francis Cheneval gives another version of this 'republican' position by proposing that '[t]owards each other, the Peoples are adequately represented and held accountable only via the systemic interaction of all the different types of highest governmental institutions'.[52] But he makes clear that this proposal for a '*demoi*cracy' may be applicable only to the relations among 'democratic peoples'.[53]

Évelyne Lagrange challenges this precedence/primacy given to the State as the 'main' or privileged representatives in IOs because, she argues, 'States and their representatives are not in a position on their own to identify objects that transcend their interests and go beyond their borders'.[54]

48 Ibid.
49 Ibid.
50 Ibid.
51 Pettit, Chapter 3 in this volume.
52 Cheneval, Chapter 5 in this volume.
53 Ibid.
54 Lagrange, Chapter 14 in this volume.

It is true that assumption of the precedence of the State has become questionable in an age when, as Jürgen Habermas rightly said, the State has lost its presumption of innocence, namely the presumption of innocence that sovereignty granted it.[55] We have good reasons not to trust excessively the State, nor to think of sovereignty as a 'benevolent power'. The 'last word' or 'veto' proposed by Philip Pettit and the '*demoi*cracy' of Francis Cheneval therefore only seem reasonable when applied to fully democratic States ... which unfortunately are not so many. Conversely, a veto recognized to authoritarian or totalitarian States is a green light to oppression of their peoples. The MIRS, on the other hand, offers the considerable advantage of trying to articulate the representativeness of various institutions – which all have their deficits – so that in the end, by complementing each other's, it would make the IO 'more' representative than it would be if it were only State-based. But the question is whether giving systemic and automatic precedence to the State and to 'public institutions' necessarily provides more democratic legitimacy in all cases. There might be hard cases, especially when thinking of peoples without States or oppressed minorities. What institution is the best representative, for instance, of the Tibetan people? Would it be China as the territorial and sovereign State? The Dharamsala government, which qualifies as a simple 'non-State actor'? CSOs that might be in close contact and get information from Tibetans living in Tibet and convey their message to the world? Or is it impossible to say which one is the best? And should all institutions be part of the MIRS? But then how to reconcile their radically divergent perspectives and figure out what the Tibetan people want, or what is in their best interest?

#### 15.5.1.3 Are Representative Institutions a Guarantee for a Qualitative Democratic Process or Procedure?

Another challenge raised is that representative institutions may not always work very well in effectively representing the people they are supposed to represent, whereas non-representative institutions may achieve excellent results in this regard. In other words, organizations may have *input legitimacy* based, for instance, on elections but very poor *output legitimacy* because they don't effectively deliver results, either because the elected are incompetent, or because the representative body is inefficient. Also, the represented may want

[55] Jürgen Habermas, 'Kant's Idea of Perpetual Peace with the Benefit of Two Hundred Years' Insight', in James Bohman and Matthias Lutz-Bachmann (eds.), *Perpetual Peace: Essays on Kant's Cosmopolitan Ideal* (Cambridge, MA: MIT Press, 1997), pp. 113–154.

to speak for themselves. Besson and Martí are assuming that 'democratic representation [is] a relation that institutes, authorizes and holds power accountable and hence contributes to the justification of political authority, including of lawmaking authority'.[56]

But precisely this assumption is challenged in many ways including in modern States democracies where many represented don't trust their representatives anymore and are willing to speak *for themselves*.[57] In his chapter, Pierre Rosanvallon recalls that even though:

> [r]epresentation remains essential in societies, but perhaps in a different sense than in the past, it appears to be gradually taking a figurative meaning: it is becoming representation in the sense of the need to explain and shed light on a complex world, a world in which, for example, the question is not simply to represent social classes, but to try to understand a whole world of social invisibility.[58]

Among other signs in domestic arenas, he sees '[t]he way of assessing the "democratic performance" of European institutions [as a] shift from an "input legitimacy" (representativeness) to an "output legitimacy" (the nature of the decisions taken)'.[59]

It is difficult to transpose the same conclusions to IOs, where no representative democracy exists. Still, the question of representativity and of its 'efficiency' and the alternatives have been posed in certain contexts. One example is the representation of national NGOs in IOs. At the UN in particular, national NGOs used to be 'represented' by international NGOs and rarely had access and were able to speak for themselves before the various bodies such as the UN General Assembly or the Economic and Social Council (ECOSOC). This was challenged in the beginning of the 1990s in the wake of 'democratic transitions' in the Global South and in Eastern European countries, which saw an unprecedented development of CSOs.[60] Among others, it resulted in the revision of the consultative status of NGOs with the ECOSOC, to make it accessible to national NGOs and put an end to what was then perceived as the 'privilege' of representation of international NGOs (mainly based in Western countries). Similarly, the Conference of NGOs (CONGOs) which was and still is supposed to be a duly elected representative

56 Besson and Martí, Chapter 12 in this volume.
57 See Dominique Rousseau, *Radicaliser la démocratie. Propositions pour une refondation* (Paris: Seuil, 2015).
58 Rosanvallon, Chapter 2 in this volume.
59 Ibid.
60 de Frouville, 'Civil Society's Role in International Organizations', fn. 14.

organ of NGOs in consultative status came under heavy criticism, showing that proper elections did not offer sufficient legitimacy in this regard.

#### 15.5.1.4 How to Avoid the Traditional Exclusionary Bias of Representation?

Pierre Rosanvallon spoke in his chapter of a new function of representation – a narrative function of representation that is shedding light on a complex world and on the world of social invisibility, the world of the forgotten and those left-behind.[61]

Can a multiple system of representation address that, and how – from the moment it is based on a *strict* conception of representation which, even if not based on election by a majority, may at least have an effect of putting forward the mainstream part of the population or of the opinions formed in a given society. By definition, minorities and even more marginalized minorities and peoples are not *representative* (in the statistic and sociologic sense) and their democratic representation is generally conditioned on positive and temporary measures of promotion to establish an effective right to participation and overcome discrimination.

### 15.5.2 *Alternative Sources of Democratic Legitimacy of IOs?*

Several contributors have put forward the idea that representation may not be the sole source of legitimacy in IOs. 'Representation' itself, as we have seen above, may be interpreted in a looser sense of 'representativity', with the concepts of 'descriptive', 'mimetic', 'statistic', or even 'altruistic' representation. Besson and Martí observe in this regard that these forms of representation 'purport to represent pre-identified traits or interests to be promoted (functional output) or, at least, knowledge or expertise in how to do so (functional input)'.[62] But in any case, they cannot be an equivalent or constitute 'democratic representation' in the strict sense, that implies 'ultimate and effective popular control'. Still, in the practice of IOs, this loose sense of representation is often considered as a superior value when it comes to participation of private actors than 'democratic representation'.

In his chapter, Pierre Rosanvallon made eloquently the point that the most important social movements today are *not* representative movements, in the strict sense.[63] Marie-Clotilde Runavot on her part showed that what was

[61] Rosanvallon, Chapter 2 in this volume.
[62] Besson and Martí, Chapter 12 in this volume.
[63] Rosanvallon, Chapter 2 in this volume.

valued in the participation of domestic parliamentarians in IOs (with the Inter-Parliamentary Union) was not so much their representative status, but rather their substantive contributions.[64] And Évelyne Lagrange made the point that linking democracy to representation (strictly conceived) does not give a clear basis for the participation of actors that are not 'representative' but are nonetheless legitimate participants. And she argues that 'decisions by IOs (even if not unanimous) can be considered legitimate through the combination of the legitimacy derived from the State's initial consent, from the IO's metafunction (deliberation) and specific functions, from the respect for its particular mandate (subject to evolving interpretation), and ultimately from the fairness of the deliberative process'.[65]

Indeed, there are other forms of legitimacies of power than 'democratic legitimacy' in the strict sense of a representative democracy:

Legitimacy based on knowledge, that is *epistemic legitimacy* or what Évelyne Lagrange called 'epistocratic' legitimacy,[66] is taking a growing part in the work of IOs, with experts, including scientific experts, or even specialized NGOs, that bring to an IO knowledge and information that it cannot acquire by itself.

*Legitimacy based on influence and/or financial impact*: one just has to think of the role played by the Bill & Melinda Gates foundation in the World Health Organization (WHO) and more generally in global health issues.[67]

*Watchdog legitimacy*, that is the legitimacy of those who are holding powers to account, like investigative journalists, human rights defenders, and whistleblowers ... that is very often persons who do not represent anybody but themselves but whose legitimacy is based on the fact that they 'speak truth to power'.

One may wonder however whether these types of legitimacies have something to do with 'democratic legitimacies'. Here Melissa J. Durkee makes the point that the question of participation of private actors in IOs reveals a tension between what she calls 'a logic of representation' and a 'logic of expedience'. Legitimacy in the first logic is based on the representativity of the private actors, whereas in the second logic, the additional value these actors can bring to realize the goal of the IOs is a primary consideration. She sees the first logic as flowing from a 'deontological perspective rather than a consequentialist or teleological one. That is, democratic self-determination and interest representation are inherent

64 Runavot, Chapter 6 in this volume.
65 Lagrange, Chapter 14 in this volume.
66 Ibid.
67 Durkee, Chapter 8 in this volume; Sophie Albert, 'La participation des acteurs non étatiques à la gouvernance de la santé mondiale: du plaidoyer à la mise en œuvre des actions', in de Frouville and Rousseau, fn. 13, pp. 181–198.

goods. Decisions made, rules developed, and actions taken through a legitimate process are right and correct because they are products of that process'.[68] Conversely, '[t]he *logic of expedience* is defined by its embrace of consequentialist and teleological reasoning. An outcome is right and correct when it advances the mission of an organization. This position values efficiency, problem solving, and progress on accomplishing public goals, whether they be public health, climate stabilization, sustainable development, etc.'[69]

The point here is that it seems that in some instances those logics seem irreconcilable: IOs would have to choose between the two logics. Either having democratic representatives, or choosing the participants for other sorts of legitimacies such as 'epistocratic', 'watchdog' or influence.

Lagrange tends to relativize this opposition in arguing that democracy is, after all, legitimizing the exercise of power and that, to this end, representation may not be the exclusive or even the best source of legitimacy. Representation, she submits:

> needlessly complicates the search for an adequate justification (by reference to a people) for mechanisms that give voice to transnational human collectivities with a community of interests but not necessarily of destiny, to collectives that do not operate on the model of democratic representation (think of colleges of experts) or to natural (or non-human) entities.[70]

In other words, she argues that democratic representation should not be seen as the sole basis for democratic legitimation, quite the contrary: 'epistocratic' legitimacy should be considered as one of the main bases of legitimization, from the moment that it is placed in a pluralist environment, and that it is linked and combined with other principles of legitimacy, including democratic representation.[71] I would add to this that the justification for participation is very often a question of point of view: IOs may see participation of actors through a logic of expedience, whereas these actors may understand their role as participating to a logic of representation and, beyond, of democratization of IOs.

### 15.5.3 *Current Processes and Models of Global Governance*

Besson and Martí are proposing a MIRS in a 'systematic and ordered approach', rather than a 'radically pluralistic' one.[72] Even though the authors

[68] Durkee, Chapter 8 in this volume.
[69] Ibid.
[70] Lagrange, Chapter 14 in this volume.
[71] Ibid.
[72] Besson and Martí, Chapter 12 in this volume.

are certainly right in pointing out that current systems of participation are not in line with a strict conception of democratic representation, several contributions suggest that they are not so disorganized. In fact, most of participatory or consultative arrangements in IOs, for actors other than States, are following similar principles. These maybe more akin to a logic of expedience than a logic of participation, but at the same time we have seen above that the two are not necessarily incompatible and that, rather, IOs are combining the two to give way to a combination of legitimacies, which, in the end, may give an appropriate foundation to the exercise of power.

Yves Sintomer has suggested during the conference that the concept of 'governance' may be looked at when trying to understand and describe those types of processes. For sure, 'governance' is a word saturated with controversies. Although Jacques Chevallier,[73] but also André-Jean Arnaud[74] have tried to overcome this confusion and get the most of a concept which, after all, may well be extremely useful to advance knowledge about how power is exercised not only in domestic societies but also at the international or global level.

Chevallier points out that the State in the post-modern age is faced with problems of 'governability', insofar as it has to deal with 'demanding citizens who are no longer satisfied with the principle of delegation inherent in the representative system but want to have a say in collective choices' – which leads to a search for 'new methods, different from traditional government techniques'.[75] These 'new methods' are generally subsumed under the term 'governance'.

Chevallier continues:

> Acknowledging the complexity of the problems to be solved and the existence of multiple powers, it is a matter of favouring flexible formulas for cooperation, aimed at involving the various players concerned in decision-making; collective action thus tends to become the product of negotiations between a very diverse set of players, both public and private, who will find themselves involved in one way or another in its development. . . . These methods imply a new style of government . . . the traditional model based on unilaterality and constraint gives way to a pluralist and interactive model.[76]

Even though not all contributors have used the word 'governance', much of what they describe fits with Chevallier's account of the concept.

73 Jacques Chevallier, *L'État post-moderne* (Paris: LGDJ, 2003), p. 209.

74 André-Jean Arnaud, *Critique de la raison juridique, Tome 2, Gouvernants sans frontières, entre mondialisation et post-mondialisation* (Paris: LGDJ, 2003), pp. 379ff.

75 Chevallier, fn. 73 (our translation).

76 Ibid., p. 211.

Global governance means that authority is dispersed between different players, at different levels and in multiple 'sites', which tend to form a 'deliberative system' through interaction between these 'interested parties'. This is not about a right to command, in the classical sense of sovereignty of the State: 'governing the globe'[77] is not of the essence of *imperium* but more of *auctoritas*. Niko Krisch uses the idea of 'liquid authority' to explain that type of power that circulates among actors, and is neither founded on force or persuasion, but rather on its capacity to create deference on the side of other actors.[78] In that, governance is different from government. More often, it is not even much about making legal norms, but rather public policies that are action-oriented. Such governance processes can be observed when IOs are entrusted or assume the responsibility of defining global public policies on global issues (such as sustainable development) involving multiple partners beyond the States at multiple levels – international but also national, regional, or local.

Participation in governance in this regard means participation in the exercise of public authority; it is a way in which 'legitimate' actors participate in the exercise of 'fluid' public authority jointly with the State and IOs. Increasingly used in IOs and governance processes, the notion of 'partnership' reflects this idea of shared power.[79] And this sharing takes place not because of a decision taken by an original exclusive holder of power, but because the actors involved – the stakeholders – are themselves originally custodians of a significant portion of a circulating power – a 'liquid' power that cannot be completely 'concentrated', 'solidified' to be concentrated in a single subject.

In this context, following Rosanvallon, 'representativeness can even come to be perceived as a burden, an insoluble constraint'.[80] This is very well illustrated in Marieke Louis' chapter, about 'classical' representative organizations like IOE being much less at ease than the International Chamber of Commerce in the context of post-2008 financial crisis economic negotiations.[81]

Another key concept to understand governance is the concept of 'orchestration', as demonstrated in Terry Macdonald's chapter on the Global Compact on Refugees. What Macdonald shows is that 'orchestration' may have the effect of putting some groups in contact and inciting them to coordinate their action and/or to act through a loose network organization based on the sense of

77 Deborah D. Avant, Martha Finnemore and Susan K. Sell (eds.), *Who Governs the Globe?* (Cambridge: Cambridge University Press, 2010).

78 Nico Krisch, 'Liquid Authority in Global Governance' (2017) 9(2) *International Theory* 237–260.

79 See in particular UNGA Res. 55/215, 'Towards global partnerships' (21 December 2000).

80 Rosanvallon, Chapter 2 in this volume.

81 Louis, Chapter 7 in this volume.

community or shared experience. As Macdonald points out, '[t]hrough so doing, IO orchestration activities can potentially support not only the functional efficacy of global governance practices, but also their democratic legitimacy'.[82] By 'orchestrating', that is *convening, endorsing*, but also *assisting*, IOs may encourage 'mimetic' or 'statistic' representatives to constitute themselves in groups that may pretend to represent their constituencies. Aspirational democratic representatives would in general take the shape of coalitions of associations, rather than a unique and unified organization. And that is because most of the constituencies – unless maybe very limited ones or localized ones – would in general produce a number of would-be representative organizations, corresponding to various groups within them, as fragmented as they are along political, social, cultural, ideological, or other lines. This pluralism within constituencies is in fact itself consubstantial with democracy. Far from being undemocratic, this scattered and multiple representation by various non-representative (in the strict sense) actors may in fact enhance democracy in IOs.

## 15.6 CONCLUSION

As mentioned before, all contributors have tried their best to maintain their work and proposals within 'non-ideal' theories. This is not to say that they intended to disqualify any ideal. And in fact, all admitted explicitly or implicitly that speaking of democracy in IOs and more generally at the international or global level somewhat relies to an 'ideal', the one of universal and equal autonomy of all human persons and maybe, beyond that, of non-human beings and parts of the biosphere, and of the biosphere itself. 'Non-ideal' theories, in this context, does not mean placing oneself within the strict confines of current 'realities' – if something of that sort does exist – but rather adopting a critical stance to existing institutions, laws, and moral ideas and in particular to existing structures of power. How is power distributed and allocated, and finally exercised is the question that every non-idealistic thinker would address in considering the question of democracy. And this keeping in mind that ideals of today often occurred in history to become the realities of tomorrow. So, the question is more what we can realistically do *now* in the light of an ideal – in other words it is what Antonio Cassese called 'realist utopia'[83] (which is not the expression of an unsolved problem, but more a methodological roadmap).

[82] Macdonald, Chapter 11 in this volume.

[83] Antonio Cassese (ed.), *Realizing Utopia: The Future of International Law* (Oxford: Oxford University Press, 2012), Introduction.

The suggestion that comes out of the volume is that there are already some complex processes of governance on going, through participatory modalities which are more akin to 'systems of deliberation' than representative institutions. But systems of deliberation also need a proper theory of representation because this is not intended that each and every person may directly participate in deliberations.

Deliberative theory as applied to global institutions has already had a powerful effect: that of giving a theoretical basis to the – not only informal, but legally founded – participation of actors other than States. In a model of international law and institutions based on sovereignty, it was plainly impossible to establish the legitimacy of actors other than the State. In the context of deliberative model, the legitimacy of an actor to participate in political processes is no longer based on sovereignty. The question is therefore no longer whether such groups should or should not participate in IOs alongside States. The question is instead *which actors* can legitimately claim to participate in *what types of activity* and, in each instance, *under what arrangements*.

At least we can be satisfied that, in the current state of things, in most IOs, the 'sovereignty' model is no longer dominant or exclusive, and the participation of non-State actors is not anymore only tolerated or admitted on a purely 'consultative' or 'instrumental' basis, but in recognition of the power of legitimization that their participation may produce. On business participation, for instance, Marieke Louis made the point that what was perceived as problematic was not business participation per se, but rather the modalities of participation and representation of those business companies.[84] Similarly, Melissa J. Durkee insisted on the need to create a separate track of participation for businesses – on the model of what some IOs have already done.[85]

Answering precisely the question of the role and function of each actor in each of the IO's activities is of major importance not only theoretically but also practically, because without proper conceptualization of what this means to participate and based on which legitimacy for each activity, this is impossible to conceive proper rules that may apply in IOs. And the risk unfolding from the absence of rule is not only poor practice and distorted results of governance processes, but also risks of instrumentalization by States, including authoritarian States, and other powerful actors like multinational companies who may use a 'democratization' of IOs discourse to promote their own interests. The

84 Louis, Chapter 7 in this volume.
85 Durkee, Chapter 8 in this volume.

so-called 'capture'[86] of IOs may not only be a goal pursued by private actors, but also by hegemonic States who are willing to take control of international institutions to strengthen their influence on world affairs.

As things currently stand, this is clear that such conceptualization of democratic participation and representation in or by IOs does not exist. A multiple system of representation, based on authorization and control, stands as serious proposal, but although non-ideal, seems extremely far-fetched. Re-instituting multiple publics would need radical reforming of IOs. 'Reforming' is by itself a challenge in the realm of interstate negotiations, especially when it comes to institutional arrangements. States form a cast of privileged 'subjects' of international law, and access of non-State actors (public or private) to IOs has been the result of piecemeal strategies, slowly developed and surreptitiously introduced through practice – and not law – at the initiative of non-State actors themselves, with the complicity of some States and of integrated organs (secretariats). Until now, all major reforms of IOs have failed. The issue of participation of civil society has once been part of the reformist agenda pushed by former UN Secretary-General Kofi Annan, on the occasion of the fiftieth anniversary of the organization in 2005. Annan appointed a 'group of eminent persons representing a variety of perspectives to review past and current practices and recommend improvements for the future in order to make the interaction between civil society and the United Nations more meaningful'.[87] The Group handed its report in June 2004, with groundbreaking proposals, none of which have been concretized since then. The main defect of the existing system, namely the ECOSOC 'Committee on NGOs', a group of elected States having the mandate to decide on attributing, suspending, or withdrawing consultative status to NGOs, has remained unchanged and continues up until today to impede access of independent NGOs and on the other side to promote Governmental NGOs (the 'GONGOs') or simply incompetent organizations so that they can use space and time to the detriment of independent, competent, and 'representative' (in the loose meanings identified above) organizations.[88] Despite all the strong lobby from hundreds of organizations throughout the world for reforms to be

[86] Ayelet Berman, 'Between Participation and Capture in International Rule-Making: The WHO Framework of Engagement with Non-State Actors' (2021) 32(1) *European Journal of International Law* 227–254.

[87] UNGA Res. 57/387 (9 September 2002), para. 141.

[88] Olivier de Frouville, 'Domesticating Civil Society at the United Nations', in Pierre-Marie Dupuy and Luisa Vierucci (eds.), *NGOs in International Law: Efficiency in Flexibility?* (Cheltenham: Edward Elgar, 2008), pp. 71–115.

adopted in the perspective of the 'Summit of the Future' there seems to be no concrete prospect for positive steps or actions in this regard.[89]

Quite the opposite, the last years have seen a powerful movement towards 'shrinking space' for civil society.[90] Authoritarian States are openly attacking independent CSOs domestically and internationally. The space that had been conquered since the 1990s is eroded, whereas in sectors traditionally not opened to participation, like climate negotiations, States are keeping the door closed for CSOs. This is even more striking that the presence of business companies, especially fossil fuel companies, is pervasive in these negotiations with high economic stakes.

Then, in these conditions, what would be our 'realistic utopia'? Democratization of IOs must be conceived as a bottom-up process much more than a top-down one. The initiatives and push towards more participation rarely came from the States themselves but rather from transnational movements and CSOs. This means putting a priority on strengthening transnational networks of actors who have the same understanding of democracy as autonomy: networks of cosmopolitan citizens and institutions, who may counterbalance the influence of the most sovereigntist States and harness the potential for change of transnational business actors. Action towards a growing access and participation to global arenas happen if grassroots movements and CSOs are able to find enough allies among States and other actors including businesses to form such multipartite transnational cosmopolitan coalitions. And this in turn can only take place through a piecemeal, step-by-step approach, in each conference, in each specific body, in each negotiation, with various and modular coalitions to be reinvented again and again, depending on the subject matter, on the institutional configuration and on the balance of power. This needs a clear vision of the goal to be achieved, a strategic vision and tactical intelligence.

Democracy in IOs may not be, as it used to be in the classical cosmopolitan idea, an 'extension' of the democratic ideal to international affairs: it may well be the ultimate guarantee for the preservation of democracies where they exist

89 See among others 'A Call for UN Charter Reform' a letter signed by eminent personalities including twenty Nobel laureates and the report *Imagining a Renewed United Nations 2023/2024* issued by the Global Governance Forum. However UNGA Res. 76/307 falls short of these ambitions notably by deciding 'that the Summit of the Future has an important role to play in reaffirming the Charter of the United Nations', UNGA Res. 76/307, 'Modalities for the Summit of the Future' (12 September 2022). No mention is made of a revised structure that would allow enhanced participation by other actors, as suggested by civil society movements.

90 See among many others the report of the UN High Commissioner for Human Rights, 'Civil Society space: engagement with international and regional organizations' (20 April 2020), A/HRC/44/25.

at the domestic levels. Interdependence of States and global challenges such as the climate emergency are inevitably leading to more transfer of powers to global institutions. And two ways are open for the evolution of the organization of global power: a democratic and federal evolution; or an autocratic and imperial one.[91]

Finding the best theories and actions to push for the democratic and federal agenda is the common goal of all contributors to this volume. Beyond theories, we now urgently need to propose practical and realistically feasible solutions …

91 Olivier de Frouville, 'Repenser le concept de constitution', in de Frouville and Rousseau, fn. 13, pp. 73–91.

# Index

Printed in the United Kingdom by TJ Clays Ltd.